Seven Quartets of Becoming

A Transformational Yoga Psychology
Based on the Diaries of Sri Aurobindo

Seven Quartets of Becoming
A Transformational Yoga Psychology

Based on the Diaries of
Sri Aurobindo

Debashish Banerji

Nalanda International
Los Angeles (USA)

PRINTWORLD
Publishers of Indian Traditions

Cataloging in Publication Data – DK
[Courtesy: D.K. Agencies (P) Ltd. <docinfo@dkagencies.com>]

Banerji, Debashish.
Seven quartets of becoming : a transformational yoga psychology : based on the diaries of Sri Aurobindo / Debashish Banerji.
p. cm.
Includes bibliographical references.
ISBN 13: 9788124606230 (hb)

1. Yoga. 2. Ghose, Aurobindo, 1872-1950 – Diaries. I. Ghose, Aurobindo, 1872-1950. II. Title.

DDC 181.45 23

First published in India, 2012
ISBN 13: 978-81-246-0623-0 (Hb) ISBN 10: 81-246-0623-4
ISBN 13: 978-81-246-0626-1 (Pb) ISBN 10: 81-246-0626-9

Published by:
Nalanda Interantional
"Nalanda", 6418, Spring Park Avenue
Los Angeles, CA - 90056 (USA)
Phones: (310)-430-8057; *Fax*: (213)-341 0156
Web: www.nalandainternational.com

and

D.K. Printworld (P) Ltd.
Regd. Office : *'Vedaśrī'*, F-395, Sudarshan Park
(Metro Station: Ramesh Nagar), New Delhi - 110 015
Phones : (011) 2545 3975; 2546 6019; *Fax* : (011) 2546 5926
E-mail : indology@dkprintworld.com
Web : www.dkprintworld.com

Printed by: D.K. Printworld (P) Ltd., New Delhi

To

Richard

patient labourer

in the quarries of the gods

Foreword

SRI Aurobindo (1872-1950) not only wrote voluminously about world philosophy, but he also practised philosophy, in the age-old Indian tradition of the *sādhu* (sage or seer). Both a scholar and a *yogī*, Aurobindo carefully documented the unfolding of spiritual consciousness starting shortly after his deep revelatory experiences while in prison, in 1908. His meticulous personal observations, about his spiritual path, were recently published in a two-volume set, *Record of Yoga*. Debashish Banerji has scrupulously analysed this work and offers a detailed, clear, systematic and inspirational interpretation of how the yoga of Sri Aurobindo may be understood and practised.

True to Aurobindo's own grounding in the Western philosophical tradition, Banerji provides bridges between the language and outlook of Asia and Europe. Heraclitus, Plato and Nietzsche helped shape Sri Aurobindo's thought, as much as the Vedas, Upaniṣads and *Gītā*. Banerji employs the insights of Nietzsche, Bergson, Heidegger, and Husserl to explain the yogic principles of will, spontaneity, and intentionality and the thinking of Deleuze and Irigaray to explore yoga's emphasis on relationality and transformation. The scientific research of Barbara McClintock and Evelyn Fox Keller similarly, provide apt metaphors employed by Banerji for understanding the complex yoga as articulated in *Record of Yoga*.

Aurobindo fashioned an architectonic for entering into

the experience of yoga, similar to the *yantra* or *maṇḍala* constructed by some advanced practitioners of tāntric or Buddhist meditation. Aurobindo's architecture of spiritual experience has seven pillars, each containing four major components. Within this edifice, the spiritual aspirant or *sādhaka* establishes a habitus, a way of being in the world, a prism through which all action and thought can be reflected and understood and made spiritual. The seven aspects emphasise one's mental outlook, advocating equanimity and strength amidst all change, the importance of knowledge, the centrality of bodily health and experience, the need for the purification of one's comportment and demeanour, and the transformation of all experience to spiritual bliss. By conveying this system in its complexity, Banerji captures both the joy to be found in laughter, beauty, and delight, and the hard work to be accomplished through spiritual austerity (*tapas*).

In addition to providing accessible explanations and charts for some of the more esoteric aspects of Indian thought, such as the *cakra*s and the five breaths, Banerji elucidates philosophical subtleties, exploring the relationships among equality, power, and knowledge. So many stellar themes abound: intuition, observing, austerity, bliss, the nature of surrender, and the vaunted state of desirelessness, to name a few. By carefully engaging and reflecting on this book, the reader will catch a glimpse of what the *Bhagavad-Gītā* celebrates as selfless action. By performing action, not for the sake of oneself or to feel the pleasure experienced by others, one does honour to the divine force, the Oversoul or Puruṣottama, through which one can know the eternality and delight of existence.

Christopher Key Chapple
Doshi Professor of Indic and Comparative Theology
Loyola Marymount University, Los Angeles

Contents

Acknowledgements

IN the summer of 2007, Richard Hartz of the Sri Aurobindo Ashram Archives visited the Gnostic Centre in Delhi and gave a series of lectures relating Sri Aurobindo's *Record of Yoga* to certain passages in *Sāvitrī*. Though the *Record of Yoga* had been published in book form a few years earlier, I had found it inaccessible, but Richard's talks and my conversations with him, fired my interest and provided the key for a renewed attempt to approach the text. Further, Richard pointed me to the glossary of Sanskrit terms in the *Record of Yoga*, available at the Sri Aurobindo Ashram website, and armed with these new resources, I turned to my own studies of this text. Hence, I dedicate this book to Richard Hartz and his many years of patient work at the archives.

In 2008, I gave a set of 10 lectures on the seven quartets of the *Record of Yoga* at the University of Philosophical Research in Los Angeles, which were turned into a course titled the "Yoga of Integral Transformation". These lectures form the basis for this text. For this opportunity, I offer my deep thanks to Dr. Obadiah Harris, president of the University of Philosophical Research and to my students at the university, who took the course for two winter quarters, helping me, thereby, to fine-tune the material. My special thanks to Jeffrey Snider, who sponsored the transcription of these lectures, which I used to create this text.

For the initial work of transcribing, proofreading and helping with the editing of the text, my thanks go to Subash

Mutsuddi, Rakesh Gade and Sundeep Pattem. For reading through the text and offering valuable suggestions, I thank Keka Chakraborty, Vincent Massa, Rich Carlson, Richard Hartz and Christopher Chapple. Others, too many to name, have read through parts of the text and have offered their suggestions, and for this my thanks go out to them. For preparing the charts to go with the text, Amrita Banerji and for the cover design, Zach Perlman receive my sincere gratitude.

Last, but not the least, my thanks to the Sri Aurobindo Ashram Trust, with whose kind permission, I have included source materials from the collected works of Sri Aurobindo and the Mother.

Los Angeles **Debashish Banerji**

November 2011

Abbreviations

AN : Sri Aurobindo, *Autobiographical Notes and Other Writings of Historical Interest*, vol. 36, The Complete Works of Sri Aurobindo, Sri Aurobindo Ashram Trust, Pondicherry, 2006.

AO : Gilles Deleuze and Felix Guattari, *Anti-Oedipus: Capitalism and Schizophrenia I*, trans, Robert Hurley, Mark Seem and Helen R. Lane, Continuum International Publishing Groups, London and New York, 2004.

ATP : Gilles Deleuze and Felix Guattari, *A Thousand Plateaus: Capitalism and Schizophrenia II*, trans. Brian Massumi, Continuum International Publishing Group, London and New York, 2004.

CP : Sri Aurobindo, *Collected Poems*, vol. 2, The Complete Works of Sri Aurobindo, Sri Aurobindo Ashram Trust, Pondicherry, 2009.

CWM : The Mother, *Collected Works of the Mother*, Sri Aurobindo Ashram Trust, Pondicherry, 1979, 2003 — followed by volume number, colon and page number.

CWSA : Sri Aurobindo, *Complete Works of Sri*

Aurobindo, Sri Aurobindo Ashram Trust, Pondicherry — followed by volume number, colon and page number.

EDH : Sri Aurobindo, *Essays Divine and Human: Writings from Manuscripts 1910-50*, vol. 12, The Complete Works of Sri Aurobindo, Sri Aurobindo Ashram Trust, Pondicherry, 1997.

EoG : Sri Aurobindo, *Essays on the Gita*, vol. 19, The Complete Works of Sri Aurobindo, Sri Aurobindo Ashram Trust, Pondicherry, 1997.

EPH : Sri Aurobindo, *Essays in Philosophy and Yoga: Shorter Works*, vol. 13, The Complete Works of Sri Aurobindo, Sri Aurobindo Ashram Trust, Pondicherry, 1998.

IU : Sri Aurobindo, *Isha Upanishad*, vol. 17, The Complete Works of Sri Aurobindo, Sri Aurobindo Ashram Trust, Pondicherry, 2003.

KU : Sri Aurobindo, *Kena and Other Upanishads*, vol. 18, The Complete Works of Sri Aurobindo, Sri Aurobindo Ashram Trust, Pondicherry, 2001.

OH : Sri Aurobindo, *Letters on Himself and the Ashram*, vol. 35, The Complete Works of Sri Aurobindo, Sri Aurobindo Ashram Trust, Pondicherry, 2011.

LD : Sri Aurobindo, *The Life Divine*, vols. 21 and 22, The Complete Works of Sri Aurobindo, Sri Aurobindo Ashram Trust, Pondicherry, 2005.

MA : The Mother, *The Mother's Agenda*, ed.

Satprem, Institut de Recherches Evolutives, Paris, 1995 — followed by volume number, colon and page number.

RoY : Sri Aurobindo, *Record of Yoga*, vols. 10 and 11, The Complete Works of Sri Aurobindo, Sri Aurobindo Ashram Trust, Pondicherry, 2001.

SABCL : Sri Aurobindo Birth Centenary Library, Sri Aurobindo Ashram Trust, Pondicherry, 1972 — followed by volume number, colon and page number.

Savitri : Sri Aurobindo, Savitri, *A Legend and a Symbol*, vols. 33 and 34, The Complete Works of Sri Aurobindo, Sri Aurobindo Ashram Trust, Pondicherry, 1997.

SoY : Sri Aurobindo, *The Synthesis of Yoga*, vols. 23 and 24, The Complete Works of Sri Aurobindo, Sri Aurobindo Ashram Trust, Pondicherry, 1999.

Introduction

SRI Aurobindo grew up in England, where he came to know very little about India or things Indian. After his schooling, he took to the study of Classics at Cambridge University, where he encountered the Sanskrit literary tradition. He returned to India in 1893 and joined the services of the ruler of Baroda, where he worked in several administrative positions and as a teacher at the Baroda College. There, he also consolidated his knowledge of Sanskrit, learnt a number of spoken Indian languages and plunged into the fledgling movement against British colonialism, becoming one of the first to declare complete political independence as India's goal. In 1905, he left Baroda to come to the forefront of the struggle for freedom, becoming one of the initiators of what has been called the *svadeśī* movement in Calcutta, the then British capital in India. It is here that he came across an instance of the exercise of paranormal power that opened his mind to the potential of yoga to affect phenomena beyond normal means. He described this event thus:

> I first knew about yogic cure from a Nāgā *sādhu* or Nāgā *saṁnyāsī*. Barin had mountain fever when he was wandering in the Amarkaṇṭak hills. The *saṁnyāsī* took a cup of water, cut it into four by making two crosses with a knife and asked Barin to drink it, saying, "He won't have fever tomorrow." And the fever left him.

An Incalculabe Yoga

Barin was Sri Aurobindo's younger brother and a collaborator in his anti-colonial efforts, as a leader of terrorist activities.

He knew a *yogī* and when Sri Aurobindo expressed his interest in yoga as a means to acquire power to liberate the nation, he introduced Sri Aurobindo to this *yogī*, a Maharashtrian by the name of Vishnu Bhaskar Lele. They met in Baroda in 1908 and Lele taught Sri Aurobindo meditation as a first step to quiet his mind. The result of this meditation was profound and beyond the expectation of both Lele and Sri Aurobindo, as it brought him the realisation of the unreality of the phenomenal world, complete cessation of thoughts, and the perception of an intangible Permanence backgrounding all things. This realisation of *nirvāṇa*, or what Sri Aurobindo would later call "the passive *Brahman*" became from then the basis of Sri Aurobindo's life experience, a condition in which he received intuitions, perceptions, directives (*ādeśa*) and further experiences leading him through the steps of what he called "an incalculable yoga" and which he later formalised under the name "Integral Yoga".

Sri Aurobindo's political activity continued through all this, and later that year (1908) he was incarcerated along with Barin and other revolutionaries on grounds of "waging war against the king". The imprisonment lasted for a year during which Sri Aurobindo's yogic activities intensified and a number of other spiritual realisations came to him. These can be summarised as:

(1) the realisation of what he would call "the active *Brahman*", a conscious energy formulating itself into all objects and entities in the universe and at work in them;

(2) the realisation of a person aspect to indivisible Reality (Vāsudeva, Śrī Kṛṣṇa), present as the essence of all things and in blissful relation with him (*līlā*);

(3) a hierarchy of impersonal planes or ranges of mind above the normal human mind, leading to a Cosmic Mind (Overmind) and a transcendental Origin of

Knowledge (Supermind) of which our universe is a manifestation as a form of Idea (Real Idea).

The Seven Quartets

After his release from the prison, he spent another year in Calcutta continuing his political activity, but departed successively to the French colonies of Chandernagore and Pondicherry, following inner directives (*ādeśa*s). In April 1910, he settled in the south Indian seaside town of Pondicherry, never to leave this city for the rest of his embodied life. Sometime in the early years of his settlement in Pondicherry (perhaps between 1911-12), Sri Aurobindo received a systematic programme of yoga made up of seven disciplinary components, each with four goals or "perfections"(*siddhi*s). He referred to this programme as *sapta catuṣṭaya* (seven quartets) and began organising his experience to himself in terms of this disciplinary structure from 1912, recording his practices and experiences along these lines in diaries or notebooks, which he titled "Record of Yoga". In November 1913, he noted down this scheme of the seven quartets on some loose sheets and began elaborating on them, a process which remained incomplete.

He may have also lectured on these quartets to the small group of disciples who stayed with him in these early years. From a number of disciples' notebooks, we find transcripts of "scribal notes" on these quartets, which are invaluable in filling the gaps and providing a closer view of what he may have meant by the distinctions he drew. From 1914 to 1920, while continuing with relative regularity his diary entries, he also wrote articles for the journal *Arya*, within which all his major writings were serialised. Among these articles, was his series elaborating his teaching of yoga, which is now available as *The Synthesis of Yoga*. This text also amplifies the teachings of the quartets and often provides a clearer key for understanding some of its obscurities.

I have drawn on all these and a few other sources, to present the description carried in this book. While such a presentation could be taken as a window into the life of an extraordinary individual practising an exotic discipline about 100 years ago, I believe the intent with which these practices were undertaken, should not be lost sight of in reference to human subjectivity in its present hour of world civilisation. Sri Aurobindo embarked upon the path of yoga as the revolutionary impulse of a modern subject at the cusp of twentieth-century modernity, marked by colonialism. Colonialism is politically no more with us, but the imprisoning forces of modernity are all around us, colonialism continues to haunt developing and underdeveloped nations socially, economically and culturally, while neo-liberal globalisation anonymises humanity across the world, populating planetary cities with complacent quasi-androids in programmed eagerness to consume packaged lifestyles coded for degrees of happiness. The gift of fire with which humanity began its ascent into self-consciousness, today burns no more in human hands, but fuels huge impersonal circulations of capital to which humanity remains imprisoned. What the seven quartets of Sri Aurobindo represents in this situation is no less than the second birth of fire, the fire of conscious evolution, the primal tool for the emergence of the infinite or plural subject out of its subjection to the shredding and pulverising of attention and quality that marks our times.

Revolutionary Impulse

1910, when Sri Aurobindo moved to Pondicherry, can be thought of as a watershed year. The revolutionary breakthroughs in science, industry and culture which characterised the turn of the nineteenth/twentieth century in Europe, were poised to inundate the world with a new chapter of civilisation, leading into our present times. What has been called the second Industrial Revolution, inaugurating the age of electricity, mass production and the world market was gathering to unleash its global regime, one whose material and psychological effects are fully manifest today. Invasive technologies would integrate the human individual into circuits of braided global information where subjectivity would be determined, fragmented and commodified, with little freedom of interiority, a behaviourism at the service of the nation state and the world market. At the still centre of this preparing epistemic storm, or perhaps the lull before its inexorable world action, we find Sri Aurobindo in a remote sheltered town in south India, surrounded by a handful of disciples and freedom fighters, searching for a wholeness of subjectivity with which to measure himself against the cosmos. Detached from the forces of the world, a luxury hardly available to anyone in today's surveilled and engineered psycho-sphere, he prepared the technologies of attention and mobilised consciousness, which became the basis of his own transformation and his teaching. One may see the same revolutionary impulse that drove him to yoke his will to an anti-colonial struggle at work here, to free humankind from dependence and subjection, not merely to an alien nation, but to the bondage, limitations and maladies of his own nature, a teleology of the Machine reversed and countered by a power of creative consciousness aiming at a perfected life. Sri Aurobindo's experiments in introspection and applied psychology were conducted with the rigour of science, using a methodical framework which was synthetic and integral. This is what he called the Seven Quartets, which are being presented here. He left his conclusions for the future, that humankind may learn to utilise, even in the midst of its subjection to the ubiquitous forces of the world, its affirmative disciplines towards freedom, wholeness, universal personhood, knowledge of oneness, creative power of a complex harmony and capacity to endure and enjoy all experiences as forms of bliss.

II

Psychology and its Alter-disciplines

Sri Aurobindo thought of these disciplines and experiments as a subjective science and a practical psychology. In *The Synthesis of Yoga*, he asserted, "All yoga is nothing but practical psychology". The modern academic discipline of psychology can be said to have its beginnings in the nineteenth century, partly as the Enlightenment's "pure" seeking for total knowledge and partly with the "applied" goal of finding a solution to human pathologies. As Michel Foucault has brought out, underlying both these aims were the modern goals of social ordering, a drive to classify and discipline human populations, establish bounds for productive use, and devise systems of containment, punishment and "cure" for those who fell outside rational and manageable bounds. The experimental and empirical structuralism of Wilhelm Wundt, the biologism of Ivan Pavlov, models of conscious-unconscious interchange as with Sigmund Freud and post-Freudian psychoanalysis, the behaviourism of John Watson and other American psychologists of the early twentieth century, such as B.F. Skinner, could all be classed in these categories.

But an alternate genealogy can be traced, which is more intimately related to philosophical inquiry into the nature of human subjectivity and its transcendence. With its nineteenth-century roots in thinkers such as William James, who challenged the structuralism of Wundt and delved into the psychology of religious experience, this lineage re-emerged around the mid-twentieth century in the USA through such movements as humanistic and existential psychology, based in European philosophical trends such as intersubjectivity, phenomenology and ontology. Instead of empirical foundations in conditioned or pathological behaviour, Abraham Maslow, one of the founders of humanistic psychology, proposed a study of human role models, positing a hierarchy of needs as part of an ascending scale of human potential, guided by a drive for self-actualisation. Probing phenomena of transcendence, Maslow theorised the category and properties of "peak experiences" and, in collaboration with others, opened up the new field of transpersonal psychology in the 1960s. Transpersonal psychology, as the name suggests, takes the human person as a site for transitional and fuzzy processes of consciousness between a recognisable socialised ego and an undefined and impersonal transcendental destination.

From another direction, the researches of Carl Jung in memories, dreams and paranormal experiences helped to open up the field of parapsychology, as well as studies in archetypal symbolism based on the possibilities of existence of extra-personal or impersonal ranges of consciousness, that Jung defined as the "collective unconscious". Jung's work on the transformative processes of "individuation" also prepared and converged with that of humanistic and transpersonal psychology. The opening made by approaches such as Jungian psychology, transpersonal psychology and parapsychology, have allowed a number of newer sub-domains of theory and research to find their niches within the academic edifice. Some of these, of relevance in trying to contextualise the present work based on Sri Aurobindo's experiments, are trans-formational psychology, spiritual psychology, yoga psychology and integral psychology.

Yoga Psychology and the Integral Movement

Most of these fledgling and specialised fields have not gathered sufficient cultural capital to claim universal acceptance in the modern academy and are construed with differing scopes and boundaries by their followers. The terms "spiritual psychology" and "transformational psychology", for example, are often used as synonyms for transpersonal psychology. More properly, spiritual psychology is often concerned with the exploration of experiences and transformations in existing world traditions of spiritual practice, whereas, transpersonal psychology usually aims at a "pure" or "neutral" vocabulary of classifications and distinctions, distancing itself from specific religious traditions. Transformational psychology is often seen as a subfield of developmental, humanistic, transpersonal or Jungian psychology, dealing with the transformative processes of self-actualisation, individuation or altered functioning of the nature following upon ontological changes. Yogic psychology may also be seen as a subset of transpersonal or spiritual psychology, in this case, as the name suggests, specifically developed around the language of the psycho-physical anatomy of yoga, along with the practices and experiences connected with it.

The term "integral psychology" has a varied provenance. It seems to have been coined by Indra Sen, a disciple of Sri Aurobindo, who thereby, attempted to open a field of specialised and comparative study into the psychological theory and process of the integral yoga, as taught by Sri Aurobindo. In more modern times, "integralism" has seen some dubious appropriations, for example, through the copyrighting of the term "integral yoga" by the *guru* Swami Satchidananda. Haridas Chaudhuri, also a follower of Sri Aurobindo, and the founder of the California Institute of Integral Studies (CIIS) in San Francisco, used the terms "integralism" and "integral philosophy" in ways that may be seen as derived from Sri Aurobindo. In more recent times, the self-styled psychologist Ken Wilber has given prominence to the term "integral" and "integral psychology" to describe his theoretical "integration" of the mind-brain paradigm of consciousness. One needs to be careful to distinguish the differing genealogies and uses of the term "integral" in all these cases, if one is to position Sri Aurobindo properly as the proponent of an "integral psychology".

Swami Satchidananda's "integral yoga", for example, is

little more than an "addition" of a few different approaches of yoga, claiming to address the entire human personality and engage it in the practices of prescribed and traditional yoga disciplines. In contrast, Sri Aurobino's "integral yoga" is the seeking for a consciousness that is integral, an ontology of wholeness which overcomes the alienated discontinuity of human existence. Moreover, it is a creative and experimental phenomenology of attention and aspiration, leading to a transformation in one's sources of knowledge, power and order; it is not a set of prescriptions. In this regard, it may be interesting to contrast the post-1960 wave of interest in yoga with that represented by such figures as Vivekananda, Sri Aurobindo and others following in their wake in the first half of the twentieth century. A transcontinental discourse of resistance to the objectification, fragmentation and functional exploitation of consciousness under the oncoming rush of modern capital converged on this term as a locus for creative technologies of the self-subjectively related and identified with the cosmos. But, by the 1960s, the regime of modernity, whose *nomos* is seduction, had infiltrated the subjective world to the extent that yoga found itself no longer a discourse of freedom and wholeness, but was compelled to speak with a forked tongue, either to the concerns of escape (the hippies) or to the eminently marketable interests of stress management (meditation), the body beautiful (*haṭha-yoga*) or the art of sexual ecstasy (Tantra). The *guru* industry proliferated and continues to expand with a plethora of techniques each patented to guarantee "success" in accumulating cultural capital in the monocultural world of neo-liberal globalisation.

From the 1980s, in addition to (and somewhat against) these transcodings within modernity, Hindu nationalism (Hindutva) has increasingly tried to claim yoga as its badge of identity in national ownership and antiquity projects. Though Sri Aurobindo participated in an anti-colonial struggle for the independence of the nation, his activism was undertaken for cultural freedom not cultural fascism. He expected that the liberated individual within the free nation would be able to draw creatively on the accumulated intersubjectivity of a national history and engage dialogically with modernity and indigeneity from this vantage; not be imprisoned by a new collective subjection in the name of the nation. At a time, nearer to Sri Aurobindo's, Aldous Huxley, in works such as, *Brave New World* and *Island* and in our present times, thinkers like Slavoj Zizek, have spelt out this inevitable assimilation of "eastern" subjective technologies by fascist states or by the desiring machine of world capital. "Yoga psychology" in this context, is often little other than a legitimisation of one or other of these packaged commodities. While sharing certain assumptions and a general psycho-physical vocabulary pertaining to subjective experience and the operations and relations of consciousness, the "yoga psychology" implied by the Seven Quartets does not privilege any techniques, formulae or rituals and steers clear of the lures of cultural capital and identity politics. What it offers instead, is a field of creative practice based on forms of attention, volition and affect.

Haridas Chaudhuri can be thought of as a founder of a theoretical philosophy of integralism. There are certain other important thinkers of Chaudhuri's era of 1950-70, such as the Harvard sociologist, Pitirim Sorokin and the Swiss philosopher Jean Gebser, who can be thought of as "integral thinkers" in the phenomenological tradition of Chaudhuri, one which belongs more closely to the scope and intent of Sri Aurobindo. The reductive developmental and systems thinking of Wilber, responsible for the contemporary popularity of the "integral" paradigm, whether in philosophy, psychology, health, culture, business management or the environment, calls itself "post-metaphysical", but is little other than a structuralist typology, with its problematic hierarchy of states and stages of human achievement, and subject to the error of all mental attempts to grasp totality, which cannot but suffer reification if represented . The use of the term "integral" in Sri Aurobindo's own texts pertains instead to an ontology of experience contingent on the silence of the mind, not a theoretical construct, and encompasses a complex oneness of being omnipresent in each of its elements. As such, it is better compared to the idea of the "plane of consistency" (or plane of immanence) theorised by the post-structuralist thinker Gilles Deleuze, as a latency of infinite possibility of experience.

Experimental Psychologies

The Seven Quartets as a "practical psychology", partakes of a number of these disciplinary formations. Backgrounded by the psycho-physical assumptions of yoga, it is undoubtedly a yoga psychology. However, whereas the field of yoga psychology is mostly concerned with an epistemology of psycho-physical consciousness and their processes and experiences contingent on practice, the Seven Quartets is a transformational yoga psychology, dealing with progressive and permanent changes in the operations of human nature through experimental practice. The relation between system and experiment in the Seven Quartets and Record of Yoga is particularly significant. Whereas all science could be said to establish or verify its systemic assumptions through experiment, and all yogas, as "practical psychologies" may be thought of as systemic blueprints related to prescriptive and introspective practice by the subject, a process involving some degree of experiment, the integral yoga implied by the Seven Quartets can be thought of as experimental in a more radical sense. Free of specific prescribed objective practices, the system of the Seven Quartets depends on the relationship between human agency expressing through attention, perception, volition, affect and skill and the unpredictable circumstances of life, seen as the movements of a transcendental field of conscious Immanence in which one's own subjectivity is inextricably involved (or "folded" to use a term from phenomenology). Such a relationship is dependent from the start (and throughout) on the progressive development of a dynamic intuition of the system manifesting itself through processes of creative experimentation.

The Seven Quartets, in their goals of a transformation of consciousness, implying cosmic potency, encompasses several functions which may be called paranormal and hence, can be said to overlap with parapsychology. At least from the mid-nineteenth century, the progress of science in Europe was accompanied by a burgeoning underworld of occult sects and cults, the resurfacing of a plethora of modern versions of medieval mystery schools. Perhaps, the most influential of these, with varied traces continuing into the present, was the Theosophical Society, an organisation for the study of occultism founded in 1875 by H.P. Blavatsky and her followers. Theosophy attempted to bestow a semblance of scientific authenticity to the study of paranormal phenomena, though an aura of magic and a rumour of charlatanism plagued its existence. In the thick of such activities, an organisation calling itself The Society for Psychical Research, with the goal of serious scientific investigations of such phenomena, was founded in 1882 by Frederic William Henry Myers and others. This research organisation (which continues to operate), counted among its members such eminent names as Henry Sidgwick, Frederic Myers, Charles Dodgson (Lewis Carroll), Alfred Russel Wallace, W.B. Yeats, Arthur Conan Doyle, C.G. Jung and William James. More recent members include Archie Roy, Rupert Sheldrake, Richard Wiseman, Susan Blackmore, Dean Radin and Charles Tart. Partly due to the influence of this society and its members, parapsychology, as an academic discipline, gained some acceptance in the Western knowledge academy, most prominently in the 1970s. It concerned itself with psychic abilities (extra-sensory perception, remote sensing, telepathy, precognition, psychokinesis), near-death experiences, out-of-body experience, crisis apparitions, retro-cognitions, reincarnation memories, regression memories, prophecy, channelling and mediumistic activities, apparitional experiences, life after death and such phenomena. The academic respectability of this field was short-lived and much fewer institutions of higher learning continue to actively promote study and research in this area today.

The parapsychological experiences, dealt with in the Seven Quartets, have to do mainly with extra-sensory perception, precognition, remote influence and paranormal capacities of the body. In his diary notes, Sri Aurobindo has a long passage discussing the legitimacy of these powers in a spiritual pursuit, concluding by justifying them as natural capacities to an enhanced human (or trans-human) consciousness.

Again, the system presented by the Seven Quartets is undoubtedly, an integral psychology, following on the definition of Indra Sen and contingent on the distinctions introduced in the previous paragraph, the scope of integrality here, arising from the ontological attainment of an "integral consciousness" in being and the transformation of the nature in the becoming, based on it. As to whether it is a transpersonal psychology, certainly the status of the egoic person is seen as transitional within it, but this does not necessarily imply the disappearance of the person in an impersonality. Perhaps, the term "trans-egoic" would serve it better than transpersonal. Finally, though Sri Aurobindo did not use the term "collective consciousness", the Seven Quartets assume the existence of extra-personal "planes" of cosmic consciousness, with which the individual can identify in being and consciousness. I would say, this too is an aspect of yoga psychology, which Jungian theory has helped to normalise in the modern academy, though here again, ideas such as that of Deleuze's plane of consistency, may be more appropriate, because related to experience, beyond the finite boundaries of mental representation.

III

Post-metaphysical Philosophies

In thinking about alternate psychologies, it is important to constellate these with a post-metaphysical tradition of philosophy which may be said to begin with Friedrich Nietzsche (1844-1900) in the late nineteenth century. At the outset of an approaching global era of contested ideologies of belief, Nietzsche concerned himself with the relative question of truth and its political establishment in human history. Acknowledging the Kantian inaccessibility of transcendentals, such as truth or god to human reason, Nietzsche showed how arbitrary genealogical histories led through operations of power to the privileging of certain ideologies. He brought the entire metaphysical tradition of post-Aristotelian philosophy under scrutiny on these grounds, seeing its attempt at establishing rational epistemologies as a surreptitious operation of the will to power, in its bid to order the inchoate and indefinable infinity of existence. Though ironically, Nietzsche was appropriated by the ultra-irrational racist ideology of the Nazis, it is the fascist implications of idealist metaphysics which Nietzsche radically critiqued, its totalitarian drive to subjugate experience and will under a transcendentally determined regime. He saw scientism, the product of the European Enlightenment, among the most dangerous of these historical and cultural regimes, an equating of human and cosmos through the defining bo(u)nds of reason, and the ideological yoking of humanity to the global enterprise of ordering all experience and all reality by an omniscient epistemology. Nietzsche identified the quintessential (late) philosopher of the Enlightenment as G.W.F. Hegel (1770-1831), who saw the impending modern reign of Reason (Logos) arising from Europe as the fulfillment of cosmic purpose and the end of history; and accordingly posited a philosophy of History which left no stone unturned in its subsumption of the past, present and future of the world. As against this vision of the inexorable predetermined progress of the *Zeitgeist*, Nietzsche looked to non-Western outlooks and presented the prophet Zarathustra, with his doctrine of the incalculable creative power of Will over every determining cosmic regime. Rather than define man and cosmos in terms of the Reason, Nietzsche displaced this power onto the Will, and posited the Will to Power as the most fundamental principle of Life, one which attempted to assert itself everywhere and in every way through political dominance but whose highest potency was creative self-transcendence, the vision of the cosmic human or *Ubermensch*.

The two most important modern streams of psychological philosophy which followed in the wake of Nietzsche and established themselves in the academy through the first half of the twentieth century are phenomenology and existentialism. Phenomenology was given its present form by Edmund Husserl (1859-1938). It proposed a method in which independent objectivity was "bracketed" in favour of grounding attention on the analysis of experience. Thus, the world that is given to us in experience was unravelled in its constitution, so as to reveal the conventions which structure the collective life-world, binding consciousness to it through intention. This unravelling enabled a purity and freedom of experience, which Husserl referred to variously as a transcendental subjectivism or a transcendental ego. A landmark and controversial figure who stood historically between Husserl and Nietzsche on one side (the past) and the gamut of postmodern philosophy on the other (the present) is Martin Heidegger (1889-1976). Heidegger provided an ontological turn to the psychologism of Husserl, and concerned himself more centrally with the relation between Being and beings (or the ontological and the ontic), thus hazing the Husserlian boundaries of the "transcendental ego", while holding fast to phenomenology in its refusal of idealist metaphysics. Opening further the approach, initiated by phenomenology, Heidegger may also be considered one of the modern founders of existentialism, in his development of the conditions for authenticity of existence and self-transcendence through the radically receptive orientation of attention, will and affect.

Postmodernism

A furthering engagement with Nietzsche, Husserl and Heidegger were in evidence in the more contemporary Francophone line of postmodern philosophy, particularly the thinking of Michel Foucault (1926-84) and Jacques Derrida (1930-2004). Both these philosophers refused metaphysics and ontology, thinking instead of the ways by which human experience is constructed at any time by historicist ideologies. While Derrida may be thought to cleave more closely to Husserl and Heidegger in his attention to unravelling the constructed nature of experience (deconstruction), he was less interested in arriving at the purity of a transcendental ego than in the creative play of signification and the openness to singularity and transcendental possibility (*l'avenir*, the democracy to come). Foucault's approach to a similar problematic can be traced more directly to Nietzsche and secondarily to Heidegger. Applying Nietzsche, Foucault sought to ground epistemology historically in the operations and mechanisms of power by which a temporal horizon becomes ontologically settled. By using the Nietzschean methods of archaeology and genealogy, he sought out the synchronic and diachronic bases for the political construction of truth for a culture at any given time. Towards the end of his life, Foucault turned his attention from the technologies of power or the will to power as technology to the technologies of the self. These subjective technologies or technologies of subject-formation or subjectivation, in Foucault's account taken from ancient Greece, included practices for the care or discovery of the soul, an ethics and aesthetics of the self through truth-telling and self-disciplines of attention (*askesis*). The exteriorisation of these practices into socially monitored forms, through confessional methods, initiated through rituals such as Christian confession in fourth century Rome, but mutating through history into the interrogations of modern disciplinary institutions such as schools, clinics, government offices, police stations and prisons, have increasingly offered the nexus for technologies of power to discipline and order subjects ideologically.

Heidegger, Derrida and Foucault all turned a good part of their attention to the unprecedented nature of modernity, the post-enlightenment epoch in which we find ourselves. All three of them identified the epistemic regime of our times as the turn towards technology or in Nietzschean terms, the will to power as technology. Heidegger noted the systemic and totalistic nature of modernity, setting out to claim all knowledge, all time and all space for its domain in the name of science, in what he called "the age of the world picture". This setting forth of the ongoing activity of research, the disappearance of the individual into the anonymity of the *subjectum* and the conversion of the world into "picture", a single representational image, marks the modern disclosure of Being, its qualitative reduction to numerical magnitude and relation. Foucault further developed the discursive and institutional mechanisms and procedures through which modern individuals are anonymised into subjects, the role of the human sciences as a cornerstone of the universal modern academy and of the pan-optical state technologies of surveillance and discipline to set in place the replicable image of "humanity". As against this ubiquitous construction of world and subject, Foucault called for the reclamation of subjectivation in individuals, an ethics and aesthetics of the self, through counter-technologies such as truth-telling and "care of the soul".

The Deleuzian Century

Apart from these thinkers, there are a number of others who have followed this train of thinking, continuing to elaborate the consequences of our age in its varied and ongoing aspects in a phenomenological vein. Among the contemporaries of Derrida and Foucault and part of the same Francophone tradition of postmodern philosophy, one may enumerate Gilles Deleuze (1925-95), Jean-Francois Lyotard (1924-98), Jean Baudrillard (1929-2007) and Michel de Certeau (1925-86). Belonging to a later generation and continuing to elaborate on the chapter of global modernity belonging to our present times, particularly its sense of historic rupture, its mnemo-technical and virtual ontology, and its alternative possibilities, some of the most prominent thinkers are the theorists of feminine subjectivity Luce Irigaray (1932-), of the ecology of speed, Paul Virilio (1932-), and of contemporary technologies of memory, Bernard Stiegler (1952-). Of these thinkers, in the context of our study, special mention needs to be made of Gilles Deleuze, who also counted Nietzsche among his forbears, but constellated his lineage of thinking with two other philosophers of the past, Enlightenment philosopher Baruch Spinoza (1632-77) and the philosopher of intuition and creative evolution, Henri Bergson (1859-1941). Deleuze, a friend of Foucault, of whom the latter said, "One day, perhaps, this century will be called Deleuzian", did not, like Foucault or Derrida, reject metaphysics or ontology, but inverted them, subordinating them to experience.

Following Spinoza, Deleuze rooted ontology in an absolute Immanence, which was knowable only as process, an univocity expressing as the radical difference and plurality of the cosmos. This field of Immanence (sometimes called field of Consistency) was conceived by Deleuze as the infinite substratum of all existence and experience, marked by infinitely varying intensities of unpredictable flows and energies, each a sensation, idea and/or feeling existing as virtual becoming or problematic, actualising itself repeatedly in different forms. It is important to note that Deleuzian ideas differ from Platonic ideas in their immanence and Deleuzian virtuality is no less real than actuality. Of his concepts, Deleuze says, "The concept they [the conditions of experience] form is identical to its object." The task of the philosopher, for Deleuze, is to intuit these fields of virtual problematics from experience and express them in the form of concepts, just as the task of the artist is to express the being of sensations, which are a compound of percepts and affects; and the task of the scientist is to express through generative functions based on fixed points of reference. Deleuze engages himself with the problematics of how one can live one's life and proposes an extension of experiencing capacity so as to become aware of the virtual field of intensities, ideas and feelings which constitute the extensive or discrete differences of the actual world. This extension in body sensation, emotion and intuition so as to experience the virtual domain, consists of an overcoming of the categories of identity, resemblance, analogy and opposition that characterise our experience of actuality and arrive through this abstraction at the experience of a scale of intensities. Deleuze and his collaborator Guattari, refer to this transformation as "making a Body without Organs (BwO)". It is only through such a transformation that the body's independent agency may be recovered and the question "Of what is a body capable?" posed by Spinoza, find its dynamic answer through experience and action. The BwO can then be thought of as a gate of entry to yet greater extensions of experience approximating progressively to the infinite plane of Immanence, marked by a simultaneity of univocity and difference, in which neither is reduced to the other. One may see in this account, a resemblance of Deleuze and Guattari's method with that of Husserl's phenomeno-logical reduction, but, whereas Husserl's phenomenology deals with concepts and percepts and is grounded in mental perception, the Deleuzian construction of the BwO deals with sensations, percepts, affects and concepts and is grounded in physical experience. While it is true that Husserl's phenomenology has been extended to include the embodied component of perception by Maurice Merleau-Ponty, the grounding of experience in intensities of sensation grants to Deleuze's transcendental empiricism a much greater integrality and an experimental method akin to yoga.

Deleuze's ontology also bears comparison with Sri Aurobindo's in terms of the way in which he conceptualises the individual and its fractal "folding" into the cosmos. Deleuze introduced the idea of the fold to theorise the integral relationship between the "inside" and the "outside" of living beings. Instead of seeing beings as autonomous, he views the collective reality of each type of being as a life on a fold of pure immanence. Such an "enfolded" existence implies an internalisation by each "monad" of the cosmic entirety following specific principles which characterise the ontology of its type of experience. Subject and cosmos, thus, integrally exist in each other and the nexus of internal and external forces determines the universal reality of cosmos for the subject. The conscious awareness of this relationship between internal and external forces is the "unfold", something which also makes possible an "unfolding" and "refolding". Existing unquestionably on a fold marks the existence of non-human beings, but humans are characterised by critical and creative subjectivity which allows them to "deterritorialise" the fixity of the relation between subject and fold. Deleuze and Guattari refer to this variously as "nomadology", "lines of flight", "becoming-other" and "making a body without organs".

In the appendix of his book on Foucault, Deleuze relates Foucault's prediction of the erasure of the human with

Nietzsche's superman-making project and his own thinking about the fold. Making it an occasion to think of the future of human subjectivity, he develops here the idea of the superfold, as the fractal ground natural to superman. The superfold is neither a fold nor an unfolding in the sense in which Deleuze conceptualised internal-external relations in the human case. It is, instead, an ontology of immanence with a protean creativity capable of an "unlimited finite". Superman represents the forces of subjective interiority which internalise the capacities of the superfold and give it monadic expression. Deleuze's intuition of the superfold as the ontological future towards which the human moves is also related to the emergence of the technologies of molecular biology, silicon-based information theory and new capacities of language use. All these technologies, portend possibilities of deconstruction and creative reassemblage, which approach the most basic building-blocks of life (genetics), matter (information), and mind (signification/language).

An "unlimited finite" is a capacity characteristic of the fulfilled potency of what Deleuze calls transcendental empiricism, which could also be nominated as a divine materialism. It implies that every fine point in space and "moment" of time is a creative actualisation of infinity. Superfold is the cosmic medium, potent with such a possibility and superman is the individualised subjectivity which can express this capacity as its native mode of existence. Superfold contains the triple folds of genetic handling (life capacity), silicon and nanotechnological handling (material capacity) and language handling (mental capacity). Superman for Deleuze, then, is the master of the triple folds of gene, silicon and language, the creative consciousness which can manipulate these forms of nature at its most basic level, manifesting infinity through their finite conditions of space-time expression. There is no habitual fixity to such a form of creative consciousness, or even if there is persistence of forms or logical development of forms, the ontology is one of pure freedom and the deployed will of omnipresence, omnipotence and omniscience at play in the finite conditions of the cosmos.

Though expressed in material terms and related to contemporary technologies of unprecedented fundamental ubiquity, Deleuze's superfold can well be thought of as close or analogous to an immanent version of Sri Aurobindo's supermind, the medium which holds unity and infinity as its conscious properties everywhere and is the nexus between the infinite and the finite in its absolute immanence. So too, the relation between superfold and superman in Deleuze is analogous to the relation between supermind and superman in Sri Aurobindo, in that the latter term in each doublet represents the subject with interiority, proper to the being and full creative expression of the capacities of the first term.

Interlocutors

Sri Aurobindo was roughly a contemporary of Heidegger and his generation of thinkers. He was familiar with Nietzsche and referred to him in a number of his writings, praising him for his existential turn as a philosopher of thought-in-life rather than of detached thought. He also, for this reason, turned his attention to the pre-Socratic thinkers of Greece, much as Heidegger and Nietzsche before him, had done. Most significantly, like Nietzsche, he proposed a self-exceeding for the human, a re-creation through *askesis* and surrender, and gave to this destining the Nietzschean name of superman. One may see the derivation of superman from the transcendental consciousness of supermind, yet the Nietzschean parallel is not fortuitous. Writing within the discursive academic culture of Indian philosophy of the early twentieth century, Sri Aurobindo had to voice his philosophical ideas in terms of idealist metaphysics. As cross-cultural expression one needs to read this as *darśana*, an epistemology arising from and necessarily coupled with a theory of practice, yoga. But entering the language community of modern specialised disciplines, it undergoes a discursive rupture and is perceived independently. In his major philosophical work, the *Life Divine*, Sri Aurobindo tried to safeguard against this conversion, pointing to the Vedāntic methodology of intuition and experience as its basis (chapter on Vedāntic methods of knowledge) and attempting to reformulate the boundaries of Idealism:

> The idealistic interpretation supposes a relation between the Truth behind and the conceptive phenomenon in front, a relation which is not merely that of an antinomy and opposition. The view I am presenting goes farther in idealism; it sees the creative Idea as Real Idea, that is to say, a power of Conscious Force expressive of real being, born out of real being and partaking of its nature and neither a child of the Void nor a weaver of fictions.[1]

Elsewhere in the same text, he uses the term "experience-concept"[2] to differentiate his thought from abstract thinking. The similarity between this and Deleuze's notion of the concept should be apparent. There are many other points of convergence between the thought of Deleuze and Sri Aurobindo's theory of practice — Deleuze's Plane of Consistency is defined in terms not far from Sri Aurobindo's Supermind, an absolute consciousness characterised by irreducible and radical univocity and infinity, Deleuze's building of the BwO is analogous to processes of liberation from "given" internal formations, including the physical, in Sri Aurobindo; Deleuze's call to experimentation is seconded by the personalisation of practice based on the emergence of consciousness by Sri Aurobindo; Deleuze's "scale of intensities" can be seen as synonymous with the conversion of all experience to forms of bliss in Sri Aurobindo.

1. LD, p. 125.
2. Ibid., p. 661.

Convergences of Sri Aurobindo's thought with other postmodern thinkers are also significant. Sri Aurobindo's political and cultural sensitivity to the forces of colonialism and modernity bring his practices in alignment with those of Michel Foucault. This establishes the contemporary relevance of Sri Aurobindo's yoga in terms of affording technologies of the self for autonomy and subjectivation of the individual and the ability to exert a transformative influence on determining regimes of global discourse in the micropolitics of power. In this regard, it is noteworthy that where Martin Heidegger, in spite of his clarity regarding the omnipresent technological power of the age of the world picture and his warnings for the authenticity of individual life, was taken in by the subjective rhetoric of the Führer of the Third Reich, Sri Aurobindo, in his distant corner of the world identified the civilisational menace of Hitler, as early as 1933, when he had just become Chancellor. He also used the enhanced powers of the self in opposing this menace. *Record of Yoga*, as a form of truth-telling connected with personal *askesis* is a quintessential example of Foucauldian ethical and aesthetic self-fashioning on one's own terms. As a strategic form of self-disclosure, it fashions its own parole, which requires a hermeneutics which is in itself the initiation to an experimental generative and transformative discourse. The Seven Quartets of the *Record of Yoga*, have to be seen as the reception of a functive in the Deleuzian sense, a functional enunciation of the problems arising in the consciousness at a certain stage in a process of self-fashioning. Today, and in texts such as the present, there lies the danger of its reduction to "received knowledge", and turned into a new orthodoxy. To prevent this, it is important to ground the theory in personal interpretation and experimental practice, a postmodern imperative. For this reason, wherever applicable, thinkers such as Nietzsche, Heidegger, Deleuze, Foucault, Irigaray and others have been used as interlocutors to our text.

Objectives

To wrap up, my primary objective in this text is to understand the processes and goals that relate to the integral transformation of being and nature in the Seven Quartets of Sri Aurobindo's *Record of Yoga*. It is also to understand the place of this particular formulation in the wider field of Indian yoga. Thirdly, it is to provide us with an approach to a hermeneutic translation of this field of yoga, a process which Sri Aurobindo himself initiated, but which must be treated as an ongoing project, because of the progress of contemporary psychology and philosophy, and their interest in paranormal, transpersonal and trans-egoic processes, as part of a dynamic understanding of the human being and its indeterminate boundaries. One of the objectives of the modern knowledge academy, as a post-enlightenment global institution, has been the discursive articulation of an integral knowledge of the human, using the human sciences, and in keeping with this objective, one of our goals here is an approach to a new psychology of process aimed at the integral, beyond the normative bounds of modernity. Finally, part of our objective is to gain a key, an opening, to understanding the inner life of Sri Aurobindo through the *Record of Yoga*, seen as a lived example, that we can learn from, and derive inspiration from, for success in experimental practice.

Prior to our entry into this study, it needs to be clearly understood that the Seven Quartets, as a "practical psychology", is not, therefore, a psychotherapy. The practice of the Seven Quartets is an aid to a self-practice, for purposes of self-exceeding into an integral consciousness and for transformation of the nature and its operations into the natural dynamic vehicles of this integral consciousness. In its positioning in the knowledge-world of the modern academy, it is not an epistemology or theoretical system, a deep structure to order experience into hierarchic forms, ripe for social ranking or exclusions and inclusions. It is rather a system of creative practice, an archive of attention, a toolbox of engagement and experience. Similarly, and perhaps most importantly, in the power-world of social life-activities, surreptitiously ordered in our times by global capital, it is not another (and even ultimate) technology at the service of social and economic advantage or, of identity politics. If anything, it is the very reverse, the possibility of a subjective reversal, the freedom, richness and wholeness of conscious Being, known through identity as one and infinite.

1

Integral Yoga Psychology and the Quartet of Perfection

"THE Seven Quartets of Becoming" outlines the system of experimental yoga practice that Sri Aurobindo followed and expressed to himself in his diary notes. Sri Aurobindo's journey in yoga could be said to have started around 1905 with the practice of conscious breath control (*prāṇāyāma*). In 1908, he had his first major yogic realisation, that of the silent spirit, known in the Indian tradition as *Brahman*.[1] While at Alipur Jail, serving a one-year sentence as an undertrial for sedition, this initial realisation was followed by others, such as that of the *Brahman* as dynamic as, the one conscious energy active in the universe; the Divine Person immanent in all beings and things; and experiences of what he was to call the ranges of cosmic mind, leading up to a transcendent source of the cosmos, which he called Supermind.[2]

Shortly after his settlement in Pondicherry in 1910, he began maintaining a diary in which he recorded the progress of his yoga experiences and experiments in terms of seven lines of transformative practice, which he called the *sapta catuṣṭaya* (Seven Quartets). These seven aspects of yoga practice, peace, power, knowledge, body, being, action and integration, formed for him an overlapping mesh through which

1. AN, pp. 91, 94, 111; OH, pp. 239-40, 244, 249.
2. Ibid., p. 94; OH, p. 249.

Sapta Catuṣṭaya (Seven Quartets) (1.1)

Śanti Catuṣṭaya **(Perfection of Equality):**
1. Samatā (Equality),
2. Śanti (Peace),
3. Sukha (Happiness),
4. Hāsya (Laughter)

Śakti Catuṣṭaya **(Perfection of Power):**
1. Vīrya (Strength),
2. Śakti (Power),
3. Caṇḍībhāva (Divine Nature),
4. Śraddhā (Faith).

Vijñāna Catuṣṭaya **(Perfection of Knowledge):**
1. Jñāna (Knowledge),
2. Trikāladṛṣṭi (Time-Knowledge),
3. Aṣṭa-Siddhi (Eight Powers),
4. Samādhi (Absorption).

Siddhi Catuṣṭaya **(General Elements of Perfection):**
1. Śuddhi (Purification),
2. Mukti (Liberation),
3. Bhukti (Enjoyment),
4. Siddhi (Perfection).

Brahma Catuṣṭaya **(Perfection of Being):**
1. Sarvam (Omnipresent)
2. Anantam (Infinite)
3. Jñānam (Omniscient),
4. Ānandam (All-Delightful)

Brahmā (Being).

Karma Catuṣṭaya **(Perfection of Action):**
1. Kṛṣṇa (Lord),
2. Kālī (Divine Śakti),
3. Karma (Work),
4. Kāma (Enjoyment).

Śarīra Catuṣṭaya **(Perfection of the Body):**
1. Ārogya (Health),
2. Utthāpana (Lightness),
3. Saundarya (beauty),
4. Vividhānanda (Varied Delight).

to address the progress of an integral transformation. He claimed to have received this system from "the Master of the Yoga" at times identified by him as Śrī Kṛṣṇa. These diaries have recently been published by the Sri Aurobindo Ashram in two volumes under the title *The Record of Yoga*, which is how, Sri Aurobindo himself titled one of these early notebooks. The diaries record Sri Aurobindo's thoughts, experiences and experiments, sometimes on a daily basis and sometimes weekly. They form a kind of scientist's log of a complex psychological experiment carried out with himself for subject. Since they were addressed to himself, these records are expressed in a shorthand, following his classification of inner processes. At the start of the *Record of Yoga*, we find a brief outline of this schema.[3] He also spoke about these practices to his early disciples, and towards the end of the second volume of the published *Record of Yoga*, an edited version of these scribal notes has been published.[4] Correlating these sources and Sri Aurobindo's later writings with the various lines of self-discipline expressed mnemonically in his outline, we will explore the transformational yoga psychology and system which Sri Aurobindo followed. We may call this the yoga of integral transformation.

Yoga is a Sanskrit word, which is understood in many different ways today. Even within the discourse of its practice in India, it has varied connotations. As touched on in the Introduction, this complexity has been exacerbated in modern times by its successive appropriation by the politics of capital. Hence, it is not easy to define this word. Literally it means union, coming into union. Sri Aurobindo has, somewhere, tried to explain yoga by calling it an applied psychology: "Yoga is nothing but practical psychology".[5] By this he meant that it concerns itself with an understanding of the processes of consciousness within the human being and an application by the self, through introspection and discipline, of these "processes" so as to arrive at certain goals — goals of personality change, and change in the powers of consciousness, that we embody and express. Through these disciplines of attention and transformation, we also come into union with suprapersonal states of consciousness (not necessarily or only impersonal). Sri Aurobindo may have been happy to hear that this view of yoga is taking its fledgling steps as the discipline of yoga psychology in the contemporary knowledge academy. This broad locus also sets the stage for our understanding of the Seven Quartets. The terms "yoga" and "yoga psychology"

3. RoY, pp. 3-29.
4. Ibid., pp. 1467-84.
5. SoY, p. 44.

here are, therefore, not limited to a set of prescriptive practices, whether of meditation, sitting postures, breathing, *mantra* repetitions, performance of ritual or any combination of these.

Moreover, the goals of yoga determine the practices of yoga. The goals of yoga are not all the same; there are a variety of goals that belong to the broad field or discipline of yoga. Why one arrives at yoga, defines or gives shape to what one does in yoga. If one is seeking health, longevity and abundance of energy, one would practise a certain yoga. If one is seeking liberation from the tyrannies of circumstances and human subjectivism, of ignorance, falsehood, suffering, one would follow another kind of yoga. If one is seeking power over others, over the world, over adverse circumstance, one would follow yet another kind of yoga. If one is seeking bliss, one would follow a certain kind of yoga. Thus, when we speak of a "yoga of integral transformation", the phrase itself provides the scope of this yoga, and the goal or aim that Sri Aurobindo lay down for himself and taught for others. As an "integral transformation", it points to the fact that he held the notion of a goal that was integral, which encompassed the totality of being and becoming.

Contemporary Social Relevance

Before we dwell further on this idea of the integral, it will be useful to consider what importance such a practice has for us today. For this, we need to reflect on modernity, the hegemonic epoch in which we find ourselves. A systemic viewing of man and world as "resources" and their deployment across the globe for the maximization of capital generation through surplus production and consumption characterizes this unprecedented age of world-being. Starting with colonialism and industrialism, its ever accelerating force, under the twin engines of capital and technology, disperses human and material resources across the globe for the pleasure of domination and the harvesting of excess. All is grist to its mill, even anti-colonial politics, religion and socialism/ communism, the troubled engagements of cultural difference rapidly surveilled and policed towards uniformity or turned into flavors of the franchised norms of neo-liberal globalization. Human subjectivity is flattened under its instrumentalizing drive, turned into surface and made into fodder for the near-instantaneous circulations of an increasingly integrated world-spanning machine to which master and serf are both subject. The term integral is more familiar to us in this sense, as the ubiquitous circuits of technology wirelessly subsume the phenomenal universe into a real-time panopticon of virtual targeting and control, which presages human disappearance in the machine.

In this era of the shredding of subjectivity, what Sri Aurobindo holds out is the inverse potential of the integral subject, in whom history lives as creative becoming and the density of whose consciousness stands master to the global forces of technology, able to utilize them as extension of self, in shaping the face of its post-human future.

In this context, it would be useful also to draw attention to Gilles Deleuze's idea of developing a "virtual body" or a Body without Organs (BwO).[6] Deleuze sees the need for this arising from the fact that what we assume as "the body" is a normative construct established through cultural assumptions and collectively kept in place through social discipline. Today, the intimate and co-dependent relation of mind and body is well accepted, so that we often refer to this interface as the body-mind. But this pervasion of body by mind, is not merely psychological, it is also cultural and political. Just as the ubiquitous interference of modernity in nature has politicised all territory so that we cannot but think of a cultural or a

6. ATP, pp. 165-84.

political geography, the entrance of humans into the symbolic domain of language subjects the body to cultural and ideological selections, so that we must properly speak of a cultural and political anatomy. We may extend the analogy to territory further, and say that in our postcolonial global era, the "organs" of such a body are functionally defined and "colonised" by cultural and political forces, so as to form a subject and bring it under social control. This cultural and political inscription affects not merely our idea of the body and its social functions, but also its micro-reality as subjective experience. The body with its functional anatomy is thus a formalised subjectivity "belonging to" an ideological text.[7]

Whether we choose it for ourselves or not, some ideology has already inscribed its mental anatomy onto our subjectivity. What we call modernity, for example, is such a text, with its normalised modes of psycho-physical expectation, behaviour, discipline, consumption, recreation, ethics, aesthetics, ideals, bliss, pain and disease, controlled by the state, the corporate market and the knowledge academy. The hegemonic universality of these norms, in today's world, have spawned a number of alternate "non-modern" ideologies, with their own sets of prescriptive psycho-physical boundaries of being, becoming and desiring. The right-wing Muslim or Hindu, for example, have very different body-mind constitutions, with their own structural and functional forms and boundaries of behaviour, consumption, ethics, ideals, pleasure and pain for this-life and the after-life. These ideological texts vie with one another for territorial authority in a global world, making their followers into unconscious agents of their violent contested wills. To free ourselves from such subjection and open ourselves to a process, in which we are creative agents in a world

7. This discursive production of the subject can be seen more prominently in the work of Michel Foucault. For example, see Michel Foucault, *Discipline and Punish: The Birth of the Prison*, Random House, New York, 1975, p. 138.

becoming, is the goal held out by Deleuze and Guattari.

But, such a creative and transformative possibility can only be generated through a reconfiguration of the subject outside the selective definitions of bio-power necessary for epistemic control. Prior to the childhood entry into the symbolic system of a cultural unconsciousness, the automatisms of the body allow little subjective agency to the physical consciousness to engage with social determinisms. But a body, which has experienced such cultural and political subjection and is aware of choice beyond it, has a form of independent physical subjectivity and agency in its engagement with the world which cannot be predicted. This is what makes Deleuze repeatedly ask, echoing the philosopher Spinoza, what the body is capable of.

This is not a question to be answered, but one to be asked continuously of the body, from a vantage of mental witnessing. This "de-territorialisation" is sought to be achieved by Deleuze and Guattari through a refusal of normative definitions for the "organs" and the presentation of a "body", which has withdrawn its discursive handles of control. Deleuze and Guattari refer to this as a nomadology. Though they do not prescribe any single method for this construction of an active or "full" BwO, leaving it to individual creativity and experimentation, they warn against destruction of the "body" through practices of burnout (one may think here of Rimbaud's "willed derangement of all the senses")[8] and recommend a body prepared through the balance of yoga, as one which, while it refuses determination by hegemonic discourses, can allow itself as creative agency for experiences of bliss and social transformation.[9]

Though Deleuze and Guattari do not specify any form of yoga, for the subjectivity to be truly free, a non-prescriptive

8. Arthur Rimbaud, *Complete Works, Selected Letters: a Bilingual Edition*, trans. Wallace Fowlie, updated Seth Widden, University of Chicago Press, Chicago, 2005, p. 377.

9. ATP, p. 167.

yoga, which is transformative in an integral sense (physical, emotional, volitional, cognitive) would be necessary. This is what the integral yoga provides. Interestingly, as we will see in the quartet of the body, the Seven Quartets propose their own psycho-physical reconstitution of the "organs", one which rests on freedom and pure consciousness in each case. Again, though Deleuze and Guattari eschew belief in transcendence, and reside the entirety of the power of creative becoming in a plane of immanence, the freedom of subjectivity opens it to acts of creative becoming, proceeding from such a plane which is one and infinite. The properties of the Supermind could easily be mapped into this Being-in-Becoming, and the goal of the practitioner can be seen as coming into identity with this integral supramental consciousness, bestowing a concrete sense and renewed scope to Nietzsche's project of supermanhood.[10]

The Divine Life: Integral Being and Becoming

The idea of "integrality" is large and complex. Add to this the idea of "transformation", and the kind of becoming implied, the application of psychological process to oneself, is clearly aimed not at an escape, nor at any limited or limiting goal, but, at the attainment of an "integral consciousness" and a thorough change of nature based on this. But, what is meant by integrality? In the Introduction, I have written about some of the confusion surrounding this term. An integral consciousness is not a piecemeal addition of different attainments; it implies a quintessential grasp of consciousness which is one and infinite, a consciousness of "the whole", not a sum, however complete, of parts. Human experience however, is fragmented, piecemeal. Our thoughts, feelings, desires, physical impulses are mostly discontinuous, a stream of consciousness where various movements interrupt each

10. See Friedrich Nietzsche, "Thus Space Zarathustra" in Walter Kaufmann (tr.), *The Portable Nietzsche*, London & New York: Penguin 1954, p. 126.

other in an unsteady flow which we take for granted. To such an experience, the idea of an "integral consciousness" seems illusory or presumptuous.

If we ponder this experience historically, we may realise that this discontinuity or dispersion of consciousness, is more prevalent in our present times than ever before. We find ourselves bombarded from all sides by an excess of information, almost always tugging at our attention. Perhaps, the complexity of our self-awareness has expanded far beyond what was common to our ancestors, but this field of awareness is far from unified or capable of agency. In earlier stages of human civilisation, for example, in ancient Greece or India of the classical period, an *askesis* of sustained attention was held up as the ideal of self-culture, a self-preservation of subjectivity necessary to the "care of the soul". The discipline of integral yoga begins with such a sustained and continuous self-gathering. Through such a discipline, if one could discover a source of wholeness, ordering one's existence and expression coherently and harmoniously not with the mind, but through the discovery of a principle of infinite oneness, so as to engage creatively with all the forces and qualities of the world, one could assert a realisation of integrality. Sri Aurobindo's experience had shown him the existence of such an integral consciousness and of man's ability to embody it, through the process of yoga.

To attempt a system of self-discipline, which will enable union with an integral consciousness, one must start with a psychology of integral being. The broad field of yoga psychology in India provides us with a number of such schema which may be called epistemologies of being. It is important to realise the difference between such an epistemology and idealist metaphysics. An idealist metaphysics, is a conceptual structure of knowledge based on transcendental axioms. What may be called a phenomenological metaphysics is a map of experience, becoming an aid to future realisation. As a structure of knowledge, it is contingent on the problematics of experience arising out of practice. Sri Aurobindo uses the term "experience-concept" to describe the metaphysical categories he uses and develops.[11] One may think of this as phenomenological, since the method of consciousness implied in its practice sidesteps metaphysics in a way reminiscent of Husserl's caveat:

> Here at the outset I require only this one thing, that one keep these sorts of prejudice, one's knowing in advance the meaning of those words that I have furnished with entirely new sense [. . .] firmly locked away in one's breast [. . .] Initially, one hears and sees what is being presented, one goes along and sees where it might lead and what might be accomplished with it.[12]

Sri Aurobindo's epistemic psychology of integral being draws on the Vedic and Upaniṣadic description of being as a continuum of seven modalities of Consciousness. Broadly, he refers to these as matter (*annam*), life (*prāṇa*), mind (*mana*), supermind (*vijñāna*), bliss (*ānanda*), consciousness (*cit*) and being (*sat*).[13] The plane of consciousness, which carries all these modalities as part of its reality and represents them in ordered form is *vijñāna* or what Sri Aurobindo calls Supermind. Thus, Supramental Being could be said to characterise the fullness of integral consciousness.[14]

Matter, life and mind are principles of consciousness familiar to us, since they constitute the foundations of our experience. The Vedāntic tradition classifies the combined

---

11. LD, p. 661.
12. E. Husserl, *Die Krisis der europäischenWissenschaften und die transzendentale Phänomenologie. Eine Einleitung in die phänomenologische Philosophie*. Husserliana 6. Den Haag: Martinus Nijhoff, 1954, pp. 439-40.
13. The classic statement of this structure of consciousness is to be found in Chapter III, Bhṛgu-Vallī of the *Taittirīya Upaniṣad*.
14. LD, p. 278.

reality and action of these three principles of consciousness as *avidyā* (ignorance). Why this is so termed, can be better understood in relation to the Vedāntic definition of knowledge (*vidyā*), a direct knowledge of oneself and others/things, through identity beyond the distinction of subject and object. Our experience, bounded by the mind-life-body complex, and structured in terms of discrete time and space, is characterised by finitude and separation, a condition in which consciousness remains subjective and unable "to know" "others" through identity. Moreover, individual consciousness is not homogeneous. It is discontinuous, made up of different forms of consciousness (mental, vital, physical) interacting with one another but unable to "know" each other through identity. This is why Vedāntic epistemology considers our assumed modality of knowing to be an ignorance. In contrast, it describes forms of experience which may be considered transcendental, in which Consciousness is undivided and self-modulating.

This is the realm of knowledge (*vidyā*), since all is known by identity here. In an absolute sense, there can be no categoric distinctions here and one can only speak of it as a singularity and an infinity. The principles of *sat*, *cit* and *ānanda* form this triune reality, often referred together as *Saccidānanda*. In itself, such an absolute reality could have no relations and could not "know" itself outside its indivisibility. But, a fourth principle of transcendental consciousness, *vijñāna*, operates as the reflexive knot that ties these two realms of *vidyā* and *avidyā* together. Supermind, as the "knowledge consciousness" can present *Saccidānanda* in the form of manifesting ideas. Thus, Supermind may be thought of as both, the knowledge consciousness and the creative consciousness of *vidyā*. The Ideas of Supermind are not static representational categories, such as Platonic ideas, but dynamic principles of immanence presenting reality as evolving fields of possibility. Accordingly, Sri

Aurobindo refers to them as Real Ideas.[15] One such field is the form of experience which characterises our existence, a structuring of reality in terms of quantised space and time and ontological finitude, the basis of an "evolving ignorance" (*avidyā*).

To transform our experience of reality, from one of ignorance in the Vedāntic sense, to one of knowledge, becomes the project of the schools of Vedāntic Yoga. Sri Aurobindo's approach to this problematic may be seen as one which attempts this transformation, while retaining the fullness of embodied experience. This approach hinges on the realisation of the supramental consciousness which presents the absolute in terms of the relative, the indivisible and infinite in terms of the discrete and finite. But, such a plane of consciousness needs to be experienced and embodied by individuals, if one is to speak of an integral yoga. Since only like can respond to like, if the supramental consciousness is to be embodied, there must be something in the individual which can take its residence in this plane of consciousness, identifying with it in being.

A centre of inexhaustible plenitude in each person, which is a precipitation of the transcendental consciousness in individual form in time, space and divisibility is identified by Sri Aurobindo as such a being. This integral Person evolving its infinity uniquely in each individual, can modulate itself in all these gradations or modalities of consciousness and thus, is capable of intuiting and realising Supermind. This is the soul personality or psychic being (*caitya Puruṣa*).[16] However, to arrive at an integral consciousness, marked by both radical unity and radical plurality, the psychic being must first enlarge itself from the personal and individual, to the cosmic and impersonal. Thus, the discovery of the psychic being and the successive attainment by it of universal and integral consciousness would constitute the goals of integral being.

15. LD, p. 125.

16. LD, p. 278.

Based on such an attainment of integral being, one's dynamic nature would need to be transformed so that what one sensed, thought, felt, wished, willed and acted out proceeded spontaneously and continually as an expression of this being. Such a consequence may seem to be obvious, since the possession of an integral being would naturally result in an experience and behaviour in consonance with such being. But, in reality, the attainments of the soul may not translate naturally to the nature. Our mental, emotional, volitional and physical nature parts act in grooves of conditioned habits which need to be brought into union with the soul consciousness through processes of transformative discipline. This aspect of the yoga of integral transformation compasses the goals of integral becoming.[17]

These twin goals of integral being and integral becoming enable the practitioner to express what Sri Aurobindo has elsewhere called a divine life.[18] We may say, the goal of all yoga is to arrive at some union with total consciousness, whether we call it God, *Brahman*, the Transcendental Subject or Integral Being, and the faith that drives this entire field of yoga is that such a union is possible. Through its validation in experience and through its repeatability, this faith is established as a general discipline. The project of the yoga of integral transformation is to find a process by which human beings can arrive at an integral consciousness and an integral action of that consciousness in the world, thereby, experiencing a divine life. However, at the outset, it is important to emphasise that such a process cannot but be existential and experiential and hence, experimental in each case.

Today's intellectual culture is justly suspicious of grand totalistic descriptions, or Theories of Everything (ToE). The

---

17. Sri Aurobindo speaks of the relation between these two, soul and nature or being and its forms of becoming in terms of cause (*kāraṇa*) and instrument (*karaṇa*). SoY, pp. 15-18.

18. LD, pp. 6-7.

justification for such scepticism arises from the mind's incapacity in grasping wholeness, as it proceeds by piecing together fragments into larger fragments, which nevertheless, arrogate to themselves "the whole" or the integral. Such a structure or schema, claiming integrality, is motivated by an ideological hegemonic totalitarianism, with its inclusions and exclusions, suppressions or eliminations, its hierarchies and gradations of distance from "the centre". In this context, it bears repeating and cannot be overemphasised that the idea of "the integral" coded into the yoga of integral transformation, does not lend itself to experience or formulation by the mind and can only be thought of in mental terms as paradoxical. Moreover, structurally it makes no sense except as a function of the process of transformation.

An unexpressed intuition of integrality leads us existentially through the process of such a transformation beyond the silence of the mind, towards an experience which refuses singular description. What Sri Aurobindo affirms is the possibility of such an experience. This experience is as much material, of the body, as it is volitional, of the will, emotional, of the heart, conceptual, of the mind and spiritual, of pure consciousness. One is reminded of Gilles Deleuze's echoing of the thought of Spinoza: "Of what is a body capable? . . . . We do not even know what a body is capable of."[19] Our discursive presumptions about "human experience" define our limits, but conscious erasure of these discursive boundaries opens up new capacities, new faculties, new forms of experience. The integral is one such form of experience whose possibility, Sri Aurobindo affirms, beyond the logic of sense or of symbolic systems masquerading in the name of God.

---

19. This inquiry into spiritual materiality or embodied spirituality is one of Deleuze's central concerns, repeatedly invoked. See, for example, Gilles Deleuze, *Nietzsche and Philosophy*, London & New York: Continuum International Publishing Group, 2006, pp. 36-38.

The Seven Quartets

As touched on before, in 1910, Sri Aurobindo travelled to the south Indian city of Pondicherry, where he "retired" from public life. Before this, he was a leader of the freedom struggle against British colonialism in India. He was already advanced in his spiritual pursuit when he came to Pondicherry, receiving a direct inner guidance (*ādeśa*) which led him to follow, in a very scrupulous and systematic manner, the path which he lay down as the *sapta catuṣṭaya* — what I have loosely translated as the Seven Quartets. The seven approaches to perfection (*siddhi*) that this involves are:

- Four approaches of more specific aspects of yoga (the *ādhāra siddhi*s), i.e. a perfection of peace or equality (*śānti* or *samatā catuṣṭaya*), a perfection of power (*śakti catuṣṭaya*), a perfection of knowledge (*vijñāna catuṣṭaya*) and a perfection of the body (*śarīra catuṣṭaya*); and
- Three approaches of general elements of perfection: a perfection of being (*brahma catuṣṭaya*), a perfection of action (*karma catuṣṭaya*) and the general approach to integral perfection (*siddhi catuṣṭaya*).

The first four specific approaches to perfection or *ādhāra siddhi*s can be thought of as forms of transformation that are instrumental in bringing about what he sought in a detailed manner. And the last general *siddhi*s refer to the kinds of processes that connect with everything else, that are followed generally in all the approaches.[20]

This may appear at first sight, a rather esoteric formulation, structured by Sri Aurobindo, mainly for himself, so as to monitor scrupulously his own experiments and progress in his diaries. As may be expected from the structure, these diary entries are peppered with Sanskrit terminology of an extremely difficult kind to decipher. But he also, as he

20. RoY, pp. 3-32.

progressed in this growth, formulated these teachings, in ways more accessible to students interested in the path of integral transformation. Among these later writings, the main text which outlines the yoga of Sri Aurobindo, is called *The Synthesis of Yoga*. It is among his best known books, and it is divided into four parts: The Yoga of Knowledge, the Yoga of Works, the Yoga of Divine Love, and the Yoga of Self-Perfection.

Comparing the scheme outlined in *the Record of Yoga* with *The Synthesis of Yoga*, we find that the first three and the last of the quartets of the record (*samatā, śakti, vijñāna, siddhi*) are elaborated in the section on the Yoga of Self Perfection in *The Synthesis of Yoga*. In the Yoga of Knowledge section of *The Synthesis of Yoga*, we find an elaboration for parts of the sixth quartet of the *Record of Yoga*, i.e. the quartet of being. And in the Yoga of Works section, we find certain keys to the quartet of action, *karma catuṣṭaya*. In his compressed quintessential text, *The Mother*, there is further elaboration of parts of the second quartet of the *Record of Yoga*, the *śakti catuṣṭaya* or quartet of power. And finally, in his last written work, *The Supramental Manifestation and Other Writings*, we find some keys to the *śarīra catuṣṭaya*, the quartet of the body. Thus, in a variety of his later writings, Sri Aurobindo re-formulated, what he presented here for himself. Over some time, he modified the approaches he recorded in the diaries. To some extent, these modifications represent changes of emphases in his conception of the yoga practice that arose with experience, or, with the need to make it more generally accessible. Hence, in our study, we will look at some of these texts in parallel. But the *Record of Yoga* provides us with a succinct and crystallised statement of terms, which helps to keep track of the various aspects of this complex transformational yoga psychology; so this will be our principal consideration, while we look at the later elaborations to explain the processes and emphases of the yoga.

The Quartet of Perfection or of Yoga

In this chapter, we take up the general elements of perfection, *siddhi catuṣṭaya* or the quartet of integration or integral perfection, which is also what Sri Aurobindo begins the section on the Yoga of Self-Perfection with in *The Synthesis of Yoga*. In *The Synthesis of Yoga*, the first ten chapters at the beginning of this section are on the general elements of perfection, relating to the quartet of perfection or *siddhi catuṣṭaya*. These chapters provide us with a broad understanding of the overall goals and processes of the yoga of integral transformation, and how these processes may be followed through the sequences of the yoga. Thus, the quartet of perfection may be thought of as the most overarching discipline describing the seeking for integrality. Emphasising the overarching nature of this quartet, Sri Aurobindo alternately named it *yoga catuṣṭaya* or the quartet of yoga. We see that he enumerated the goals of this quartet as *śuddhi, mukti, bhukti* and *siddhi*. These terms Sri Aurobindo himself translated broadly as: purification, liberation, enjoyment and perfection, respectively. Of these, we may say that the core, the meaning of the quartet of perfection, and of what Sri Aurobindo considered the goal of his own yoga, is to be found in the two central elements: *mukti* and *bhukti* (liberation and enjoyment). They also give us an insight into what Sri Aurobindo considered to be the telos of the human being. The human being, he has written, is a transitional being.[21] He did not see the human being as a static, defined reality, there is no such thing as "man" that can be defined once and for all, a structure of consciousness, but, it is an ongoing transition to something else; in a sense, he echoes

---

21. "Man is a transitional being, he is not final; for in him and high beyond him ascend the radiant degrees which climb to a divine supermanhood." Sri Aurobindo, "Man and the Supermind" in EDH, p. 157.

Nietzsche here who sees man as a rope thrown between the animal and the god, the overman or superman.[22]

Thus, as overall ideals of integral transformation, we find Sri Aurobindo identifying two central goals — liberation and enjoyment. We may say, these are the primordial needs that Sri Aurobindo has reduced human psychology to. If we think of it, we realise that these primordial goals are intimately related to two views of Reality that human beings find themselves affirming, as a result of their life experience. Human beings are pre-figured into a life to which they find themselves responding in two major ways. One of these is that the world is a prison, and we are imprisoned here. We feel bound, shut in, constrained within painful limits from which we seek release. Many of the different paths of yoga assume this as the fundamental human condition. Considering our own existence we find, at the very outset, that we are a consciousness bound in a physical body, which is like a cage or prison. Our consciousness often feels, or finds itself, operating as if from outside the confines of the body, in its dreams, in its idealisations, its visions and aspirations; and yet, we are constantly brought back to the fact that we are shut in a body; a body which is irreducibly unconscious, has its roots in material inconscience, and is surrounded by inconscience.

The body is dust, which will return to dust. Several modern philosophers, existentialists, have identified the quintessential human condition as one of being conscious in an unconscious world. Apart from this physical entrapment, we find ourselves bound by the laws of mental and emotional response, psychological laws which can be used to manipulate us; and we are subject to social, cultural and political laws, not of our personal making. So, this is the sense of entrapment in which

22. Friedrich Nietzsche, "Thus Space Zarathustra" in Walter Kaufmann (tr.), *The Portable Nietzsche,* London & New York: Penguin, 1954, p. 126.

we find ourselves. This sense of entrapment cries out for liberation; and that provides one direction to our understanding of reality and our urge towards self-development. But, if this was all, we would all be unreservedly and constantly seeking for some way to leave life. The easiest solution, which would be rampant, would be suicide, the escape through denial of the physical basis of life. At the other extreme, what would have solved the unhappy persistence of bound consciousness would have been the erasure of consciousness itself, the solution of *nirvāṇa* offered by the Buddha more than 2,500 years ago. But, Buddhism notwith-standing, most human beings want to stay back in life, they wish to enjoy it and they think of it as a field of fulfillment.

In one of his narrations Sri Aurobindo says that man is everywhere bound, but he is in love with his chains.[23] Humankind does not wish to escape from its bondages, because there is something delightful in life itself. Power and enjoyment draw us, but at the same time they slap us in the face. Every act of power is constrained by its opposite, every mastery is constrained by limitation and opposition: someone has more power than you, some cosmic reality will resist or oppose your actions. And if we think about enjoyment, we realise that happiness comes in equal measure with sorrow, in our lives. And yet, there is something in us that chooses life over death, enjoyment over escape. We enjoy and we seek power.

The Two Traditions

In world traditions, there are two major paths that have developed along these two lines: one is spirituality, the movement towards liberation, the seeking for a consciousness which does not need anything for its existence; and the other

23. "The whole world yearns after freedom, yet each creature is in love with his chains; this is the first paradox and inextricable knot of our nature." Sri Aurobindo, "Thoughts and Glimpses" in EPH, p. 204.

is technology, the attempt to control and master visible and invisible forces, and thus enjoy the world around us. In the Indian tradition these two primordial drives find two theories of practice, very early philosophies that have persisted. One can say that they are not exclusive to each other; these two drives are in a perpetual dialectical relationship. One of them is the field of Vedānta, leading towards liberation; the other is Tantra, leading to the exploration and maximisation of power and enjoyment in the world. Each of these blends elements of the other into itself. In terms of integral transformation, Sri Aurobindo tells us that both these goals of liberation and enjoyment are necessary to an integral perfection, that, in fact the condition of a perfect enjoyment is a perfect liberation.

One may derive this necessity from Sri Aurobindo's view that Conscious Being has entered into an evolutionary Becoming in this material universe. This Divine Being, always liberated, self-conscious, infinite, free, has assumed the form of a material inconscience, and explores its own evolution here into greater and greater forms of consciousness, an evolution that is essentially a play of delight. In the process of this evolution out of the inconscient, forms of sentience emerge. Each of these forms represents a gradation and modality of consciousness. It is through this manifold emergence of consciousnesses that the divine individualises itself and actualises itself multiply in a play of delight.

To Being-in-the-Becoming, there is no imprisonment. Even in the forms of its own self-limitation, it is always free. But the individualised forms of relative consciousness within which this being hides itself and through which it explores itself in multiple ways, experience their reality as one of being conscious but bound, an imprisonment. Thus, the experience of imprisonment belongs to the evolving forms in a graded field of relative consciousness. If any of these beings were to become fully conscious of the one who has assumed all the forms of becoming in the universe and is present in each of them, it would know itself to be a free self-determination of Conscious Being, and be enabled to enjoy this creative self-becoming in its own development and in its relations with other forms of becoming.

This leads us to the goal of integral transformation, which intends to arrive at a perfection of the conditions and experience of becoming based on a perfection of being. The perfection of becoming implies a perfect enjoyment (*bhukti*); while the perfection of being implies the intrinsic freedom of divine being (*mukti*). An integral transformation must, thus include both liberation and enjoyment (*mukti* and *bhukti*). And we see that these two are related causally as per the relation of being and becoming — that is, a perfect *mukti* is the condition for a perfect *bhukti*. But these two, *mukti* and *bhukti* are surrounded by something which precedes them and something which follows them. That which precedes them is purification (*śuddhi*). Neither liberation nor enjoyment is possible without a purification of the being. And what follows them is a fulfillment, and this is the seal of perfection (*siddhi*).

Śuddhi, the Starting Point

When we consider more deeply the Seven Quartets of transformation, formulated by Sri Aurobindo, we find that they are often expressed in recursive terms. In recursion, a term being described appears in its own description. This arises due to the nature of integrality, where the whole is contained in each of its parts. This "self-enfolded" or fractal nature of integral reality is seen in the quartet of perfection (*siddhi catuṣṭaya*) in the fact that *siddhi*, perfection is to be understood as the realisation of the other six quartets of integral transformation. Thus, there is no need for us to elaborate this aspect at present as we will consider these quartets in turn in our study. But, our starting point for the quartet of *siddhi* is best approached by looking at what Sri Aurobindo means by *śuddhi*. Here is what he says about purification in *The Synthesis of Yoga*:

> We have not to doctor symptoms of impurity, or that only secondarily as a minor help, but to strike at its roots after a deeper diagnosis. We then find that there are two forms of impurity which are at the root of the whole confusion. One is a defect born of the nature of our past evolution which has been a nature of separative ignorance. This defect is a radically wrong and ignorant form given to the proper action of each part of our instrumental being.[24]

In other words, as human beings, we are born with a psychological constitution which is marked by error. And its defect lies in the fact that there has been a past to it, an evolutionary past with its root in a sense of separation and a blind wish to survive and enlarge one's separate reality. This evolutionary past has introduced distortions to the working of our intstrumental parts, which we are unconscious of and take for granted. Sri Aurobindo sees this as the first root of impurity in human nature. Moreover, evolution of consciousness among living things has been a progression through *ad hoc* steps, which have been added on to previous steps without sufficient integration. This leads to the second form of impurity.

Sri Aurobindo describes this second form of impurity in these terms:

> The other impurity is born of the successive process of an evolution, where life emerges in and depends on body, mind emerges in and depends on life in the body, Supermind emerges in and lends itself to, instead of governing mind; soul itself is apparent only as a circumstance of the bodily life, of the mental being and veils up the spirit in the lower imperfections. This second defect of our nature is caused by the dependence of the higher on the lower faculties; it is an immixture of functions by which the impure working of the lower instrument gets into the characteristic of action of the

---

24. SoY, p. 645.

> higher function and gives to it an added imperfection of embarrassment, wrong direction and confusion.[25]

These defects or impurities define the scope of *śuddhi* within the quartet of perfection, as Sri Aurobindo sees it. But to grasp this better, we need to understand certain philosophical and psychological concepts that are assumed or coded in the quotes we have considered. These concepts and elements, basing the psychological make-up of the human being, arise from general assumptions, which belong to the historical discourse of Indian philosophy, which Sri Aurobindo adapts to his purpose. These merit our consideration as some of the bases of the yoga of integral transformation.

Yoga Philosophy: Vedānta

First, as we saw in the section on *The Life Divine*, in Sri Aurobindo's *darśana*, which is another way of saying philosophy, but a philosophy of experience arising out of a realisation of being, an altered ontology — there are two major principles of being: *vidyā* and *avidyā* (knowledge and ignorance). This distinction is not peculiar to Sri Aurobindo, but originates in the Upaniṣads and is common to the entire discourse of yoga philosophy and yoga psychology.[26] As we saw, knowledge here does not mean a mental understanding of things and an expansion, piecemeal, of various fragmentary concepts that we try to accommodate into a system, or a systemic theory. Knowledge is the self-consciousness of the One Being there is. Knowledge is an intrinsic property of the consciousness of Conscious Being. When we speak of knowledge as a principle, we mean the attribute of consciousness that can be experienced as identity — knowledge that arises because it is what it knows — as an act of self-consciousness.[27]

25. SoY, pp. 645-46.
26. IU, pp. 8-9, 51-55.
27. Ibid., pp. 51-55.

But, this is not our normal experience. We do not experience ourselves as beings of knowledge of this kind — very far from the case. We find ourselves as beings of ignorance (*avidyā*). By ignorance is meant the normal form of terrestrial experience in which each individual is a monad, a separate organ of knowledge, an organ of separative experience. Each of us is a centre of our own knowledge-universe. If we assume this to be the permanent form of human experience, then we could affirm with the eighteenth-century German philosopher Immanuel Kant, that it is never possible for humans to know anything as it truly is. All we can know is what our self-consciousness translates of its experience of a separate and transcendent world of beings and things. And, this subjective translation or representation is what each of us takes to be his or her universe. Unfortunately, there is only one universe we have been given, in which we all have to rub shoulders, and compete in order to claim for ourselves. This is what gives one of the great disturbances and defects to our human existence, the basis of the trouble of egoism. *Avidyā* starts from this kind of separation. In the Indian philosophies, the name given to the transcendental agency, that is said to have caused this experience of separation is *māyā*. *Māyā* is a power of Supreme or Conscious Being that can create such a projective appearance of separated being-experience. It is the projection of a self-multiplication of being in the form of its infinite possibilities and a granting of independent reality to this variety of selves.[28]

But, the work of *māyā*, which is often taken to be a creator of illusions, is only a self-operation of Being or *Brahman*, and is not without purpose. Sri Aurobindo points out that *avidyā* as an appearance of *vidyā* has *vidyā* involved in it.[29] In other words, as touched on at the beginning of this chapter, this world of

28. LD, pp. 44, 109, 116, 123-24.

29. Ibid., pp. 39-40, 46.

separation is an appearance which becomes the basis for a graded and phased evolution of consciousness. The self-consciousness of infinite Being is latent behind this appearance of fragmentation, yielding up successive degrees of consciousness, grades of consciousness, in an evolution of consciousness. But this kind of evolution is to be distinguished from intelligent design, or the inexorable Hegelian dialectic, where a transcendental *Zeitgeist* (Time Spirit) determines the stages of evolution and history. Though Sri Aurobindo accepts an independent transcendental domain of *vidyā* in relation to the cosmos of *avidyā,* it is the freedom of the Ignorance and the agency of conscious beings which accounts for the experience of evolution here. Hence, similar to the ontological ideas discussed in the philosophy of Gilles Deleuze, evolution must be considered an immanent problematic, in which the relations among forces are instantiated into actuality along gradients of becoming.

Such processes occur through *ad hoc* and unpredictable events, marked by a play of necessity and chance. Human beings may become agents in this process through conscious experimental transactions. In Sri Aurobindo's view, these forms of evolving consciousness aim for a horizon where the individual may know its identity with Supermind, or the wholeness of reality, its principle of simultaneous unity and infinity. As human beings, we are at a stage in this evolution of consciousness, when such a modality of consciousness is possible to us as an eventuality of supramental transition. Such an intuition has been affirmed in the wisdom literatures of several ancient cultures. The statement in the Bible that man is made in the image of God may be fruitfully read in these terms, as an affirmation of potential identity requiring *siddhi* through *śuddhi* and conscious evolution (*yoga*). Thus, according to Sri Aurobindo, the human being, though a creature born of *avidyā* may be able to manifest *vidyā* here. Sri Aurobino's philosophical work, *The Life Divine,* is principally an exploration of this theme, and he draws on a very powerful but succinct Upaniṣad, the *Īśa Upaniṣad*, to bring out the lines of this evolutionary movement within cosmic nature, and of human possibility within this purpose.

Here it cannot be over-emphasised that what is received by us as tradition, whether the categories of Vedānta or the quartets of Sri Aurobindo, is handed down like a fossil, etched into place by an authorised interpretation. It is only the creative engagement of an inner life, an *askesis* of liberatory self-becoming that can release the fossil from its entrapment into what Deleuze calls a "line of flight". A metaphysics of becoming is hardly a fossil, but a theory of praxis and a call to experiment based on the growth of creative consciousness. Moreover, as with Deleuze, Sri Aurobindo's evolutionary problematic is infinite, not a teleology which stops with the attainment of Supermind. Conceptually, Supermind may be considered the horizon of our present becoming, a significant "event" or punctuation mark in Being's self-exploration without end.

Sāṁkhya

An intuition of our existence already noted here, which visits us sometimes is that of being conscious in an unconscious world. If we try to probe this further, we enter into a line of reasoning and a line of "applied psychology", of yoga, because our probing can yield a progression in the identification of consciousness. We can ask ourselves the question, how much or what in us is conscious and what is unconscious. Those, who have carried out this introspection, have arrived at a clean cleavage between Nature and Spirit. It seems to us that our body is unconscious; it is made up of matter and functions through a set of unconscious mechanisms. Our life energies, our feelings, our will, etc. seem to be conscious, they are living, but they are biologisms, they are a kind of automatism. They can be classified into forms; we can arrive at a behavioural science of desire, of need, of will, of enjoyment. Our mentality is another set of cognitive automatisms; automatisms of sensing, of logical and symbolic reasoning, of imagining based on suggestions of upbringing, environment and natural propensities. All these are held up by a certain sense of individual consciousness which is an illusion of the mind. Behind all these, there must be something they are borrowing their consciousness from. That something is a nameless conscious being, which certain schools of Indian philosophy have called *Puruṣa* (the Conscious Person).[30]

The above is an exercise, proposed by a dualistic Indian school of philosophy named Sāṁkhya. We may be struck here by the analogy of this exercise to that of Methodological Scepticism as prescribed by Rene Descartes (1596-1650). Descartes' reduction through doubt led to the equation of existence and thought, and became the basis of the Mind-Body dualism that we largely take for granted in our modern world. The reduction of Sāṁkhya is more radical, treating even thought as conditioning and aiming at a purity of consciousness beyond thought. Coming closer to our time, the analogy may be pressed further with the phenomenological reduction of Edmund Husserl (1859-1938). Husserl's self-interrogation goes beyond Descartes' in questioning the constitution of thought. Thinking can no longer be taken as an axiomatic given for Husserl, but arises according to the constitution of the object of thought in one's attention. Thinking itself is a form of consciousness and all forms of consciousness attach themselves to their objects through intention. Thus, Husserl's reduction found a purer essence of consciousness than thought in what he called the "transcendental ego", a purity of subjective existence that nevertheless remained individual. It may be instructive to sound this analogy some more by considering the treatment of the phenomenological reduction

30. SoY, p. 215.

by Husserl's student, Heidegger. Heidegger eschewed the subjectivism and relativism of Husserl's transcendental ego and developed an articulation which located the subject in terms of the way in which a common spatio-temporal horizon (the being of beings) constitutes humans as conscious beings (or makes itself available to beings and reciprocally, makes beings available to itself, to each other and to themselves, thus, constituting a world). This ontological turn moves beyond the personal horizon of consciousness to the horizon which makes the personal possible in every case in a common world.

To return to Sāṁkhya, it sees the indefinable conscious element in us as radically distinct from our nature. Moreover, it sees all human nature as the workings of the same enumerable automatisms, and hence, universalises this principle. Hence, we may think of it as extrapersonal and call it Nature. Nature is called *Prakṛti* by Sāṁkhya, and the conscious part in us is termed *Puruṣa*. *Puruṣa* is the foundation of experience.[31] But in Sāṁkhya, this reduction brings us the freedom and purity of *Puruṣa* at the cost of nature, because its goal is an escape from the conditioning instruments of nature. The tendencies towards activity in nature can be put to sleep because if one identifies with *Puruṣa*, one finds that it is not only a pure conscious witness (*sākṣī*), watching the movements of Nature, without participation; but it is also the giver of sanction to the movements of *Prakṛti* (*anumantā*), or rather, in Husserlian terms, a withholder of intention. It thus has a veto power over the automatisms of Nature, and if it exercises this power — the desires fall off, the motivations drop, the thinking stops, finally the body itself collapses and one is left with a pure witnessing centre of consciousness.

Though the founding of Sāṁkhya is attributed to Sage Kapila, the earliest canonical text on the subject is *Īśvara*

31. SoY, pp. 428-30.

Krishna's *Sāṁkhya-Kārikā*. An early Sāṁkhya conceived of one *Prakṛti* but many *Puruṣas*, analogous to Husserl, as many as there could be experiencers. But later, this notion of many conscious beings was itself conceptualised as an illusion of *Prakṛti* experienced due to an identification with ego (*ahaṁkāra*). This further reduction can be seen as analogous to Heidegger's ontology, the experience of a single impersonal *Puruṣa* that made every individual experience possible. Among the best known systems of yoga in India, is Patañjali's *Rāja-Yoga*, which was founded in the second or third century CE and is considered to be based on Sāṁkhya. However, as pointed out by Ian Whicher, whereas Sāṁkhya as elucidated in the *Sāṁkhya-Kārikā*, grafts experience onto a metaphysical structure, in Patañjali's *Yoga-Sūtras* (as with Sri Aurobindo), the metaphysical schematic is abstracted from yoga experience, leaving it more open-ended in terms of the relation of *Puruṣa* and *Prakṛti*. Instead of a trenchant dualism

Psychology of Self-Perfection (1.2)

Kāraṇa (Cause):	*Karaṇa* (Instrument):	In *Avidyā* (Ignorance), dual principle:	In *Vidyā* (Knowledge), dual principle:
• Spirit (*Brahman/ Īśvara*)	• *Manaḥ* (Mind) – *Citta* (subconscient mentality), *Manas* (sense mind), *Buddhi* (intelligence), *Ahaṁkāra* (ego) • *Prāṇa* (Life) – physical life-force, nervous life-force, feelings, vital instincts • *Śarīra* (Body) – *Sthūla* (Gross), *Sūkṣma* (Subtle)	• *Puruṣa* (Soul/ Conscious Being/Person)/ *Prakṛti* (Nature): • *Manomaya* (Mental) • *Prāṇamaya* (Vital) • *Annamaya* (Physical) • *Caitya* (Psychic)	• *Īśvara* (Lord)/ *Śakti* (Power of Consciousness)

between soul and nature, what we have here, is the operation of the reduction exercise of Sāṁkhya, so as to reclaim experience from a vantage of freedom and availability to the horizon of Being's disclosure in the world.[32]

Later in our consideration we will see how powerful this veto power of *Puruṣa* is, in the purification and control of the nature, *Prakṛti*. But, as with Ian Whicher's interpretation of Patañjali, the attainment of *Puruṣa* is not treated as an end in itself in the yoga of integral transformation.[33] To understand why this is so, we should see that if we followed the path of exclusionary identification, we would attain liberation, but we'd lose the world; we'd find *mukti* but we'd lose that other desirable goal of *bhukti*. But, can we have both? Here Sri Aurobindo points to a different relation between *Puruṣa* and *Prakṛti*. The apparent duality of *Puruṣa* and *Prakṛti* is an artefact, an illusion of *avidyā*. There is another possibility of experience in which these two are seen as complementary forms of the same Reality, Being and Becoming, *Īśvara* and *Śakti* (Lord and his Power of Consciousness). An aspect of the yoga of integral transformation lies in being able to attain a consciousness where this separation of *avidyā* is overcome and one experiences not the duality of *Puruṣa* and *Prakṛti*, but the two-in-one, *Īśvara-Śakti*, coupled power of consciousness and master of consciousness, as two sides of the same Being and Reality (*ParaBrahman, Parameśvara*).[34]

The Instrument and the Cause, Karaṇa and Kāraṇa

It is important to understand this action of duality, because it is ongoing in us at every level. It is happening at the level of mind, at the level of the life-forces and at the level of the

32. Ian Whicher, *The Integrity of the Yoga Darsana*, SUNY Press, New York, 1998.
33. SoY, pp. 432-33.
34. Ibid., pp. 123, 637-38.

body. But mind, affect, volition and body, which we take to be ourselves, are seen in the systems of yoga and by Sri Aurobindo as instrument only, *karaṇa*, while the mover, the cause, is not any of these; it is Spirit, *Brahman* or *Īśvara*, who is *kāraṇa*.[35] Understood thus, the primary key to yoga lies in making a change of faith. As mental-vital-physical beings, we have a faith in ourselves as the doers of our actions, our own thinking, of our own feeling and willing. But, what we take to be ourselves is a nature-complex (*Prakṛti*) which is meant to be the instrument of something or someone that is our true Being but has put on our nature, along with its sense of separate identity, like masks: it is *Puruṣa* in its aspect transcending the duality of *Puruṣa* and *Prakṛti*, its aspect of *Īśvara* or lord, that is *kāraṇa* (cause).

Our instrumental nature operates ordinarily through a set of conditionings, determinisms of physics, chemistry, biology, and beyond these, of psychology, sociology, economic and political forces, and of invisible predilections. We take these determinisms or forms of subjection to be our free will. To arrive at our true self and our true freedom of will, our cosmic agency, we need to replace the conditioning of our instrumentation and our false identification with the instrument. Thus, this is a major aspect of transformation that we need to accomplish in each of our instrumental actions. This requires a change of faith. This change of faith is to be exercised in all the instruments of nature — body, will, feelings and thoughts. This higher power to which our receptivity is demanded, is the self-disclosure of the Being of beings. Our orientation towards this power opens us to the cause. That central openness to a cause that is using us and that yet is our own Self and the One Self, is one of the driving engines of the yoga of integral transformation.

---

35. SoY, pp. 17, 628-31.

Śuddhi or Purification

To return to *śuddhi*: all Yogas have some idea of a process of purification, which is to be followed as preparation. In this, these practices can be constellated with the practices of austerity (*askesis*) for "the care of the soul" prescribed by pre-modern schools of self-culture in Greece, as discussed by Michel Foucault. In Patañjali's yoga, we have the *yama*s and *niyama*s (the rules and regulations) of mental and moral self-discipline that are to be followed. There are also purification processes for the inner channels of vital energy in the body (*nāḍī śuddhi*). The subtle (*sūkṣma*) anatomy of the human being is said to be pervaded by these channels, which form the basis of many systems of non-modern medicine, such as Ayurveda and Acupuncture. All the channels through which the energy runs in our body have to be kept clean. They are cleansed through a variety of cleansing practices. This forms a part, also of the yoga of integral transformation, the last of the elements of *śuddhi*, which is *śarīra śuddhi* (the cleansing of the body). But here, though one may use some of the physical means of cleansing as taught in traditional *haṭha-yoga*, the dependence is more on a direct inner action of consciousness. What is more important for us to consider now are the inner instruments, the make-up of the mental and vital being in yoga psychology, and the purification related to that.

Purification of the Life energy (Prāṇa-śuddhi)

Yoga psychology posits a life being and body (*prāṇamaya Puruṣa, prāṇamaya kośa*) in humans, which Sri Aurobindo calls the vital instrument.[36] The life-being in us is the vehicle of the vital energy (*prāṇa*), that pervades the being and circulates in it. *Prāṇa* is what gives the basis for animal responses, cravings, desires, possessive and devouring appetites, the blind instinct for survival, the sex drive. In humans, the immixture of mental

36. *Taittirīya Upaniṣad*, II.1-6; SoY, pp. 461-62.

and psychic influences modify the operations of this vital being, producing behaviours such as our ambitions. It also gives us our enthusiasm, our generosity, our courage, our creativity. Based on the Upaniṣads, yoga psychology assumes a disjunction between the mental, vital and physical beings in us. It names them in terms of different bodies (*śarīra*), each with different qualities of *Prakṛti* and a different sense of *Puruṣa*.[37] Sri Aurobindo assumes this disjunction as a fact of experience and explains it as a consequence of the *ad hoc* discontinuous evolution of consciousness in nature and the emergence of new holistic properties with each grade of consciousness.[38] As with Gilles Deleuze, these have to be seen as differences of kind, not of degree.[39] So, *prāṇa* has to be approached in terms of its own properties from the viewpoint of purification. The purification of *prāṇa* lies in understanding that the movement of the life-being is composed of dualities, of attractions (*rāga*) and repulsions (*dveṣa*), polarities within which we are pulled and pushed at all times. To bring inner control over *prāṇa*, it is necessary to identify these polarities and to establish a power of equality in our responses to these dualities.[40]

Here, Sri Aurobindo locates three kinds of prāṇic defect of duality: the duality of craving pertaining to the will, the duality of attachment pertaining to the emotions and the duality of preference pertaining to mental tastes. The duality of craving is experienced in the nervous constitution of the human being, its physical-vital constitution. There are a variety of cravings in us; cravings that very easily become habits, addictions. These habits and addictions of the nervous nature, have to be understood in terms of dualities. These cravings

37. *Taittirīya Upaniṣad*, II. 1-6.

38. SoY, pp. 645-46.

39. See Gilles Deleuze, *Bergsonism*, tr. Hugh Tomlinson and Barbara Habberjam, Brooklyn: Zone Books, 1998.

40. SoY, pp. 659-60.

are related to the pleasure principle — cravings for food, sex, chemical intoxicants of various kinds or objects of obsessive interest which exert a fetishistic attraction, such as the diverse array of consumer products, often also coded for social status. Cravings are also what lend themselves most easily to conditioning. Our present world, driven by the engines of capital accumulation through the expansion and penetration of markets, targets most prominently this pleasure principle through desire production, using visual media and other forms of simulated and surrogate experience.

Technologies of information acquisition and memory storage, combined with technologies of behavioural conditioning and non-local access, are bringing worldwide populations increasingly under subjection to personally marketed forms of instant gratification based on the stimulation of craving. The only defence against this entrapment of the subject is the practice of the counter-technologies of the self, which bring the choice of acceptance and rejection in equal measure. On the flip side, for everything that we crave, there is something that we are repulsed by, or that we otherwise shrink from. Shame, repulsion and fear at this level include natural and socialised responses, such as the fear of attack, repulsion for refuse or products of decomposition, shame at exposure of privacy, etc. Careful study of these patterns of response is the first step; and a scrupulous avoidance, not of action, but of being drawn, swayed by either the craving or its opposite — repulsion — is the practice towards the purification of craving in the *prāṇa*.[41]

At a more conscious level of our vital nature, is our affective or emotional being. This also constitutes part of the prāṇic action. Here, we have our strong emotional attachments, likes and dislikes, obsessions and repulsions which trouble our affections with exultation, excitement or grief, heartbreak and

41. RoY, p. 1478.

other responses of emotional loss. Here too, we have to learn to impose equality. As with our cravings, here too we must develop a power of detached observation, a perception of the positive and the negative, that which causes trouble and that which causes pleasure, and moderate the response so as to bring to them an equality of inner reaction.[42] These processes will be considered in greater detail when we take up the quartet of equality or peace.

Siddhi Catuṣṭaya (Quartet of Perfection) (1.3)

Śuddhi, Mukti, Bhukti, Siddhi, Śuddhi

Prāṇa	*Citta*	*Manas*
Dualities of desires: craving; emotions: attachment; mentality: preference – capacity for equal enjoyment (*rasagrahaṇa*)	sensational subconscious mentality: established stillness	sense-mind: purification of the senses (doors of perception) by removing preference and conditioning from senses and stilling the habitual mental responses.

Buddhi	*Śarīra*
disengage intelligence from subjection to ***prāṇa, citta*** and ***manas***; change of faith in intellect from knower to instrument of knowledge; surrender to intuition and divine knowledge above mind.	Cleansing of body, celibacy (transformation of ***retas*** to ***ojas***)

In the general discipline of purification there needs to be a constant exercise of consciousness, one needs to carry on a persistent self-observation and control of inner reaction to craving, emotional attachments, and mental preferences. In our era of overchoice and conditioning seduction, this discipline may feel like a struggle, since the prized individuality of the

42. RoY, p. 1478.

modern subject is premised on its free will and power of choice. It is only when we realise that our "natural" choices are largely conditionings of socialisation and that we can have subjective freedom from them, that this discipline can gather strength.

At the level of mind, we have our own preferences. Our mental pride makes each of us believe that our knowledge and our personal taste is the best, is perfect. Thus, there is a power of enjoyment that arises from our mentality, but this is also based in duality, attraction and repulsion or positive and negative attribution, which is a cause of trouble for us. As with the vital nature, in mind too, we must develop a capacity for equal enjoyment of all tastes. This is called *rasagrahaṇa*. Again, this will be considered further in the quartet of peace or equality.[43]

The natural basis of prāṇic action in living beings is desire. This is a consequence of *avidyā*, because the development of individuality of consciousness out of an amorphous inconscience is marked by the automatism of survival and separate satisfaction. Desire governs human action to such an extent that it is supposed by behavioural psychologists that desire is the root of all actions. The premise of *prāṇa śuddhi* (the purification of the *prāṇa*) is that this is not true. Nature's evolution has created the conditioning of desire to ensure the persistence of individuality of consciousness, but desire draws its sense of choice from the free creative will of the true conscious individual, the *Puruṣa* or *Īśvara* within us. The de-conditioning of desire brings us into contact with this true psychic or spiritual will within, which can then use the prāṇic energies as its instrument.[44]

The Mental Instrument

The ignorant action of the *prāṇa*, based in desire, influences and utilises the mental being and its constituents. Through

43. SoY, p. 717.

44. SoY, pp. 660-61, 669.

this influence, the patterns of individual desire become habits of character and personal preference/identity. The mental being in humans is composed, according to the psychology of Vedānta and Sāṁkhya, of a gradation of refinements and organisations of mental consciousness. This "inner instrument" (*antaḥkaraṇa)* needs to be distinguished from the *prāṇa* which acts in it. Purification of the *antaḥkaraṇa* is aimed at eradicating the more conscious identifications, attractions and repulsions, which recur as patterns in our behaviour. In exercising these patterns, we have a sense of personal choice. It is because prāṇic desire has been internalised in mental substance and infected with *ahaṁkāra,* that there is an individuation of desire in the mental instruments and a greater danger of confusion with the will of the true self or soul.

The constituents of this mental being are given as *citta* (subconscient mentality), *manas, buddhi* and *ahaṁkāra.*[45] The most primordial form of mental consciousness, identified by yoga psychology, is known as *citta. Citta* is a pervasive layer of mentality present in all of life.[46] In fact, we may speak of a kind of subconscient mind within matter itself. It makes its emergence in life. In plants, there is a distinct mentality. It has no nervous organisation (organs of sense) but it is present as a subconscious mentality that responds to external stimuli. This is the *citta,* a mentality of feelings and sensations, not of the senses which are specialised according to sense organs, but primordial sensations more basic than the senses. This layer of subconscient mental consciousness pervades the physical system. These sensations, mediated by the attractions and repulsions

45. For the Vedāntic description of *antaḥkaraṇa,* see Dharmaraja Adhvarindra, *Vedānta Paribhāṣā,* I.58, Venkateshwar Press, Bombay, 1968, p. 57. The Sāṁkhya description may be found in Īśvara Kṛṣṇa's *Sāṁkhya-Kārikā* XXXIII, XXXV. This Sāṁkhya text gives three constituents — *manas, buddhi* and *ahaṁkāra* — for *antaḥkaraṇa.* For Sri Aurobindo's treatment, see SoY, p. 647.

46. Īśvara Kṛṣṇa, *Sāṁkhya Kārikā,* op. cit.; SoY, pp. 647-48.

of the *prāṇa*, get recorded as a memory of habitual response and reaction of feelings, reflexes and semi-automatic behaviours. Here too, it is necessary to bring a power of detachment and establish a stillness of response, an equality, in the life of our sensations and primitive responses of subconscious mentality. We have to be able to bring a perfect calm into these excitations of the sensations and turn the subconscious memory into a conscious passive receptacle of heuristics, or learned behaviours which a higher consciousness can utilise flexibly at will.

The next more organised form of mental consciousness, identified by Sāṁkhya, is the sense-mind, known as *manas*.[47] The sense-mind receives the messages of the senses, and translates them into interpreted perceptions. The differentiation of the sense organs of sight, hearing, touch, taste, smell are implied here. Our sense organs, each possess their own consciousness, a distributed intelligence which already determines our selective reception of the world. What are the properties of these objects of sense and how do they relate to our world of meanings and responses? Behind the consciousness of the sense organs lies, what is often called "the sixth sense" — a kind of essence of sense which processes each of the senses in the mind and translates its experience to a foundational perception.[48] This is also the part of the mind responsible for what is known as *synaesthesia*, where the sense experiences may be experienced interchangeably. For example, one may see sounds, hear smells or touch flavours. These experiences all belong to the central *manas*. Here again, the action of the *manas* comes with the duality of liking and disliking, and here again, purification involves a removal of preference and conditioning from the senses and an expansion of sense capacity.

The well-known English mystic and poet, William Blake, has written about this purification of the *manas* as a key to

47. SoY, p. 650.

48. Ibid, p. 664.

spiritual experience. Blake's famous sentence pertaining to this purification is: "If the doors of perception were cleansed, everything would appear to man as it is: Infinite."[49] This statement was revived in modern times by Aldous Huxley, who wrote a book titled *The Doors of Perception*, and closer to the present, by the leader of a Los Angeles rock band which named itself after it: The Doors. But, whereas Huxley and Morrison thought of this purification more in terms of a forcible opening of the inner senses through psychoactive substances, what Sri Aurobindo is referring to here, is a process of attention as the key to a systematic de-conditioning of sensory preference. In other words, our senses, when they are purified, will themselves become witnesses or recorders of the oneness of being all around us. It will become a concrete, sensed reality, that there is one infinite being whom we meet in all our contacts. This is the true meaning of the Indian term *darśana* (non-dual seeing) where consciousness in the observer and the observed recognises itself in identity of Being.

In this context, here is a passage from Sri Aurobindo, dealing with the purification of the *manas*:

> *Manas* depends in our ordinary consciousness on the physical organs of receptive sense for knowledge, and the organs of the body for action directed towards the objects of sense. The superficial and outward action of the senses is physical and nervous in character and they may easily be thought to be merely results of nerve action. They are sometimes called in the old books *prāṇas*, nervous or life activities. But still the essential thing in them is not the nervous excitation, but the consciousness, the action of the *citta*, which makes use of the organ of the nervous impact of which it is a channel. *Manas* is the activity emerging from the basic consciousness which makes up the whole

---

49. William Blake, *The Marriage of Heaven and Hell*, Plate 14, 1790, facsimile reprinted by Dover, London, 1994.

> essentiality of what we call sense. Sight, hearing, taste, smell, touch are really properties of the mind, not of the body. But the physical mind, which we ordinarily use, limits itself to a translation into sense of so much of the outer impact as it receives through the nervous system and the physical organs. But the inner *manas* has also a subtle sight, hearing, power of contact of its own which is not dependant on the physical organs, and it has moreover, a power not only of direct communication of mind with object, leading even at a high pitch of action to a sense of the contents of an object within or beyond the physical range, the direct communication also of mind with mind. Mind is able to alter, modify, inhibit the incidents, values, intensities of self-impacts. These powers of the mind, we do not ordinarily use or develop, they remain subliminal and emerge sometimes in an irregular and fitful action, more readily in some minds than in others, or come to the surface in abnormal states of the being. They are the basis of clairvoyance, clairaudience, transference of thought and impulse, telepathy, most of the more ordinary kinds of occult powers so called, though these are better described less mystically as powers of the now subliminal action of *manas*.[50]

The third component of the mentality is the *buddhi*. In fact, in modern cognitive psychology, it is intelligence which is equated with consciousness. But, to the understanding of yoga psychology, intelligence is a form of consciousness. *Buddhi* is the rational faculty in us, it is that which allows us to deduce using logic, interpret, classify, create rules and laws, give a rational explanation or description of the world to ourselves. We must disengage the intelligence from its subjection to *prāṇa*, which forms the conditioned action of the *buddhi*.[51] This is a common functional defect. Our intelligence is constantly subverted by our wishes, desires and cravings, our attatchments and ambitions, supporting these with its biased justifications.

50. SoY, pp. 650-51.
51. SoY, pp. 651-53.

But, we have a part of the intelligence which is disinterested and impersonal, a faithful seeker for truth, which can come to the aid of a scrupulous rejection of this subjection to personal interest. In fact, the amazing progress of science in the modern age rests largely on the foundation of this impersonal part of the intellect turned upon the material world for its understanding. But this power of mental purity can also be a helper in the necessary change of faith in the intellect from a knower to an instrument of knowledge, through receptivity to an intuition and higher sources of knowledge, as will be seen later.

The intellect, particularly in our rational age, is generally the repository of the greatest pride for human beings. For it to open to a higher source of knowledge, it needs to be confronted with its relative ignorance. Sri Aurobindo presents us with the discipline he himself followed to arrive at this altered functioning:

> The capital period of my intellectual development was when I could see clearly that what the intellect said may be correct and not correct, that what the intellect justifies is true and its opposite also is true. I never admitted a truth in the mind without simultaneously keeping it open to the contrary of it. And the first result was that the prestige of the intellect was gone.[52]

This is what the intellect needs to recognise, that it is a groping seeker, never a possessor of knowledge, that it can arrive only at relative truth or at schema, a variety of models of existence. But, if it knows that this model forming capacity is an instrument that can be receptive to expression by a power in relation with the identity of consciousness, then it can become an instrument of that power, leading to the transfer or transition of the intellect to a faculty of intuition and finally, its transformation to an organ of knowledge.

---

52. A.B. Purani, *Evening Talks with Sri Aurobindo*, Sri Aurobindo Ashram Trust, Pondicherry, 2007, p. 199.

The final constituent of the mental being, according to yoga psychology, is *ahaṁkāra*. This is our sense of separate self. The infinite self-conceptions of the one, each experience themselves, as a fragmented centre of existence in the ignorance. These centres may be seen to have a double constitution — an indeterminate interiority and a constructed personality, where agency must be negotiated in a field of plural contested codes and destinations. In thinking of the purification of the ego, we may bring to mind Husserl's phenomenology, where the awareness of intention in the constitution of objects and ideas through the play of power in the life-world, arrives at a purity of the mental ego. Heidegger's ontological turn pushes beyond the subjective relativism of Husserl in grounding consciousness reflexively in existential inquiry on the being of beings, the horizon of consciousness which makes beings possible. Between construction and interiority, this introduces a transpersonal or trans-egoic dimension.

The monadology of Gilles Deleuze and Felix Guattari, best developed in Deleuze's late work on Leibniz, could be considered a trans-egoic treatment analogous to that of Heidegger, but one which bases ontology in an embodied immanence. In their treatment, each individual centre of consciousness or "monad" operates along two registers, which may be thought of as two floors, the world of matter, open to the universe (exteriority), and the world of the soul, closed in on itself and lacking apertures (interiority). On the lower floor there exists the constructed ego, in and of the world and connected, as a body, to all other bodies. On the upper floor there exists pure interiority, that may be likened to private apartments, although each involves "variants of the same interior decoration", the signs of immanence.[53] For Leibniz the upper floor is the soul, or what we might call, following

53. Gilles Deleuze, *The Fold: Leibniz and the Baroque*, tr. Tom Conley, Minneapolis: University of Minnesota, 1993, p. 100.

Guattari, the incorporeal aspect of subjectivity. Deleuze refers to it thus in an interview:

> Leibniz's most famous proposition is that every soul or subject (monad) is completely closed, windowless and doorless, and contains the whole world in its darkest depths, while also illuminating some little portion of that world, each monad, a different portion. So, the world is enfolded in each soul, but differently, because each illuminates only one little aspect of the overall folding.[54]

The relation between these two floors determines our sense of self in its "becoming world" or worlding. Deleuze, following Michel Foucault, calls this subjectivation. The immanence of world in soul, following a fractal definition of being by Deleuze, coincides with the integral ontology of Sri Aurobindo. Similarly, the notion of the unique aspect of the whole illuminated in each case, coincides with the soul personality or psychic being in Sri Aurobindo; and the plural constructed nature of the ego, drawing its independent sense of self by reflection from the soul is equally coincident with the Sāṁkhya ideas of *ahaṁkāra,* as with Sri Aurobindo. Finally, where both Deleuze and Sri Aurobindo differ from Sāṁkhya, is in thinking of the relations between soul and ego or the upper and lower storeys in their monadology, as neither fixed, nor watertight. Deleuze posits changing relations between these two forms of self and hints at a future possibility, where the soul's chambers in the upper floor may develop doors and windows and communicate actively with the constructed self on the lower floor. This possibility may be thought to coincide with Sri Aurobindo's idea of a psychic transformation of self in nature.

The notion of the transformation of self and subjectivity through practices that alter ontology, ultimately equating the

---

54. Gilles Deleuze, *Negotiations*, tr. Martin Joughin, New York: Columbia University Press, 1990, p. 157.

human with a cosmic and transcendental consciousness which is lord of nature, not through domination but through identity, is the goal of the integral yoga, a goal which coincides with the lineage of modern thought launched by Nietzsche in the image of the superman. Deleuze returns to this ideal and sees it in the form of a transformed habitation of subjectivity, the occupation of a "superfold":

> The superman, in accordance with Rimbaud's formula, is the man who is even in charge of the animals (a code that can capture fragments from other codes, as in the new schemata of lateral or retrograde). It is a man in charge of the very rocks, or inorganic matter (the domain of silicon). It is a man in charge of the being of language (that formless, "mute, unsignifying region where language can find its freedom" even from whatever it has to say).[55]

It is only a mastery of physical (silicon), vital (biotic) and mental (significatory) consciousness, the possession of the trident of Śiva (or of Poseidon, lord of cosmicity), which can launch the human beyond the enormous subjection which constitutes our times, not an escape from the modern, but an endownment and an exceeding.

Mukti or Liberation

Śuddhi leads to the second perfection of this quartet. This is *mukti*. For Sri Aurobindo, liberation is of two kinds: the liberation of the spirit from its encasement in nature and the liberation of nature from its conditioning. Liberation of spirit refers to the realisation of our essential freedom beyond all conditioning. We are so naturally constituted that what we call ourselves, our identity, is wrapped up with our nature. But all the elements of nature are in fact, instrumental and conditioned. Hence, while we harbour a mental sense of absolute independence of being and consciousness, we are tied in bondage to the

55. Deleuze, *The Fold*, op. cit., p. 132.

chains (*pāśa*) of nature (*paśu*). However, the sense of individual independence intrinsic to human experience is not an illusion; it has its basis in the fact that each human being is truly a self-presentation of *Brahman*, eternally free, but bound by self-choice within *Prakṛti*. The primary realisation of *mukti* would then be a release from subjection to nature and a replacement of human identity by the true unchanging essence, one with the One. To arrive at this liberation of the spirit, Sri Aurobindo points to two levers of change in nature, the replacement of desire by the divine will and the replacement of the ego-sense by the true unchanging person, free of all determinations.

Siddhi Catuṣṭaya (Quartet of Perfection) (1.4)

Mukti **(Liberation)**

Of Spirit	**Of Nature**
Replacement of: ***kāma*** (desire) by ***tapas*** (divine will), ego (***ahaṁkāra***) by ***Puruṣa*** and ***Ātman*** (true universal and transcendental Person and Self) through (a) contemplation on the One Being (***Brahman/Īśvara***) in all things; (b) surrender to the One Being in action.	Transformation of the three **guṇas** (qualities) of ***Prakṛti*** (Nature) by the triple qualitative power of the higher existence; Transformation of ***Sattva*** (mental light) into ***jyoti*** (light of Knowledge) by celibacy and silent receptivity to intuition and Knowledge; Transformation of ***Rajas*** (kinesis) into ***Cit-Tapas*** (conscious force) by silent receptivity to divine will; and Transformation of ***Tamas*** (inertia) into **Śama** (conscious repose) by equality and indifference.

We have already touched on the discipline leading to the freedom from our subjection to desire (*kāma*). Sri Aurobindo points out that desire has behind it, a power of divine will; what he calls *cit-tapas*. He also sometimes uses the Greek word *askesis*. But *askesis*, in his view, is not restricted to ascetic practices, disciplines of the self. The coherent appearance of the world may itself be thought of as the manifestation of a cosmic *askesis*, a concentration of consciousness as creative will. This is distorted in the medium of *avidyā/Prakṛti* into desire, the sense of lack and of wanting. Thus, desire can and should be replaced by that which is self-possessed and acts out of its own delight, the creative will.[56]

Here again, one may fruitfully invoke Nietzsche and Deleuze, though one must not be misled by terminology. What Sri Aurobindo refers to as "desire" is closer to the Freudian economy of lack, though for Freud, such an economy is absolute and structures all life, especially human psychological and social life. But this naturally conditioned life of individual desire has, underlying it, an economy of cosmic *askesis* (*tapas*) a creative will to power as enlargement through association and self-exceeding. It is this impersonal productive force which Deleuze refers to as "desire", while he reads the sense of lack as a "territorialisation", or the effect of an exploitation of desire by self-interested orders of social and political control. While the psychology of desire posed by Deleuze and Guattari may be debated, their extension of its operations beyond the individual open human potential, to powerful creative forces of will, which are impersonal and cosmic.

On the other hand, the economy of a "territorialised" desire is what is more common to our experience, socially ensured through pleasure and fear. Sri Aurobindo's analysis of *kāma* in the *Record of Yoga*, also sees two different operations of one force in it, the usual operation to be transformed into

56. SoY, pp. 675-76.

the other power of will. This normal (or normalised) operation of desire is activated and exploited by power interests more strongly than ever before in our times. Once more, we are brought into the remembrance of our contemporary predicament, where an unthinkably complex and impersonal global machinery is continuously manufacturing desires for the consumption of its insatiable productive surpluses and perfecting evermore its technologies for targeting these at the shattered fragments of subjectivity within the human mind-life-body complex. The reversal of consciousness proposed here springs from the awareness that an internal stillness, as with the cessation of response to the tugs of the world, is the basis for a clear intimate perception of what needs to be done in any given situation and the dynamic intuition and executive force of how to do it. As we will see, when we consider the quartet of action (*karma catuṣṭaya*), the realisation prepared by this receptive and impersonal stillness is the action of the conscious force (*cit-śakti*) at work in the world as the single becoming of Integral Being or *Brahman*. A concentrated receptivity puts one in the flow of the will (*tapas*), of this becoming, making one a channel and dynamic instrument of its work, filled with its *śakti* and creative *ānanda*.

Similarly, our sense of identity is a distorted separative *ahaṁkāra* formed by reflection of the true divine self (*ātman*) on the instruments of nature. Earlier, we have discussed this dual constitution of the self. The *ahaṁkāra* can and should be replaced by the *Puruṣa* and *ātman*.[57] We have to distinguish the difference between this self and the universal Self or Person, that has its station within us. That is the *Puruṣa* and the *ātman*, accessible as the immanent psychic being and the universal and transcendental Person and Self. This is to be achieved through the use of two powers, or two kinds of actions. The first of these is the discovery of the liberated self. There is something in each human

57. SoY, pp. 676-77.

being which is always free, it is the unborn part in us, which remains untouched by the movements of nature. One may arrive at this part through meditation.[58] Sri Aurobindo himself was taught and practised a radical version of *rāja-yoga* meditation to arrive at this awareness of the silent Self (though in his case, the realisation which resulted brought the *nirvāṇa*, an impersonality beyond the sense of Self).

The more traditional process of *rāja-yoga* consists of making a conscious effort at watching one's thoughts. Though at first this may seem difficult due to our absorbed identification with our thoughts, the effort to watch one's thoughts is based on the faith that there is something to the mind which does not participate in thinking and can watch the thoughts as if occurring in a separate medium. The attainment of this ability is the realisation of the mental *Puruṣa* mentioned earlier in this chapter. The mental *Puruṣa* is the most accessible aspect of the *Puruṣa* in human beings, since the mind as an instrument of *Prakṛti* is self-aware and impersonal in the higher operations of its *buddhi*. This relative freedom from the ego in the mental nature, allows the soul or conscious part, mental *Puruṣa*, to more easily disentangle itself from the operations of mind and be experienced as a pure silent witness, not participating in one's thoughts, desires or actions. This silent witness is also experienced as a silent *ātman* supporting the individuality of the nature. The settled awareness of the mental *Puruṣa* also brings the realisation of its power of sanction — that is, the *Puruṣa* can be invoked to silence any thought, desire or impulse to action arising from the ego. Thus, one can see that in the task of *śuddhi* the emergence of the mental *Puruṣa* can be a powerful aid.

But the silent self achievable by the meditation of *rāja-yoga* is a quietistic experience and may not bring so easily a dynamic realisation of the One infinite Self in the universe. One may

---

58. SoY, pp. 677-80.

arrive at this through another kind of meditation, the contemplation on the One Being in all beings and phenomena. Sri Aurobindo, in responding to the question "What is the best meditation?" answered that the best meditation was the meditation on the One Being in all things, everywhere and at all times. Keeping one's attention focused on this idea in one's active and passive moments, is a powerful meditation for the replacement of the ego by the liberated self. However, this cannot compete itself easily due to the complexity of our nature. A more dynamic practice, involving one's active self, needs also to be mobilised. This is surrender to the One Being in action: to keep the active consciousness always in a poise of surrender, of remembrance, that in whatever one does, one is an instrument of the Śakti, the Conscious Force or Being-in-Becoming. We invoke Being, as that which is present everywhere and in all things, to express itself through us and identify its consciousness with ours so that we may know it by identity.[59]

The other aspect of *mukti* is the liberation of the Nature from its conditioned action to its conscious participation through choice. The liberation of the Spirit by itself can bring us the knowledge of our essential freedom, from all determinations of Nature, but does not transform our Nature into a potent centre of the divine action. For this possibility, a second liberation is necessary. This is the liberation of the Nature. This is achieved by a transformation of the three *guṇa*s (qualities) of *Prakṛti* that are the active in us. All *Prakṛti* is characterised in yoga psychology, as expressive in three qualitative modes of consciousness, *tamas, rajas* and *sattva*.[60] The text that is best known for the discussion of these modes and liberation from these modes, is the *Bhagavad-Gītā*.[61] The

59. SoY, pp. 680-81.

60. Īśvara Kṛṣṇa, *Sāṁkyha-Kārikā* XI-XIV; the *Gītā* deals with the liberation from the *guṇas*: *Bhagavad-Gītā*, XIV: 5-20; SoY, pp. 683-87.

61. *Bhagavad-Gītā*, op. cit.

active human nature also operates through these three modalities or qualities. There is a mental light in us, a light of consciousness tending towards clarity, but limited in being a reflected or more properly, a refracted light, not a light of self-awareness. This is *sattva*. This operation of *sattva* needs to be transformed into the light of self-aware knowledge (*jyoti*).[62] The kinetic part in us, which is the blind animal energy, *rajas*, needs to be transformed into an action of the puissant omnipotence of consciousness, *cit-tapas*, which is another way of seeing in nature, what we saw in Being.[63] And the *tamas* in us has to be transformed into *śama* (conscious repose), a power of being not sunk in an unconsciousness of sleep but in a state of conscious repose, awake with the fullness of one's consciousness, completely immobile, but also completely awake.[64]

This transformation of *tamas* is achieved by equality and indifference. We need to learn how to refuse to be pulled into any action, unless we are sure of its origin, not by impulse, desire, preference or attachment. We would rather not act. One part of us must become independent, just like the judiciary is independent of the executive branch of the government, the *tamas* transformed into *śama* has to become an independent power of inaction in us, a power that refuses action unless it is sure that the action is coming from a source that is truth itself. Similarly, the transformation of *rajas* is to be achieved by a silent receptivity to the divine will. Here we return, as in the case of the intelligence, to a surrender to the divine will, as the conscious power that will allow us to be its channel through receptivity. The *sattva* as a limited power of light, also needs transformation. The transformation of *sattva* is accomplished through continence and silent receptivity to intuition and

62. SoY, pp. 687-89.

63. Ibid., pp. 688-89.

64. Ibid., pp. 689-90.

knowledge. Here again, the utility of continence will be further discussed when we consider *śarīra*, and its perfections.

But we can certainly see how a power of altered activity can emerge, if there are these transformations.[65] Philosophically, we can understand the three qualities of transformed *Prakṛti*, in terms of the transformation of the consciousness of *avidyā* to that of *vidyā* in the individual. We can also see how these transformations in the responses of nature can reverse our subjection to the ubiquitous regime of capital which targets our unconsciousness, desire, greed and selfish ambition. *Tamas* transformed can then be seen to be the quality of consciousness of *sat*, pure immobile presence of infinite Being, with consciousness latent within it; *rajas* transformed can be seen as the quality of dynamic omnipotence of self-energism (*tapas*), of the One Consciousness at work in the universe (*cit*); and *sattva* can be understood as the quality of consciousness as self-awareness of Being, radiance of knowledge (*vijñāna*).

Bhukti or Enjoyment

The results of *śuddhi* and *mukti* are *bhukti* and *siddhi*. Sri Aurobindo enumerates the various forms of *bhukti* which are the results or goals of *śuddhi* and *mukti*. They are of seven kinds, pertaining to the seven modalities of cosmic consciousness, touched on towards the start of this chapter while outlining Sri Aurobindo's epistemic psychology.[66] These modalities are matter, life, mind, supermind, bliss, consciousness and being. The forms of bliss pertain to each of these forms of consciousness.

The first is *kāmānanda*, (physical bliss) which belongs to the *śarīra* (body). This is the coursing of delight in the nerves and senses. Sri Aurobindo gave special attention to physical

65. RoY, p. 1480.
66. RoY, p. 1481.

bliss, dividing it further into five kinds, which he discussed under the *siddhis* of the body. We will consider these under the quartet of the body (*śarīra catuṣṭaya*). The second form of delight is *premānanda*, which belongs to the *citta* or the emotional or affective mind. This is the delight of universal love in all things, a constant exaltation and delight in the feelings. The third form of delight is *ahaitukānanda*, which belongs to the *manas*. This is a causeless delight in the basis of sense. In other words, whatever meets us through our senses, doesn't need a cause to give us delight. It is intrinsically delightful because the One Delight-Being, the Being of delight is realised as expressing through it. We can see how this connects with the purification of the senses and the quotation cited earlier from William Blake. All experiences, received mentally through the senses, awake the *rasa* (taste) of an intrinsic causeless bliss.

***Siddhi Catuṣṭaya* (Quartet of Perfection) (1.5)**

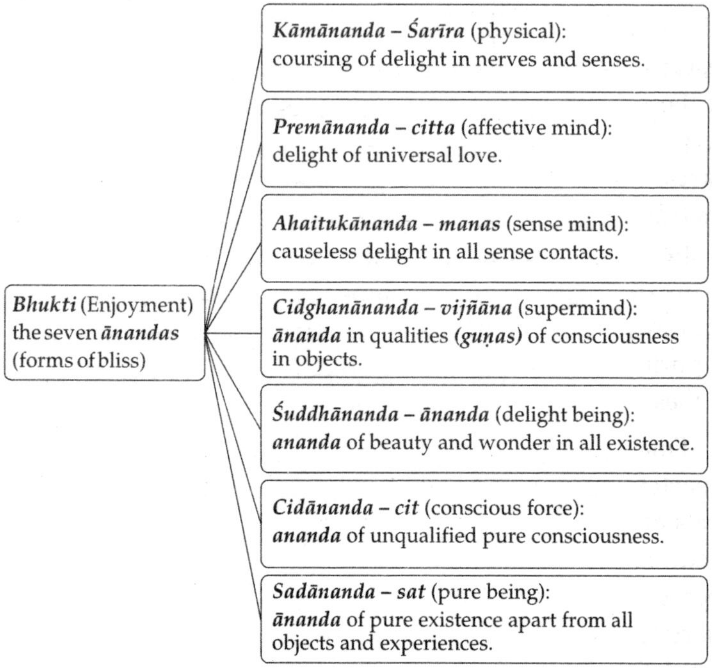
Bhukti (Enjoyment) the seven ānandas (forms of bliss)
Kāmānanda – Śarīra (physical): coursing of delight in nerves and senses.
Premānanda – citta (affective mind): delight of universal love.
Ahaitukānanda – manas (sense mind): causeless delight in all sense contacts.
Cidghanānanda – vijñāna (supermind): ānanda in qualities (guṇas) of consciousness in objects.
Śuddhānanda – ānanda (delight being): ananda of beauty and wonder in all existence.
Cidānanda – cit (conscious force): ananda of unqualified pure consciousness.
Sadānanda – sat (pure being): ānanda of pure existence apart from all objects and experiences.

Citghanānanda is the next form of delight and belongs properly to *vijñāna*. This is the essence of *ānanda* in the qualities or *guṇa*s of consciousness in objects. Whereas *ahaitukānanda* is a varied causeless delight in all mental reception of sense experience, *citghanānanda* is full of the density of consciousness of the Real Idea which has become this evolving universe and is present in all its objects and experiences. *Śuddhānanda,* the next form of delight, is the *ānanda* of the Being of Delight, *Ānandamaya Puruṣa,* the *ānanda* of the Being of infinite beauty and wonder in all existence. *Cidānanda* (*ānanda* of *cit*), conscious Force is the bliss of unqualified pure consciousness, the delight of being conscious. And finally, *Sadānanda* (the *ānanda* of pure being) *sat*, which is the *ānanda* of pure existence, apart from all objects and experiences, the very fundamental bliss of existence of infinite Being.

These are the varied forms of Bliss to be experienced on all the different planes and parts of the Being as an overall result, *siddhi* of the yoga of integral transformation. Several of these forms are hardly possible to human beings, until a very advanced stage of transformed existence. But others, particularly the first three — *kāmānanda, premānanda, ahaitukānanda* — may be experienced sporadically by us even at the outset, and we may have a better grasp of these in terms of the goals of human aspiration. All these forms of bliss are intrinsic to Being and develop automatically as a result of purification (*śuddhi*) and a settled state of liberation (*mukti*) in these various aspects of being.

Finally, the *siddhi* (goal/perfection) of the *siddhi catuṣṭaya* (quartet of perfection) is achieved in the attainment of the goals of the other quartets, and hence, the achievement of the conditions of the quartet of perfection — i.e. purification and liberation, become the general accompaniments for the other quartets, and when complete, are seen to coincide with the completion of all these goals and hence, with the attainment of the *siddhi* of integral transformation.[67] One sees here why Sri Aurobindo considered the quartet of perfection to be synonymous with the quartet of yoga, the foundational quartet of the yoga of integral transformation. As demonstrated here, the twin goals of this most general quartet are *mukti* and *bhukti*. In terms of *siddhi*, then, we will find that the goals of each of the other quarters can also be divided into aspects or forms of liberation and enjoyment. We turn then to these other quartets.

67. RoY, pp. 23, 1481.

2

The Quartet of Peace

In the previous chapter, we considered the general elements of integral transformation, which Sri Aurobindo classed under *siddhi catuṣṭaya* (the quartet of perfection), and also sometimes referred to as *yoga catuṣṭaya* (the quartet of yoga). There we saw that the primary pre-requisite for the goals of this approach, liberation (*mukti*) and enjoyment (*bhukti*), was purification (*śuddhi*). Hence, a major part of our consideration dwelt on this aspect, drawing out the different elements of the yogic psychology which needed to be purified. We saw how almost all the elements there — the elements of the nervous being, the will, the emotional being, and of the various aspects of the mind — *citta*, *manas* and *buddhi* — (the mentality of sensations, the mind of sense and the rational mind), with its gradations — are to be subjected to the power of equality. Equality is the great purifier. This primary importance of equality was further developed by Sri Aurobindo by turning this discipline into the first of the specific formulations of perfection or *ādhāra siddhi*s.

The Progression of Equality

Sri Aurobindo referred to this as *samatā catuṣṭaya* (the quartet of equality) and alternately, *śānti catuṣṭaya* (the quartet of peace). Sri Aurobindo translated the Sanskrit term *samatā* as equality. Perhaps, a word is necessary to explain this translation, when the term more commonly used is "equanimity". Equanimity does not quite capture the sense of *samatā*. Equanimity means to maintain a balanced mental attitude in the face of all circumstances. Equality is to react to all events and circumstances with an undisturbed inner consciousness in one's mind, emotions, sensations and physical actions and reactions, not only a mental attitude but a habit of consciousness at every level, an integral ideal. The difference between these two translations also highlights a fundamental conceptual difference regarding consciousness. At least, since Aristotle, and more so with Descartes, with his mind-body dualism, consciousness in the West has been equated with reason, while in Indic thought, the radical dualism of Sāṁkhya has located consciousness entirely in soul (*Puruṣa*), treating all the operations of nature (including thinking) as *Prakṛti*, unconscious except by reflection of *Puruṣa*. But, though Sri Aurobindo utilised the method of Sāṁkhya to arrive at a kind of freedom for practical purposes, the metaphysics more proper to his goals of integral transformation, had their roots in Vedānta and Tantra in affirming a reality, in which nothing was devoid of consciousness. This consciousness may take many forms, not merely mental, and each of these forms of consciousness would have its own qualitative responses.

Sri Aurobindo, in his writings, often invoked the Indian nationalist scientist, Jagadish Chandra Bose, to refer to non-human forms of consciousness, such as the consciousness of plants or of matter. For example, Bose sought to demonstrate that what is referred to as "tolerance" or "fatigue" in metallurgy, is not merely an anthropomorphic or animistic substitution, but a subjective response of metal consciousness. For Sri Aurobindo, it was possible and necessary for humans to identity with the independent movements of these forms of consciousness, participating in their "becoming". As in several other instances, this may be seen to have an analogue in the ideas of Gilles Deleuze, here the idea of "becoming-other". Sri Aurobindo wished to distinguish such processes of participation from a stoic culture of the mind, implied in the term "equanimity". So he used the term "equality" as an elemental reference to translate *samatā*.

Equality is the first term in the progression of this quartet and its last term is ecstasy. It is an interesting series which deals with the growth of quietude, of calm as a progression of consciousness leading ultimately to bliss and ecstasy. Again, we see those two wings on which the yoga of integral transformation moves, the wings of *mukti* and *bhukti* (freedom and enjoyment). This progression too, as a quartet, has four stages or four *siddhis*, connected with it. They are *samatā* (equality), *śānti* (peace), *sukham* which means happiness or contentment, and *hāsya* (laughter). *Samatā* and *śānti* can be seen as attributes of *mukti* while *sukham* and *hāsya* are forms of *bhukti*. This quartet begins with equality. The other terms in this progression are peace and contentment and the series ends with the powerful positive laughter of the gods. In *Savitri*, Sri Aurobindo has a phrase: "The vast golden laughter of truth's sun."[1] This is a vast sense of delight, an intense causeless ecstasy, carried in an oceanic equality experienced as the basis of truth. The foundation of this entire progression is *samatā*.

Equality and the Puruṣa

In the quartet of equality, the power of equality is further developed and seen not only as a purifier but as a dynamic power for the full emergence of the *Puruṣa*. In the last chapter, we saw the Sāṁkhya distinction between consciousness and nature, that which is conscious in us and that which is

1. In the vast golden laughter of truth's sun
like a great heaven-bird on a motionless sea.
Is poised, her winged ardour of creative joy,
On the still deep of the eternal's peace.
(*Savitri*, SABCL 29, Book X, Canto 3,
The Debate of Love and Death, p. 632).

conditioned, whether these principles of conditioning come from the cosmos itself or are individualised and picked up in the process of our present and past life journeys. According to Sāṁkhya, that which is conscious in us is the *Puruṣa*, and that which is conditioned instrumentation of nature is known as *Prakṛti*. In the schools, that prioritise liberation over the activities of the world, the trend is to separate the *Puruṣa* from the *Prakṛti*, so as to put the movements of nature to rest. This is done through a process of progressive refusal, a refusal of identification in consciousness with the body, with the various aspects of the life being, with the thinking, with the sensing, leading to a realisation that there is something not touched by any of these, the *Puruṣa*.[2] The *Puruṣa* is experienced initially, as a pure witness, *sākṣī*, and subsequently as a power of sanction to the movements of nature, something that can veto the activities of nature.. And in this, it is a giver of sanction (*anumantā*). These are the powers of the *Puruṣa*.[3]

In quietistic schools of yoga, that aim to put an end to all the movements of nature, the separation of *Puruṣa* from *Prakṛti* through a progressive refusal of identification is the way followed. This way can also be followed in Sri Aurobindo's path of integral transformation, but only as one process among a number of parallel processes to be practised, and with a different goal. In the perfection of equality we find that the process of developing equality is an inner discipline, through which the emergence of the *Puruṣa* is sought while continuing the activities of *Prakṛti* and purifying them at the same time. It

---

2. This Advaitic discipline of progressive negation is referred to as *neti, neti* (not this, not this) and takes its origin in the colloquy of Yājñavalkya at the court of King Janaka in the *Bṛhadāraṇyaka Upaniṣad*. See *Bṛhadāraṇyaka Upaniṣad* III.9.26.

3. In *Bhagavad-Gītā*, XIII.23, the *Puruṣa*'s status as witness (*upadraṣṭā*) and sanctioner (*anumantā*) is followed by its emergence into the fullness of its capacities as enjoyer (*bhoktā*) and lord (*Īśvara*). Also see Sri Aurobindo, SoY, pp. 122-23.

is a purification of the activities of nature, which overcomes the distortions cast by nature upon *Puruṣa*, so that *Puruṣa*'s reality is reflected in a transparent and complete manner by the activities of nature. The foundation for this is equality. Here is, a passage from *The Synthesis of Yoga* where Sri Aurobindo shows how equality becomes a foundation of the yoga of integral transformation:

> A divine action or even a perfect human action is impossible if we have not equality of spirit and an equality in the motive forces of our nature. The Divine is equal to all, an impartial sustainer of his universe, who views all with equal eyes, assents to the law of developing being, which he has brought out of the depths of his existence, tolerates what has to be tolerated, depresses what has to be depressed, raises what has to be raised, creates, sustains and destroys with a perfect and equal understanding of all causes and results and working out of the spiritual and pragmatic meaning of all phenomena. God does not create in obedience to any troubled passion or desire, or maintain and preserve through an attachment of partial preference, or destroy in a fury of wrath, disgust, or aversion. The Divine deals with great and small, just and unjust, ignorant and wise, as the self of all who, deeply intimate and one with the being, leads all according to their nature and need with a perfect understanding power and justness of proportion. But through it all he moves things according to his large aim in the cycles and draws the soul upward in the evolution through its apparent progress and retrogression towards the higher and ever higher development, which is the sense of the cosmic urge. The self-perfecting individual, who seeks to be one in will with the divine and makes his nature an instrument of the divine purpose must enlarge himself out of the egoistic and partial views and motives of the human ignorance and mold himself into an image of this supreme equality.[4]

4. SoY, p. 700.

This is why equality becomes the foundation through which the *Puruṣa* can emerge in the midst of action, can illuminate our actions and determine choice in the truth of free will. Prior to this, what we call free will is a conditioning, a kind of forcing of the hand by nature which the ego takes to be its own doing and therefore, mistakes as free will. But, it is only when equality can be established that the *Puruṣa* can emerge and, as Sri Aurobindo has pointed out, bring into the being the true will (*cit-tapas*) through which that which needs to be done can be manifest without distortion.

> This equal poise in action is especially necessary for the *sādhaka* of the integral yoga. First he must acquire that equal assent and understanding which will respond to the law of the divine action without trying to impose on it, a partial will and the violent claim, of a personal aspiration.[5]

Taken from the same passage, in *The Synthesis of Yoga*, this is an interesting sentence, showing the impurity of our inner will, even our most exalted or noble aspirations. Even our aspirations for the realisation of the divine are marked by partiality, preference and ignorance. Hence, they need to be brought under the action of equality.

> A wise impersonality of quiescent equality, a universality which sees all things as the manifestations of the Divine, the One Existence is not angry, troubled, impatient with the way of things, or on the other hand, excited or over-eager and precipitate, but sees the law must be obeyed and the pace of time respected, observes and understands with sympathy the actuality of things and beings, but looks also behind the present appearance to their inner significances and forward to the unrolling of their divine possibilities, is the first thing demanded of those who would do works as the perfect instruments of the Divine. But, this impersonal

---

5. SoY, p. 700.

> acquiescence is only the basis. Man is the instrument of an evolution which wears at first the mask of a struggle, but grows more and more into its truer and deeper sense of a constant, wise adjustment and must take on in a rising scale the deepest significance now only underlying the adjustment and struggle of a universal harmony.[6]

The Passive Disciplines of Equality

Sri Aurobindo, in his *samatā catuṣṭaya* (quartet of equality), details how we are to approach this equality in our lives. Here, he outlines two aspects to equality: a passive equality and an active equality. He outlines the passive *samatā* in terms of three practices of consciousness: *titikṣā* (endurance), *udāsīnatā* (indifference to dualities), and *nati* (submission to the divine will).

When we look at these elements of perfection, we begin to sense a logic to the formulation of these progressions of consciousness. There is an aspect in each of these elements, related respectively to a discipline of the sensational or nervous part of the nature, to the affective or emotional part of the nature — what we loosely call "the heart" — and to the mental part in us, the reasoning part of our nature. The physical-vital complex, the vital-mental complex, and the pure mental being and its constituents — these are the three stations of nature which Sri Aurobindo approaches in this progression of the practice of equality.

Titikṣā

Thus, we find, when we consider the three terms he introduces as the disciplines of a passive equality, that these can operate separately, they can operate simultaneously, or they can operate in conjunction in any form or combination. *Titikṣā* may

---

6. SoY, pp. 700-01.

be translated as endurance. This brings to mind the Greek ideal of the stoic, someone who faces his lot with fortitude, an attitude of endurance. And indeed this is the beginning of the discipline of *titikṣā,* though *titikṣā* is also an attitude of our active parts, our parts of the life-being, of the will, and of our sensational and physical reactions. It is related to pleasure and pain of the body, the sensations and our nervous responses to life. To bear all these with endurance, there must be within us the faith or experience of a strength or presence, which upholds even through extremes of pain or pleasure. This is the essence of *titikṣā*.[7]

Here, one may ask what is meant by forbearance as a response to pleasure. It is easy to think of pain, suffering that makes us wince, smart or cry out and to counteract these with faith, that we have something within that can endure these things stoically. But what may it mean to "bear" pleasure? Sri Aurobindo refers here to the conditioned responses of pleasure, being subject to the compulsions of pleasure. Once we embark on the discipline of equality, we realise that something in us is enslaved to pleasure, not at all its master. This is part of our animal constitution which nature utilises to ensure certain predictable responses. We carry this with us as part of our active constitution, but unlike the animal, we also have something in us which seeks the realisation of its intrinsic freedom. As this need for freedom comes more to the front of our existence, we begin to feel trapped by our desires, our conditioned responses to pleasure. The English poet W.B. Yeats has brought this sense of helpless entrapment out very well in his poem "Sailing to Byzantium". Here he speaks of old age as a state of helplessness, not merely a helplessness of the loss of faculties or of illness, a condition of suffering, as the Buddha realised and taught, but a helplessness in the realisation of one's bondage to desire.

7. SoY, pp. 711-12; RoY, p. 3.

Even the failure of our capacity for enjoyment does not stop the driving compulsion of pleasure and the poet feels most acutely this human enslavement: "Consume my heart away; sick with desire/And fastened to a dying animal/It knows not what it is; . . ."[8] However, it need not take the stern teaching of old age to bring this to our attention. The need for inner freedom and causeless bliss, lives in us, as perhaps the most characteristic truth of the human condition, and the disciplines of equality only help to bring this need to the front of our experience.

Another aspect of this forbearance in the face of pleasure that we can think of has to do with its intensity. Facetiously, we sometimes say or hear others saying, "Oh stop! I'll die laughing!" This expression, as of a pleasure too great for one's physical capacities, becomes no more a "laughing matter" in the case of some of the experiences of subjective bliss that come through the opening of the gates to cosmic consciousness. The sensational apparatus experiences burn-out. One loses consciousness in a painful excess of bliss. From a certain point of view, Sri Aurobindo points out, what we call pain is also a convention of nature defining a range of responses to the variations or gradations of bliss.[9] All that we called pain can in this sense, be thought of as a whiplash or sting of bliss too intense to bear. Even the terminal experience of death may be thought of in these terms, as an irreversible disruption of physiological functioning, under the stress of forces, too strong or intense, for it to bear. Here we come into closer contact with the true power of *titikṣā*. It takes its strength in the faith of the indestructible, eternal, omnipotent spirit within us. If we can bring this faith and its discipline dynamically and constantly into all our responses, at every level and in every

8. W.B. Yeats, "Sailing to Byzantium", *The Collected Poems of W.B. Yeats*, London: Wordsworth Editions, 2000, p. 163.
9. RoY, p. 4. See also the line "He stung himself with bliss and called it pain" in Sri Aurobindo's poem "Parābrahman". CP, p. 218.

faculty and instrument of our being, the capacity for our nature to respond to and recognise itself as a form of action of this spirit develops and we begin to experience a stretching of the limits and a transformation of functioning of our nature. But, it is important to realise that the discipline of *titikṣā* is not merely a stoic attitude of the mind, not the proverbial British "stiff upper lip" of external reserve in expression. It is the active exercise of the faith in the power of endurance of the spirit within, or faith in the presence of the divine seated within us in every aspect of our nature and modality of our consciousness.

While on the subject of *titikṣā*, it is useful to consider that in contemporary times the stoics and their disciplines of the self have been adulated by Michel Foucault as an "aesthetics of existence".[10] Foucault has drawn attention to this Greek past as a historical instance of the operation of an ethical imagination without reference to the socially hegemonic discourses of religion, science and law. He sees the possibility of such an ethics, a "care of the self" or "care of the soul" as a counter to the determining regime of modernity, enforced by state, religion, science or techno-capitalism. While *titikṣā* is not seen by Sri Aurobindo primarily in ethical terms, the enterprise of self-discipline in an integral yoga certainly has its ethical dimension and likewise reverses the subjection of the self through an "aesthetics of existence".

Udāsīnatā: Being Seated Above

The second discipline in the progression of passive *samatā* is the power called *udāsīnatā*, which can be translated as indifference to dualities. *Udāsīnatā* literally means "being seated above". If *titikṣā* can be thought of as a lateral movement, or movement at the same level as the impact of the world, *udāsīnatā* implies a

---

10. Michel Foucault, ed. Frederic Gros; tr. Graham Burchell, *The Hermeneutics of the Subject*, New York: Picador, 2005, pp. 416-17.

level of ascent. *Udāsīnatā* means that there is something in us, not only as a response of strength or endurance to all the movements of the world, but something entirely untouched by the movements of the world. This has more to do with the mental element in us. It is this that gives us the freedom to apply an action of indifference upon the movements in our life. It can neutralise the conventions and preferences with which the shocks of life come to us. Our mind plays an important part in giving us interpretive values to our experience; and the way in which we can utilise the mind as an instrument to bring indifference to the dualities of our reactions, both in mind and in life, is an aspect of *udāsīnatā*.[11] To cultivate *udāsīnatā*, one must develop the intuition of the unborn self which we are. To this self, the structure of our phenomenal lives and their experiences is a representation only, from which it can withdraw or which it can inhabit in freedom. To come into contact with the power and discipline of *udāsīnatā* is to have a fundamental detachment from one's experiences, a realised sense of being free from them, even while some part of

Śānti Catuṣṭaya (Perfection of Equality) (2.1)
Samatā, Śānti, Sukha, Hāsya

***Samatā* (Equality)**

Passive Samatā
Titikṣā (endurance);
Udāsīnatā (indifference to dualities);
Nati (submission to divine will).

Active Samatā
Rasa (experience of taste and quality);
Prītiḥ (pleasure of mind in all *rasa*);
Ānanda (equal bliss beyond all dualities).

11. SoY, pp. 712-13.

one's being experiences them. In Sri Aurobindo's yoga, *udāsīnatā*, however, is not used as an escape from the experiences of the nature but a leverage to rid these experiences of extreme reactions.

Nati

Finally, there is the aspect of *nati*, which has to do with *bhakti* or the devotional element.[12]

Neither *titikṣā* nor *udāsīnatā* can complete itself until and unless there enters into the practice of equality the sense of a glad submission, what in its essence is the very meaning of the word *Islam* — a submission to the Divine Will. As the common-sense saying goes, no practice can endure, unless there is some "heart" to it. This is a loving submission to the Divine Will as an aspect of a devotional relationship with the One Being that is guiding us. This is based on the intuition and growing experience of the fact that there is a living presence and power which is bringing us our experiences of

Śānti Catuṣṭaya (Perfection of Equality) (2.2)

***Śānti* (Peace)**: a vast joyous calm

***Sukha* (Happiness)**: complete release from all possibility of *duḥkha* (grief).

***Hāsya* (Laughter)**: the active side of *sukham* — internal state of divine joy and ecstasy.

12. SoY, pp. 713-14.

the world, whether of pleasure or pain, happiness or sorrow, so that we may grow through these experiences into the likeness of that Divine. It may be useful to introduce here, the nature of the object of our submission. In the *Record of Yoga*, what emerges as the master of the yoga is an intensely personal relationship, which is yet beyond any sectarian limitation. By a constant practice of trust and submission to the impersonal and illimitable *ParaBrahman* who is yet the Supreme Person, *Puruṣottama* at the heart of its reality, we attain to an equality which is glad, unshakeable and full of the gift of gratitude.[13]

Active Disciplines of Equality

This *nati* becomes the central change in the affective part that completes the triple aspect of the passive *samatā*. But, if this were all, we would hardly be agents for any powerful action in the world. We would be merely receptive beings. We would practise the discipline of receiving the shocks of the world and at best be equal to them. But what of the creative aspect of our own being, the dynamic response from within us of the divine, if indeed it is the divine whose life is to be lived in us? What about the divine delight, *ānanda* and unrestrained laughter (*hāsya*) that is at the heart of all things and indeed, is all things, according to Sri Aurobindo? This cannot be over-emphasised. For this aspect, one needs to develop what Sri Aurobindo calls an active or dynamic equality. Both the passive and active disciplines of *samatā* must be practised simultaneously. As with passive *samatā*, active *samatā* relates to three kinds of practices (*abhyāsa*) and their resulting experiences — the discipline and experience of an equal active enjoyment in the mind, the life-energy (*prāṇa*) and the spirit. The first kind of experience is called *rasa*, the second, *bhoga* and the third, *ānanda*.[14]

---

13. RoY, pp. 4, 28.
14. SoY, pp. 716-17; RoY, p. 4.

Rasa

Our affective experiences can be divided into those which are pleasant, unpleasant and neutral. But these responses of our subjectivity are based on values which the mind gives to our experiences. Such values, which we take to be "natural" and unchanging are, in fact, also conditionings. Though we often take these affective responses to characterise ourselves, they are the products of innate tendencies of nature (*saṁskāras*) or upbringing and environmental or ideological forces. We are surrounded by the mythologies of the politics of capital and power which infiltrate our affections, conditioning feeling. As such, they are relative and can be interchanged by force of mind or spirit. If our mind deliberately refuses the binary simplification of experience into pleasant and unpleasant, and tries instead to acquire a habit of neutrality towards our experiences, we will find that they can be divided into combinations of qualities. A study of this kind lay behind the Indian theory of aesthetics (*rasa-sūtra*).[15] Aesthetics divides subjective experience into distinct qualities; but the idea of *rasa*s applies to all our senses, as the gateways to mental experience. Sense experiences are interpreted in the mind which perceives the qualities being transmitted by the senses and translates these into values. These values become then, the basis of our affective, nervous and sensory experiences.

The building-blocks of "taste", for example have been divided into six categories: sweet (*madhura*), sour (*āmla*), salty

15. The first extant passage to deal with this is the 6th chapter of Bharata's *Nāṭyaśāstra*, a text on dramaturgy, believed to have been written sometime between 200 BCE and CE 200. But this psychological theory of affect was elaborated extensively through the medieval period and applied to all arts, mystical experience and life itself. Apart from an aesthetic understanding of *rasa*, there are also the more obvious psycho-physical understanding of taste as a sense belonging to the tongue and an (al)chemical understanding of *rasa* as material quality.

(*lavaṇa*), bitter (*kaṭu*), pungent (*tikta*) and astringent (*kaṭu*). But if we think more deeply about it, we realise that all such classifications are also conventions and a convenience. We can understand this more clearly if we think of odours rather than tastes. Odours are much less easy to classify, though they are distinct. If we make an effort to overcome our "natural" mental valuation of odours into pleasant and unpleasant, we become more conscious of the unnameable yet distinct identity of an odour. The science of Indian aesthetics extended such an idea of classification of tastes to our sense experiences of sight, hearing and emotional responses. Such subjective states are undoubtedly, more complex than the six tastes of the tongue. The Indian theory of subjective or aesthetic taste, divides experience into nine *rasa*s — the amorous (*śṛṅgāra*), the humorous (*hāsya*), the courageous or heroic (*vīra*), the pathetic or compassionate (*karuṇa*), the wonderful (*adbhuta*), the terrible (*raudra*), the fearsome or horrible (*bhayānaka*), the odious (*bībhatsa*) and the peaceful (*śānta*).[16] Further, subdividing affective experience, Vaiṣṇavism introduced additional *rasa*s related to devotion (*bhakti*), such as parental love (*vātsalya*), friendship (*sakhya*), love of service as of a servant or slave of god (*dāsya*), and supraphysical love (*mādhurya*).[17] The last two of these have an important part to play in the quartet of power, *śakti catuṣṭaya* of the *Record of Yoga*.

---

16. Bharata's *Rasa-Sūtra* enumerates eight *rasas*, but *śānta* as the ninth and most privileged *rasa* was added in *Abhinavabhāratī*, the very influential tenth-eleventh-century commentary on Bharata's *Nāṭyaśāstra* by Abhinavagupta, a teacher of Kāśmīr Śaivism. See *Abhinavaguptācārya*, ed. Pushpendra Kumar; tr. M.M. Ghosh, *Natyasastra of Bharatamuni : Text, Commentary of Abhinava Bharati*, Delhi: New Bharatiya Book Corporation, 2006, 3 vols.

17. The theory of *bhakti rasa*s in Gauḍīya Vaiṣṇavism was developed by the Brindavan Gosvāmīs, Rūpa and Jīva Gosvāmī. See Rupa Gosvāmī, *Bhaktirasāmṛtasindhu* and *Ujjvalanīlamaṇi*; and Jiva Gosvāmī, *Bhaktisandarbha*.

What is important here, is not so much the specific classification of subjective experience but the attempt in Indian aesthetics to direct the mind beyond its binary response of good and evil, and towards an enjoymnent of reality in its varied qualities as manifestations of the One Delight. To arrive at this, the mind has to learn to neutrailse our "natural" responses. This is only possible through an impersonal detachment of the intellect, which knows how to observe experiences in themeslves and perceive their distinctive qualities. Again, it is not important that one gives a name to these distinct qualities, but is able to perceive and recognise them as manifold manifestations of the differential One. A mental exercise of this kind, against a backdrop of neutrality, predisposes the subjective experience in certain ways. This is why Indian aestheticians have debated which of the *rasa*s is the most primary. If we prioritise the neutrality, necessary for the clear perception and experience of qualitative distinction, the primary *rasa* can be thought to be *śānta*. The great tenth-century *yogī*, aesthetician and teacher of Kāśmīr Śaivism, Abhinavagupta, privileged *śānta rasa* in this way. If, on the other hand, a more active aspect of the ability to perceive quality without attraction or repulsion is seen as primary, we realise that the underlying affect is one of *adbhuta*. Then again, if this is the case, a further intensification of wonder is seen as a powerful experience of *śṛṅgāra,* between the experiencer and the one Beloved who manifests in all things as its varied relationships of delight. As a result, the Indian devotional schools of Vaiṣṇavism have seen these *rasa*s as primary. In Buddhism, the *rasa* of sublime sadness or *karuṇā* is prioritised, since this foundational sorrow and its awareness is thought of as the basis of temporal experience. An extension of this is seen in the quality of the beauty of transience in Japanese aesthetics, known as *mono-no-aware*. Again, without labouring this point, what we can take away from this in terms of the disciplines of an active equality, *samatā*, is a detachment of the intellect and the development of a perception of distinctive quality of each subjective experience outside of the dualities of pleasure and displeasure. A part of our mind then treats our experiences, as if they were staged phenomena, to be savoured as forms of subjective taste. This is the development of the capacity of an equal taste of *rasa* in experiences, *rasagrahaṇa*.[18]

Bhoga

This consequence of an equality of the mind and the development of an active capacity for the perception and enjoyment of quality can be taken further into an active enjoyment by the life energy, the full grasp and transformed experience in the senses and nerves. Thus, in this discipline there is a leveraging of the power of impersonality of the *buddhi* to transform the experience of the *manas*, the *citta* and the *prāṇa*. The perception of equal but differentiated quality in the *buddhi*, may be imposed on what we call the sixth sense, or the part of the mind behind all the senses and that which is responsible for the experience of synaesthesia (*manas*).[19] This is then further extended to the *citta*, which is the aspect of rudimentary mentality, where sensations turn into feelings or affects. A feeling of distinct quality, devoid of the push and pull of attraction or repulsion, is experienced here, through this extension. This feeling is further extended into the nervous experience of the *prāṇa*, in what may be thought of as a vital-physical layer of experience.

This practice can be brought to a focus in the reactions of the senses, thus, approaching the discipline of equality in the experience of *rasa* through the subconscious *citta*. Thus, one can work towards establishing both an equality, and a fullness of the experience of taste in the sense organs or taste-buds, in

18. SoY, pp. 354, 656, 717.

19. RoY, pp. 5, 1467-68, 1478-79.

one's sensations. We are not to reject the intensity of taste. We are to accept them all equally with a seeking for their specific quality. Of course, the question may be asked: Is Sri Aurobindo then making a case for masochism here, are we supposed to inflict pain on ourselves as a form of delight? This is not what is meant; we have no need to seek out experiences of pain, such experiences will find us, there is no need to inflict pain on oneself. Sri Aurobindo draws attention to this in terms of the invisible hand, which takes us through life, granting us experiences to make us progress in consciousness. The phrase he uses for this "invisible hand" is his epic poem *Savitri*, is the "Assigner of the ordeal and the path".[20] This is what he also identifies as the "Master of the Evolution" or "Master of the yoga" in his own diaries. This is also the one to whom we are asked to make our *nati* at the outset; this Master of the Evolution assigns pain to us just as he assigns happiness to us, because without this we will not be able to emerge into the fullness of our consciousness.

Transforming Pain to Bliss

Thus *bhoga*, the experience of taste in the nervous sensational being, received equally, may be understood as an aspect of the active equality of *rasa*, which Sri Aurobindo calls *rasagrahaṇa*. Equality to the natural attractions and repulsions of sense reactions results in the perception of specific quality in each taste as a form of enjoyment, equal in degree, but different in kind. We may wonder, is this possible? Is it even desirable? What is interesting here, is that Sri Aurobindo has a number of entries in the *Record of Yoga* relating to this. In his letters on yoga and in his conversations, he also elaborates on the ability to bring an equal power of reception to experiences, painful

20. Assigner of the ordeal and the path
Who chooses in this holocaust of the soul
Death, fall and sorrow as the spirit's goads, . . .
— Savitri, 17.

and pleasurable. Experiences, which are normally felt as painful, are here transformed into bliss. Sri Aurobindo writes, for example, of being stung by ants, or by a scorpion, but experiencing these as forms of intense bliss. We saw above how some aesthetes take the amorous *rasa*, *śṛṅgāra*, as the pre-eminent "taste". In the case of the scorpion sting, Sri Aurobindo writes about this experience not merely as a divestment of its lethal or poisonous content, or even as an impersonal transformation to an experience of bliss but as a concrete experience of blissful physical contact with the divine beloved, an act of love.[21] As mentioned above, what we call pain is an intensity of bliss that our system cannot bear. Similarly, death is an intensity of bliss that our body cannot bear, so it breaks under the impact. If there was a perfect equality in the system, this would become the basis of a transformation through higher consciousness, and the nerves would turn to "burning threads of joy", as Sri Aurobindo writes in his epic *Savitri*.[22] This is perhaps the most difficult form of *samatā*, being the least under our control. Here, we can also see more clearly why Sri Aurobindo uses the term equality to translate *samatā*, rather than equanimity. The latter is a mental attitude, but *samatā* pertains to forms of behaviour, which are non-mental and seem commonly to be unconscious. But we can make note of the fact that though not mental, these disciplines also pertain to forms of consciousness. With the progress of *samatā* in the physical, vital and subconscious mental system, this possibility opens up for us.

In contemporary theory, the work of Deleuze and Guattari,

21. Sri Aurobindo, "The Meditations of Mandavya" in CP, p. 509.

22. A divinising stream possessed his veins,
His body's cells awoke to spirit sense,
Each nerve became a burning thread of joy:
Tissue and flesh partook beatitude.

— Savitri, 334.

may be seen as touching on, or intersecting with several of the possibilities raised by Sri Aurobindo, in terms of the potentia of experience related to equality. In *Anti-Oedipus* and more pointedly, in *A Thousand Plateaus*, Deleuze and Guattari introduce the idea of the "BwO" (Body without Organs) and relate it to the larger idea of the "Plane of Consistency" or "Plane of Immanence". The BwO is a "virtual body" which refuses the territorialisation of the desiring subject and replaces this with an expanding potential of experience beyond the conventional valuation of pleasure or pain. Deleuze and Guattari refer to these experiences in terms of a scale of intensities.[23] In *A Thousand Plateaus*, they distinguish between empty and full BwO and hold up the body prepared by the balance of yoga to be more suitable for the full BwO.[24] This condition is one in which psycho-physical subjectivity can allow a plurality of experiences to pass through or upon it, bearing all these as intensities. This expansion of the body towards an unformed but potentially infinite richness of experiential possibility takes it towards identity with the virtuality of "the earth", also referred to as the Plane of Consistency or Plane of Immanence by Deleuze and Guattari.[25] Such a plane of absolute immanence is conscious rather than dead and is in a condition of perpetual experience of an infinite variety of transformative intensities which they also equate with absolute bliss:

> We will say of pure immanence that it is A LIFE, and nothing else. [. . .] A life is the immanence of immanence, absolute immanence: it is complete power, complete bliss.[26]

23. This finds expression throughout the work of Gilles Deleuze and later in his collaborations with Felix Guattari — e.g. AO, pp. 20-21, 93-94, 373.
24. ATP, p. 167.
25. Ibid., p. 297.
26. Deleuze, *Pure Immanence, Essays on a Life*, trans. Anne Boyman, Urzone, New York, 2001, p. 27.

Deleuze and Guattari emphasise the radical plurality (molecular) of existence and experience for both the BwO and the Plane of Consistency, but it is also clear that such radical plurality is an ontology, the experience of a univocal being, both one and infinite.[27] This expansion of capacity and ability to experience the potentially infinite simultaneous movements and impacts of the cosmos at the material, vital and mental levels is also largely what the seven quartets are meant to prepare — towards identification with the consciousness of Supermind. Though all of the seven quartets may be brought into this comparative frame, the quartet of equality (*samatā catuṣṭaya*) and the quartet of the body (*śarīra catuṣṭaya*), with their goals of realising a consciousness in the body marked by plurality of causeless and unnegatable bliss, may be thought of as the closest analogues to this thinking of Deleuze and Guattari.

Prīti

Prīti is the next form of active equality in the nature. This form of equality belongs to the affective nature. We discussed *premānanda* earlier, as the experience of universal love in all things. *Prīti* is similar to the experience of *rasa* and relates to an unshakeable feeling of sweetness, goodwill and affection in the *citta, manas* and *prāṇa*. In this sense, *prīti* implies an eradication of habitual responses and an equal pleasure in the reception of the emotional content of things we sense and feel.[28] Here too, we have conditioned preferences. But, once again, in all tastes, smells, sights, sounds, there exists a qualitative action of delight. In a correspondence with a disciple, who complained of bad odours, Sri Aurobindo once responded that there were no bad odours. Nature prepares us through the conditioning of our responses with preferences

27. ATP, pp. 281-82.
28. RoY, p. 1479.

that make us gravitate towards forms of experience that will help us better to survive. But, as the consciousness awakens and moves towards self-determination, we seek to become free of the habits of Nature and discover that we can give arbitrary values of liking and disliking to the experiences that come to us, just as we can receive them with neutrality and experience them for what they are in their essence. This, one may say, is a kind of Zen of the senses, for such indeed is the aim of Zen. Zen Buddhism aims at the development of a perfect neutrality of consciousness in which things can be received as they truly are, without distortion in the taste.[29] We have touched on this aesthetic equality of *rasa* experience. Both the *rasas* of sensations and feelings in the *citta* and the *rasas* of affections and habitual thoughts in the *manas* can further be extended to a full-bodied enjoyment in the nerves and the *prāṇa*.[30] This extension requires a further transformation, that of the *prāṇa*, through its neutrality or equality. This is known as *bhoga*. The experience of the scorpion bite, referenced earlier, is one such complete example of the transformation of sense experience, extending through the *rasa* of the *citta* and *manas* into the *prāṇa* of vital/physical experience.

Ānanda

Finally there is *ānanda*. Sri Aurobindo defines *ānanda* as "the divine *bhoga*, superior to all mental pleasures with which God enjoys the *rasa*".[31] In *ānanda* the opposition of the dualities

29. See, for example, D.T. Suzuki's discussion of the Zen aesthetic of Haiku poetry in Daisetz Teitaro Suzuki, ed. William Barrett, *Zen Buddhism: Selected Writings of D.T. Suzuki*, New York: Doubleday, 2006, pp. 325-26. Though it is true that Suzuki and scholars following in his wake have been largely responsible for turning Zen into an Orientalistic essence identified with Japanese national ontology, my point here is about the psychology of aesthetics attributed to Zen and described in an accessible way here by Suzuki.

30. RoY, p. 1479.

31. Ibid., p. 5.

entirely ceases, because it is the self-delight of *Puruṣa* (Conscious Being). Delight is intrinsic to Conscious Being just as Consciousness is intrinsic to it. Indeed, it is this intrinsic self-consciousness of Being which brings it Knowledge, which is why the Upaniṣads characterise existence without separation as *vidyā*. So too Conscious Being (*Brahman*) can be given the name of *ānanda* because that is its intrinsic property. From the viewpoint of experience we may catch a glimpse of this causeless property of Delight in the infinity of the One Being. Sri Aurobindo points out how we experience true delight with every exceeding of boundaries. Whenever our horizons recede, whenever we feel a true expansion of being, there is an experience of freedom and with it, of bliss.[32] Consideration of this experience may grant us an insight into *Puruṣa*'s intrinsic property of Delight. Conscious Being is infinite and hence, has no horizon. Every horizon it may conceive leads inevitably to a greater horizon, because what confronts it at all times is the illimitable infinity of Pure Being.[33] Thus, we can see how the infinity of Being implies bliss as its intrinsic property. From this standpoint of intrinsic and unchangeable bliss, all the responses that we give to nature, are not only conditioned responses, but also responses that can be experienced as bliss. Whatever their qualities of relative delight, as we have discussed above, there is also an absolute delight, a delight in the world and in all things of the world, irrespective of their qualities, and a delight irrespective of all things in the world — a delight of self. The seven forms of delight that were enumerated under *bhukti* in the quartet of perfection, *siddhi catuṣṭaya*, are also the goals of *ānanda* arising from the fullness of *samatā*. Thus, we find that the twin goals of liberation and enjoyment belong here as well — if the receptive or "negative" forms of equality pertain to liberation, the active or "positive"

32. LD, p. 99.

33. Ibid.

ones are forms of enjoyment, with their culmination in *ānanda*. Under *bhukti* of the quartet of perfection, we also found Sri Aurobindo writing of the delight of *vijñāna*, which he termed *citghanānanda*, and the delight of pure Consciousness (*cidānanda*). *Cidghanānanda* was the one delight in the varied qualities of all things — the essential Delight of the Real Idea manifesting as cosmos. But, the one delight outside of all qualities is *cidānanda*, and the one delight of existence outside of all manifestation, the pure self-experience of being is *sadānanda*. Thus, *sadānanda* and *cidānanda* are to be understood as aspects of *ānanda*, which we may experience within and beyond the world, and therefore, experience as forms of response to the world in our progress of equality.

Śānti

This practice of equality, if continued, brings about a deepening of its settled condition, reaching a point where practice is no longer necessary: it becomes a consciousness — not a habit, but natural quality of the being. This is *śānti*. *Śānti* is defined by Sri Aurobindo in these terms:

> Only when *samatā* is accomplished can *śānti* be perfect in the system. If there is the least disturbance, or trouble in the mentality, we may be perfectly sure that there is a disturbance or a defect in the *samatā*. For, the mind of man is complex and even when in the *buddhi* we have fixed ourselves entirely, in *udāsīnatā* or *nati*, there may be revolts, uneasinesses, repentings in other parts. The *buddhi*, the *manas*, the heart, the nerves, *prāṇa*, the very bodily case must be subjected to the law of *samatā*. *Śānti* may be either a vast passive calm based on *udāsīnatā* or a vast joyous calm based on *nati*. The former is apt to associate itself with a tendency to inaction and, it is therefore, in the latter that our yoga must culminate.[34]

34. RoY, p. 5.

In other words, a peace that nothing can shake, an inner silence as the consequence of a calm equality, not only a passive, receptive calm of the being, but also a powerful positive peace that is the consequence of our happy surrender to the Supreme Being. *Nati* brings that kind of active, affective surrender and its quality of glad silence, that pervades our being and cannot be touched or shaken by any kind of reaction. This is why Sri Aurobindo points out that *udāsīnatā* and *titikṣā* are ultimately only completed when *nati* enters the being in its fullness and one doesn't feel the need to effect any kind of positive resistance to the experiences of the world. But, this freedom from all touches of the world, does not mean that Sri Aurobindo is prescribing docility in the face of injustice. As we know well from Sri Aurobindo's own life as a political freedom fighter, resistance to circumstances may be what is required under certain conditions and may come as a direction of the *tapas śakti*. This belongs to other aspects of the yoga of integral transformation, for example, the *śakti catuṣṭaya*, but as far as the perfection of equality goes, it must be understood that it doesn't strive or struggle to better one's lot in the world, to increase one's comfort or convenience. The *nati* is equally happy to accept whatever circumstance is given to it, and whatever action is dictated to it from within; from a calm equality that receives the Divine Will.

Sukham

Śānti further deepens, and the third term of this *catuṣṭaya*, is *sukham*. *Sukham* is an intrinsic happiness in the being and it is based on the realisation of the active power of *śānti*. *Śānti* must establish itself unshakeably for *sukham* to anchor itself as a substance of consciousness. One may get an indication of the power of *śānti* as a settled consciousness in Sri Aurobindo, not merely as an ideal, but as an active power, peace, as the transformed *Prakṛti* itself. This example pertains to an early period of the stay in Pondicherry, of Mirra Alfassa, Sri

Aurobindo's spiritual collaborator and referred to by him as the Mother, at a time when there was a fierce cyclone. Cyclones are violent storms that shake up everything, uproot trees, throwing things topsy-turvy, tremendously powerful destructive storms. Such a cyclone was in progress, and in the house in which Sri Aurobindo lived — several people lived in that house, including the Mother — people started closing the doors and windows and looking to their own safety. The Mother realised that Sri Aurobindo was in his room, writing, and she went to check on him. She found him seated at the table, writing. The window was open. There was not a breath of wind in the room. Sri Aurobindo was oblivious to the storm. The cyclone was raging outside, but it couldn't enter the room because of the power of silence. The Mother refers to the active silence there that was inviolable, that could not be violated by the forces of nature. This is the nature of *śānti* arising as a consequence of perfect *samatā*.[35]

Śānti further refines itself or deepens into *sukham*. *Sukham* is the complete relief and release from *duḥkha*, from *vīṣāda* — these are different descriptive words for suffering or sorrow of any kind — which comes by a fulfillment of *samatā* and *śānti*. *Sukham* can be literally translated as deep happiness or contentment. The perfected *yogin* has never in himself, any touch of sorrow, any tendency to depression, cloud or internal repining and weariness, but is always full of a sāttvic light and ease, a glad condition of the being — "a large, easy, quiet, amiable condition", is how Sri Aurobindo described himself once to a disciple, who complained to him that he was austere and aloof.[36] This happiness, that no opposite can affect, is *sukham*.

---

35. Satprem, *Sri Aurobindo: Or the Adventure of Consciousness*, tr. Tehmi, New York & London: Harper & Row, 1968, p. 87.

36. Nirodbaran, *Twelve Years with Sri Aurobindo*, Sri Aurobindo Ashram Trust, Pondicherry, 1988, p. 224.

Hāsya

Finally, there is *hāsya*. This is the greatest intensity of the positive quality of *samatā*. *Hāsya* literally means laughter. *Hāsyam* is an intense delight, blissful and ecstatic, a laughter in the face of adversity, a comic appreciation of the entire spectrum of manifestation. Sri Aurobindo says of it:

> *Hāsyam* is the active side of *sukham*; it consists in an active internal state of gladness and cheerfulness, which no adverse experience, mental or physical, can trouble. Its perfection is God's stamp and seal on the *siddhi* of the *samatā*. It is in our internal being, the image of the smile of Śrī Kr̥ṣṇa, playing *balavat*, as the eternal *bālaka* and *kumāra* in the garden of the world.[37]

Bālaka and *kumāra* mean child and boy, respectively. This is the delight of the Supreme Being in the guise of the young child, playing carelessly in the garden of the world, in the fullness of delight, and this manifest ecstasy, a carefree delight of infinite exploration, is the culmination of the yoga, or the perfection of *samatā*.

I end, with a few lines from Sri Aurobindo on this condition of the action of equality, the nature of action which results from equality, from *The Synthesis of Yoga*, the chapter called "The Action of Equality" in the section, The Yoga of Self-Perfection:

> The calm established in the whole being must remain the same, whatever happens, in health and disease, in pleasure and pain, even in the strongest physical pain, in good fortune and misfortune — our own or that of those we love — in success and failure, honour and insult, praise and blame, justice done to us or injustice, everything that ordinarily affects the mind. If we see unity everywhere, if

37. RoY, pp. 5-6.

we recognise that all comes by the Divine Will, see God in all, in our enemies, or rather our opponents in the game of life, as well as our friends, in the powers that oppose and resist us, as well as the powers, that favour and assist, in all energies and forces and happenings, and if, besides, we can feel that all is undivided from ourselves, all the world is one with us, within our universal being, then this attitude becomes much easier to the heart and mind. But, even before we can attain or are firmly seated in that universal vision, we have, by all the means in our power, to insist on the receptive and active equality and calm. Even something of it, *svalpam api asya dharmasya*, is a great step towards perfection. A firm, a first firmness in it, is the beginning of liberated perfection. Its completeness is the perfect assurance of a rapid progress in all the other members of perfection, for without it we can have no solid basis, and by the pronounced lack of it, we shall be constantly falling back to the lower status of desire, ego, duality, ignorance.

This calm once attained, vital and mental preference has lost its disturbing force, it only remains as a formal habit of the mind.[38]

Sri Aurobindo then indicates a stage beyond this:

We have then to get beyond this stage even. For the perfect action and experience is not to be determined by any kind of mental or vital preference, but by the revealing and inspiring spiritual will which is the Śakti in her direct and real initiation. When I say that as I am appointed I work, I still bring in a limiting personal element and mental reaction.[39]

This is the ego of the instrument, as he describes it.

But, it is the Master who will do his own work through myself as his instrument, and there must be no mental or

38. SoY, p. 724.

39. Ibid., p. 725.

other preference in me to limit, to interfere, to be a source of imperfect working. The mind must become a silent luminous channel for the revelations of the Supramental Truth and of the will involved in its seeing. Then, shall the action be the action of that highest Being and Truth and not a qualified translation, or mistranslation, in the mind. Whatever limitation, selection, relation is imposed will be self-imposed by the Divine on himself in the individual at the moment for his own purpose, not minding, not final, not an ignorant determination of the mind. The thought and will, become then an action from a luminous infinite, a formulation not excluding other formulations, but rather putting them into their just place in relation to itself, englobing or transforming them even, and proceeding to larger formations of the divine knowledge and action.[40]

40. SoY, p. 725.

3

The Quartet of Power

THE yoga of Sri Aurobindo is called the Integral Yoga because it seeks for a power of integration in our lives; a power that can take the fragmentation of our being and find behind it something which is united, coherent, single, integrating us within, and integrating us with the world. However, this should not be confused with a seeking for mental control, which would amount to just one fragment bossing it over the others. Nor is this some finite personal identity which binds our forces in a separate fixity in the universe. What we seek is, a pre-individual and impersonal power of being to which order is intrinsic as an aspect of its univocity or self-recognition in all things. A fragmented being means that we have many independent parts within us, each of which has, as we sometimes say, a mind of its own. Thus, it is as if our sense of being a person is more like the address of a house, the physical body, within which dwell many lodgers, each of whom claims to be its owner. One may imagine the chaos that this can cause in terms of running the house.

Moreover, in our everyday lives, each of these parts in us is subject to dualities, which seem innate or inherited. One of these primary dualities, is that of being a conscious being in an unconscious world. We have a sense of being conscious, but all around us, are varying degrees of unconsciousness, starting from matter which presents the face of a complete unconsciousness, an inconscience, going through the manifestations of life, such as the multitude of plants and animals, and then onto other human beings including ourselves — we encounter different forms or degrees of consciousness, or, looked at from our state of subjection, degrees of unconsciousness. These degrees of unconsciousness are experienced by us as automatisms, automatic actions and reactions, predictable, definable through laws. Of course, to realise that things are predictable, is an acknowledgement of the presence of mind in matter, and a certain pride of control by human mind, but at the same time, it is a source of profound loneliness, a lack of true or conscious contact in the heart of things, since the predictability of things is unconscious, mechanical or else partial, hiding a gulf of meaninglessness.

The experience of this lack has been spoken of by existentialist philosophers as *angst*.[1] This is the human condition, not created by human beings but "given" — it is our sense of inheritance as a species, our sense of "thrownness", born into this condition.[2] We are faced with the question of how to deal with it. This becomes one of the general issues of philosophy and of spiritual practice through the centuries, in different cultures. One way this question has been approached is through culture, the attempt to discipline the Unconscious and build a home in it, for example the Greek ideal of a sound mind in a sound body; or alternately, through a perfection of the spirit, of consciousness, of identifying that something in us which is conscious and can know its freedom or liberation from the imprisonments of the unconscious world.

1. The concept of *angst* in existential philosophy may be traced to Soren Kierkegaard (1813-55) who used the term in a religious context to refer to human anxiety in the face of responsibility to God. Later existential adaptation of this term, by thinkers such as Martin Heidegger (1889-1976), Jean Paul Sartre (1905-80) and Albert Camus, refer to a more primordial anxiety arising from the dichotomy of human consciousness, freedom and will to meaning in a world whose meaning eludes us or is irrelevant.
2. Martin Heidegger, *Being and Time*, tr. Joan Stambaugh, Albany: SUNY Press, 1996, p. 127.

Schools, that have taken this second kind of stand, have attempted to analyse what is conscious and what is unconscious in us. As we saw in Chapter 1, this led to the dichotomy of what is known in Indian philosophy as *Puruṣa* and *Prakṛti*; *Puruṣa* being the conscious part, the "soul", if we wish to use that term, and *Prakṛti* being the unconscious part or "nature".

A Different Relation between Soul and Nature

Sri Aurobindo, in discussing this dichotomy, saw it as practical rather than factual and noted that if we were to isolate our consciousness from the automatisms, we could attain a liberation of consciousness by rejecting the movements of nature. But, this *mukti* (liberation) — as we have dealt with earlier, was understood by him as only one (though a primary one) of the general elements of perfection in the yoga of perfection, or the perfection of yoga. The other key fulfillment was seen to be *bhukti* (enjoyment). In other words, we are here not only to be liberated: this world is not a prison out of which we must escape, it is also a field of manifestation, of expression, delight, creativity, mutuality and of a divine nature at work. So, as Sri Aurobindo saw it, this field of nature presents the appearance of an *angst*-ridden irreconcilable duality of *Puruṣa* and *Prakṛti* in ignorance (*avidyā*).[3] But, while this appearance is the universal condition in which we find ourselves, it does not need to be the eventual condition. We find ourselves on earth as participants in an evolution of consciousness, which could lead us to a different relation between *Puruṣa* and *Prakṛti*, where they are seen, not as dichotomies, but as two aspects of the same integral reality — Divine Spirit that can be seen in a personal form as conscious *Puruṣa* with its own expressive and qualitative *Prakṛti* or conscious force (*śakti*).[4]

3. LD, p. 361.
4. Ibid.

Seen thus, our understanding of the unconsciousness of nature, in which we find ourselves as alienated conscious beings, also changes. We realise that the material and organic processes of nature, including its operations in our own living bodies, are a concealed action of this Śakti, which has subjected its consciousness to a "sleep" or "forgetting", so as to appear unconscious.[5] Still, its latent intelligence is at work in nature as a power of evolution, pushing towards manifestations of greater consciousness and individuality. What we earlier considered as the conscious part in us, is then seen as only a drop of self-consciousness, floating on an unfathomable sea of universal nature-consciousness. This nature-consciousness, of which our own organic processes are a part, is directed by an evolutionary intelligence. To surrender to this intelligence in its originary form and allow it to live, act, feel and think in us, using all our functional parts as its instruments of expression and self-becoming, and moulding them to forms which give it its perfect means, is the basis of the quartet of power or *śakti catuṣṭaya*.[6]

Gendered Considerations

In the gendered terminology of the Sāṁkhya philosophy, which most later schools of Indian thought and yoga practice adapt, the *Puruṣa* (or conscious soul) is male and marked by its capacity of freedom through refusal to the movements of nature, which is gendered female as *Prakṛti. Prakṛti,* as power of becoming, manifests *Puruṣa,* carrying it as its essence in all things, beings and activities.[7] We find such a gendered

---

5. LD, pp. 614-15.

6. This theme is repeated by Sri Aurobindo in a number of places. One of the most cogent and concise summaries of this process can be found in the chapter "Equality and the Annihilation of the Ego" in the Yoga of Works section of *The Synthesis of Yoga*. See SoY, pp. 230-31.

7. LD, p. 371.

signification also in Christian theology; for instance, in the Virgin Birth, the self-birth of Being (*swayambhu*) in its own manifestation through its power of becoming. Hence, it is this power of becoming, in its originary intelligence, which can reveal the reconstituted mystery of integral and inextricable Dual-Oneness, which it has unravelled into the polarities of cosmos.[8] Contemporary feminist discourse approaches this realisation in its perception of the phallocentric regime of domination and mastery, through separation from nature and the will to transcendental identity.[9] On the flip side, it recognises the feminine as qualitative differential flow of becoming, embodied, open-ended, infinite and participatory. Among contemporary feminist thinkers, it is perhaps Luce Irigaray, who gives the profoundest articulation to this polarity of subjective experience, calling for an embodied development of a feminine subjectivity and as ideal of divine becoming, marked by its radical alterity from a masculine subjectivity.[10]

In Sri Aurobindo's treatment of subjectivity in his yoga psychology, we find an acknowledgement of these two

---

8. LD, pp. 371-72.
9. Phallocentrism and its synonym, phallogocentrism (which splices the word "logos" into the former term to connote a rational investment in truth), are neologisms coined by Jacques Derrida to refer to the historically established patriarchal dominance of masculinity and its "colonisation" (read subjugation, possession, disciplining, exploitation and enjoyment) of Nature, the non-rational and the feminine. Ideologically, the term may be seen to have its precursor in Sigmund Freud and has been adapted by other contemporary thinkers such as Jacques Lacan and feminists such as Helene Cixous and Luce Irigaray.
10. Irigaray associates feminine subjectivity with the "sensible transcendental" and conceives of the divine as an immanent and "multiple becoming incarnated in sensuous bodies". See Luce Irigaray, *An Ethics of Sexual Difference*, tr. Carolyn Burke and Gillian C. Gill, Ithaca: Cornell University Press, pp. 17, 32; Margaret Whitford, *Luce Irigaray: Philosophy in the Feminine*, New York: Routledge, 1991, p. 144.

approaches co-existing in each human, though there are natural inequalities in their predominance in each case. *Puruṣa* and *Prakṛti* follow their own paths towards the arrival at full or integral consciousness, the first by withdrawal of consciousness and will to mastery, and the second, by embodied social practices of creativity, will and emotion.[11] But, if they are to arrive at integral consciousness, each must discover and include the other at some point. The withdrawal of the *Puruṣa* would stop short at an impotent silence of consciousness, were it to attempt escape from or domination of *Prakṛti*; and the aspirant movements of *Prakṛti* would remain an infinite longing intuiting celestial beatitudes or an entrapment in machinery, without the plenitude arising from the Presence of the One, were they to remain bound in process.[12] However, if the twin goals of *mukti* and *bhukti* are to be attained, even the transition of the *Puruṣa* from its status as witness (*sākṣī*) in the ignorance (*avidyā*) to its knowledge of oneness with *Prakṛti* (*Īśvara*) in the integral consciousness (*vidyā*) would be impossible without the transformative action of the Supreme *Prakṛti* (*Parā-Prakṛti*) and to that must be our surrender.[13] If the quartet of equality or peace, *samatā catuṣṭaya*, relied largely on the emergence of the *Puruṣa*, the quartet of power, *śakti*

11. See the discussion of Vedānta and Tantra in Sri Aurobndo, SoY, p. 43.

12. A historical basis for the withdrawal of the *Puruṣa* has been discussed by Sri Aurobindo in the chapter "The Refusal of the Ascetic" in *The Life Divine*, pp. 27-28. For his critique of the method of *Prakṛti*, see the discussion on Tantra in SoY, p. 43.

13. "If we would affirm our independence of Nature, she reveals to us the supreme and omnipresent power of the *Īśvara* and ourselves as beings of his being, but that power is herself and we are that in her supernature. If we would realise a higher formation or status of being, then it is still through her, through the Divine Śakti, the Consciousness Force of the Spirit that it has to be done; our surrender must be to the Divine Being through the Divine Mother: for it is towards or into the supreme Nature that our ascension has to take place and it can only be done by the supramental Śakti taking up our mentality and transforming it into her supramentality." LD, pp. 371-72.

catuṣṭaya opens up this imperative discipline of surrender to the originary power of becoming, Supreme Nature, *Parā-Prakṛti*, or Divine Mother, who carries the soul as its portion and possibility of individuation in its evolutionary self-unfoldment. Though this surrender can be mediated by the mind, it belongs properly and naturally to the soul or psychic being, and thus, the fullness of the *śakti catuṣṭaya* is premised on the purification of the nature (*śuddhi*) allowing the psychic being as the inmost person to emerge and become the central being in us.[14] In the *Record of Yoga*, Sri Aurobindo does not explicitly mention the psychic being, whose emergence and leadership with dynamic surrender to the transcendental Śakti, becomes the cornerstone of the Integral Yoga in his later formulations. But, it is clearly implied in the quartet of power.

The psychic being intuitively recognises the messages and directives of the evolutionary intelligence of the Divine or Transcendental Śakti or Divine Mother and makes its dynamic and integral surrender to that power of becoming. Thus, such a surrender is not a call to a neo-primitivism or a reversion to an aboriginal or "animal" condition, rather, it is an attempt to unite with a creative potency of nature which is that of the god, exceeding the power of consciousness expressed so far in nature and capable of transforming matter, life, mind and their processes to their divine manifestations. One may bring to mind once more the thought of Nietzsche, and the will-to-power as art, the universal creative consciousness which he invoked for his superman-making project.[15] In Sri Aurobindo,

---

14. "The cultivation of this second perfection need not wait for the security of the equal mind and spirit, but it is only in that security that it can become complete and act in the safety of the divine leading." See "The Power of the Instruments" in Sri Aurobindo, SoY, p. 729.
15. In each section of *Thus Spoke Zarathustra*, Nietzsche invokes a "going under" as the basis of the "going over" required of the Overman/

a similar power of consciousness is sought in its originary form, not from below but from above, from that which plunged into oblivion to mission the beginningless beginning and endless end of things; in terms of the immanence, a movement back to the future, as Martin Heidegger poetises it.[16]

This *Parā-Prakṛti* is the consciousness-force of the spirit. This is the true meaning of Śakti; because, though I have loosely translated *śakti catuṣṭaya* as the quartet of power, the term "power" can be misleading. Power gives the sense of a development of force within us. This is certainly an understanding of *śakti catuṣṭaya*, but it is force understood in a specific way, the qualitative force of unbounded divine nature which needs to be identified, generated, activated and expressed in and through us. For this, the whole essence of the perfection of power, or the perfection of nature, is an opening to that higher qualitative activity of nature, the energy which is free and conscious, and which can enter the unconscious and transform it. Since it is this expressive power

---

→ Superman. This is a surrender to the creative evolutionary Will, the foundation of the "eternal recurrence". In the context of Irigaray's "sensible transcendental", Lawrence Lampert provides an important insight to Zarathustra's "going under" – "... he descends to demonstrate that transcendent things are products of earth and body, thereby calling for a revaluation of both the things descended to and the traditional ideal of ascent, with its hatred of the earthly and the bodily." Lawrence Lampert, *Nietzsche's Teaching: An Interpretation of Thus Spoke Zarathustra*, New Haven: Yale University Press, 1986, p. 16.

16. Martin Heidegger intuited the Mystery of the disclosures of Being through its Power of Becoming and the need for surrender to this Power, but had insufficient access to the psychology of purification and the emergence of the psychic being. This lacuna led to his tragic (if temporary) misidentification of the "Führer" as a messiah figure. For Heidegger's treatment of the anteriority of the future, see Martin Heidegger, *Introduction to Metaphysics*, tr. Gregory Fried and Richard Polt, New Haven: Yale University Press, 2000, p. 47.

of *Puruṣa,* which has produced the appearance of subjection and limitation, which we experience as the condition for evolution, it is the same power which can transform this condition. So, this is a transformative process and a process of manifestation. We may talk about a union in consciousness with spirit, but if this union is to manifest or express itself through our instruments of nature, these instruments too need to be perfected — they cannot remain the unconscious instruments that they are in our normal reality.[17]

Relationship with the Divine Mother

This perfection of nature is what lies at the centre of the quartet of power. The approach to this quartet arises out of a central practice — that of surrender to the Divine Śakti, or to the full consciousness of a Divine Nature. In many world cultures and perhaps all ancient cultures, this real idea of Divine Nature, being conscious, has been considered a being and named Mother, identified according to her attributes in various forms and functions. Many proto-historic cultures seem to have identified this Motherhood with fertility processes in Nature. The Abrahamic tradition, however, whose theologies have a dominant influence in the modern world, privileges the masculine and reads material and organic processes as "fallen" or separated from a transcendent spirit, the monotheistic Absolute as Father, in need of Judgement or Redemption. Eastern spiritual traditions which preach escape, such as the *nirvāṇa* of the Buddhists or *mokṣa* of the Advaitins, presuppose a similar trenchant divide and subordination or rejection of nature by consciousness. "Western" civilisation, pervaded by Judeo-Christian traditions, merely displaced this patriarchal model to the mind-body dualism, which is commonly attributed to Descartes, but belongs properly to the European enlightenment and the entire rational phase of post-

17. SoY, pp. 759-61.

enlightenment modernity, in which we find ourselves. Of course, alongside our increasingly technologising civilisation, there has run a constant undercurrent of romanticism and mysticism, affirming a presence and wisdom in Nature or attempting to unearth secret energies through schools of alchemy, predictive arts or hermetic and other magical practices.[18] These have continued in contemporary times, when a number of voices are being raised, often in confusion, to validate Mother Earth (Gaia) and her processes, or various Pagan Mother cults or the celebration of the Divine Feminine in embodied women. From a more scholarly angle, feminism, postmodernism and schools of new psychology have made their counter-cultural critiques against the regime of the Father, opening up new possibilities of being and becoming in our times.

Perhaps, the most powerful "psychological justification" for Judeo-Christian patristic norms has come from Sigmund Freud and his Oedipal model of ego formation and socialisation.[19] The privileging of the phallus is treated by him as a basic ahistorical human structure. Following the dynamics of this "deep structure", psychoanalysis attempts to socialise pathologies into the conventional norms and expectations of civilised life, free of the confusions of the unconscious. Freud's models are also adopted by the very influential postmodern cultural psychologist and psychoanalyst, Jacques Lacan.

---

18. Paul Valery, referring to early modernity, writes: "Magic, alchemy, divination by the stars, and stimulated dreams coexisted in more than one brain with the most limpid classic culture and the discipline of the exact sciences. Never have scepticism and credulity been more closely associated than at that time." Louis Pauwels and Guy Breton, *Histoires magiques de l'Histoire de France 2*, A. Michel, Paris, 1977, pp. 226, 268.

19. See, for example, Chapter V "The Material and Sources of Dreams," Sigmund Freud, *The Interpretation of Dreams*, Avon books, New York 1980, p. 296.

Though Lacan takes a step in the direction of affirming a symbolic cultural intelligence in the unconscious when he says "The unconscious is structured like a language",[20] he nevertheless also privileges the phallus as the ahistorical signifier of the symbolic order, into which the child must be initiated for normal ego development,[21] though, as in Nietzsche's dialectic between the irresolvable Appolonian and Dionysiac drives, Lacan's conflicted adult, it seems to me, lives out, at best, a sense of tragedy.[22]

Other contemporary thinkers, such as Jacques Derrida, Gilles Deleuze and Luce Irigaray, have contested these patristic characterisations of the symbolic order of civilisation and pointed to other ontologies meant to break the historical stranglehold of the phallocentric regime. Of these, Deleuze in his book *Anti-Oedipus*, co-authored with Felix Guattari, challenges the obsessive absolutism of the Oedipal model and points to the self-organising processes of a decentred desire (desiring machines) as the productive unconscious life, giving birth to new forms of order.[23] Though Deleuze and Guattari are far from identifying these processes with any idea of a Mother Goddess, their underlying assumption of the univocity of life and the operation of ideas as fields of exploration, open the possibility of a hidden intelligence immanent in Nature.[24]

---

20. Jacques Lacan,, *The Seminar, Book XX: Encore, On Feminine Sexuality, The Limits of Love and Knowledge*, Norton, New York, 1998, p. 48.
21. Jacques Lacan, "The Signification of the Phallus", tr. Alan Sheridan Écrits*: A Selection*. London: Tavistock, 1977; New York: W.W. Norton & Co, 1977, pp. 281-91.
22. Lacan's work has sometimes been seen as a Nietzschean interpretation of psychoanalysis. See, for example, Luc Ferry, *What is the Good Life*, trans. Lydia G. Cochrane, Chicago: University of Chicago Press, 2005, p. 293, fn.18.
23. AO, Chapter 6, "The Whole and its Parts", pp. 45-57.
24. This Intelligence, however, is not something which unites or totalises a radical plurality, it co-exists with this infinite plurality and is its hidden name. This is why it cannot be comprehended or

Similarly, Luce Irigaray, a feminist student of Lacan, challenges the ahistorical premise of Oedipal phallocentrism, seeing it, instead, as a structure in a historically bounded discourse, which has little place in it for independent feminine subjectivity. Focusing on the embodied basis of language and thought, she points to altered practices of language, thought and imagination to transform the dominant order of civilisation to one which has room in it for an embodied female subjectivity or divine-becoming.[25]

Rooted Traditions

Early mystic practices in Judaism and Gnosticism provide evidence of a continuation of Mother Goddess worship. Designated Shekinah in the Kabalistic tradition, and Sophia in Gnosticism, the Mother in these traditions, exceeds the cyclical processes of nature and includes the intelligence which informs human knowledge and creativity.[26] Though clearly suppressed in both Judaic and Christian orthodoxies by the second century CE, the recognition of these mystical potencies of the Mother is continued in Catholicism, with its emphasis on the Virgin Mother, as the intercessor between man and god. Symbolically, this virgin motherhood is, once more an acknowledgement of a property exceeding the subjection to unconscious processes, Nature as feminine subject, a transcendent or Divine layer of Nature which houses and births the Divine Soul. Apart from this embodied form, Christianity also retains the impersonal principle of the Mother in the form

→ apprehended by mind, which can grasp only finites. D&G refer to the "molecular", "desiring machines" as the "attributes" and their infinite ground to be the "Immanence" or "Substance" of Spinoza. See AO, p. 110.

25. See for example, Luce Irigaray, *Speculum of the Other*, tr. Gillian G. Gill, Ithaca: Cornell University Press, 1985, pp. 87-89.

26. Karen Armstrong, *A History of God: the 4000-Year Quest of Judaism, Christianity and Islam*, New York: Ballantine Books, 1994, p. 249.

of the Holy Ghost, or divine mysterious animating essence immanent within the earth and its natural processes as well as transcendent beyond it.[27]

In Indian spiritual traditions, it is Tantra which prioritises the worship and identification with the Divine Mother. The central image in Tantra, is that of the black naked female form of Kālī, wearing a garland of skulls and holding a scythe in one hand and a skull in the other and dancing on the breast of a supine Śiva. The fertile archetypal ambiguity of this image and its corporeal concreteness lend themselves to many variations and interpretations, which become alternate discursive codes in the historical politics of culture. These then determine cultural and individual goals and practices. In modern Hindu discourse, which is dominated by masculinist Advaita Vedānta, Śiva represents pure existence, with consciousness hidden or asleep in it. Thus, this could be seen as immanent spirit, inert without consciousness and alien to Nature. The black and naked ferocious Kālī represents the blind unconscious Energy of Nature, driven by the power of separation from, or abandonment by its conscious source, and seeking it back through the destruction of fetishised appearances. Each skull in her necklace may be seen as a form of unconsciousness in human desire, hiding the truth of spirit from the aspirant, which her relentless drive destroys, so as to create the "clearing" where spirit may be experienced. Kālī's work is then complete and the aspirant free to merge into the experience of Śiva as transcendent spirit.[28]

But, as in our earlier explanation, this discovery of spirit

---

27. J.J. Van Der Leeuw, *The Fire of Creation*, Whitefish Montana: Kessinger Publishing, 2004, p. 121.

28. The symbolism of Kālī is discussed in a number of texts and poems/songs. See, for example, Sir John George Woodroffe, *Śakti and Śākta: Essays and Addresses on the Śākta Tantraśāstra*, London: Luzac & Co., 1918, pp. 365-68.

could form the beginning of a renewed expression based on a new relation between Spirit and Nature. It is towards this end that some schools speak of Kālī's blackness being replaced by a golden body at the end of the process. Or even that the blackness is an appearance of excessive light, a mystic darkness which reveals its true nature of golden light as our consciousness develops the capacity to see her as she is.[29] In passing, one may note the pre-textual "language" in which this imagery is couched. Though it is possible to interpret in certain ways and thus guide into a semiotics of experience, the pure visual power of the image gives it the capacity to work directly at the level of the unconscious, effecting transformative changes when related to specific practices. One is reminded again of the famous sentence from Jaques Lacan: "The unconscious is structured like a language." In this, Lacan may be thought to have problematised Freud, for whom the unconscious was a pre-lingustic reservoir of oedipal repressions. We noted earlier how Luce Irigaray exploits this linguistic potential of the unconscious for her politics of feminine subjectivity, seeing it as historically mutable. Like Irigaray, Deleuze and Guattari challenged the structuralist assumptions of Freud and Lacan in describing an unconscious in which passive syntheses of time-consciousness and a virtual field of Ideas and intensities sought actualisation. Again, in Carl Jung, we find an alternate understanding of the unconscious, as a collective subjectivity with extra-human agents, the archetypes. The fertile and polysemic image of

29. See, for example, Sri Aurobindo, *Record of Yoga*, p. 420; Karen Pechilis, ed., *The Graceful Guru: Hindu Female Gurus in India and the United States*, New York: Oxford University Press, 2004, p. 160; Shambhavi L. Chopra, *Yogic Secrets of the Dark Goddess*, New Delhi: Wisdom Tree, 2008. This kind of imagery also occurs in a number of poems/songs on Kālī — e.g. Kamalakanta's Bengali song *Shyama Maa ki Amar Kalo* (Is my Mother Shyama Black) — "People say she is black, but my mind does not say she is black/In black form she is sky-clad and lights up my heart-lotus."

Kālī lends itself to a number of creative transformative possibilities in these post-structuralist models of the unconscious. Perhaps for this potential complexity, Sri Aurobindo preferred to distinguish between the "subliminal" and the "unconscious". Sri Aurobindo's "subliminal" includes the cultural agency of a post-Freudian unconcious (though it appears to include a larger ontological sweep).[30]

Bengal, where Sri Aurobindo was born and spent his early years, and where he returned for conducting the struggle against colonial rule, was and continues to be a regional centre for tāntric practices, involving the worship of Śakti as Kālī and Durgā. Pervasive to the popular imaginary of Bengal is the mythos of the sacrifice of the Mother Śakti in the guise of Satī and the distribution of her body parts across the length and breadth of India.[31] It is easy to see how this dissemination implies a faith in the intervention of a higher power of consciousness into the unconscious processes of earthly and living Nature at the "national" level. When Sri Aurobindo began his work of political mobilisation against colonial rule in Bengal, he utilised the symbology and sentiments, proper to the Śakti mythos.[32] In fact, he was hardly the first or only person to do this, for almost a century before his action, a cultural movement, now known as the Bengal Renaissance, had prepared the ground partly by invoking these ideas of Śakti and calling for the sacrifice to the cause of her liberation. Sri Aurobindo promoted and himself practised the attitude of surrender to the geographic territory of India as the Mother,

---

30. Sri Aurobindo, "The Cosmic Illusion: Mind, Dream and Hallucination", in LD, Book II, Part I, Chapter 5, pp. 440-41.
31. Constance Jones and James D. Ryan, *Enclyclopedia of Hinduism*, New York: Checkmark Books, 2006, p. 400.
32. See for example "Bhawani Mandir", in *SABCL* 1:69; "Hymn to Durga" in *SABCL* 4:39.

of which he was a part.[33] Of course, the sentiment of "motherland" is a common one in binding national or ethnic cultures, but in India, due to its background in the intensely devotional processes of Tantra, it had much deeper transformative mystical effects, with many of the revolutionaries becoming disciples of spiritual masters and having numinous experiences. Later, in his post-revolutionary phase in Pondicherry, we find this kind of practice further generalised and systematised in the *śakti catuṣṭaya*. Even later, Sri Aurobindo was to make this practice the cornerstone of his teaching, as expressed succinctly in his book *The Mother*, directing the surrender of his disciples to his spiritual collaborator, Mirra Alfassa, who he declared to be the embodied form of the Divine Mother.[34]

But, while writing the *Record of Yoga* (as brought out also in the quartet of action, *karma catuṣṭaya*), it was Kālī who stood for the integral Śakti and Divine Mother, free and all-conscious beyond the cosmos and immanent in all the processes of universal Nature; and surrender to her became the basis of his progress in the goals of being and becoming.[35] The specific name of this Śakti is not of prime importance, or, put differently, the Śakti may make herself known uniquely to each person. However, since the basis of this surrender is not an unconscious *Prakṛti*, radically and eternally separate from an all-conscious *Puruṣa*, the surrender acknowledges her inextricable identity with *Īśvara*, the Two-in-One or inexhaustible Being-in/as-Becoming.[36] Representing the

---

33. See Sri Aurobindo's "Letter to his wife, August 30, 1905" in A.B. Purani, *The Life of Sri Aurobindo*, pp. 79-84.

34. Sri Aurobindo, *The Mother and Letters on the Mother*, SABCL 25:1.

35. SoY, p. 251.

36. Chapter XI, "The Master of the Work", in *The Yoga of Works*, SoY, p. 243; Chapter XVII, "The Action of the Divine Śakti", in *The Yoga of Self-Perfection*, SoY, pp. 768-70.

potential of Śakti to transcend any specific form of Becoming, this transcendental *Īśvara* polarity of Kālī is seen in the *Record of Yoga*, as Kṛṣṇa, and the surrender of the individual is thus equally made to him.[37] As a biographical detail, it is this surrender to Kṛṣṇa and experience of identity with him, which is better known in the life of Sri Aurobindo.[38] In several instances, Sri Aurobindo acknowledged the importance of the *Bhagavad-Gītā* in his own yoga and the central practice in the *Gītā* is one of a dynamic surrender to Kṛṣṇa, seen as the embodied *Brahman* (Transcendental Being) which has become this universe and all its creatures.[39] In the *Record of Yoga* too (as expressed in the Introduction), Sri Aurobindo identifies Kṛṣṇa as "The Master of the Yoga".[40] This polarity of being as transcendental Lord is present in the quartet of power as well, though in the background. We see that Śakti, Kālī or the Divine Mother is the principal source of the yoga here, her aspects or emanations, active as energies and soul powers in the individual, but behind or united with these emanations of the Śakti are situated their male counterparts or *Īśvaras*.[41]

Thus, the Divine Mother presents Herself through a double relationship — on the one hand, her relation with Conscious Being (*Īśvara*) and on the other hand, with the creation which has emanated from her and into which she has entered, as substance, being and force, driving its processes so as to provide to it the power of evolution. This relationship, on the

---

37. SoY, p. 740.
38. Peter Heehs, *Sri Aurobindo: A Brief Biography*, New Delhi: Oxford University Press, 1989, pp. 93-94.
39. Ibid.
40. See RoY, pp. 158, 236, 401, 405, 542, 567.
41. Sri Aurobindo's nomenclature for these Īśvaras coincides with, the *vyūha* or emanation system of Pāñcarātra Vaiṣṇavism. See RoY, p. 1455.

one side as the consort of *Īśvara*, on the other side as the Mother of all the creation and its creatures, is the place and function of the Divine Mother as transformative agent in the process of conscious evolution we know as yoga.[42]

The Siddhis of the Śakti Catuṣṭaya

The quartet of Śakti is concerned with invoking the action of this Śakti in our lives so that it enters as a transformative power into our mind, life, body and all their various instruments, turning these into divine capacities, and using us as its embodiment, so that our identity is one with its consciousness and our instruments are its adequate expressive means.[43] To achieve this goal, Sri Aurobindo introduces the four *siddhi*s or perfections of the *śakti catuṣṭaya*. These are *vīrya*, which can be translated as "soul force", *śakti*, translatable as power, *caṇḍī bhāva* or *daiva Prakṛti*, which can be thought of as the manifestation of the qualitative being of the Divine Śakti in the personality of the individual, and *śraddhā* which is translatable as faith.[44] These are the four perfections of Śakti. Sri Aurobindo later elaborated on the central aspects of this quartet in his synoptic text, *The Mother*. This work was developed by Sri Aurobindo as an encapsulation of his teaching, because looked at from a certain angle, the entire teaching of Sri Aurobindo hinges on the transformation of the nature and its use by a divine consciousness. The Divine Śakti as the most intimately constituting consciousness of all created entities in substance, being, force and expression, and as the creatrix responsible for the appearance of the ignorance can prepare our nature, transform it and change our consciousness to become identified in being and nature with

---

42. *The Mother and Letters on the Mother*, op. cit., 6, pp. 19-20.
43. Ibid., 41.
44. RoY, p. 7.

her own divine reality, always at one with the Supreme Puruṣa.[45]

If we consider these four perfections of the *śakti catuṣṭaya*, we find that Sri Aurobindo describes them in terms of qualities or capacities that relate to our innate tendencies of self-expression (*svadharma*), firstly a cultivation through purification and practice of our expressive powers, and secondly by a surrender to the Divine Śakti, calling her to express these through us. In this, our relationship to the Śakti is taken, as explained above, as that of a child to its mother — with the inner perception that She acts in us and opens up or develops these powers of expression.[46]

Vīryam: Soul Force and the Fourfold Personality

The first of these perfections is *vīryam*, which, Sri Aurobindo translates as "soul force" or "the energy of divine temperament".[47] Sri Aurobindo also dwells on this in *The Synthesis of Yoga* in a chapter titled "Soul Force and the Fourfold Personality". As he explains in this chapter, soul force proceeds as the power of becoming along four expressive lines which emanate from four manifesting powers of the Divine Śakti.[48] Just as the *śakti* is accessible to us through relationship as the Divine Mother, these four powers are also perceivable as four mother goddesses. These four goddesses are at the qualitative and functional manifesting root of the entire cosmos, what Sri Aurobindo calls the cosmic *mahāśaktis*. They are named Māheśvarī, Mahākālī, Mahālakṣmī, and Mahāsarasvatī. To each

45. Chapter II "Self-consecration" in "The Yoga of Divine Works", *The Synthesis of Yoga*, p. 86; Sri Aurobindo, Chapter VI, "The Four Powers of the Mother", in *The Mother and Letters on the Mother*, SABCL: 25, pp. 25-41.
46. SoY, pp. 742-43.
47. Ibid., p. 740; RoY, p. 7.
48. See also Chapter VI, *The Mother and Letters on the Mother*, SABCL 25: pp. 19-41.

of these goddesses or forms of qualitative will, as explained above, there also corresponds a god or aspect of *Īśvara*, its being. In the *Record of Yoga*, Sri Aurobindo identifies these gods in terms of two alternate traditions, one an ancient cult based on emanationism with Vāsudeva Kṛṣṇa at its centre, known as *Pañcarātra*; and the other, a more mainstream Purāṇic nomenclature — Mahāvīra or Śiva as counterpart of Māheśvarī, Balarāma or Rudra as counterpart of Mahākālī, Pradyumna or Viṣṇu as counterpart of Mahālakṣmī and Aniruddha or Kāma as the counterpart of Mahāsarasvatī.[49]

We know that, in Hinduism, there exists the social institution of a caste system, derived from the Veda. In the modern world, marked by the ideals of egalitarianism and universal human rights, the notions of hierarchy and heredity associated with the social construct of the caste system are regressive, to say the least. But, Sri Aurobindo draws on the roots of this idea as a system of psychological expression present universally, not as a hierarchy but as an equivocity. The four castes, brāhmaṇa, kṣatriya, vaiśya and śūdra, are then seen to be expressive becomings of these four cosmic *mahāśakti*s, Māheśvarī, Mahākālī, Mahālakṣmī, and Mahāsarasvatī respectively.[50] The brāhmaṇa is one whose principal mode of expression is knowledge. The kṣatriya's mode of expression is power. The vaiśya's is exchange or mutuality — love, harmony, an interchange of energy. And that of the śūdra is the power of service or skill in work.[51] Applied psychologically, we may think of each human soul or psychic being, the innermost psychological centre of the person, as something with a qualitative predisposition. One may think of this as

49. RoY, p. 1455. See also diary entry of 8 February, 1912 in RoY, pp. 72-73.

50. SoY, pp. 742-43.

51. Ibid., p. 742, *The Mother and Letters on the Mother*, SABCL 25:, pp. 19-20.

having been psychically born from one of these four aspects of the Mother. But it is a misunderstanding to have a rigidly structuralist view of this explanation or to believe in some fixed exclusivity of expression. All four soul qualities are present in each human being, in a specific proportional arrangement which constitutes the qualitative uniqueness of the person. We are meant to develop all four in each of our expressions. However, one is likely to predominate.[52]

This is powerfully addressed in the *Bhagavad-Gītā* through the ideas of *svabhāva* and *svadharma* — *svabhāva* can be translated as soul-type, and *svadharma* as soul-expression, which arises naturally from *svabhāva*.[53] If we become sufficiently equal to ourselves, if we are not pushed by the pressures of society, or of all the various conditionings that make us choose careers for ourselves, we would discover this *svadharma* dynamically as a natural predominance of expression which gives us a sense of growth and delight. This is an intrinsic delight which relates to a specific expression of these four soul powers. In *śakti catuṣṭaya* these soul types are recognised as proceeding from the *Īśvara*s and the soul forces from the Divine Mother and her four cosmic emanations or *mahāśakti*s.[54] In opening our expressive capacities to the Divine Mother, these soul forces are developed through the Śakti's dynamic guidance as Her expressive means. With this development, the soul or psychic influence proceeds to transform the human instrumentality, psychicising the intellect, the will, the emotions and the body and thus moving towards the effectuation of what Sri Aurobindo calls the psychic transformation and beyond that, as the Divine Mother fully occupies and manifests in the nature, the spiritual and supramental transformations.[55] The

52. SoY, p. 743.
53. EoG, pp. 508-10.
54. RoY, p. 7.
55. Sri Aurobindo, *Letters onYoga I*, SABCL 22, p. 282.

development of all these under the predominance of the inner qualitative expression which develops under the influence and power of the Divine Śakti relates to *vīryam*.

The Soul Force of Knowledge

The soul-force of knowledge is termed *brahmatejas*, fiery radiance of cognition, and the presiding deities for this perfection are the Goddess Māheśvarī and her Lord, Mahāvīra or Śiva. Māheśvarī is the goddess of wideness, knowledge, compassion, and an all-embracing quality infinite in its acceptance. She is the source of knowledge and the force of knowledge. She is the power that acts in us to develop the qualities necessary for the perfection of knowledge.[56] The

Śakti Catuṣṭaya (Perfection of Power/Nature) (3.1)
Brahmatejas: Māheśvarī
Vīryam (Soul Force — energy of divine temperament)

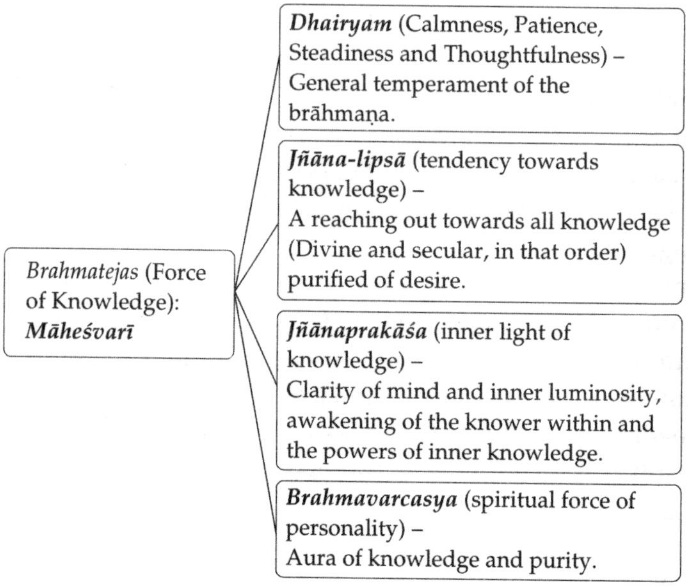

Brahmatejas (Force of Knowledge): Māheśvarī
Dhairyam (Calmness, Patience, Steadiness and Thoughtfulness) – General temperament of the brāhmaṇa.
Jñāna-lipsā (tendency towards knowledge) – A reaching out towards all knowledge (Divine and secular, in that order) purified of desire.
Jñānaprakāśa (inner light of knowledge) – Clarity of mind and inner luminosity, awakening of the knower within and the powers of inner knowledge.
Brahmavarcasya (spiritual force of personality) – Aura of knowledge and purity.

56. *The Mother and Letters on the Mother*, SABCL 25:26-28.

perfection of knowledge will be dealt with in greater detail when we consider the *vijñāna catuṣṭaya,* and during our consideration of the quartet of being (*brahma catuṣṭaya*) which reveals the original basis of knowledge as knowledge by identity. But to become a manifesting centre of knowledge, the qualities we need to cultivate are dealt with under *brahmatejas* in the quartet of Śakti. The last of these qualities, but perhaps the first which lends itself to practice, is described by Sri Aurobindo as *dhairyam,* which can be translated as patience, calmness, steadiness and thoughtfulness. It implies a rock-steady consciousness, which refuses to jump to conclusions, and can wait patiently for the fullness of knowledge to develop in us. This is the general temperament of the brāhmaṇa.[57]

The first quality of *brahmatejas* enumerated in the *Record of Yoga* is *jñāna-lipsā,* a tendency or desire — *lipsā* means thirst or attachment — for knowledge. The word "thirst" carries in it a sense of craving, desire, need or compulsion. But, in this quality of divine Śakti, all compulsion must cease from us. It is only when compulsion is entirely eradicated in the nature, that the truth of a desireless seeking for knowledge can awaken in us.[58] This is *jñāna-lipsā,* the aspiration for knowledge. In *The Synthesis of Yoga,* Sri Aurobindo describes this as "a hunger and passion for knowledge".[59] Sri Aurobindo uses the term *lipsā* to point to the transformative process involved in moving from a more ego-driven natural condition to a condition of desirelessness — the desireless aspiration for knowledge grows only with exercise. The thirst for knowledge, even if there is desire, has to find expression. It must be subjected to the aspiration for purity so as to grow

57. SoY, pp. 743-44; RoY, p. 9.
58. RoY, p. 8.
59. SoY, p. 743.

desireless, but we must not kill it under the sterile injunctions of conventional morality. This seems less telling an example when applied to the "thirst for knowledge" but we will find that Sri Aurobindo introduces the quality of *lipsā* in the culture of each of the soul forces. No power of becoming should be maimed in us because of an exaggerated ascetic purism. So *jñāna-lipsā* is a seeking for all forms of knowledge.

We can note here that Sri Aurobindo classes knowledge in terms of two main kinds — divine knowledge and secular knowledge, in that order.[60] This order is important because, even if we are of a studious disposition, we are normally accustomed to conducting our lives firstly, through a study of various kinds of "secular" literature so as to "increase our knowledge". But Sri Aurobindo reverses this equation, pointing to the insight that the reason most human beings are like cripples in the world of knowledge — constantly dependent on books and lectures — is that we have lost our faith in the knowledge that is within. In an early nationalist text on education, Sri Aurobindo was already pointing out that in truth, nothing can be taught, because all knowledge is contained in each of us.[61] Taking this in its extreme implications, we could say that if we wanted, we could become aeronautical engineers or possessors of any other specialised professional skill, just by the knowledge which is within; every form of knowledge can be tapped into from within. The basis of this insight comes from the intrinsic unity of all being — there is a root of conscious identity we share with all things and this root can be actualised in the form of knowledge from within, if we knew how to do so. The foundation of all knowledge, according to the Upaniṣad, is the discovery of "the knowledge by which all else can be known" (*yasmin vijñate sarvam idam*

60. "Jñāna includes both the Parā and the Aparā Vidyā", RoY, p. 8.
61. Sri Aurobindo, "A System of National Education", SABCL 17, p. 204.

vijñātam).[62] The Knowledge of Being (*Brahman*) implies the knowledge of all things by identity. There is only one Absolute Being, and everything that we know of is an aspect of that Being. By extension of identity we can know whatever we wish to know. This becomes the foundation of the Yoga of Knowledge, which will be developed later, but this also provides the foundation in the development of *jñāna-lipsā* — to cultivate a progressive trust in the fact that knowledge dwells within us, in our own innate intuitive capacity, in the primary ability to arrive at knowledge directly from within and only secondarily from the evidence of our senses and our external sources of information.[63]

The next quality of the *brāhmaṇa* is *jñāna-prakāśa.* As this dependence on inner knowledge becomes more regularised in us, there develops a clarity of mind and an inner luminosity.[64] This clarity of mind is also aided through the purification of the mental instruments, as discussed while dealing with purification of the mental being — the *citta śuddhi*, the *śuddhi* of the *manas* and the *śuddhi* of the *buddhi*. These three purifications develop a foundation of disinterest in the mind, a detachment from self-interest, which is a condition for the operation of intuition, and in this condition, there develops a quality of clarity and an inner luminosity.

The one who expresses *jñāna-prakāśa*, has luminosity in knowledge. Those who have a subtle vision of things can see a radiance emanating from such people or their expressions of knowledge. That is *jñāna-prakāśa*. It is the presence of the awakened knower within and the powers of inner knowledge. Finally, as if a more intense degree of the *jñāna-prakāśa*, is *brahma varcasya*, which can be translated as spiritual force of

62. *Muṇḍaka Upaniṣad*, 1.1.3.

63. RoY, p. 8.

64. Ibid.

personality, a concentrated aura of knowledge and purity that is carried by the perfection of the *brāhmaṇa*, the expression of knowledge in the individual.[65]

The Soul Force of Power

The perfection of the soul-force of power is expressed as *kṣātra-tejas*, the fiery force of will, and the deities behind this are the Goddess Mahākālī with her Lord, Balarāma or Rudra. The qualities that relate to this perfection are first, *abhaya* (fearlessness) which can be thought of as a passive form of courage. The second enumerated quality in this perfection is *sāhasa*, what can more properly be thought of as active courage. Both *abhaya* and *sāhasa* are forms of courage, but *abhaya* is a fearlessness, it is unafraid of danger or misfortune. This quality implies freedom from the fear of danger, even the danger of death. Nor is there, to the person who possesses it, fear of any kind of misfortune, because one rests in the inner

Śakti Catuṣṭaya (Perfection of Power/Nature) (3.2)
Kṣātratejas: Mahākālī
Vīryam (Soul Force — energy of divine temperament)

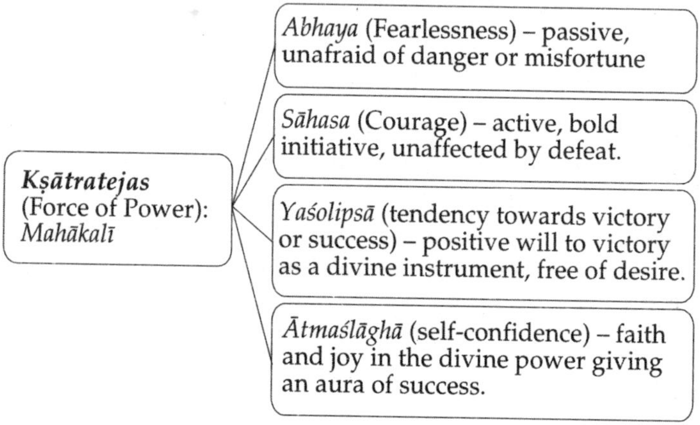

Kṣātratejas (Force of Power): Mahākalī
Abhaya (Fearlessness) – passive, unafraid of danger or misfortune
Sāhasa (Courage) – active, bold initiative, unaffected by defeat.
Yaśolipsā (tendency towards victory or success) – positive will to victory as a divine instrument, free of desire.
Ātmaślāghā (self-confidence) – faith and joy in the divine power giving an aura of success.

65. RoY, p. 8.

confidence of a knowledge that we are intrinsically free, we have the strength of complete independence within us, we are not dependent on anything, including even the instruments of our own external nature.[66]

In pre-modern times, the lives of human beings were much more precarious than our lives today; torture, pain, disease and death came frequently and unpredictably in every culture of the world. Our largely predictable and highly sanitised and "insured" world has brought an external comfort and security, but has also numbed us from the sources of our own inner courage. Under these circumstances, one must make a greater effort to contact the roots of one's intrinsic freedom; free because unborn and immortal, something to which the entire structure of one's body, life and mind is merely a temporal expression in a certain place and time. This absolute fearlessness is the foundation of *abhaya*, something which can be developed through a meditation on a sense within that nothing can condition us, one is not dependent on anything. Thus, one fears no loss, not even the loss of one's life. We are ultimately, totally and absolutely free at all times and in every circumstance. This is *abhaya*.[67]

The next quality for the kṣatriya to achieve is *sāhasa*. *Sāhasa* is the active aspect of *abhaya*. It is courage, the urge for adventure, the ability to take bold initiatives, unaffected by the fear of defeat. The inner attitude here is:

> Even if defeat, dishonour or death be the consequence for what I feel is right, it will not prevent me from taking bold action, against all odds, if need be. I will call on the Divine Mother and move forward.

This kind of strength, courage, is a quality to cultivate, in

---

66. RoY, p. 9; SoY, pp. 744-45.

67. Ibid.

becoming an instrument of Mahākālī, and expressing *kṣātratejas*.[68]

The third property for the kṣatriya is *yaśolipsā*. In its type, it is similar to *jñāna-lipsā* — as discussed, each of the qualities of *vīryam* has a *lipsā* associated with it, a thirst or attachment which is to be purified and made a desireless expression of *śakti*. In a state of desirelessness, each *lipsā* reveals a positive impersonal will towards the expression of its quality. *Yaśolipsā* is the positive will to success. What this implies is a powerful self-confidence — "I will be victorious". This kind of confidence is the hallmark of heroes. A hero is recognisable by a positive will to victory, free of desire, not for the ego, but for a higher cause, a warrior of the Divine. Whether in the field of knowledge or in politics, or business, or general work, this desireless will is necessary to be a victorious instrument of truth.[69]

The fourth and final quality for this type is given as *ātma-ślāghā*, which is the counterpart in this type, of the radiance of the man of knowledge. The hero also carries an aura, an aura of invincibility. Once again, we must distinguish this from arrogance, which is an impurity of self-confidence stemming from the ego. That kind of crudity is unfortunately all too common. But, there is something more refined in the confident warrior of Truth, who draws this power neither from ego, nor from ideology, but from inner contact with the manifesting source of unity and truth (*dharma*). This emanation of faith and joy in the divine power, giving an aura of success, is the quality or attribute of *kṣātratejas*.[70]

---

68. RoY, p. 9; SoY, pp. 744-45.
69. Ibid.
70. Ibid.

Śakti Catuṣṭaya (Perfection of Power/Nature) (3.3)
Vaiśya *śakti: Mahālakṣmī*
Vīryam (Soul Force — energy of divine temperament)

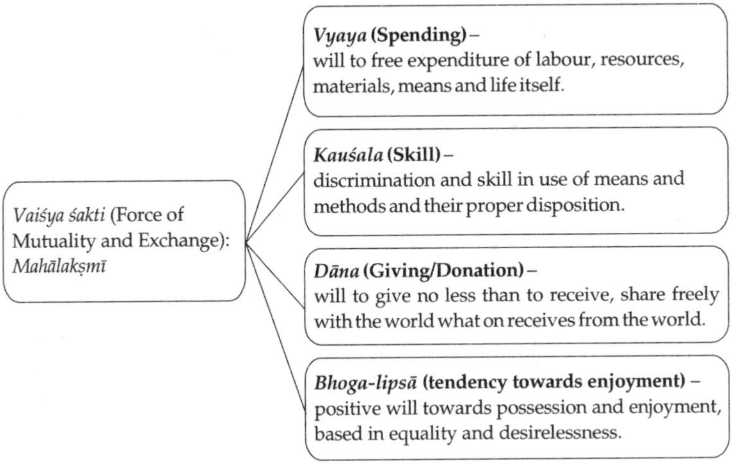

Vaiśya śakti (Force of Mutuality and Exchange): Mahālakṣmī
Vyaya (Spending) – will to free expenditure of labour, resources, materials, means and life itself.
Kauśala (Skill) – discrimination and skill in use of means and methods and their proper disposition.
Dāna (Giving/Donation) – will to give no less than to receive, share freely with the world what on receives from the world.
Bhoga-lipsā (tendency towards enjoyment) – positive will towards possession and enjoyment, based in equality and desirelessness.

The Soul Force of Harmonious Interchange

We now move to the third of the soul forces of *vīryam*. This is the force of mutuality and exchange, *vaiśya śakti*. In general, this is taken to be the quality associated with business people. In a wider formulation, it can be seen behind great communicators, diplomats, people whose natural dynamism moves towards exchange. But closer to its qualitative truth, it is a power of harmony and universal love, an embracing of all beings in a freedom of give-and-take. The deities behind this are the Goddess Mahālakṣmī with her Lord, Pradyumna or Viṣṇu. This soul force also has four qualities or attributes that one may cultivate, to become an instrument of Mahālakṣmī. First, there is *vyaya* (spending). *Vyaya* implies a will to free expenditure of labour, resources, materials, means and life itself. The attitude here can be summarised as, "I will spend freely towards the goal which I have set, without fear that by spending I will lose what I have".

Prudence will immediately suggest that this attitude of free-giving is something foolhardy. Indeed, it can be so, unless accompanied by the second quality in this type, which is skill (*kauśala*). *Kauśala*, is a quality powerfully highlighted in the *Gītā* where, in a famous epigram attributed to Kṛṣṇa, skill is equated with yoga — *yoga karmasu kauśalam* (yoga is skill in works).[71] That skill arises from the intuitive power of discrimination and the skill in the use of means and methods and their proper disposition. How much to use, how much to give, what is the necessary measure in a particular place and time, what is the needed proportion, the just energy, the proper pressure to apply in a certain situation. This is the intuition of skill. This intuition is a practical knowledge. It is not a knowledge of theory, it is a knowledge that comes in the performance of works, to the expressive being by opening oneself to a practical intuition in relation to the totality of Being. It relates to *dharma*, and even further, to the Vedic quality of *ṛtam* which pertains to how the one expresses itself in its many parts. If one were completely integrated, one would have the perfect harmonious operation of all one's limbs and all one's faculties. The divine integral being is of this kind. Because, in a condition of separation and fragmentation (*avidyā*), there is a loss of that sense of harmonious cosmic integrality in its constituents, we have discord and disharmony in the world. As we develop this dynamic intuition of integrality within us, we find that there is the increasing sense of a skill which brings success and happiness in all that we do, not only to ourselves but to those we exchange with. Every transaction, whether it is a business transaction or a political transaction or something else, becomes a transaction of harmony marked with an inner sense of justness, with the development of *kauśala*.[72]

---

71. *Bhagavad-Gītā*, II:50.

72. RoY, p. 10; SoY, p. 746.

The third property for this soul force is *dāna* (giving or donation). This relates to *vyaya,* because in *vyaya* one spends with a certain end in mind. It's the idea of spending to get. But behind *vyaya* there must be a more unconditional power of giving, and that is *dāna*. In fact, the English word "donation" has the same Indo-European root as *dāna*. It is the will to give freely. For this, there must be a clear equality and a positive will to give, arising from that equality — to share freely with the world what one receives from the world. The attitude here is, "whatever I have received from the world is not mine, I don't possess it, I am a trustee for the world of what the world has given me". This is the basis of action that can, in essence, be called non-profit action. And, its joy is much greater than the delight of possession. It is the joy of the One Being in its power of exchange.[73]

The fourth quality of the *vaiśya śakti* is *bhoga-lipsā,* or the will towards enjoyment. This is a positive will towards possession and enjoyment based in equality and desirelessness. Again, as in the earlier cases, where a positive will resulted in a radiance of personality, so too *bhoga-lipsā* results in its own radiant aura. This is a radiance of universal love, which is a property of the will to enjoy. In this intuition, the essence of the will to enjoy is not a possessive urge, but as a kind of a wide, equal, desireless power of sharing. Some of these *śakti*s, as for example *kṣātratejas* and *vaiśya śakti*, are not conventionally perceived as spiritual powers in most spiritual schools, particularly those which are quietistic or pietistic in nature. However, they are addressed in the tāntric schools of India where *śakti* (power) becomes the primary means of spiritual expression and experience. In the Integral Yoga, where a transformed world action is the aim, they are indispensable, and hence, it becomes necessary to pay attention to the development of all these expressive powers in its practitioner.

73. RoY, p. 10; SoY, p. 746.

Śakti Catuṣṭaya (Perfection of Power/Nature) (3.4)
śūdra śakti: Mahāsarasvatī
Vīryam (Soul Force — energy of divine temperament)

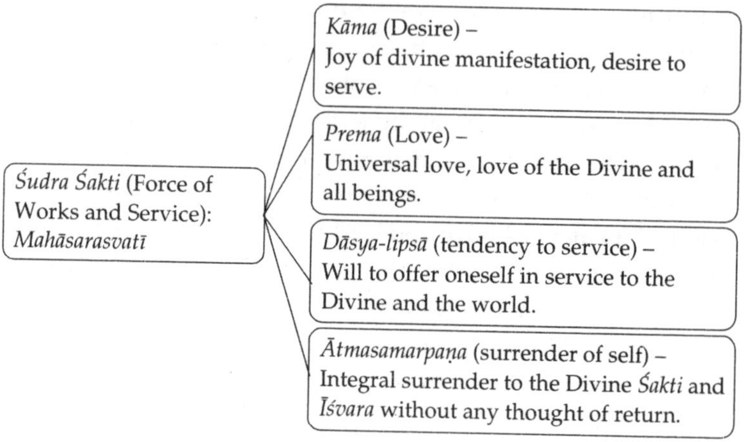

Śudra Śakti (Force of Works and Service): Mahāsarasvatī
Kāma (Desire) – Joy of divine manifestation, desire to serve.
Prema (Love) – Universal love, love of the Divine and all beings.
Dāsya-lipsā (tendency to service) – Will to offer oneself in service to the Divine and the world.
Ātmasamarpaṇa (surrender of self) – Integral surrender to the Divine Śakti and Īśvara without any thought of return.

The Soul Force of Loving Service

Finally, and in some key sense, the most important of the soul powers of *vīryam* is *śūdra śakti* (the force of works and service). The aspect of the cosmic *śakti* connected with it is Mahāsarasvatī and its *Īśvara* is Aniruddha or Kāma. As with the others, there are four perfections associated with this power. The first of these is *kāma*. As with *lipsā*, one may justifiably ask here what part desire plays in a yoga which makes desirelessness one of the bases of its fulfillment. The indication here, again, is that we utilise the energies as they are given to us. Desire is present as a powerful motivational factor in the human being. We are being asked to recognise this and utilize its force. We are not asked to maim desire, we are asked to purify it. Once we purify it through equality, we discover behind it, an impersonal will towards the acceptance and enjoyment of things in the world. So, *kāma* is the fundamental joy of the Divine Manifestation, it is the Divine Mother's delight in her own self-creation, and it is quintessentially expressed as the desire to serve. Sri Aurobindo is presenting here the idea that this desire to serve is in truth, the essence of desire. This master intuition springs from an attitude of wonder towards the manifestation of the Divine in the world, and its difficult but miraculous evolution towards perfection. From this perception, a fundamental impulse that arises is, the desire to serve: "My whole life should become a service to this piecing together of conscious unity in the world". This is the nature of the *kāma* of *śūdra śakti*: one-pointed desire to serve the Divine Manifestation.[74]

The second attribute of this soul force is *prema*. This is a universal and unbounded capacity to love, in various ways and forms, all the beings and creatures of the creation. Again, in its character as *śūdra śakti*, this love is based on the urge to serve, it is a service to the Divine felt as the Beloved, in himself and in all beings. The third attribute here is *dāsya-lipsā* (the will to serve) to surrender oneself in service to the Divine and to the world. And the fourth attribute of this *śakti* is *ātmasamarpaṇa* (surrender of self).

This may be seen as the central power of the entire *śakti catuṣṭaya* and from a certain perspective, of the entire integral yoga. This quality forms the essence of what Sri Aurobindo calls the psychic being or the inmost soul in us. The prime property of the psychic being is a complete and unconditional surrender to the Divine Śakti, the Divine Mother, who can transform us. Surrender of self, an integral surrender to the Divine Śakti and to the *Īśvara*, that is, the Conscious Being whose Consciousness Force is the Divine Śakti — without any thought of return, is the essence of this quality. That can be a most valuable meditation that one can carry out everyday — a dwelling on the sense of surrender to the Divine, without

74. RoY, pp. 10-11; SoY, pp. 746-48.

any expectation of return, a joyful abandonment to the power that understands us better than ourselves, and that will inform us as a result of that surrender, a power that will express through us and transform us into its own nature.[75]

Śakti or Divine Power

What we have discussed so far constitutes *vīryam*, the first perfection of the quartet of power. The second perfection of Śakti is *śakti* itself, or divine power. This is the proper working and expression of consciousness in the instruments, *karaṇa*, of the being. Though Sri Aurobindo positions this discipline of the quartet second, after *vīrya* in *Record of Yoga*, in *The Synthesis of Yoga*, he introduces it as the first of its *siddhis*.[76] This is because he presents this as a preparation of the specific forms of *śakti* in the instrument, prior to its proper use by the Divine Śakti. However, such a preparation may proceed simultaneously with the development of the soul forces and the expression of the Śakti through these. In developing the discipline of the *śakti*s of the instruments, Sri Aurobindo identifies four kinds of instrumentalities — the intelligence, the emotional being, the volitional being and the body.[77]

The *śakti* of the body is *deha śakti* or physical power. The specific properties of physical power will be dealt with in greater detail in the *Śarīra Catuṣṭaya* (the quartet of the body). In *The Synthesis of Yoga*, Sri Aurobindo foregrounds one of these capacities of the body. This is *dhāraṇa sāmarthya* (the physical capacity to sustain intensity). This is a very important capacity of the physical body, a body which does not tire, which carries within itself such repose that it can constantly renew itself in a powerful unceasing activity in its expression.

---

75. RoY, pp. 10-11; SoY, pp. 746-48.
76. Ibid., p. 7; Ibid., p. 729.
77. SoY, p. 729; RoY, pp. 11-12.

Śakti Catuṣṭhaya (Perfection of Power/Nature) (3.5) *Deha-śakti* and *Prāṇa-śakti*

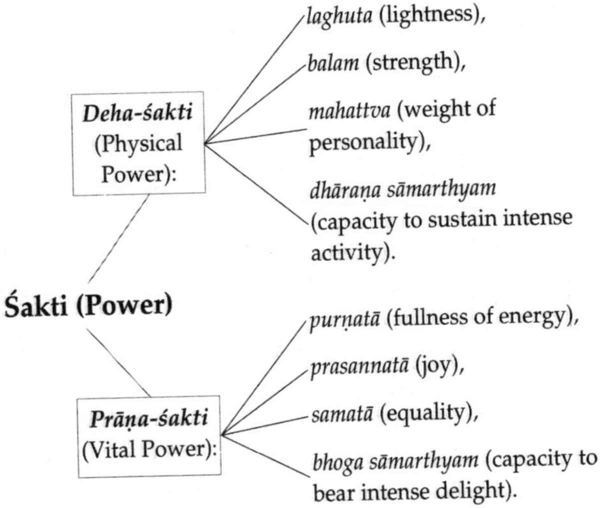
Śakti (Power)
Deha-śakti (Physical Power):
laghuta (lightness),
balam (strength),
mahattva (weight of personality),
dhāraṇa sāmarthyam (capacity to sustain intense activity).
Prāṇa-śakti (Vital Power):
purṇatā (fullness of energy),
prasannatā (joy),
samatā (equality),
bhoga sāmarthyam (capacity to bear intense delight).

To arrive at this, it is necessary to develop the body's faith in its capacities of endurance and extend its power of responsiveness. For this, Sri Aurobindo invokes the high degree of mental control to which many spiritual disciplines subject the body. Though the aim in the Integral Yoga is not a subjection of the body to the mind, but rather the awakening of the body's own consciousness, the disciplining of the body by the mind can be useful as a stage towards the preparation of the body consciousness to be perfectly responsive to the directives of the soul or spiritual Self.[78]

Sri Aurobindo invokes the remaining powers of the body in a quintessential way under *śakti*. These are *laghutā*, *balam* and *mahatva*. We will encounter the bases of these physical *śakti*s in the quartet of the body, as the qualities of *laghimā*, *aṇimā* and *mahimā*, respectively. *Laghutā* is the sense of

78. SoY, pp. 730-31; RoY, p. 11.

lightness. This is a power that results in the paranormal capacity of levitation. It is an anti-gravitational force in the body. Here it can be thought of as a consequence of the action of the Divine Śakti perfecting the instruments of nature. Then, there is *balam,* the body's ability to tap into earthly sources of impersonal and universal energy which are locked within it. Finally, there is the weight of personality, *mahatva*. We perceive a power of personality which may be translated as a sense of greatness in some people. This is not a surface impression caused by external paraphernalia, such as dress or grooming. Irrespective of costume or expression, we are sometimes conscious of people as carriers of a gravity, a power of physical personality. This is *mahatva.*[79]

Elsewhere, at a number of places, I have noted the work of Gilles Deleuze and Felix Guattari with respect to the consciousness of the body — the formation of the BwO and the form of physical attention embodied in the question "Of what is a body capable?" In our age of deep mental alienation from the life of the body, and the resulting massive environmental dislocation, a growing number of thinkers (or scholar-practitioners) have begun to draw attention to *deha-śakti*, the consciousness of the body as a form of earthly consciousness, part and parcel of the consciousness of other material and vital beings. The work of David Abram may be mentioned here. I quote here a passage from Abram's *The Spell of the Sensuous*, dealing with an experience of body language communication with the animal world within a milieu in Java, Indonesia, which supported such an ontology. Abram also notes, however, that a return to the US with its very different universal mind-body relations, gradually eroded this power, imposing its normative suggestions on his perceptions, sensations and possibilities of experience:

---

79. RoY, p. 11; SoY, p. 732.

> While at Pangandaran, a nature preserve on a peninsula jutting out from the south coast of Java ("a place of many spirits", I was told by nearby fishermen), I stepped out from a clutch of trees and found myself looking into the face of one of the rare and beautiful bisons that exist only on that island. Our eyes locked. When it snorted, I snorted back; when it shifted its shoulders, I shifted my stance; when I tossed my head, it tossed its head in reply. I found myself caught in a non-verbal conversation with this Other, a gestural duet with which my reflective awareness had very little to do. It was as if my body were suddenly being motivated by a wisdom older than my thinking mind, as though it was held and moved by a logos, deeper than words, spoken by the Other's body, the trees, the air, and the stony ground on which we stood.[80]

The second instrument for the action of *śakti* is the life being and the *śakti* working in it is *prāṇa-śakti* (vital/volitional power). In traditional paths of yoga, the exercises of *prāṇāyāma* are used to bring the *prāṇa-śakti* under the control of the *yogī* and develop *siddhi*s (paranormal capacities) through this control. Sri Aurobindo points out that one may use *prāṇāyāma* for some degree of control over the *prāṇa*s (life energies) but this should not be a necessity, because then it would be a subjection and a dependence. The Integral Yoga rests on the powers of conscious attention and aspiration and these direct powers of the *Puruṣa*, are to be developed to the degree, where they can achieve what would otherwise be possible through the mechanical exercises of *Prakṛti*.[81] Vital power also has four attributes. The first is *pūrṇatā* (fullness of energy) unflagging energetic force. The second is *prasannatā* (joy) — this may, more properly, be called gladness or contentment. There is certain kind of equal

---

80. David Abram, Chapter 1, "The Ecology of Magic", *The Spell of the Sensuous*, New York: Vintage Books, 1997, p. 21.

81. SoY, p. 734.

contentment which becomes part of the unchangeable fabric of one's character.

This aspect of *śakti* is related to equality. In our discussion on the perfection of equality, we had occasion to consider this gladness or contentment (*ātma-santoṣa*) as equality deepens into peace, peace deepens into happiness, and happiness deepens into ecstasy. This is the natural progression of the consciousness of equality and this is related at the level of the life-energy to *prasannatā*. In keeping with this progression, the third attribute of this soul force is equality itself (*samatā*). The last of the attributes of *śakti*, in the life-instrument, is *bhoga*

Śakti Catuṣṭaya (Perfection of Power/Nature) (3.6)
Citta-śakti and Buddhi-śakti

Śakti (Power)

- ***Citta śakti* (Emotional Power):**
  - *Snigdhatā* (gladness of feeling),
  - *Tejas* (strength of character),
  - *Kalyāṇa śraddhā* (confidence in universal good),
  - *Prema sāmarthyam* (capacity for unbounded love for all beings).
- ***Buddhi śakti* (Thought Power):**
  - *Viśuddhatā* (mental purity),
  - *Prakāśa* (light of knowledge),
  - *Vicitrabodha* (high resolution in intellectual perceptions and distinctions).

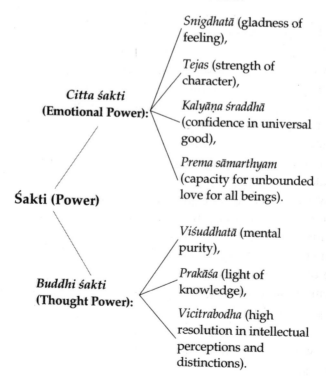

sāmarthyam (the capacity to experience intensities of delight). The word "delight" here should not be mistaken. By delight is meant the fundamental affective property. Delight includes, in our experience, both joy and sorrow. *Bhoga Sāmarthyam* refers to the capacity to bear intensities of all affective states. Intensity of pleasure or intensity of pain should not overwhelm us; the nerves develop an unshakeable equality to bear these intensities as forms of *ānanda*. A major factor associated with this attribute is the preparation for spiritual experience. The intensities of spiritual bliss (*ānanda*) can be overwhelming. This is why some fall into trance, or leap, jump and dance, unable to contain the ecstasy in sustained activity, but it is possible for much greater intensities of delight to descend into and be experienced in the nerves, without excitement, so as to become a constant condition of one's active being.[82]

The third instrument for the action of *śakti* is the *citta*. *Citta* is characterised by Sri Aurobindo as the subconscient mentality pervading all things in an unorganised form. *Citta* is present in its latency even in matter, but much more manifest in the nervous responses of plants and animals. It forms part of the sensational mentality, the mental consciousness related to sensations, which cascade up to become feelings, sentiments and emotions. The action of *śakti* in the *citta* is *citta-śakti* (broadly speaking emotional or affective power).[83] Emotion does not fully characterise the operation of *citta-śakti*. It is better understood as the action through which we experience the dualities of pleasure and pain, at first at the level of sensations, then at that of the senses, further at the level of the mind and also of what we generally refer to as the heart, the affective or emotional being.

In his treatment of the *prāṇa-śakti* and *citta-śakti* in *The*

82. SoY, pp. 733-35; RoY, pp.11-12.

83. RoY, p. 12; SoY, p. 736.

Synthesis of Yoga, Sri Aurobindo uses the terms psychic *prāṇa*[84] and psychical being[85] respectively. These terms should not be confused with what he calls the psychic being in his later writings. The later use refers to the soul personality, the immanent divine element forming the deep centre of the human psychological constitution, which is eternal and persists from life to life. In the section on *citta-śakti*, Sri Aurobindo does refer to this soul personality also, referring to it as "the pure psychic being", and saying of it that it "is of the essence of *ānanda*" and "comes from the delight-soul in the universe".[86] In this earlier usage, the psychic *prāṇa* can be taken as a soul of desire, responsible for the conditioned life of feelings. This needs purification, leading to the qualities of the perfected *citta-śakti*, which include an established gladness of feelings, *snigdhatā* and a concentrated strength of character (*tejas*).[87] There is a power of health in the consciousness of truth. This gathered constancy of attention is *tejas*, and to it belongs a certain radiance.

The third quality is *kalyāṇa-śraddhā* (a confidence in well-being) *maṅgala* (a sense that universal goodwill prevail) — a condition of auspiciousness and success in the will to self-exceeding and the works that enable it. And finally, there is *prema sāmarthyam*, or the capacity for unbounded love for all beings.[88] In Sri Aurobindo's description one sees how this last quality captures the essence of the perfection of *citta-śakti*:

> The wider and more universal the capacity of love, a love self-sufficient and undisturbed by want or craving or disappointment and the more fixed the faith in God and the

84. SoY, pp. 734-35.

85. Ibid., p. 736.

86. Ibid., p. 737.

87. RoY, p. 12. in *The Synthesis of Yoga*, Sri Aurobindo uses the term *saumyatva* instead of *snigdhatā*. SoY, p. 737.

88. SoY, p. 737; RoY, p. 12.

> joy in all things as *maṅgalam*, the greater becomes the divine force in the *citta*.[89]

One can see that these properties of *citta-śakti* are closely related to the *vaiśya-śakti* and the *śūdra-śakti* and the development of these two soul forces.

Finally, there is *buddhi-śakti* (thought power). This again has four aspects. The first of these is mental purity (*viśuddhatā*) which was introduced earlier when dealing with the perfection of purity (*śuddhi*) while discussing the *siddhi catuṣṭaya*. The second is *prakāśa* (the light of knowledge) — this relates again to *brahma-śakti* or *brahmatejas* (the radiance of knowledge). The third is *vicitra bodha*. This is an interesting and important capacity to develop in thought power — a fine resolution in intellectual perceptions and distinctions. We should be able to make subtle qualitative distinctions with our intellect. The intelligence should become a perceptive instrument, so as not to render things roughly or crudely, but to make sophisticated representations and judgements, to know how to split hairs, as the saying goes — not for the joy of sophistry, but for the perfection of the expression of knowledge.[90]

Sri Aurobindo writes about the culture of the logical intelligence, developing it as an instrument which is open to higher powers of intuitive mentality in these terms:

> The developed logical intelligence uses the imagination for suggesting new discovery and hypothesis, but is careful to test its suggestions fully by observation and a sceptical or scrupulous judgement. It insists too on testing, as far as may be, all the action of the judgement itself, rejects hasty inference in favour of an ordered system of deduction and induction and makes sure of all its steps and of the justice, continuity, compatibility, cohesion of its conclusions. A too

89. RoY, p. 12.
90. SoY, p. 738; RoY, p. 12.

> formalised logical mind discourages, but a free use of the whole action of the logical intelligence may rather heighten a certain action of immediate insight, the mind's nearest approach to the higher intuition, but it does not place on it an unqualified reliance. The endeavour of the logical reason is always by a detached, disinterested and carefully founded method to get rid of error, of prejudgement, of the mind's false confidence and arrive at reliable certitudes. . . . [But] a time must come . . . when the mind perceives the necessity of calling to its aid and developing fully the intuition and all the great range of powers, that lie concealed behind our vague use of the word and uncertain perception of its significance. In the end, it must discover that these powers can not only aid and complete but even replace its own proper action. That will be the beginning of the discovery of the supramental energy of the spirit.[91]

The final perfection of the intelligence is the capacity for integral thinking. The mind intuits unity in the infinite plurality of the universe, but finds it difficult to grasp it. This intrinsic faith in unity is what drives the scientist's seeking for a Unified Field Theory, or the philosopher's thinking of a unitive ground of Being. However mind, in its constitution, cannot grasp opposites together. Thus, unity and plurality remain incommensurables, unless one is reduced to the other. True integrality is that which grasps a unity which does not obliterate plurality, but manifests in and as plurality. It is the simultaneous identity of the one and the infinite. To aim at such an integrality in the intelligence, is an aspiration towards the fullness of Supermind, a capacity for an all-round or global thinking, which yet does not lose the irreducible particularity of its elements. This is *sarva-jñāna sāmarthya*, which Sri Aurobindo translates as "integral capacity" in thinking.[92]

---

91. SoY, pp. 854-55.

92. Ibid., p. 738.

Embodying the Divine Śakti

The two final aspects of the quartet of power are *caṇḍī bhāva* and *śraddhā*. *Caṇḍī bhāva* is a culminating result — from this viewpoint, one may think of it as the last of the four. Sri Aurobindo uses three synonymous terms, *caṇḍī bhāva*, *devī bhāva* and *daivī Prakṛti* to refer to the embodiment of the Divine Śakti by the human being. In other words, our individuality becomes completely identified with the Divine Mother; we experience Her living in us and acting through us — we are a soul one with and carried on the wave of the Divine Mother. She expresses in us her attributes, qualities and powers through our instruments which she has perfected and made her own. This implies the possession of the four *śakti*s: Māheśvarī, Mahākālī, Mahālakṣmī and Mahāsarasvatī and their respective *Īśvaras*. Sri Aurobindo's text *The Mother* provides a mantric description of this fulfillment. Here he says:

> The last stage of this perfection will come when you are completely identified with the Divine Mother and feel yourself to be no longer another and separate being, instrument, servant or worker, but truly a child and eternal portion of her consciousness and force. Always she will be in you and you in her; it will be your constant, simple and natural experience that your thought and seeing and action, your very breathing or moving come from her and are hers. You will know and see and feel that you are a person and power formed by her out of herself, put out from her for the play and yet always safe in here, being of her being, consciousness of her consciousness, force of her force, *ānanda* of her *ānanda*. When this condition is entire and her supramental energies can freely move you, then you will be perfect in divine works; knowledge, will, action will become sure, simple, luminous, spontaneous, flawless, an outflow from the Supreme, a divine movement of the Eternal.[93]

93. *The Mother and Letters on the Mother*, SABCL 25, p. 14.

Faith and the Divine Śakti

Just as *ātmasamarpaṇa* was seen to be a key to the entire yoga of integral transformation, a key lever to the entire *śakti catuṣṭaya*, is what Sri Aurobindo enumerates as its fourth limb. This is *śraddhā* (faith). In *The Synthesis of Yoga*, Sri Aurobindo devotes two chapters to the Divine Śakti, and a chapter each to the other *siddhi*s of the quartet of power. One of these, is the chapter on faith and the *śakti*.[94] Faith is an innermost intuition we carry within ourselves leading us to the future. It is of the nature of an occult memory, a psychic memory of what we already are in essence and must become in the manifestation. It is the basis of the future-orientation of human beings and what the *Gītā* considers to be the very definition of the human, when it says: *yo yacchraddhaḥ sa eva saḥ* — you are what your faith is.[95] Faith, as Sri Aurobindo puts it here, is of two kinds : one is faith in the arranger of circumstances and leader of the way, the *guru* and the Lord; the other is a faith in the Śakti at work in our own selves and all our instruments.[96] This can also be seen as faith in the love and wisdom of the *Īśvara* and the power of the Śakti within us. In other words, there is a Being who is leading us, and I have faith that that being knows more than my limited intelligence and is providing for me, what I need at every moment for me to make progress and become one with it in consciousness and nature. That is the first faith. The second faith is in the power of the *śakti* within us. In other words, not only is this transcendental Being leading us in every aspect through the circumstances of our lives, through the opportunities and challenges that are given to us, but also from within us in every energy, every faculty, every expressive power. It is that

---

94. SoY, pp. 771-82.
95. *śraddhā-mayo'yam puruso yo yacchraddhaḥ sa eva saḥ* — *Bhagavad-Gītā* 17.3; SoY, p. 771.
96. RoY, p. 13; SoY, p. 771.

Divine power within us, that knows how to do the things, that we don't know through our conditioning. So, we need to have faith in our own selves, not as egos, but as instruments of a divine force that is working in us.[97] Thus, the *śraddhā*, which is to be held firmly and consciously in the being is both in the wisdom of the *Īśvara* and the power of the Śakti within us and above us, leading us and working out the yoga in our instrumental parts. Sri Aurobindo points to the centrality of faith in an epigrammatic line: "Without *śraddhā* there is no *śakti*; imperfect *śraddhā* means imperfect *śakti*."[98]

In the *Record of Yoga*, Sri Aurobindo points to two progressive aspects of faith. He says that there is a force of faith and an illumination of faith. Roughly speaking, we may say the force of faith is what is sometimes called "blind faith". It is a faith to which there is no clear knowledge of either a Divine leading, or the presence or power of the Divine within us. Sri Aurobindo writes: "It is sufficient at first to have full force of the faith, for, we cannot from the beginning of the yoga, have full illumination."[99] However, it should be noted that this faith is not a blind belief. It is important to make the distinction between belief and faith. Blind belief is mental indoctrination. Faith already assumes access to an inner intuition of truth, an existential destining; it is a faculty of consciousness. This is quite different from a belief that affirms some vital desire or ideological conditioning. *Śraddhā* is an intuitive faith in the Divine leading, and that proceeds from a power of unity and a seeking for identity with the Divine; we may not have the knowledge of it, but we can still have the force of it.

The force of faith is close to the experience of surrender. We feel that whatever happens does so by the sanction of the

97. SoY, p. 780.

98. RoY, p.13.

99. Ibid.

Divine Mother, and we also have the confidence that we can't ultimately go wrong because whatever we do in our ignorance, the Mother holds our hand and will set us right. Of course, this is not a license to falsehood; even in ignorance, sincerity must be our watchword, if we are to be safe in the Mother's leading. This is a very subtle but important, even critical aspect of the transformative journey; it's not a belief, but a power that helps to set us right, because we are moving from ignorance to knowledge, and in that movement we cannot ever be completely right. Whatever we do, is marked by error, but, if we have faith in the Divine and surrender to the Divine, that conscious power, our own transpersonal origin and destining, guides our steps and we are progressively set into the right path in fullness of knowledge. Thus, Sri Aurobindo continues:

> Then, however we err and stumble, our force of faith will sustain us. When we cannot see, we shall know that God witholds the light, imposing on us error as a step towards knowledge, just as he imposes on us defeat as a step towards victory.[100]

This, again, is a powerful meditation one can conduct each day. One can bring into one's mind all the various activities and decisions that one is given for that day — "sufficient to the day is the evil thereof" — and offer these to the Divine Mother, the Śakti within us and the Divine Lord (the *Īśvara*) dispenser of circumstances and results in the universe, with the sense that I will do the best I can, but I surrender it to you — you do what is right for me, to set me right, to place me where I need to be. That is the full force of the faith. "Then, however we err and stumble, our force of faith will sustain us."[101] This is the primary power of the quartet of power, and the primary quality with which its fourfold perfection concludes.

---

100. RoY, p.13.
101. Ibid.

4

The Quartet of Knowledge

THE *vijñāna catuṣṭaya* forms the third of the *ādhāra siddhis* and may be described as the quartet of knowledge. *Vijñāna* is a term from the Upaniṣads which Sri Aurobindo has translated as Supermind, so it becomes pertinent to clarify further his use of the term in this context. What are the general distinctions that background Sri Aurobindo's understanding of Knowledge, what may be called his epistemology? Firstly, taken from the viewpoint of the human being and the manifestation of Reality as an Ignorance, the Vedic distinction of three forms of Knowledge, is intrinsic to his understanding. These three forms are known as *ādhibhautika, ādhidaivika* and *ādhyātmika*.

Three Forms of Knowledge: Ādhibhautika, Ādhidaivika, Ādhyātmika

In the *Life Divine,* Sri Aurobindo deals with these three forms of knowledge, though he does not identify them explicitly by name. If we were to attempt a translation, *ādhibhautika* knowledge, in Sri Aurobindo's terms would be knowledge by external or indirect contact, that is, sense-knowledge.[1] *Bhūta* means "element", and refers to the constituents of the phenomenal world. We apprehend these elements through our senses. This is our usual mode of knowing. We contact

1. LD, p. 544.

reality as being "outside" of ourselves by instruments of sensing, and the results of this sensing are cognised and interpreted in the mind, to arrive at what we call knowledge. This is the knowledge characteristic of the world of separation or *avidyā* (ignorance).

However, in consonance with the Vedas and Upaniṣads, Sri Aurobindo affirms that all knowledge exists within each person. The origin of this intrinsic root of knowledge lies in the fact that Being is self-conscious and present in its infinite fullness in each of its constituents. Infinite conscious being has knowledge of itself by its own power of self-consciousness. This characterises the pole of reality, known in the Upaniṣads as *vidyā* (knowledge). *Ātma* means self, hence this most directly experienced self-knowledge is *ādhyātmika*, knowledge by identity.[2] But, we have not developed this knowledge by identity in ourselves; hence, we are sceptical about it and give no place to it in our lives. This brings up the relativity of human development, and particularly, the history of modernity. If the history of human development had been different, we may conceivably have questioned the necessity of the entire advancement of technology. For example, if we wanted to look at things in the dark, we could have developed our inner powers of sight, or we could have invented electric lamps. The privileging of objective knowledge, *ādhibhautika*, has normalised the technology of the electric lamp. But, an alternate possibility of development may have privileged the inner powers of sight so that we could penetrate the darkness with our sight.

Similarly, in the domain of knowledge we can acquire knowledge through cognitive interpretation of objective data obtained through our senses and their extensions — scientific observing mechanisms — but this indirect knowledge can only

2. LD, pp. 543-44.

provide us with models more or less adequate to describe realities "outside" of ourselves. Alternately, we could develop the power of knowledge that is within us, which arises out of the knowledge by identity of the self, that is, by experience of identity with the object of knowledge. But, this second or alternate development is not obviously accessible to us, which is why, we cannot trust it until it can be established fully in ourselves. In between these two polarities of knowledge, we have a variety of intuitive forms of knowledge. These are what are known as *ādhidaivika* knowledge — knowledge by inner contact.[3] The word *ādhidaivika* comes from *deva*, which refers to the gods, those who span the differences of the world through interiority, the intensities of virtual or inner space. Through inner mental concentration or through the development of subtler potencies of the senses, through lucid imagination or dreaming, through the powers of empathy or sympathy, or through a nervous instinctive sensing, we may arrive at intuitive forms of knowledge, that are partially available to us in our normal existence, but can be more fully developed through discipline. *Vijñāna catuṣṭaya* (the quartet of knowledge) may be understood as the progression from *ādhibhautika* to *ādhyātmika* knowledge, through the intermediate development of an intuitive or *ādhidaivika* knowledge instrumentality.

Four Forms of Knowledge in Supermind: Vijñāna, Prajñāna, Saṁjñāna, Ājñāna

Elsewhere, Sri Aurobindo introduces the idea of *vijñāna* as Supermind and writes about the four forms of knowledge native to Supermind in a way that opens up the scope of the term *vijñāna*. These four forms of knowledge are available both in the *vidyā* which is the knowledge by identity of the One Being, and in the *avidyā*, characterised by separative

3. LD, pp. 543-44.

knowledge.[4] They work as universal principles having different modalities in these two realms. These four terms, taken from the *Aitareya Upaniṣad*, are *vijñāna*, *prajñāna*, *saṁjñāna* and *ājñāna*.[5] *Vijñāna* itself is the foundation of this foursome, that is, the direct knowledge of the One, knowledge by identity. In other words, *vijñāna* can only be availed of in the realm of *vidyā*. However, in its very etymology, *vijñāna* refers to *viśeṣa jñāna* (qualified knowledge). This implies the possession of a knowledge which is simultaneously unified and differentiated.[6] We may compare it analogously with our individual sense of identity. We possess an overall sense of being "someone", but this *ādhyātmika* "grasp" of the self lacks content or even extent. Latent within this overall sense, is a diffuse sense of indefinable parts and operations. A concentration of consciousness can bring this differential knowledge into focus out of its amorphous presence in the overall knowledge. *Vijñāna* can be thought of as such an overriding sense of Oneness with the possibility of differentiation present in it at hand. The other forms of supramental knowledge can be thought of as the operations of such specialised actions of *vijñāna*, bringing specific differential forms of knowledge.

Of these, *prajñāna* becomes the first deployment of the knowledge by identity, whereby, its possibilities become knowable in themselves, as independent realities.[7] This makes it possible for the One to know itself as the Many. It is important to understand this notion of the One and the Many in terms of the Supermind, as Sri Aurobindo explains it, since this is necessary for a resolution of the fragmented and separative condition in which we find ourselves in our

4. KU, p. 51.
5. *Aitareya Upaniṣad*, III:2; KU, p. 51.
6. SoY, pp. 862-63.
7. Ibid., p. 862.

experience of being. Are the Many here related to some invisible but experienceable One? And, if there is such a One, what is the nature of its relationship with the Many? Of course, it might be possible to construe the experience of reality in terms of a fundamental dualism, to say that there is the One and there are the Many, but there is no relationship between them. In such a case, if we are to arrive at the One, we would have to divest ourselves entirely from the experience of the Many, taking it as an illusion. It is easy to arrive at this conclusion logically, since one and infinity are logically incompatible.

But, if we contemplate the Master Word (*mahāvākya*) of the Vedānta, that there is nothing other than the One,[8] then the infinite Many could only have reality as forms of the One; and what, for lack of a better word, we are forced to call One, can only be an infinite One, inexpressible, except through paradox. Sri Aurobindo affirms this Vedāntic viewpoint as a truth of realisation, *darśana,* that what we call the Many, the fragmented reality that characterises our normal experience in this world, is a simultaneous multiple self-conception of the One.[9] We can think of ourselves as having a self-conception — this is like a partial mirroring of ourselves. I can turn within and form an image of who I am. We are familiar with this exercise — we create *avatāra*s of ourselves on cyber-space. These are self-conceptions. But, can we extend this to conceive of a Being who is infinite enough to create infinite simultaneous self-conceptions? Such an idea boggles the mind, because mentality operates in the domain of finites. However, *Brahman* is inifinite and thus, so are its self-conceptions. Each of these would have an independent life, and yet each of these would be none other than the infinite One, who had conceived himself

8. *ekam eva-advitiyam brahma, Chāndogya Upaniṣad,* VI:2:1; *Sarvam khaluvidam brahma, Chāndogya Upaniṣad,* III:14:1.

9. LD, p. 158.

in it. Gilles Deleuze affirms the time reality of this truth of being by noting that what Nietzsche referred to as the eternal recurrence of the same is indeed the eternal or perpetual return of difference. This is the multiple self-concentration of the Divine One, as and in the ever-changing Many.[10]

In this self-conception, each of these Many would always be integrally related to the One. By "integrally" here is meant, that the One would be entirely present in each of its self-conceptions. In each part is the Whole. However, because these self-conceptions have independence, each one of these Many, would also have the capacity to arrive at its specific kind of self-knowledge — that is, a prismatic angle on the totality of truth. These multiple self-conceptions, may each be considered a soul; and its journey, along a line of inclusiveness to totality of cosmic self-identification, and further to the exceeding of that identification in the radically Infinite One, would constitute the self-becoming of Being, in an evolutionary manifestation.[11]

Thus, the differentiation of Being into its infinite possibilities of quality, is what characterises the One and the Many, in their relationship in Supermind, in the *vidyā*. The operation of that relationship as knowledge is what is called *prajñāna*.[12] *Prajñāna* is an operation of knowledge, where the One can hold its infinite multiplicities at an observable distance from itself. It has objectified its parts through a concentration (*tapas*) in accordance with a master self-conception or Real Idea of itself. Out of this objectification it derives specific knowledge of its potentia, and these potentia likewise, derive specific knowledge of themselves, of each other and of the One. Therefore, *prajñāna* can be thought of as a knowledge of

10. LD, p. 158.
11. Ibid., p. 176.
12. Ibid, pp.175-76.

the Many as the One, that is, each of the Many is the One, the One knows each of these Many as its own self, and as a self-conceptions of itself.[13] This form of knowledge (*prajñāna*) would be the source of a manifested cosmos, where the One and the Many co-exist in their unitary and separative knowledge, all as forms of the One's self-knowledge. This implies a representation of the One as cosmos or a cosmos of representations, which are nevertheless, all and each not other than self-presentations.

In fact, if *prajñāna* did not exist, we couldn't even imagine the possibility of a divine life, or a supramental manifestation. Also, we could not conceive the possibility of the truth of our own creation in the fragmented *avidyā*. Our creation is one in which *prajñāna* hides its oneness. The One and the Many that are the self-conceptions of the One co-exist, but the One veils itself so, that only the Many remain to think of themselves as many Ones. This is the phenomenon of Ignorance, *avidyā*. Therefore, in *prajñāna* itself, we can see the way by which we could arrive at a divine life by the restoration of the root of the One in the Many. Like *prajñāna*, the other forms of knowledge are also forms of the knowledge of the One, as the Many, or of the Many as the One, that is, in each of the Many there is the One.

The third form of knowledge, in this sequence is, *saṁjñāna*. Like *vijñāna* and *prajñāna*, *saṁjñāna* and *ājñāna* are forms of direct knowledge in the *vidyā*, but in the *avidyā*, *prajñāna*, *saṁjñāna* and *ājñāna* are forms of indirect knowledge. By direct knowledge is meant knowledge by identity; knowledge which does not need instruments to arrive at its knowing, though it may use instruments to represent its self-knowledge. Knowledge by identity is self-evident knowledge. For example, our most fundamental under-

---

13. LD, p. 176.

standing of ourselves arises by identity. We know ourselves as "someone", not because we have been told this; nor because it is a label that we have acquired; nor because we possess the property of language. It is self-evident. This is knowledge by identity. I know I am. Similarly, direct knowledge, knowledge of the Many as the One, or knowledge of the One, directly, is a knowledge by identity of the same kind. But knowledge by identity may use instrumental forms to represent itself. We have already seen this in the example of imaging oneself as an *avatāra* in cyber-space. This identification may go further — we may experience the sensations of such an *avatāra* through neuro-sensory contacts in virtual game-playing. However, in the case of the human actor, the knowledge of the world acquired by these means remains a knowledge through instrumentation, a knowledge by indirect contact, since the world remains distinct from the self, is not a self-conception. But this is not the case for *Brahman*, the only One there is, since self and world are both self-conceptions to it. To *Brahman*, all knowledge is knowledge by identity, or by extension of identity through representational instruments.

Prajñāna, *saṁjñāna* and *ājñāna* are such forms of knowledge. *Saṁjñāna* is the sense-knowledge of the One and of the Many as the One.[14] In other words, an objectification of sensible properties — what may be seen, heard, smelt, tasted, touched, felt — is possible, but in the *vidyā*, this is a representational objectification by which the One experiences its self-conceptions through a primordial Sense. These self-conceptions, the Many, on their part, also experience their oneness with the One and with others through this Sense — what in the Upaniṣads has been called the Sense of the senses.[15] The indivisible Reality has taken a certain figure in each of us and we may see with

---

14. KU, 51.
15. Ibid., p. 54.

its Sight. This is not a mental concept, but a seeing; that is, the senses themselves have the property for this kind of knowledge — direct sense-knowledge (*pratyakṣa*). This is the basis of what has been called *darśana* in Indian culture.[16] This also relates to what William Blake meant when he wrote that when the doors of perception are cleansed, you will see reality as it truly is — infinite.[17] In all things, one can see the Infinite One, without losing the specific qualities of self-representation of that Infinite One. This is applicable to the other senses as well. Each particularity is experienced as a qualitative contact with the Infinite Being. This is *saṁjñāna*. Gilles Deleuze, in writing of the transcendental conditions which make possible our empirical experience of sense, refers to a being of sensation present in all sense reality. The apprehension of this comes intimately close to Sri Aurobindo's *saṁjñāna*.

The fourth form of knowledge is *ājñāna*, which is practical knowledge through will and skill. Knowledge of effectuation and knowledge by effectuation — that is, knowledge which comes only in the performance of action — is the domain of *ājñāna*. *Ājñāna* in *vidyā* relates to power of control and development of things as aspects of the One Self.[18] To truly control something, one needs to be identified in will with it, *ājñāna* also relates to skill, perfection in handling materials and effecting results. There is an intuitive skill in any action or work. That is also an aspect of *ājñāna*, because the will enters into intimate contact with its object through the active instruments of being, and deploys a practical knowledge, of handling, working and effecting. As a form of Supramental knowledge, this is the knowledge by the One of itself and of the Many as forms of itself, held together by self-relations

16. KU, p. 429.
17. William Blake, *The Marriage of Heaven and Hell*, Plate 14, 1790, facsimile reprinted by Dover, London, 1994.
18. KU, p. 51.

Vijñāna Catuṣṭaya (Perfection of Knowledge) (4.1)

Jñānam

Jñānam (Knowledge), *Trikāladṛṣṭi* (Triple Time Vision), *Aṣṭa-siddhi* (The Eight Powers), *Samādhi* (Absorption)

Forms of Knowledge (*Jñānam*):

- 1. ***Ādhibhautika*** (knowledge by external contact)
  2. ***Ādhidaivika*** (knowledge by inner contact),
  3. ***Ādhyatmika*** (knowledge by identity).
- 1. ***Vijñāna*** (direct knowledge of the One)
  2. ***Prajñāna*** (direct knowledge of the many as the One)
  3. ***Saṁjñāna*** (sense knowledge of the many as the One)
  4. ***Ājñāna*** (practical knowledge through will and skill of the many as the One)
- 1. ***Dṛṣṭi*** (revelation, truth-seeing)
  2. ***Śruti*** (inspiration, truth-hearing)
  3. ***Smṛti*** (intuition, truth-remembrance)
  4. ***Viveka*** (truth-discrimination)

following the possibilities of self-conception, what Sri Aurobindo has referred to as Real Idea. This knowledge by identity of the One and the Many, is the basis of an automatic action of will, what Sri Aurobindo calls Knowledge-Will, in evolving the intrinsic potential of each of its objects through self-relations.[19] In the *avidyā*, this is the domain of technology, instrumental handling of external objects to achieve preset goals. This may require specialised cognitive and practical knowledge, as well as physical skill of action, which, when it is truly skillful, cannot but rest on some intuition of identity. Again, its root, though hidden, is knowledge by identity. These are the four forms of Supramental knowledge. They may all be thought of as forms of *vijñāna*. When we think about *vijñāna catuṣṭaya* (the quartet of knowledge), we envisage the emergence of these powers of self-knowledge — knowledge by identity of Being in each self, which is ultimately none other than the One Self.

---

19. KU, p. 56.

The Intuitive Mind

Though, historically, humanity has evidenced instances of intuitive knowledge, these have not been taken seriously as reliable sources of general cognition. Extraordinary cases of mysticism or prophecy have been rarer than instances of genius and treated with scepticism, as possibly sporadic paranormal activity, or fodder for the credulous and gullible. A full-fledged and normalised activity based on a knowledge by identity has not been considered within the range of human possibility. Sri Aurobindo was well aware of this and hence, saw the arrival at this condition as a systematic effort proceeding by stages. In his words:

> In man, any emergence of the supermind, must be a gradual and at first an imperfect creation and to his customary mind the activity of an exceptional and supernormal will and knowledge. In the first place it will not be for him a native power always enjoyed without interruption, but a secret potentiality which has to be discovered and one for which there are no organs in his present physical or mental system: he has either to evolve a new organ for it or else to adopt or transform existing ones and make them utilisable for the purpose.[20]

This "evolving" of a "new organ", brings us back once more to the Nietzschean project of self-exceeding, which initiates the existential quest of modernity. Deleuze, in times closer to our own, speaks of making a "body without organs". This can be seen as a precursor to creating a body with "new organs". Indeed, in Sri Aurobindo's cases, the creation of an intermediate mentality, between the mental and the supramental, becomes possible through a receptive transformation of the mind. This intermediate mentality is what he called the Intuitive Mind.[21]

---

20. SoY, pp. 799-800.
21. Ibid., pp. 799-810.

In *The Synthesis of Yoga,* Sri Aurobindo indicates four alternate processes to arrive at a normalised action of this intuitive mentality. The first of these proceeds through a silencing of the mental activity, a process familiar to the meditative disciplines of *rāja-yoga, zazen, vipassanā* and other such practices. However, here this silence is sought as a permanent state of the mind, not an experience conditioned by specific practice. This silence also does not aim at a cessation of life-activity (*cittavr̥tti nirodhaḥ*) but becomes a state of conscious stillness open to a transcendental action. This, indeed, is the method Sri Aurobindo himself was led to follow.[22]

Instead of proceeding to silence the mind completely following a traditional meditation method, another way described by Sri Aurobindo, recognises a division of the mind into an inner and an outer part. Many thinkers and poets are conscious of such a division of the mind — an inner part, where some sustained mental or imaginative activity of a high intensity is undertaken and an outer part which continues to respond to the stimuli of the environment through established mechanisms of interaction. The inner mind can be made receptive and concentrated on a hidden centre of thought and impulsion, above the mind, relying more and more on a "descent" of idea, will and consciousness from this source. Sri Aurobindo invokes the tāntric theory of the mystic centres (*cakras*) in discussing this method, writing of the thousand-petalled lotus (*sahasrāra*) as the centre through which this descent occurs. In this method, the "thinking" is experienced at first as happening in some omniscient source above the mind and transmitted by descent to the mind; but later, the mind consciousness itself is experienced as shifting its centre to a position "above the head" in the subtle body and becoming permanently stationed there.[23]

---

22. SoY, pp. 802-03.
23. Ibid., pp. 805-06.

For those of a more emotional bent, Sri Aurobindo indicates a method which proceeds through mystic communion with the cosmic and transcendental Being in all things, opening through a receptive silence of the mind to the inner "heart", or emotional centre. This practice relies on the psychic being, the soul personality or innermost being hidden in the heart and its intuitions, proceeding from an intimate relationship with the cosmic and transcendental Being/Person. Sri Aurobindo points out that this method is more prone to error of impurity than reliance on the centre above the head, since the emotional and volitional being are tainted with the self-centred ego responses of nature, and a high degree of psychic purification is required before these intuitions can attain a degree of regular credibility.[24]

A fourth method proceeds by heightening and amplifying the subtlety and depth of thought, to the point, where it begins opening to intuition. Interestingly, a wave of contemporary, particularly Francophone, philosophy and art has moved in this direction. With a faith in the intellect turning it receptive to intuition, the mental apparatus of modern man can itself be made a medium for its own self-exceeding.[25]

These approaches, however, are not exclusive of each other and Sri Aurobindo recommends a combination of all of them, depending on the specific needs of each person at any time. He also points to the long and careful process and the need for developing an intuitive discrimination and a selective tact in effecting the transformation from normal human mentality to something approaching a more pure intuitive action of the mind.[26]

Here, it might be worth mentioning that the approach to

---

24. SoY, pp. 803-05.
25. Ibid., pp. 806-07.
26. Ibid., p. 807.

intuition, taken by Gilles Deleuze, following Henri Bergson. Deleuze, in his early text *Bergsonism*, looks for the transcendental conditions of experience through a methodical use of intuition. For this, he turns to Henri Bergson, lauding him as the founder of intuition as a philosophical method. This method consists of distinguishing true from false problems, ultimately reducible to differences in degree and differences in kind. Delueze points out, whereas differences in degree are homogeneous and quantitative and belong to objective space, differences in kind are heterogeneous and qualitative and belong to subjective time or "virtuality". A deep-rooted fear of instability and extinction, inherent in the monadic ego, makes us reduce time to a function of space, or subordinate becoming to being, substance and identity. To be able to separate these two forms of apprehension, is the critical point of intuition as a method. The mind is then freed to a new apprehension of experience, one in which becoming is privileged over being, and the experiencer steps outside of the charmed circle of spatialised appearances and outside too of one's own personal historicity to intuit duration. Duration, a term given prominence by Bergson, may be thought of as the co-extensive continuing history of heterogeneous becoming. This depth dimension, may be thought of as the nexus of the psychic and cosmic being-in-becoming, reaching towards knowledge by identity. Arriving at such an apprehension, there should, then be a reintegration of experience through the univocity of duration; space now becoming extensity, a continuous function of differential becoming.

In the *Life Divine*, Sri Aurobindo has a chapter titled "The Methods of Vedāntic Knowledge", in which he makes a distinction, similar to Deleuze and Bergson, between thought and intuition, pointing to the methodical use of the latter in a Vedāntic epistemology, something he himself followed. It is interesting to note that Sri Aurobindo carries out a similar analysis of Space and Time as dual properties of self-experience of Conscious Being-in-Becoming. In this analysis he proceeds, like Deleuze/Bergson, through a separation in kind of Space and Time to arrive at an intuition of Conscious Being, from which Space and Time are reintegrated as its properties of self-experience. He writes:

> Time and Space are that one Conscious-Being viewing itself in extension, subjectively as Time, objectively as Space. Our mental view of these two categories is determined by the idea of measure which is inherent in the action of the analytical, dividing movement of Mind. Time is for the Mind a mobile extension measured out by the succession of the past, present and future in which Mind places itself at a certain standpoint whence it looks before The Supreme Truth-Consciousness and after. Space is a stable extension measured out by divisibility of substance; at a certain point in that divisible extension, Mind places itself and regards the disposition of substance around it. In actual fact, Mind measures Time by event and Space by Matter; but it is possible in pure mentality to disregard the movement of event and the disposition of substance and realise the pure movement of Conscious-Force which constitutes Space and Time; these two are then merely two aspects of the universal force of Consciousness, which, in their intertwined interaction comprehend the warp and woof of its action upon itself. And to a consciousness higher than Mind which should regard our past, present and future in one view, containing and not contained in them, not situated at a particular moment of Time for its point of prospection, Time might well offer itself as an eternal present. And to the same consciousness not situated at any particular point of Space, but containing all points and regions in itself, Space also might well offer itself as a subjective and indivisible extension — no less subjective than Time. At certain moments we become aware of such an indivisible regard

> upholding by its immutable self-conscious unity the variations of the universe.[27]

The analogy with Deleuze's discussion of a method for intuition seems apparent here, as are the differences. Deleuze differentiates between difference in degree and difference in kind, relating these to Space and Time, respectively. He notes the predominant tendency to reduce temporality to a form of spatiality, or becoming to being. This is, even more so, in our technological age of objectification, where knowledge has been normatively reduced to "knowledge by external contact". Instead, he privileges becoming over being, time as heterogeneous process over space as homogeneous dispersion. Though this may bring us the intuition of duration, the presence of the cosmic past in every time-unit and spatial configuration, along with a creative openness to the future, this qualitative apprehension may be thought of as *ādhidaivika* knowledge (knowledge by inner contact). This is the reduction of space to a form of time. In the passage by Sri Aurobindo, he indicates an experience in which both Space and Time, substantial extension and perpetual mutation, are independent infinites, and self-presentations of That which appears as them. Neither can be reduced to the other, but each gives evidence of the other and yet retains its dimensional independence as self-experience of infinite Being and perpetual Becoming. This simultaneous co-existence in self-experience of infinite Being, substantial extension and perpetual Becoming, heterogeneous mutation, is the condition for supramental or *ādhyātmika* knowledge. Sri Aurobindo refers to glimpses of this kind of experience which are simultaneously of the form of memory and of unpredictable spontaneity, at once Being and Becoming (*Īśvara* and *Śakti*).

---

27. LD, pp. 142-43.

The Goals of the Quartet of Knowledge

Under the *vijñāna catuṣṭaya*, Sri Aurobindo lists four goals. These are *jñānam, trikāladṛṣṭi, aṣṭa-siddhi* and *samādhi*.[28] Of these, *Jñānam* translates literally to knowledge and our discussion above of knowledge relates directly to it. The other enumerated goals are specific conditions for the perfection of knowledge. In further elaborating *jñānam*, Sri Aurobindo divides it into *jñāna* of thought, *jñāna* of experience and *jñāna* of action.[29] We can relate these broadly to cognitive knowledge, subjective knowledge and practical knowledge or *prajñāna, saṁjñāna* and *ājñāna* respectively.

While dealing with the transformation of cognition into an intuitive mentality, Sri Aurobindo also points to the extension of this activity to the feelings, will and bodily and psychic activities:

> The most prominent change will be the transmutation of the thought heightened and filled by that substance of concentrated light, concentrated power, concentrated joy of the light and the power and that direct accuracy which are the marks of a true intuitive thinking. It is not only primary suggestions or rapid conclusions that this mind will give, but it will conduct too with the same light, power, joy of sureness and direct spontaneous seeing of the truth the connecting and developing operations now conducted by the intellectual reason. The will also will be changed into this intuitive character, proceed directly with light and power to the thing to be done, *kartavyam karma*, and dispose with a rapid sight of possibilities and actualities the combinations necessary to its action and its purpose. The feelings also will be intuitive, seizing upon right relations, acting with a new light and power and a glad sureness, retaining only right and spontaneous desires and emotions,

28. RoY, p. 16.
29. Ibid.

so long as these things endure, and, when they pass away, replacing them by a luminous and spontaneous love and an *ānanda* that knows and seizes at once on the right *rasa* of its objects. All the other mental movements will be similarly enlightened and even too the prāṇic and sense movements and the consciousness of the body. And usually there will be some development also of the psychic faculties, powers and perceptions of the inner mind and its senses not dependent on the outer sense and the reason.[30]

Cognitive Knowledge: Jñāna of Thought

Sri Aurobindo further divides the first of these, *jñāna* of thought, in terms of *dṛṣṭi, śruti, smṛti* and *viveka*.[31] A loose and literal translation of these terms would be sight, hearing, memory and discrimination, respectively. These four forms of cognitive knowledge can be thought of as each having two modalities — those of knowledge by inner contact (*ādhidaivika*) and those of knowledge by identity (*ādhyātmika*). We may, thus, think of them in terms of progression: we start by relating to them and establishing them as forms of intuitive knowledge, and they end up becoming forms of knowledge by identity. Even seen as inner or intuitive knowledge, these four forms of knowledge make a hierarchy, a higher and lower doublet.[32] The higher doublet consists of *dṛṣṭi* and *śruti* (revelation and inspiration) and the lower of *smṛti* and *viveka* (intuition and discrimination) respectively. The word *smṛti,* here, is interesting, because *śruti* and *smṛti* are terms used generally in Hindu theology or epistemology, to describe the difference between *ādhyātmika,* divine and *ādhibhautika,* human knowledge. *Śruti* is thought of as Truth-hearing, the Word of God, that which is received as revealed scripture, and thus,

30. SoY, p. 808.
31. Ibid., p. 17; See also KU, pp. 429-30.
32. RoY, pp. 1472-73; SoY, pp. 814-15.

ādhyātmika. We may say, all religions have some foundational idea of revealed scripture. God gave Moses the Ten Commandments; the prophet Gabriel came to Mohammad and dictated the Koran. Similarly, the Vedas are supposed to be "unauthored"(*apauruṣeya*). These form the general understanding of *śruti* (truth-audience).

Both, Truth-seeing and Truth-hearing (*dṛṣṭi* and *śruti*), are related to what is generally referred to as *śruti* in the Indian cognitive system. The aspect of "direct sight" *pratyakṣa dṛṣṭi*, which gives us revealed knowledge, is more commonly called *darśana*. If "hearing" and "seeing" are related to direct and divine knowledge, "remembering" is a subjective function, resting on human agency. This is *smṛti*. *Smṛti* literally means memory, things remembered, and what we generally understand by this is a compilation of revealed knowledge, *śruti*, as remembered, interpreted and narrated by humans. Thus, this is considered a secondary form of knowledge. In the Indian *āstika* tradition, the Vedas (Saṁhitā, Āraṇyaka and Brāhmaṇa) and Upaniṣads are considered Śruti, the Purāṇas, Tantras and Itihāsas (the mythical histories narrated in the epics *Rāmāyaṇa* and *Mahābhārata*) are classed as Smṛti.

Cognition: The Lower Doublet

But, when discussing knowledge in the quartet of knowledge, Sri Aurobindo uses the term *smṛti* in a different sense. He uses it firstly, as a form of knowledge by inner contact, an intuition, a truth-remembrance.[33] It arises, because we carry within ourselves, the hidden root of Oneness, which was present in the *prajñāna* but has veiled itself as the *avidyā* or *ājñāna*. Because it is within us, we remember it. We all have a faint remembrance of our truth, our reality. That is the beginning of our journey towards the One. To open up this memory, to bring it to the front, becomes a part of the yoga

33. SoY, p. 854.

of the *vijñāna catuṣṭaya*. This intuition, in the nature of a psychic memory of Origin, of the One Self in all selves, is what we often think of as faith.[34] When dealing with the quartet of power, we had occasion to consider *śraddhā* as a form of memory, an intuition like a remembrance of the truth that is hidden, but present in us. We touched on this in the section on the intuitive mind, and will later see the root of this memory to lie in Supermind. This is what stirs within us, as an invitation to trust, to have an increasing faith in this knowledge of all things that is within us, active in every moment. As we follow its thread, we receive recollections, we capture this sense of memory. This is a very important aspect of intuition. Sri Aurobindo also calls it the "suggestive intuitive mind".[35] We gradually wake to a sense of a knowledge, already known to us. There is nothing exotic about this, its quality is one of the deep intimacy of remembering experienced things. In fact, this is its distinguishing character — if it carries the dazzle of the exotic, we can be sure that this is a masquerade, it is not the *smṛti* of the inner knowledge.

It may be useful to relate this aspect of knowledge as memory with the notion of innate knowledge of Plato as discussed by him in *Meno*. Similar to Sri Aurobindo, Plato here holds that all knowledge is of the form of memory, due to the soul's familiarity with ideal essences prior to its incarnation in earthly bodies. But, as with the dualistic division in Indic philosophies which see watertight permanent realms of *vidyā* and *avidyā*, Plato's realm of Ideas provides the original prototypes for manifest existence but remains pure beyond them, while it (the manifestation) remains capable only of approximations to these truths. In Sri Aurobindo, the immanence of the ideal, or the realm of knowledge in the

---

34. SoY, pp. 112-13, 245.
35. Ibid., p. 817.

manifestation, makes the memorable nature of knowledge dynamically present within it at all times, not as static essences but as dynamic fields of evolutionary possibility. This may be intuited by us in our normal consciousness, but a methodical cultivation of it brings us closer to a realisation whose natural operation is supramental.

The other form of knowledge in this doublet is *viveka*.[36] Sri Aurobindo refers to *viveka* as truth-discrimination. Discrimination means the distinction between right and wrong; what is to be chosen and what is to be rejected.[37] Note that this is not some absolute judgement for distinguishing the chosen of god from the accursed, but a dynamic and pragmatic judgement pertaining to existential choice. In dealing with the perfections of the *vaiśya* in the *śakti catuṣṭaya*, the property of *kauśala* (skill) was discussed. This implied a spontaneous improvised selection from a variety of possibilities, a practical knowledge of selection, proportion, priority and emphasis.[38] How do we arrive at this practical skill? This is also a form of discrimination and has an aspect related to the intellect. One of the properties of the intellect we dealt with when discussing Śakti, was variety and subtlety of distinction, *vicitra bodha*.[39] This development of a high resolution in intellectual judgement and taste and its expressive aspect, a fine precision in language use, prepares the intellect to open to the intuition of *viveka*.

Viveka (discrimination) first arises in the normal rational intelligence. This is what we commonly call judgement. We are constantly judging, putting things in schema of prioritisation, classificatory systems. But, these are shifting, relative systems. They are usually based on a mixture of sources — some universal ideology that we have bought into, some

36. SoY, p. 816.
37. RoY, pp. 17-18, 1472.
38. Ibid., pp. 10, 1469.
39. Ibid., p. 1470.

preferences and desires of nature or upbringing, some practical goal which we wish to achieve. This implies more of an automatism of judgement than discrimination. But one of these may predominate and form a more predictable basis for judgement. If I have a goal to achieve, all the means at my disposal will be organised in terms of priorities based on this goal. Another, and more settled basis for judgement, may arise out of ideology. But, however, effective or comforting, these are ignorant bases for judgement, founded on relative presuppositions and preferences. They lack the insight of an identity which can portion out or proportion out its objects, known intimately as its own parts and faculties, to achieve its ends, through spontaneous skill. This would require an intuition, which belongs to the self-knowledge of the One. Closer to this, is the proportional intuition of the artist (*pramāṇāṇi*), who captures a knowledge of typal limits (*sādṛṣya*) and variances or irreducible specificities (*rūpabheda*), the configuration of forces and the way in which infinite power formulates its ideas as immanent problematics. Sri Aurobindo refers to this as the critical intuitive mind.[40] At the human level, the development of this intuitive discrmination in the inner mind would be the starting point of *viveka*, but, its progress would lie in a spontaneous certitude based in a knowledge by identity with the One. That is, what Sri Aurobindo means by *viveka*, seen as a perfection of *jñānam* of thought (cognitive knowledge) in the *vijñāna catuṣṭaya*.[41]

Thus, we find that the lower two forms of knowledge under *jñānam* of thought are *smṛti* and *viveka* (truth-remembrance and truth-discrimination). These are both, forms of intuition. The first comes to us from within, from the psychic sources of immanence, as these emerge with the purification and equality of the desires and emotions; and the second

40. SoY, p. 817.
41. RoY, pp. 16-17.

comes to us from above, as the mind becomes more and more silent and receptive to self-evident cosmic or supramental knowledge by identity of the One. The heart and the mind become channels for these intuitions. We see, as in a flash, what is pre-existent, and how things are to be done; what is to be given a certain importance, what else is to be included, what is to be avoided, what is to be put beside or aside. So, these form a progressive understanding of intuition, which begins at a lower level of the operation of *jñānam* through inner contact, from an inner remembrance of the oneness of things.

These two powers of intuition and discrimination complete and complement each other. Intuition without discrimination leads to visionary flashes, which remain isolated or incoherent, a condition well known in the history of mysticism, and characterising all the "mad" prophets and mystics. There are even traditions that glorify such visionary incoherence as the mark of authenticity in mysticism. However, the development of intuitive discrimination helps to stabilise this power, relating the intuitions to each other and to wider idea-forces or bodies of understanding, so as to arrive at harmonious or synthetic visions and judgements. Discrimination by itself, on its part, can help to order, what is already known, but does not advance the field of knowledge with new and original insights. Here is, where it rests on the visionary intuition or intuitive memory to complement it.[42]

Dṛṣṭi and Śruti: The Higher Doublet of Cognition

The higher doublet of the *jñānam* of cognition are *dṛṣṭi* and *śruti*, the faculties, respectively, of revelation and inspiration, or truth-seeing and truth-hearing.[43] This requires, not merely an operation within the mind through inner contact, but also

42. SoY, p. 816.
43. Ibid., pp. 816-17; RoY, pp. 17, 1472-73.

rising to a power of knowledge beyond thought, where truth represents itself in visionary and vibratory realities. One directly sees — *pratyakṣa* — as non-dual *darśana* of the truth,[44] or one receives in the hearing, the original Word or vibration, the *oṁkāra,* that pervades the universe and modulates itself into the inner structure of all ideas and forms and travels on the wings or progressions of world rhythms (*chandas*).[45] *Dṛṣṭi* and *śruti* imply the existence of faculties of divine representation, by which the One becomes manifest to itself in varied sensible form. They are, thus, aspects of *saṁjñāna*. Existing impersonally as powers of cosmic mind and supermind, these divine faculties have entered into the fragmentation of the ignorance as instruments of indirect knowledge. But, if our seeing and hearing, our eyes and ears, were to resist nature's outward pull and open to their inner potential, this could initiate a progression where, tuned to a cosmic key, these visionary and auditory capacities could rise beyond thought to realms of revelation and inspiration. Sri Aurobindo writes that the lower doublet and higher doublet of intuitive knowledge must work together. They are all necessary in establishing the *jñānam* in us. In the chapter "The Gradations of the Supermind" in *The Synthesis of Yoga,* Sri Aurobindo writes how these two doublets are related, how they can operate together, and why they are necessary to each other: "The two higher powers in the same way make a higher intuitive gnosis."[46] This implies a progress in knowledge arriving at a higher working. With the disciplining of the faculties of knowledge, as we replace our normal operations of knowledge by these intuitive operations, it is as if "new organs" form in us. Gradually, these become the normal ways of knowing for us, and we can replace by them our expected

44. SoY, pp. 832-33.
45. Ibid., pp. 836-37.
46. Ibid., p. 816.

modes of reasoning — inference, deduction, induction, analysis that were natural to us. So, as he writes, these "two higher powers in the same way make a higher intuitive gnosis. Acting as separate powers in the mentality, they too are not, in themselves, sufficient without the companion activities."[47] (By the companion activities is meant, the doublet of *smṛti* and the *viveka*.) "The revelation may indeed present the reality, the identity of the thing in itself and add something of great power to the experience of the conscious being,"[48] — because the basis of this revelation or *dṛṣṭi* is a knowledge by identity, not only is it "seen" or envisioned, but experienced as Self. It's experience is both, objective as well as subjective.

> but it may lack the embodying word, the outbringing idea, the connected pursuit of its relations and consequences and may remain a possession in the self, but not a thing communicated to and through the members.[49]

In other words, one may have this visionary experience in identity but without the *śruti*, the *viveka* and the *smṛti*, one is unable to understand it, or turn it to something practical in one's life. This is why, the higher faculties of knowledge need each other and the lower doublet to make them effective. These are all needed for perfection of expression, since these are the manifesting powers of knowledge.

> There may be the presence of the truth, but not its full manifestation. The inspiration may give the word of the truth and the stir of its dynamis and movement, but this is not a complete thing and sure in its effect without the full revelation of all that it bears in itself and luminously indicates and the ordering of it in its relations.[50]

---

47. SoY, p. 816.
48. Ibid.
49. Ibid.
50. Ibid., pp. 816-17.

"Ordering of it in its relations" refers to *viveka*, and revelation refers to *dṛṣṭi*. Thus, Sri Aurobindo here gives us the example of the operation of *śruti* aided by *viveka* and *dṛṣṭi*. In fact, one may view all of Sri Aurobindo's own writing as *śruti*, since he explains *śruti* as a form of *mantra*. He explains this, not only as what one receives from above as truth-audition, but also what one receives from the word of experience — the writing of the seer, which has received its power through truth-audience and can express experience of truth.

We see him writing here of the "stir of its dynamis and movement".[51] This phrase can be thought of as the English translation of the Sanskrit term *dhvani* which means vibrational power, the character of the *mantra*.[52] The vibrational character of the *mantra* is that, which extends the subjective quality of experience in the expression. When someone, who has experienced something speaks of it, you receive not merely the mental understanding, but some power of subjective experience with it. This power of experience is received subliminally through tone and vibration, and it makes the words alive in one's experience. In such cases, one often realises that though one lacked the ability to understand cognitively, one understands perfectly well. This understanding has been carried by the power of *śruti*. Sri Aurobindo points out that this is one form of experiential knowledge, but this form of knowledge becomes even more prominent and realised, when the experience it extends is so integral that we hear it, know it and see it in itself and its relations. It is our normal sense experience, our *pratyakṣa dṛṣṭi*, our *darśana*. This is why *śruti* and *dṛṣṭi* must lean on one another. At the same time, for it to become active and manifest in our lives, we need *smṛti* and *viveka*, particularly *viveka*, which gives

51. SoY, p. 816.
52. Ibid., p. 879.

the sense of relations; as he says, "to the ordering of it in its relations".

He continues:

> The inspired intuitive mind is a mind of lightnings, lighting up many things that were dark. But the light needs to be canalised and fixed into a stream of steady lustres that will be a constant power for lucidly ordered knowledge. The higher gnosis by itself, in its two soul powers, would be a mind of spiritual splendours, living too much in its own separate domain, producing perhaps invisibly its effect on the outside world but lacking the link of a more close and ordinary communication with its more normal movements, that is provided by the lower ideative action.[53]

This is why, we find that in the writings of Sri Aurobindo himself, there is such a clarity of rational content. It seems as if it is rationally organised, but one also senses the light of gnosis shining through that rationality in its coherence and integrality, and its suggestive visionary and vibrational power. That is, how it turns experience into expression. "It is the united, or else the fused and unified action of the four powers that makes the complete and fully armed and equipped intuitive gnosis."[54] This is the *jñānam* of the *vijñāna catuṣṭaya*.

In concluding this section, we may note that Einstein, one of the greatest scientists, relied heavily on his intuition, and proposed that the scientific method be revised so as to make hypothesis formation dependent not upon the intellect but on intuition. This proposal, of course, was not taken seriously by the scientific community.[55]

---

53. SoY, p. 817.
54. Ibid., p. 817.
55. For Einstein on intuition, see William Hermanns, *Einstein and the Poet: In Search of the Cosmic Man*, Branden Books, 1983, pp. 70, 94, 103, 109, 138.

Knowledge of Time

The next *siddhi* of *vijñāna,* enumerated by Sri Aurobindo, is *trikāladṛṣṭi,* which he translates as the "triple time vision". This is an esoteric and paranormal power. It includes the power of prophecy and also of cosmic memory, both backward and forward in time. In terms of the reversal of time's arrow, it implies the direct knowledge of the past. In other words, one could know the past by experience as if living it, not indirectly by reading about it or being told about it or even remembering it as mental memory-image of something experienced at another time and place. We touched on this nature of memory experience in the section on the Intuitive Mind. There we saw that *smṛti,* intuition as memory supports *śruti* and *dṛṣṭi,* intuition as direct transcendental perception. *Trikāladṛṣṭi* may be thought of as the origin of such transcendental perception, where a faculty of infinite consciousness is directly cognisant of all becoming. Such a limit condition of temporality, where all time becomes spatialised, is transcendental, and exceeds the expectations of our human modality of experience, which is finite. The attempt at such an experience, pulls us out of the becoming into the homogeneity of pure Being. To arrive at an experience of co-extensive Being and Becoming, the simultaneous grasp of the river of time as noumenon and phenomenon, perception of the three times and spontaneous lived experience, one must form a "new organ" of consciousness, different in kind from our present organisation. This is supermind.

However, in approaching this new formation, the extension of our time experience is possible through the becoming itself, in a dimension, which is not transcendental but immanent. This approach is privileged by Henri Bergson and following him, Gilles Deleuze, through the intuition of duration. In thinking about the experience of time, Henri Bergson has noted that indeed, all the past is present in every present object.

This continuing presence and continuous passage of time is what he calls duration. Gilles Deleuze points to this in his discussion of Bergson's methodical use of intuition. It is due to the continuing duration of time that one can intuit, that is, directly apprehend the past and the future in the present, for the sum total of developing realities in the present comprise the virtual space of the future.[56] It is the extension of this intuition that Sri Aurobindo seeks, a conscious identity with the body of time. The Bergsonian intuition of Deleuze bears comparison in its extended possibility in this quote from Sri Aurobindo:

> If we could be aware of all the present, all the action of physical, vital, mental energies at work in the moment, it is conceivable that we would be able to see their past too involved in them and their latent future or at least to proceed from present to past and future knowledge. And, under certain conditions, this might create a sense of real and ever-present time continuity, a living in the behind and the front as well as the immediate, and a step farther might carry us into an ever-present sense of our existence in infinite time and in our timeless self, and its manifestation in eternal time might then become real to us and also we might feel the timeless Self behind the worlds and the reality of his eternal world manifestation. In any case, the possibility of another kind of time consciousness than we have at present and of a triple time knowledge, rests upon the possibility of developing another consciousness than that proper to the physical mind and sense and breaking our imprisonment in the moment and in the mind of ignorance with its limitation to sensation, memory, inference and conjecture.[57]

---

56. Gilles Deleuze, Chapter II "Duration as Immediate Datum", *Bergsonism*, tr. Hugh Tomlinson and Barbara Habberjam, New York: Zone Books, 1991, pp. 37-49.

57. SoY, p. 890.

Duration, the continuous river of becoming, in which all time is present in every present, may be intuited by a concentration on cosmic process in all instances. But immanence (the space of virtuality) may also have many strata (planes, plateaus), in which time may be intuited in different degrees of cohesion or wholeness. The co-existence of all time, though ever present, is accessible in its wholeness (integrality), once again only in the consciousness of supermind. In Deleuzian terms, one may think of this as the superfold which grants the subjective access of superman. In Sri Aurobindo's experiments with *trikāladr̥ṣṭi* in the *Record of Yoga*, it is both immanent and transcendental experiences of time-knowledge that he deploys, as approaches towards a supramental consciousness.

Experiences of *trikāladr̥ṣṭi* may also be fruitfully studied in the life of Mirra Alfassa, the collaborator of Sri Aurobindo, whom he designated as the Mother. We read of certain experiences in the Mother's childhood, as related by her in The *Agenda*, which are significant in this regard. In the Mother's telling, when she was a child, people would give her history books; and as she would read its descriptions, she would also relive them, see their events happening as if before her in real time. Further, her living experience of the events would often be different from their descriptions in the books. Yet, the lived experiences carried such self-evident power, that she could judge the written texts to be factually inaccurate based on these experiences. She also mentions that she realised, only later, that this was not common human experience. She believed that this was how all people experienced history — by reliving in reality the events written about.[58]

This is an example of acquiring the direct knowledge of the past by immanent intuition or identity (duration). In its origin, this is a power natural to *vijñāna* or Supermind, by

58. Georges van Vrekhem, *The Mother: The Story of her Life*, New Delhi: Rupa & Co, 2007, p. 12.

dint of time being its subjective ontology — we could call it poetically, the owner of the house of undivided time, through whose rooms it could range at will, experiencing its events with the immediacy and intimacy of identity.

Bridging Time and Eternity

Trikāladṛṣṭi is phenomenal knowledge by identity of past, present and future, an intrinsic property of Supermind. This is because Supermind is the Eternal Being who knows itself dynamically as time. The coexistence of Eternity and Time is a paradox to our minds, because time is constrained by beginnings, middles and ends. Eternity, on the other hand, is beginningless and endless. How are we to reconcile these? As we are constituted, it seems impossible to contemplate, because we are entirely subject to the stream of time. In drawing back mentally from phenomena, we may experience an aspect of our consciousness that escapes from this stream and knows eternity. But, how do we relate the two? It is a similar problem as that of relating the One and the Many. We can only relate the two, if we think about the stream of time as co-extensive with a beginningless and endless eternity, a dynamic self-conception of the infinite. Any self-conception of infinity must itself be infinite. Yet, it may order its infinity through an Idea. Such an idea organises events in relative causal structures with infinite possibilities of beginnings, middles and ends, each of which can be encompassed in its totality as a single time-unit, and at the same time as infinitely fractionated instants of time.

This leads to the notion of the cycles of time in Indic cosmology. Such a Real Idea in Supermind can encompass the eternal emergence and manifestation of the infinite potentia of conscious Being, *sat* out of its own self-negation, *asat* as an evolution towards cosmic embodiment and further cosmic self-creation. Indeed, if this is the case, then in the knowledge of its own progress, of its own distributed sequences, there must be stages of time-experience, moving from a state of unmanifest timelessness and spacelessness to a level, where time is a property of space — in other words, in some Divine Mind, some level of Supermind, all virtualities of Becoming are held in the Eternal Presence of the unfathomable time-unit, an infinite memory in which everything that has happened, is happening and will happen, lives. At another level, the immanence of becoming, there would be the deployment of a creative consciousness actualising the potentia that are yet to manifest. This creative power is not entirely alien to us since creativity is a property of the human. When humans deploy the power of creativity — when one writes a great poem, or produces music, for example, there is a sense of expansion, as of a vast background of possibilities from which an instantaneous seeing selects the inevitable word relating to an ordering intuition within the subjective dictates of the context. There is the sense of picking a pre-arranged sequence of objects from an infinite archive. There is an ordering that is already inevitable and implicit in the making of such selections in real time. This is the way in which eternity and time are bridged by Supermind, and the knowledge of the three times is related to phenomenal experience.[59]

Purification of the Sense Mind

A beginning approach to such experiences could come, as we have discussed earlier, through the purification of the *manas*, what Sri Aurobindo calls the sixth sense, the consciousness of the sense-mind.[60] In dealing with mental apprehension, we saw that a subconscient mentality (*citta*) pervades all matter and records traces of all phenomenal impressions, which can be accessed by the sense-mind (*manas*) through direct inner

59. SoY, pp. 885-86.

60. Ibid., p. 864.

contact. Similarly, the sense-mind or sixth sense can contact mental impressions of phenomena remote in space and time, even from the present or the near future. Events to come precipitate their images as possibilities in a subtle physical medium and the sense-mind may develop the capacity to receive these images subliminally. The sense-mind or sixth sense can use any of the senses as its instrument to receive these impressions, leading to the phenomena of clairvoyance or clairaudience, or it may operate directly through an inner mental sentience translating itself telepathically into knowledge. The development of such an ability through the inner possibilities of the senses and the sense-mind is one approach towards the growth of the triple time vision (*trikāladr̥ṣṭi*) as a *siddhi* of *vijñāna*.[61]

As with the past, our normal experience of the present is also largely indirect. As pointed out by Kant, even our experience of the present is a subjective translation of reality, not reality itself. Moreover, our experience of the present is localised in space as defined by our physical existence and we cannot normally know what is remote to this physical location except indirectly, through extensions of our senses by magnifying or telecommunicative instruments. A direct knowledge by identity of events, both experienced in the body and remotely, would be the fullness of our knowledge of the present. But, this too must start with an intuitive grasp through the inner subliminal mind or sense mind extending itself in identification with its objects of immediate experience and also extending itself remotely.

The development of the sixth sense in its fullness yields a direct power of sight, hearing, touch, smell and taste and a direct sensing though the essence of sense is not dependent on one's physical organs or one's location in space. It is an

61. SoY, p. 864.

immanent intuitive method, similar to Bergson or Deleuze's seeking for duration. This approach is also referred to by Patañjali, in what is known as the Vibhūti Pada (Chapter 3) of

Vijñāna Catuṣṭaya (Perfection of Knowledge) (4.2)
Trikāladṛṣṭi

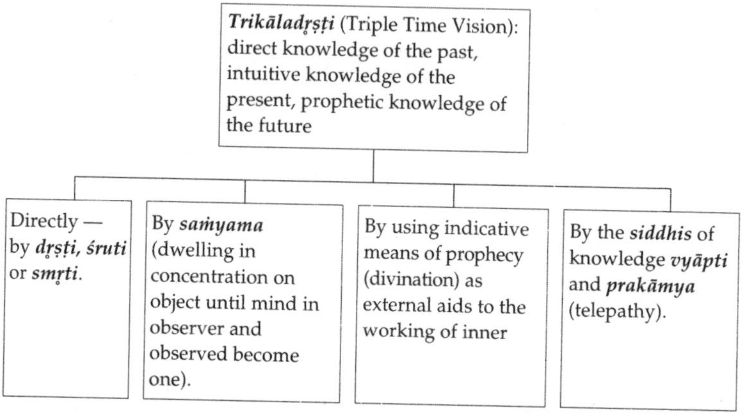
Trikāladṛṣṭi (Triple Time Vision): direct knowledge of the past, intuitive knowledge of the present, prophetic knowledge of the future
Directly — by dṛṣṭi, śruti or smṛti.
By saṁyama (dwelling in concentration on object until mind in observer and observed become one).
By using indicative means of prophecy (divination) as external aids to the working of inner
By the siddhis of knowledge vyāpti and prakāmya (telepathy).

the *Yoga-Sūtras*.[62] In this chapter, Patañjali refers to a substratum in which latent (past), active (present) and unmanifest (future) impressions are contained.[63] This substratum is present in all objects and qualities. Earlier in the chapter, Patañjali refers to *saṁyama*, an exclusive and intense concentration, through which the mind in the observer becomes one with the mind in the observed.[64] Such a *saṁyama* brings the mind into contact with the substratum (*dharmī*), thereby yielding its sedimented knowledge of process, a subjective archaeology.[65] This relates to the action of the purified sense-mind on the subconscient mentality (*citta*)

62. Patañjali's *Yoga-Sūtras*, III: pp. 1-6, 14-16.
63. Ibid., III: p. 14.
64. Patañjali's, op. cit., III: pp. 1-6; See, for example, RoY, pp. 81, 196, 207, 231, 316, 402, 594.
65. Patañjali, op. cit., III: pp. 14-16.

present in all things, discussed earlier. *Citta* is the latent or subconscient presence of mind in all things, what is referred to as the substratum (*dharmī*) in the third *pada* of the *Yoga-Sūtras*. The presence of mentality in matter, evokes immanent ideas ordering the possibilities of actualisation. However, instead of thinking of these as transcendental Platonic ideas, of which material objects are only more or less bad copies, we are concerned more with an empirical mental contact with embodied and evolving ideas.[66] If we dwell on this, we come into contact with the mental impress of the object's history, an inner intuition of what it is. This form of knowledge can be obtained from objects, not merely in the present. The intuition of *saṁyama* can also yield knowledge of objects in the past and in the future. Therefore, this kind of concentration can give us access to knowledge of past, present and future in particular beings, events and objects, though with a lower level of certitude than that of the Supramental knowledge by identity, but one which is derived from and leads towards the supramental time vision (*trikāladṛṣṭi*) obtained by the supramental *saṁjñāna*.

This supramental *saṁjñāna*, which has specialised itself as sense in mind, would receive everywhere and in all things, the delight of the infinite in sense contact and extend itself infinitely. Sri Aurobindo refers to this operation thus:

> The supramental sense can act in its own power and is independent of the body and the physical life and outer mind and it is above too the inner mind and its experiences. It can be aware of all things in whatever world, on whatever plane, in whatever formation of universal consciousness. It can be aware of the things of the material universe even in the trance of *samādhi*, aware of them as they are, or appear to the physical sense, even as it is of other states of experience,

66. See Deleuze's treatment of the Platonic Idea in Gilles Deleuze, *The Logic of Sense*, Continuum, London, 2004, p. 65.

> of the pure vital, the mental, the psychical, the supramental presentation of things. It can, in the waking state of the physical consciousness, present to us the things concealed from the limited receptivity or beyond the range of the physical organs, distant forms, scenes and happenings, things that have passed out of physical existence or that are not yet in physical existence, scenes, forms, happenings, symbols of the vital, psychical, mental, supramental, spiritual worlds and all these in their real or significant truth as well as their appearance. It can use all the other states of sense consciousness and their appropriate senses and organs adding to them what they have not, setting right their errors and supplying their deficiencies: for it is the source of the others and they are only inferior derivations from this higher sense, this true and illimitable *saṁjñāna*.[67]

Similarly, in approaching prophetic knowledge of the future, one may make use of indirect tools of divination for starting approaches, but use these as channels through which the *manas* or higher mental perceptions and intuitions may contact the images of the future.[68] The awakening or active awareness of the subliminal subjective consciousness also brings intuitions of events past or future through images, sounds, symbolic transcriptions or other experiences. From all such intuitive means, one may progress towards the truth-vision and truth-audition discussed earlier, which are powers of knowledge proper to *saṁjñāna* of supermind and carry the certitude of truth in the experience of the future. Such forms of knowledge tend in their advanced condition, to become increasingly experiences of identity in being. Sri Aurobindo's diaries are replete with many interesting examples of his development of this power of *trikāladṛṣṭi*, with and without the use of various external divinatory devices and/or symbolic images or sounds,

---

67. SoY, p. 867.
68. Ibid., pp. 892-94.

expressed through means such as "sky-writing" (*lipi, ākāśa lipi*), astral imagery (*dṛṣṭi, rūpa, chāyā, citra*) or paranormal hearing (*vāṇī*).[69]

The *Record of Yoga* is full of experiments that Sri Aurobindo conducted in *trikāladṛṣṭi*, using a number of these methods. He received certain kinds of time-knowledge directly, some by means of *saṁyama*, some by divination and some by exteriorised sensory representation. To develop and test these means, he conducted many experiments on animals and humans in his neighbourhood — the flight of crows, the flitting of butterflies, the movement of ants.[70] For example, he observed butterflies moving from plant to plant, and attempted to predict their movements.[71] He recorded his intuition and then the actual result. These experiments were conducted with the impersonality of a scientist — recording faithfully instances of success, failure and partial success.

Other Means Towards Trikāladṛṣṭi

We have discussed a progression in the formation of this power of time-knowledge. The supramental aspect of this knowledge is accessible through forms of knowledge by identity. We have touched on these forms of direct knowledge as *dṛṣṭi, smṛti* or *śruti*. We have discussed the use of *manas* and the practice of *saṁyama* as intuitional approaches to this knowledge. We have also touched on the use of indicative means of prophecy as external aids to the working of inner knowledge faculties. These include the various kinds of divination that we are familiar with — astrology, numerology,

---

69. SoY, pp. 893-96; Examples abound in the Record. See for example, RoY, pp. 54-55.
70. Eg. RoY, p. 72.
71. RoY, p. 133. See also the psychological note of RoY, pp. 1283-84, where the mental movements of a butterfly are predicted using mind contact.

etc. Sri Aurobindo frequently utilises something he calls sortilege. Sortilege is the random opening of the pages of a book — one concentrates and opens the pages randomly, and allows one's eyes to fall on a passage. This is taken to be a message relating to a specific question whose answer one is seeking.[72] Another means for developing *trikāladṛṣṭi*, which Sri Aurobindo indicates, leads us to the *siddhi*s of knowledge, *vyāpti* and *prakāmya*, which together constitute the paranormal power of telepathy. Though these are also used as predictive capacities, they belong more properly to the next major property of the quartet of knowledge — what is known as the eight occult powers (*aṣṭa-siddhi*).

Siddhis: Justification, Dangers and Use

In his notes on *vijñāna catuṣṭaya*, Sri Aurobindo begins with a section titled "Siddhis, Their Justification, Dangers and Use". At the start of this section, he introduces the paranormal aspect of the goals of this quartet and that of the body (*śarīra catuṣṭaya*), in terms of what is different and controversial in this from the goals of the other quartets. He begins:

> The two first *catuṣṭaya*s of the *ādhāra* have reference mainly to the central principle of man's existence, the *antaḥkaraṇa*; but there is one superior faculty and one inferior instrument which have each its peculiar *siddhi*, the *vijñāna* or supraintellectual faculty and the body. The *siddhi* of the *vijñāna* and the *siddhi* of the body belong both of them to that range of experience and of divine fulfilment which are abnormal to the present state of humanity. These are called specially *siddhi*s, because of their abnormal nature [,] rarity and difficulty; they are denied by the sceptic and discouraged by the saint. The sceptic disbelieves in them

72. The *Record of Yoga* has too many instances of sortilege for all to be enumerated here. Some examples are RoY, pp. 44, 71, 78, 1285-87, 1311.

Vijñāna Catuṣṭaya (Perfection of Knowledge) (4.3)
Aṣṭa-siddhi

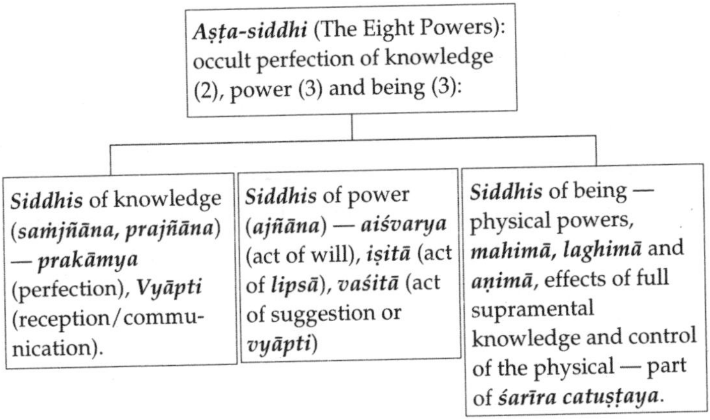
Aṣṭa-siddhi (The Eight Powers): occult perfection of knowledge (2), power (3) and being (3):
Siddhis of knowledge (*saṁjñāna, prajñāna*) — *prakāmya* (perfection), *Vyāpti* (reception/communication).
Siddhis of power (*ajñāna*) — *aiśvarya* (act of will), *iṣitā* (act of *lipsā*), *vaśitā* (act of suggestion or *vyāpti*)
Siddhis of being — physical powers, *mahimā, laghimā* and *aṇimā*, effects of full supramental knowledge and control of the physical — part of *śarīra catuṣṭaya*.

> and holds them to be impostures, fables or hallucinations, as a clever animal might disbelieve in the reasoning powers of man. The saint discourages them because they seem to him to lead away from God; he shuns them just as he shuns the riches, power and attainments of this world, and for the same reason.[73]

But, since the goals of integral transformation take in an activity more natural to an integral being, the development of powers, now underdeveloped or in their latency in normal human functioning, and their creative utilisation as part of the instrumentation of a divine Śakti, is within the scope of Integral Yoga. The development and expression of paranormal powers is not uncommon in Tantra, and this aspect of the seven quartets can be thought of, in consonance with the tāntric goals of enhanced potency. From the perspective of the rethinking of human being and becoming in modern times, this is also in consonance with the Nietzschean project of supermanhood,

---

73. RoY, p. 14.

understood in the Olympian sense of a universalised ontology and potency. Power is ubiquitous to human functioning and a world-affirming yoga has perforce to deal with the hierarchy of power which structures an interdependent (and co-dependent) worldly existence. In this, it is the vision and consciousness using power which is critical in determining the objectives of world becoming, within which such a deployment is operational.

One must remember, as touched on in the introductory chapter of this text, that Sri Aurobindo's interest in yoga was initiated by the possibility of the enhancement and extension of the power of consciousness to aid the struggle for national independence. In an age of world-dominating technology and the mechanisation of man, human power becomes the last bastion for protection and action against powers of oppression and social conditioning, which saturate the global psycho-sphere, and can find easy actualisation. When Sri Aurobindo was experimenting with these powers, the Age of Colonialism was still at its height and the powers of chauvinistic nationalism were in the ascendant and staking their claim in the first global war of planet earth. Sri Aurobindo's diary entries, testing the steps of the development of these powers, include those of remote sensing and action pertaining to two main domains — the immediate environment of domestic activities and urban nature; and the shifting international political theatres of First World War. On 15 December 1912, we find Sri Aurobindo recording his conviction regarding the truth and extent of operation of these powers:

> The truth of telepathy is now thoroughly established; the proofs of its correctness when received from persons in the house or town [occur] daily, as by it I know when one is coming from one room to another, what an animal is about to do, when someone is returning to the house and often who it is. . . . Also the proofs of it, when it comes

> from hundreds or thousands of miles away, are now coming in. . . .[74]

It is again these powers that he claimed to have utilised in Second World War.

As part of the diary entry of 29 November 1912, we find an example of predictive *trikāladṛṣṭi* intuition related to the politics of First World War:

> For some days there have been continual proofs of *vyāpti prakāmya* e.g., the presence of an Austrian warship at Durazzo, the rumour of the Austrian consul being killed, etc. Yesterday, there came in the mind the positive idea that Turkey had asked to be included in the Balkan Confederacy; today the same is given (in yesterday's evening paper reaching here this morning), as a strange piece of news from Constantinople and Sofia. This is striking as there was neither data nor probability and the knowledge, of the fact or rumour, came suddenly without previous thinking in that direction.[75]

The Eight Occult Powers (Aṣṭa-siddhi)

There are a number of traditions in written and oral yogic traditions pertaining to eight occult powers, *aṣṭa-siddhi*. Sri Aurobindo's enumeration of these eight powers coincides with several from one of the most common of these lists, but some are different and even the coincident ones assume meanings variant from their traditional interpretations.[76] Though these "eight powers" belong to the *vijñāna catuṣṭaya,* we must understand that Knowledge is ubiquitous — it is not merely cognitive knowledge, as we commonly understand it, it includes knowledge of the senses, feelings, actions, even

---

74. RoY, pp. 149-50.

75. Ibid., p. 120.

76. The traditional enumeration closest to Sri Aurobindo's lists *aṇimā, mahimā, garimā, laghimā, prapti, prakāmya, isiśita* and *vaśita*.

Vijñāna Catuṣṭaya (Perfection of Knowledge) (4.4)
***Aṣṭa-siddhi* (The Eight Powers):**
*Siddhi*s of knowledge (*saṁjñāna, prajñāna*)

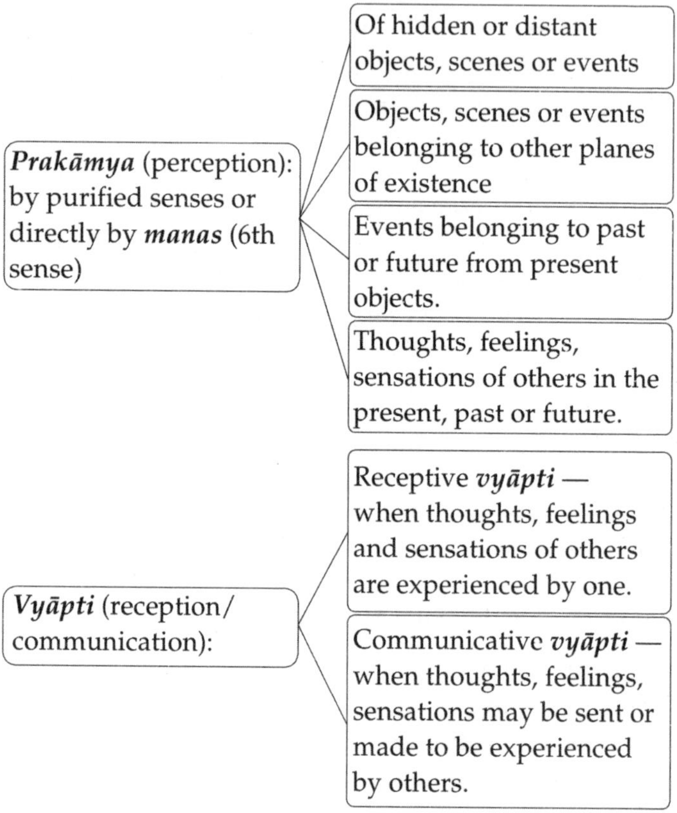

Prakāmya (perception): by purified senses or directly by *manas* (6th sense)
Of hidden or distant objects, scenes or events
Objects, scenes or events belonging to other planes of existence
Events belonging to past or future from present objects.
Thoughts, feelings, sensations of others in the present, past or future.
Vyāpti (reception/ communication):
Receptive *vyāpti* — when thoughts, feelings and sensations of others are experienced by one.
Communicative *vyāpti* — when thoughts, feelings, sensations may be sent or made to be experienced by others.

knowledge of the body. So, under *aṣṭa-siddhi,* Sri Aurobindo classes two perfections of knowledge as cognition, three perfections of power, or knowledge as will, and three perfections of being, or ontic knowledge. The *siddhi*s of knowledge as cognition relate to *saṁjñāna* and *prajñāna,* introduced at the beginning of this chapter; they are the two *siddhi*s of remote knowing and telepathy and are termed *prakāmya,* and *vyāpti.*[77]

---

77. RoY, pp. 19-20.

The Powers of Knowledge

These two powers of remote knowledge and telepathy, *prakāmya* and *vyāpti*, occupy a very important place in Sri Aurobindo's own experiments. In traditional nomenclature, the two *siddhis* that come closest to these and may be considered powers of remote-sensing are *prakāmya* and *prāpti*, though *prāpti* is usually thought of as a *siddhi* of power rather than of knowledge. *Prakāmya* implies hidden or remote perception by the concentration of the intellect (*buddhi*), purified senses or directly by the *manas*, which is the sixth sense. We may recollect here the earlier discussion on Blake, regarding the purification of the doors of perception. The sixth sense is the synaesthetic sense in us, it is the sense behind the five senses. Thus, it is the power of this sixth sense that perceives things directly with an essence of sense or represents perception interchangeably in terms of any of the senses. The reason that experiences of synaesthesia are possible, why for example, in experiments with hallucinogens, people have been able to smell colours, taste lights, etc. is because this aspect of the *manas* became activated independently. But the *manas* can also come to the front of the sensory system and be the master of the all the five senses. If this happens, one can sense without using the normal senses: a blind man can bypass the eyes and see, for example. This is also part of the progression of *prakāmya*. Through its development, we start receiving perceptions of hidden or distant objects, scenes or events — or those belonging to other planes of existence, or events belonging to the past or future from present objects, as we discussed under *trikāladr̥ṣṭi*. This also includes the telepathic power to perceive thoughts, feelings and sensations of others in the present, past or future through mental concentration. We find these powers also included by Patañjali under this discussion of *saṁyama* in the Vibhūti Pada of the *Yoga-Sūtras*.[78]

78. Patañjali, op. cit., III: pp. 19, 26-29.

Thus, *prakāmya* can be thought of as extrasensory perception through active or willed mental contact using *manas* or *buddhi*. Sri Aurobindo describes it thus:

> *Prakāmya* is when you look mentally or physically at somebody or something and perceive what is in that person or thing, thoughts, feelings, facts about them, etc. There is also another kind of *prakāmya* which is not of the mind but of the senses. It is the power of perceiving smells, sounds, contacts, tastes, lights, colours and other objects of sense which are either not at all perceptible to ordinary men or beyond the range of your ordinary senses.[79]

This is the wide scope of *prakāmya* as an aspect of the eight powers but also of the *trikāladr̥ṣṭi* because Sri Aurobindo points to this as the fourth way by which *trikāladr̥ṣṭi* opens; he also sometimes clubs these two powers of remote knowledge under *trikāladr̥ṣṭi* in his diary entries.

The other *siddhi* of knowledge is *vyāpti. Vyāpti* can be receptive or communicative and works *in tandem* with *prakāmya*. Receptive *vyāpti* is when thoughts, feelings and sensations of others are experienced by ourselves. Whereas *prakāmya* has to do with perception, *vyāpti* has to do with reception. In Sri Aurobindo's words, "*Prakāmya* is the sight of one looking from a distance and seeing an object; *vyāpti* is the sensation of that object coming towards us or into contact with us."[80] Sri Aurobindo gives the example of Ramakrishna, who once exclaimed that he felt the whips of a bullock driver on his body. Outside, indeed, there was a driver whipping his bullock and, without knowing it, Ramakrishna, identified in a part of his consciousness with the bullock, was experiencing its lashes. The experience of stigmata by Christian mystics can also be taken as an example. In mystic literature

---

79. RoY, p. 1474.
80. Ibid., p. 20.

of all traditions, there have been records of those who have had this kind of transference of physical or emotional experience of others, often without even knowing who they were. More common are thoughts from others, which are received, often unknowingly, by all human beings. This kind of power is the receptive aspect of *vyāpti*. It is a way of expanding one's sympathy or mental consciousness and bringing it into contact with the universal consciousness. The other aspect is communicative *vyāpti*. This operates in the reverse direction, where thoughts, feelings and sensations may be sent out or made to be experienced by others.

Vyāpti literally means pervasion and refers to the receptive or communicative pervasion of one's field of consciousness. Like *prakāmya*, which involves a willed or selective process of perception, *vyāpti* may also proceed by a tuning of the receptivity or the intent to the object of knowledge or communication; but it may also operate in a generalised form, bringing a rush of thoughts and experiences which one suffers (or enjoys) as one's own. Thus, without an inner freedom (*mukti*) from thoughts and feelings and the development of the intuitive discrimination (*viveka*) to choose between the true and the false, *vyāpti* can be at best an uncomfortable and at worst a deranging *siddhi* to attain. In the *Record of Yoga*, *vyāpti* is often used in tandem with *prakāmya*, the two together translating to the general paranormal power of telepathy. As illustrated under the discussion for *trikāladr̥ṣṭi*, this was one of the means Sri Aurobindo used for informing himself about near and distant persons or events of interest, as for example the First World War. Conversely, in his diary entries and conversations, he noted that he used the communicative *vyāpti* to transmit thoughts and ideas into the minds of others at a distance. Along with the *siddhis* of power, this facility was used by him to play an active part in world events. It is worth noting that Sri Aurobindo used these powers only when he felt it was critical or imperative. He also did not make any claim of invincibility for them. His diary entries show a generally high degree of success in predictive phenomena but more mixed results in cases of determining events through the powers of will.

The Powers of Will

The *siddhi*s of remote power relate to *ājñāna*, or knowledge by will. These are *aiśvarya* or the action of will, *iśitā* or the action of *lipsā* (which we introduced while discussing *cāturvarṇya* in the *śakti catuṣṭaya* as a kind of desireless tendency or aspiration), and *vaśitā* which is the action of suggestion or *vyāpti*.[81] In the traditional system, two of these *siddhi*s of will are mentioned — *iśitā* and *vaśitā*; but Sri Aurobindo introduces a third modality of remote volition — *aiśvarya*, though he sometimes clubs all these powers of the will under *tapas*.[82] In Sri Aurobindo's classification, *aiśvarya* can be thought of as a power of mental will, *iśitā* of emotional will and *vaśitā* of the essence of will. Action of the mental will, *aiśvarya*, implies that one possesses a knowledge of things or beings around one, so that one can make them will something. This action of will can occur at such an independent level of being that it bypasses the thinking mind, one doesn't think it, one directly does it, the knowledge is implicit in the will — an invincible knowledge-will that carries out exactly what it wants in one's surroundings or in the world.[83] This is also a perfection which comes through identity with the One, the assumption of the power of the One over its constituents through identity — this is the root of *aiśvarya* as an action of will. It is by *aiśvarya* that one individual can hope to transform the entire world, because if s/he knows his/her true absolute oneness in will, s/he can wield the power of oneness and make everything

81. RoY, pp. 20-21.

82. See, for example, RoY, p. 229.

83. RoY, p. 21.

experience that oneness. Sri Aurobindo has a line in his epic *Savitri* — "One man's perfection still can save the world."[84] Of course, this is easier said than done, but that is the ultimate perfection of *aiśvarya* in Supermind.

Iśitā as an action of *lipsā*, is more subtle than *aiśvarya* and it has to do with reception rather than direction. By *iśitā*, Sri Aurobindo implies that, if there is a pure emotional desire or aspiration, it will be brought to one by this power. This is also an act of will, at a subtle level of willing. Sri Aurobindo indicates that all human beings utilise this power unconsciously to some extent. At a certain level, *iśitā* can be thought of as a power of concentrated desiring, which produces the energy which magnetises its object of desire. Much of what is known in esoteric traditions as "magic", consists in exercises meant to focus and amplify such an energy of desiring. Methods, such as visualisation, are other examples of *iśitā* at this basic level of operation.[85]

At a subtler level, one may think of prayer as affording a mechanism for the action of *iśitā*. In prayer, one gathers one's emotional state and invokes a higher power to help in the attainment of one's need or amelioration of one's condition. In such a process, there is a reciprocity which obtains between the devotee and the object of prayer, the deity or the divine. The prayer is "offered" to this higher presence and power, whose will is invoked in its attainment. The notion of a *lipsā* is much like a prayer which lifts its aspiration to a higher power and leaves it with confidence to the action of this power. One has transferred one's burden and thinks no more of it. But, the intensity of the faith and the offering ensure a secure transmission, so that one rests in the confidence of one's aspiration being answered in the best way that the higher

---

84. Savitri, p. 531.

85. RoY, pp. 14-15.

power decides in its greater knowledge. For this, there may be no content of words as in a conventional prayer, but a silent concentration of visionary aspiration (the Mother uses the phrase "clairvoyant aspiration" in a statement referring to this kind of action);[86] and there need be no recognisable deity, but the sense of the integral Śakti, whose partial and ignorant manifestation we experience as ourselves, in our present condition.

Just as *aiśvarya* is a power of *Īśvara, iśitā* is a power of Śakti, and Śakti's operation is to bring the creatures what they need. Of course, what Śakti understands by what we need, may not be what we ourselves understand in our blindness. Śakti's understanding of creatures' needs pertains to the evolution of consciousness in the creature and the cosmos. If one is meant to develop and express something as part of its growth and experience in the world, Śakti effects the inner formations which attract the kinds of knowledge and experiences that one needs, they will come to one even if one doesn't seek them. To develop this ability in a conscious way is the perfection of *iśitā*. It implies a perfect surrender to and faith in the Divine Śakti.

Finally, there is *vaśitā* or the action of vital suggestion. Here, Sri Aurobindo describes having inner control over the natures of things so that when one speaks or transmits suggestions to them, they obey.[87] *Vyāpti*, particularly its communicative variety, which was dealt with as a cognitive *siddhi*, is a form of *vaśitā*.[88] If the *Prakṛti* of a being is identified with so perfectly that there is a sense as if speaking to or acting

86. "All those who want to collaborate for the progress of humanity and for India's luminous destiny must unite in a clairvoyant aspiration and in an illumined work." *The Mother*, CWM 13: 35.

87. RoY, p. 21.

88. Ibid.

on oneself, the control seems automatic. It obeys, not because it is an external will, but because it's a will that is felt as its own. Once again, one can see how this *siddhi* too, can only reach its perfection in Supermind, as an aspect of the *ājñāna* of the One.

The Mother's Yoga of the Cells

Here, it is instructive to consider the Mother's Yoga of the physical, in the last phase of her life, after Sri Aurobindo's passing. In this phase, the Mother was actively working on supramentalising her body consciousness and recorded her experiences through the conversations included in her *Questions and Answers* and later, in *The Agenda*. Among these experiences, one can particularly note the action of *iśitā* and *vaśitā* (in the form of communicative *vyāpti*) working at the level of the consciousness of the cells. We find the earliest references to these experiences in her conversations of May 1954. On 5 May, she noted that the power with which she could transform circumstances in her environment, was felt to be descending into the cells of the body, so as to give the body a direct mastery over the beings and things surrounding it.[89] This seems like an experience of communicative *vyāpti* at the level of the physical consciousness. Soon after, on 19 May, she noted the decentralisation of physical consciousness at the level of the cells.[90] We have referred earlier to Gilles Deleuze's idea of deterritorialisation and the building of the body without organs. The decentralisation of consciousness experienced by the Mother, can be read as an extreme edge of such a destabilisation of constructed form. The Mother had noted even earlier that this phase was preceded by the disappearance of the mental and vital personalities and realisations. These established formations of world realisation were put aside so

89. CWM 6, pp. 123-24.

90. Ibid., p. 140.

as to experience the body consciousness in its singularity, and further decentralise even this through the levels of the consciousness of the form and the consciousness of the organs down to the radical plurality of the cells. Here, the reconstruction of a new body was attempted by seeking a direct conscious power of creative choice at this level of the unbound cells. The working of this power was attested to on 19 May as a direct and spontaneous aspiration for the Divine in the cells of the body.[91] It should be clear that the mention of the Divine here, has nothing to do with "the idea of God". Such a spontaneous aspiration, as a form of will, can be alternately read as *iśitā* working at the level of the cells.

On 16 April 1958, the Mother noted an even further degree of the decentralisation of physical consciousness, a level which might be thought of as analogous to subatomic particles in the case of material substance. This analogy is supported by the fact that the Mother's experience of cellular consciousness as a "conglomerate of vibrations", at this stage, made it possible for her to unravel living matter into its universal building-blocks.[92] The practical effects of this experience were noted by her on 7 October 1964, when she repeated her perception of physical life as made up of "conglomerates of vibrations" and extended this perception in an experience of physical ubiquity, which this universalisation afforded:

> . . . In the last few days, yesterday or the day before, there was this experience: a kind of consciousness wholly decentralised (I am speaking always of the physical consciousness, not of the higher consciousness at all), a decentralised consciousness which happened to be here, there, there, in this body, in that body (in what people call "this person" and "that person", but this notion does not exist very much any more). . . .[93]

91. CWM 6: 140
92. CWM 9: 314-15.
93. The Mother, *Notes on the Way*, CWM 16: 4.

Such an experience can certainly be thought of as *vyāpti* in its most singular action at the level of the building-blocks of living matter.

Similarly, one finds in the Mother, a continuing progression with the power of *iśitā* through the surrender and aspiration of the cells. This was experienced increasingly by her, in the form of a spontaneous *mantra* arising from the cells. From the late 1950s, there are two such *mantra*s of the cells which she recorded. One of these was the English phrase "What Thou willest".[94] The other, which became more and more constant and predominant was the Sanskrit *mantra "oṁ namo bhagavate"*. This *mantra,* arising independently in the cells, made them coherent, bringing them into a functional density as of a single compact block.[95]

Powers of Being

The remaining *siddhi*s are those of being, and are related directly to the body. In a way, one may have expected these powers to appear in the *śarīra catuṣṭaya*. But their appearance in the quartet of knowledge occurs because the body rests for the fullness of its powers on the Supermind; it is as the supramental body that it can exceed fully its material limitations, and is thus, more intimately linked to *vijñāna* than any other aspect or line of the seven quartets. The *siddhi*s of being, for Sri Aurobindo, are *aṇimā, mahimā* and *laghimā*.[96] These three are also included in the traditional *aṣṭa-siddhi,* which add a fourth power of the body, called *garimā,* the power of enhancing one's weight.

---

94. CWM 16: 168, 332.

95. Since 1958, this mantra gains increasing importance in the Mother's yoga of the cells. There are many references to this mantra and its effects in *The Agenda*. See, for example, MA, volume 9, pp. 236-37.

96. RoY, pp. 19, 22.

In the scribal notes, one finds Sri Aurobindo's description of *aṇimā, mahimā* and *laghimā*:

> *Mahimā* is unhampered force in the mental power or in the physical power. In the physical it shows itself by an abnormal strength, which is not muscular, and may even develop into the power of increasing the size and weight of the body, etc.
>
> *Laghimā* is a similar power of lightness, that is to say, of freedom from all pressure or weighing down in the mental, prāṇic or physical being. By *laghimā* it is possible to get rid of weariness and exhaustion and to overcome gravitation. It is the basis of *utthāpana*.
>
> *Aṇimā* is the power of freeing the atoms of subtle or gross matter (*sūkṣma* or *sthūla*) from their ordinary limitations. By this power one can get free of physical strain or pain or even make the body as light as one chooses. It is by this power that *yogīs* were supposed to make themselves invisible [and] invulnerable or [to] free the body from decay and death.[97]

Powers, similar to this, also appear in the Vibhūti Pada of Patañjali's *Yoga-Sūtras,* though seldom named explicitly, with the exception of *aṇimā*. They are mostly related to the exercise of *saṁyama* on a variety of objects and in specific ways. For example, verse 25 pertains to attainment of strength and magnitude as in *mahimā,* through the performance of *saṁyama* on entities which possess such properties, such as elephants; verse 40 deals with the control of a life energy, *uḍāna,* leading to lightness and the power of levitation, as in *laghimā;* verse 21 deals with making oneself invisible by *saṁyama* on one's own body, and verse 22 extends this to freedom derived from other forms of sensing, such as, hearing, touch, taste and smell. These may be related to *aṇimā,* as may be verse 41, which

97. RoY, p. 1475.

deals with radiance or efflugence. Verses 45 to 47 deal with the exercise of *saṁyama* on material elements leading to indestructibility, smallness, perfection of form, beauty, strength and hardness. This is the only verse in which one of Sri Aurobindo's *siddhis* of being is explicitly named, but in an inclusive way — *aṇimādi*, meaning "aṇimā, etc.". Sri Aurobindo's *siddhis* of being are contingent on supramental control over the laws of matter, so, properly speaking, it is only verses 45-47 in the text of Patañjali's third chapter, which are close in essence to these *siddhis* of being. However, as in the case of *trikāladṛṣṭi*, these may, very well be starting points to the development of these *siddhis* of being.

In Sri Aurobindo's *siddhis* of being, one can see that the scope of *mahimā* includes *garimā*, the power of increasing one's size or weight; but it also includes physical vitality manifesting as extraordinary strength. *Laghimā*, on the other hand, proceeds in the direction of lightness, both in vitality and in a physical anti-gravitational effect. Sri Aurobindo relates this power to *utthāpana* (levitation). Interestingly, *utthāpana* becomes one of the four goals of the quartet of the body, and is therefore, considered as a general power of the "body" over the laws of physical nature. In his diary entries, Sri Aurobindo sometimes clubs all these powers of the body under *utthāpana* and lists them under the quartet of the body. In his own description, he says of this set of the *siddhis* of *vijñāna* that "they are strictly part of the physical *siddhi*".[98] Finally, *aṇimā* seems to be the most far-reaching in its control of materiality, envisaging such phenomena, as invisibility (de/materialisation), invulnerability and immortality. It thus seems to be the essence of supramental physicality.

Ontological Identity with the States of Brahman

The fourth *siddhi* in the quartet of knowledge is *samādhi* or

98. RoY, p. 22.

absorption. In most yogas, particularly the traditional yogas of knowledge, the notion of *samādhi* as absorption into an unmanifest infinity, is largely considered the goal of yoga. The Upaniṣads speak of four *avasthā*s (states of consciousness): *jāgrat, svapna, suṣupti* and *turīya* (the waking, dreaming, dreamless sleep and unmanifest transcendental conditions) respectively.[99] *Samādhi* is supposed to pertain to the last two of these conditions — *suṣupti* and *turīya*. In both these conditions, there is an immersion in a state of unconditional freedom, where all relation to manifestation ceases. But, in the Integral Yoga, where manifestation and expression are key aspects, such forms of trance can only be

Vijñāna Catuṣṭaya (Perfection of Knowledge) (4.5)
Samādhi

Samādhi (Absorption): an aspect of ***vijñāna*** or ***prajñāna*** by entering into identification with objects or beings through a full placement of the energy of consciousness in it/them.

- ***Jāgrat*** (Waking): focusing one's consciousness on an object or being or event and seeing it in one's physical atmosphere or inner being with eyes open or eyes closed, respectively.
- ***Svapna*** (trance or sleep): part of the mind remains in waking condition and another part goes into trance, sending the record of its experiences to the waking part – utility in access to divine being or universal planes and powers.
- ***Suṣupta*** (supramental or *satcidānanda* consciousness): borders of suṣupti need to be pushed further.

99. *Māṇḍūkya Upaniṣad*, pp. 3-7.

temporary expedients.[100] Here, in its completeness, *samādhi* or absorption is an aspect of *vijñāna* or *prajñāna* acting in the different conditions of consciousness by entering into identification with objects or beings through a full placement of the energy of consciousness in it or in them. For Sri Aurobindo, this could happen in all of the four states, but particularly in the first three *avasthā*s, spoken of in the Upaniṣads: *jāgrat*, *svapna*, and *suṣupti*. Moreover, the aim being a transformed waking existence, these trance states are meant to lead to a continuum of waking consciousness, where one can pass at will from state to state without loss of consciousness at the more outer levels:

> [A]s it becomes the master of its *samādhi*, it is able to pass without any gulf of oblivion from the inner to the outer waking. Secondly, when this has been once done, what is attained in the inner state, becomes easier to acquire by the waking consciousness and to turn into the normal experience, powers, mental status of the waking life. The subtle mind which is normally eclipsed by the insistence of the physical being, becomes powerful even in the waking state, until even there the enlarging man is able to live in his several subtle bodies as well as in his physical body, to be aware of them and in them, to use their senses, faculties, powers, to dwell in possession of supraphysical truth, consciousness and experience.[101]

Jāgrat is the waking state: in other words, in our waking condition we can receive knowledge of the realities of things in the material world, with eyes open or with eyes closed, through identification with the cosmic Being in the material world. In the fullness of its *siddhi*, identification of consciousness with the aspect of *Brahman* manifest as the material world is what this implies. In the scribal notes, Sri

100. SoY, p. 519.

101. Ibid., p. 525.

Aurobindo described *jāgrat samādhi* as an experience of the waking consciousness, when "we are able to concentrate and be aware of things beyond our consciousness".[102] This may happen with eyes open, when images and other sensory impressions may be seen in one's physical atmosphere; or, seeing things in the inner being with eyes closed, but still in a waking condition. One closes one's eyes to receive images in an inner subtle space (*cittākāśa*).[103]

The second state is the so-called "dream" state (*svapna*) which pertains to a trance of the subliminal being. In meditation, one may cross the threshold of objective experience and enter into a state of inner realities, where it receives subtle sense experiences in an etheric medium, *cittākāśa*. In this condition, too, as far as the *vijñāna catuṣṭaya* is concerned, part of the mind remains in a wakeful state while another enters into trance, sending the record of its experiences to the waking part.[104] This has great utility in accessing the occult and universal planes and powers. It takes a good deal of training to enter into this condition. This is something that the Mother learned and practised from an early stage, while she was training under an occultist in Algeria. She learned at this stage, how to put her body to sleep in seven successive stages. The body would enter into sleep and a subtler body would emerge from it and enter into a trance state, but the apparently sleeping body would retain some consciousness into which the record of that trance state was transferred. She would remember it perfectly and even be able to describe it while in a state of trance.[105] This is the knowledge of *svapna samādhi*.

---

102. RoY, p. 1475.
103. Ibid., p. 1476.
104. Ibid., p. 1476; SoY, p. 525.
105. The Mother quoted in Georges van Vrekhem, *The Mother: The Story of Her Life*, New Delhi: Rupa & Co., 2007, p. 60.

Finally, we have *suṣupti*. *Suṣupti* in the normal understanding, is what is known as dreamless sleep, or it is sometimes called the sleep of trance, from which nothing returns. In Sri Aurobindo's interpretation of this, a trance from which nothing may be brought back does not really exist. It is only a limitation of consciousness. Since Being is infinite, there will always be a point where we will fall into a trance of unknowing, where consciousness falls to sleep in a swoon of luminous ecstasy. But, with practice the link with the waking consciousness can be made to persist, pushing further the ceiling of what may be called *suṣupti*.[106] This is why for Sri Aurobindo, the perfection of *suṣupti* included a constant breaking of its borders, pushing it further, ever deeper into the planes beyond the known and the unknown. What is Unknowable at any time, even in a cosmic sense, can enter the realm of the Unknown, and what is Unknown, can be progressively known through a pushing of these lines as one extends one's consciousness.[107]

What is described as *suṣupti* in the Upaniṣads, refers to the status of consciousness of what Sri Aurobindo calls the Supramental Being.[108] The goal of the Integral Yoga can be formulated in terms of the waking possession of this Being and the naturalised action of this Being through one's transformed nature. This is the enormously expanded scope of knowledge that Sri Aurobindo gives us in the *vijñāna catuṣṭaya*. Much of it is beyond any sense or semblance of our present operation of knowledge, but, the key to its understanding is that all knowledge dwells within us, and to develop gradually our powers of intuitive understanding and

---

106. SoY, p. 526.
107. RoY, p. 1476.
108. SoY, p. 525. He calls it here "Self of the Gnosis" and "Īśvara, the Lord of Being."

rely on these more and more with faith, while using our rationality and our sense of discrimination, to test the ground, is the way to its progress.

I wish to end this chapter by quoting Sri Aurobindo on this aspect of testing each step in the achievement of these powers of knowledge. Here, Sri Aurobindo writes about *viveka*, which is a foundational factor in the development of the powers of knowledge, starting with the intuition:

> The importance of *viveka* for the purposes of man's progress in his present stage is supreme. At present in the greatest men, the powers of the *vijñāna* act not in their own power, place and nature, but in and through the intellect, as helpers of the intellect and occasional guides. Directly, we get an intuition or revelation, the intellect, memory, imagination, logical faculties seize hold of it and begin to disguise it in a garb of mingled truth and error, bringing down Truth to the level of the nature, *saṁskāra*s and preferences of a man, instead of purifying and elevating his nature and judgements to the level of the Truth. Without *viveka*, these powers are as dangerous to man as they are helpful. The light they give is brighter than the light of the intellect, but the shadow which the intellect creates around them is often murkier than the mist of ignorance which surrounds ordinary intellectual knowledge. Thus, men who use these powers ignorantly, often stumble much more than those who walk by the clear, though limited light of the intellect. When these powers begin to work in us we must be *dhīra* and *sthira* and not be led away by our enthusiasm. We must give time for the *viveka* to seize on our thoughts and intuitions, arrange them, separate their intellectual from their *vijñānamaya* elements, correct their false extensions, false limitations, misapplications, and assign them their right application, right extension, right limitation, make, in the image of the Upaniṣad, the *vyūha* [which means formation], or just marshalling of the rays of the sun of knowledge, *sūryasya raśmaya*. Knowledge is not for the hasty mind but

only for the *dhīra* [the patient], who can sit long, accumulating and arranging his store and does not rush away with fragments like a crow darting off with the first morsel of food on which it can feed.[109]

109. RoY, pp. 17-18.

5

The Quartet of the Body

THE quartet of the body (*śarīra catuṣṭaya*) is located by Sri Aurobindo as the last of the *ādhāra siddhi*s (perfections of the instrument). This is, in some ways, the most advanced of the perfections and represents some extremes in terms of its results, including physical immortality. It includes much which is not discussed by Sri Aurobindo in his other writings and pertains to his personal practice, at an occult level. The four perfections of this quartet are *ārogya* which means freedom from disease; *utthāpana* which literally means levitation and more broadly, freedom from the physical laws of nature; *saundarya*, which means beauty; and *ānanda* which is bliss.[1] Here too, in keeping with the principal goals of the quartet of yoga, we find the first two *siddhis*, *ārogya* and *utthāpana*, to be those of *mukti* (liberation); and the last two, *suandarya* and *ānanda*, to pertain to *bhukti* (enjoyment).

In an age, which bases reality in matter and refuses independent status to consciousness, the industries of flesh and skin have taken predominance in defining human self-concern and can be seen to imitate the objectives of the quartet of the body. This is why, perhaps of all the seven quartets, it is the quartet of the body which resonates most strongly in the contemporary social imaginary. Today, the entire complex discourse of Indian Yoga has been reductively redefined in

1. RoY, pp. 23, 1477.

terms of physical *āsanas* (*haṭha-yoga*), and franchised in chains across the world. These packages promise health and fitness (*ārogya*), coupled with the prospect of enhanced stamina for capital advantage and sexual performance (*ānanda*). The maximisation of physical ecstasy is also sought through the cultivation of the body beautiful (*saundarya*) and the secrets of sexuality, mystically marketed through the equation of Tantra with *ars erotica*.

Yoga, however, cannot claim any special prerogative in the achievement of these goals and has to compete through its claims for romantic excess, the exotic allure of the secret Orient, its unchanging roots lost in the mists of the Golden Age of Origin. More properly, this is the domain of cosmetology (*saundarya*), gyms, vitamins and the pharmaceutical and health industry (*ārogya*), mood enhancing drugs (*ānanda*) and in the horizon of things to come, *ārogya* realised through genetic engineering and cryogenics (immorality). The body translated into a pattern of information, de-materialisation and re-materialisation (*utthāpana*) is no longer unimaginable, the exceeding of the human made possible through lateral splicing of universal genetic materials.

In his justly famous work on the archeology of knowledge, *The Order of Things*, Michel Foucault traces the appearance of "the human" as a defined essence, the central object of anthropology, in itself a discipline at the centre of the knowledge academy, at the end of the eighteenth century. He points out that this discourse of "the human" has been historically contingent to the modern arrangement of knowledge and that, as it appeared historically, it is likewise doomed to disappear. In the last paragraph of this work, he foresees the approaching erasure of "man", "like a face drawn in sand at the edge of the sea".

Friedrich Nietzche, who profoundly influenced Foucault, saw such a disappearance of the human through its self-exceeding in the superman. Martin Heidegger, one of Nietzsche's spiritual children and another forebear of Foucault, declared himself an anti-humanist, refusing the rationally defined essence of the human which forms the cornerstone of the age of humanism. Sri Aurobindo, in a similar vein, refused a static definition of the human, choosing rather to affirm a perpetually transitional identity. This erasure of the human in the second decade of the twenty-first century, however, has other ramifications than that of a transformation of the human through power of consciousness. Donna Haraway has shown how human integration within global circuits of a binary information space has inaugurated the post-human age of the cyborg. Thinkers, like Jacques Derrida and more recently, Bernard Stiegler have pointed to the co-dependent implication of technology in human consciousness, problematising thus, the culture/nature dualism and drawing attention to their systemic co-evolution. At the other end of the spectrum, the symbiotic, syncretic and competitive unstable processes of natural genetic interactions across species boundaries and the artificial interventions of gene splicing have opened up the cosmic soup of post-human zoo-genesis.

Clearly, we are passing through a destabilisation of the human, a tending towards post-human chaos with untold possibilities. The prospect of androids and cyborgs as neo-colonialism's subhuman serfs, as that of the arrival of the eugenically engineered superman, stand in sharp contrast to Sri Aurobindo's vision of the conquest of human limitation by power of consciousness, but may be more imminently real to the predictable shape of the future. Still, in answer to these prospects, Sri Aurobindo points out that the body is a structure of consciousness and that though it cannot be reduced to mental, vital or psychic consciousness, it needs to be integrated with these through a more primordial quality of consciousness, to which these differences in kind turn out to be differences of degree.

Sri Aurobindo does not deny or eschew the co-evolution of human-technological systems and/or of human-non-human biological systems, seeing these as parts of a cosmic expansion, a "becoming-cosmos" which is an aspect of Nature's Yoga through the evolving human species. But, these processes are ambiguous, as we saw above and need both, an ethics of the post-human and agency to critique and liberate from subjection to technology and neo-racial politics. Gilles Deleuze, in his work on Michel Foucault, reflects on the disappearance of the human and the emergence of the superman in terms of the emergence of the hyper-technologies of genetics, silicon and language. Human imbrication within these technologies must be seen as an experimental and creative release of human forces in an "unlimited finity", something whose ambiguity and danger can only be overcome through a human transition out of its present fold of immanence to a superfold, where it can realise a new ontology as master of the new envelopments of nature possibility. Gene, silicon and language can only then be no longer subjections, but the natural tools of the superman. This description of superman can be seen to come close to Sri Aurobindo's view of the discovery of a level of transcendent/ immanent consciousness to which mental, vital and physical nature are its self-modulations.

Body and Spirit

Pertaining to the way to these perfections, it is useful to prelude this consideration with three statements on the body by Sri Aurobindo that open up a blueprint for practice. The physical body is considered by many schools to be irrelevant to spiritual realisation, something to be denied or neglected. But, as may be expected in an integral yoga, Sri Aurobindo takes a stand in which the body serves a progressive role in spiritual realisation. The first statement comes from his commentary to the *Īśa Upaniṣad*. Here, Sri Aurobindo says, "Every creature is His eidolon or manifestation, and everybody His temple and dwelling place."[2] This is the idea of the body as the temple of God, of the *Īśvara*. This statement validates the very first line of the the *Īśa Upaniṣad*. *Īśa* means Lord and this Upaniṣad begins with the line: "All this is for the habitation of the Lord."[3] This idea of habitation is what is referred to in the phrase "Everybody is His temple and dwelling place". The body is the habitation of the Lord. The second statement by Sri Aurobindo on the body, comes from the text, *The Supramental Manifestation on Earth*. This was written in 1950, shortly before he left his body. In a chapter called "The Perfection of the Body", he quotes a certain line from Sanskrit literature: *śarīram khalu dharmasādhanam*;[4] and he translates it: "the body is the means of fulfilment of *dharma*".[5] Sri Aurobindo explains the word *dharma* here as "the ideal" of an integral perfection, which may be thought of or called a divine life. Thus, the means to the fulfilment of this integral perfection is the body. The third statement comes from another chapter of the same text. This chapter is "The Divine Body". Here he makes the role of the body a little more explicit: "A divine life in a divine body is the formula of the ideal that we envisage".[6] We may recognise this, of course, as an alternative form of the Greek ideal of a sound mind in a sound body — a divine life in a divine body.

In each of these statements, we see a perspective on the body relating it to spiritual practice and realisation. In the first, the body is the temple and dwelling place of the Divine. That itself represents an attitude to the body which gives us access to the Divine; the Divine is housed within this thing that we know of as the body and we must treat it in a way

2. IU, p. 281.
3. Ibid., p. 5.
4. Sri Aurobindo, "The Supramental Manifestation on Earth", EPY, p. 521; quoted from Kālidāsa, *Kumārasambhavam*, 5:33.
5. Ibid.
6. EPY, 5:36.

befitting a habitation of the Divine. The second goes farther to make the body instrumental, not merely a location but an instrument for the fulfilment of an integral perfection. It is the means to the fulfilment of *dharma*. Thus, it becomes an active site of processes, which will lead to an integral perfection. The third goes yet further in saying "a divine life in a divine body is the formula of the ideal that we envisage". Here, the body is more than a lame human instrument: it is a divine agent of expression. This is a further step from instrumentality into the perfection of the body. The body itself becomes here a part of the divine manifestation. In other words, the body is not merely a temple of divinity, nor an instrument aiding in the realisation of divinity, but a formation of consciousness manifesting divinity. Thus, these three statements provide us with a progression in our attitude and in the role of the body in the practice and realisation of the integral yoga.

Freedom from Disease

The first item in the quartet of the body is *ārogya*, which means freedom from disease.[7] To start with, let us consider the practices related to the freedom from disease in Sri Aurobindo's own teaching. The first is *samatā* (equality), the second is sexual continence, the third is faith, the fourth is the consciousness of the body, and the fifth is the action of the divine Śakti. Equality, as a way to the freedom from disease, *ārogya*, means that the body has to develop the capacity to be unshaken by extremes.[8] In other words, this relates to endurance (*titikṣā*) and beyond endurance, to the settled and effortless experience of peace (*śānti*) in the physical being, in the midst of the most extreme conditions that the body is subjected to. This invokes a higher consciousness which can

7. RoY, pp. 23, 1477.
8. Ibid., p. 1477.

support and stretch the limits of the body. A realised equality is the presence of the divine in the body, a presence which always finds the reserves within itself to sustain the body through all conditions. The practice of equality would lead to a realisation where peace would be established as a natural thing in the body under every condition that it is subjected to.

The second of these practices is continence, something critical to the quartet of the body, because it is concerned with energy transformations which could be called "alchemic".[9] Continence is enjoined in a variety of traditions to some of their members, a practice which has been ridiculed in our times of "sexual revolution" as a form of social repression. It is important to note that in yoga, this is not a mental act of suppression, or of flesh-denying transcendence, and involves processes leading to an alternate functioning of consciousness in the physical system. To think about a divine body, a body transforming from a mortal body subject to ageing, disease and death, to a body free from these conditions, is also to think about going against the grain of nature. Nature has set all living things in their grooves — and human beings are among the creatures of nature — conditioned in certain ways so as to propagate its motives of preservation and survival. The preservation of the species is ensured through the act of sex, which is why, there is so much natural investment in this act.

Indian Yoga psychology has a well-developed discourse around the reversal of nature's processes so as to make its unconscious forces available for the sustenance of the body and to generate consciousness. Sri Aurobindo draws on these teachings of occult energetics in the matter of celibacy.

---

9. Sri Aurobindo, "The Divine Body" in *The Supramental Manifestation on Earth*, EPY, p. 543; The Mother, "The Four Austerities", *On Education*, CWM:12, p. 54.

According to this, the crude consciousness-energy involved in sexual activity, which is known as *retas*, is sublimated and transformed into a higher quality of energy called *ojas*, which is responsible for stamina in the body, endurance and ecstasy in the nerves, force in the dynamic will and radiance in the mind.[10] This transformation is considered to be natural and automatic to a degree, in all human beings and forms as part of the occult anatomy of Indian medicine. But, in yoga, it becomes a conscious and systematic process mediated by acts of aspiration in the mind and body, as well as operations of the vital forces (*prāṇa*s) that act within the physical system. The word *prāṇa*, literally means life-force, and the action and control of *prāṇa*s in the body are important elements related to physical transformation. In traditional *haṭha-yoga*, these processes of purification (*śuddhi*) and control of the vital and physical energies are achieved through *āsana* (body posture) and *prāṇāyāma* (breathing), but in the Integral Yoga, these are not indispensable. One may take their aid, but depends more properly on the eradication of sexual desire from the mind and the development of consciousness in the mind-body nexus with the direct ability of the vital and physical *Puruṣa*s to control the *Prakṛti* (nature) at these levels; or an invocation through surrender to the transformative action of the Divine Śakti. Continence leads to a reversal of the energetics in physical functioning, opening the door to an alternate functioning of the body.[11]

Certain aspects of contemporary feminist theory, particularly in the work of Luce Irigaray, bear reflection in this context of rethinking physical existence and enjoyment. Whereas, continence or celibacy has been conventionally related, both in Western and Eastern spiritual tradition, with

---

10. EPY, p. 554.
11. CWM 12, pp. 54-55.

the denial of the flesh and the seeking for a spiritual freedom transcending the body, for both Irigaray and Sri Aurobindo's *śarīra catuṣṭaya*, continence is a practice of embodiment and a transformed and enhanced basis for physical enjoyment or *jouissance*. Irigaray sees this as the proper type of feminine sexuality and contrasts it with orgasmic masculinity, but beyond essences, her feminist discourse is important as a potential for physical existence:

> For the female, everything right away is not the equivalent of death. It is more like the quest for infinite life. An openness on the infinite in *jouissance*. Man sets the infinite in a *transcendence* that is always deferred to the beyond, even if it be the beyond of the concept. Woman sets it in an *expanse* of *jouissance*, here and now, right away. Body-expanse that tries *to give itself exteriority*, to give itself in an unpunctuated space-time that is also not orgiastic in the limited sense of that word. To give itself to a space-time without end. Or, very resistant to definition.[12]

The third general practice applied to the body is faith (*śraddhā*). The specific faith as far as the first perfection, *ārogya* in the quartet of the body is concerned, is the faith of the body in itself.[13] The body's faith in itself, its self-regeneration, is also present to some degree as a natural factor in all human beings. That is why "faith-healing" is not so unbelievable. Closer to common experience, all human beings recognise consciously or subconsciously that the body has its natural healing powers: when we receive a surface cut we seldom jump to the conclusion that we may die of bleeding. This is because the body carries its own faith in wellness, a faith that the cut will heal, and it does. We have a similar response to a

---

12. Luce Irigaray, *An Ethics of Sexual Difference*, tr. Carolyn Burke and Gillian C. Gill, Ithaca: Cornell University Press, 1993, p. 64.

13. RoY, p. 1477.

variety of diseases — fevers, stomach upsets, skin eruptions. The body conveys a confidence that it will overcome these things. With success, this innate faith of the body grows stronger and appears in the surface of our nature, a faith in its ability to not be broken by disease. However, due to a number of factors, this faith gets compromised over time — through attacks by serious diseases, fear, dependence on external cures — and this shaken confidence grows with the sense of advancing age, as the physical faculties diminish in their functional effectiveness, and through collective suggestion. In the development of *ārogya,* there is the need to support the innate faith of the body by a higher faith in the indestructibility of a perfect physical consciousness, in union with the divine. This is an extension of the natural faith in the body; by yoga that faith is amplified and transformed into a faith which believes in the immortality of the divine body, accessible to the degree of completeness of one's union with the divine.

Awakened Body Consciousness

The fourth, in this series of general powers related to *ārogya,* is the consciousness of the body. This is part of the complex and diversified field of consciousness. Normally, we are given to thinking of consciousness as limited to mental understanding and volition. We speak of the cerebrum as the conscious part of the brain, we apply the term consciousness to the carrying out of cognitive functions and decisions based on these. However, yoga psychology tells us that consciousness in not limited to the mind, there are other forms of consciousness. For example, there is the consciousness of the emotions which is a distinctly different kind of consciousness than that of mental cognition; similarly, there is the consciousness of the sensations, the consciousness of the will. These are all forms of consciousness because they operate in a way distinct from the operation of the cognition and are experienced differently, yet, each of these is a way of being conscious. It is a common experience that one may think of doing something but cannot accomplish this intention, because another form of consciousness, for example one's emotions or physical needs, has interfered with the thought and dominated it. So we find ourselves in a field of consciousness and in that field, the body has its own distinct consciousness. This consciousness of the body is usually highly compromised. In habitual behaviour, this consciousness is overridden and spoken for by some other more dominant consciousness. The mind dominates the body with its morals and its purposes; the will dominates the body with its desires and ambitions; the emotions dominate the body with their blind passions. The body consciousness is seldom given a chance to determine its own existence. But, in the *śarīra catuṣṭaya*, the yoga of the perfection of the body, a very important part is to become conscious of the body's own consciousness and to liberate it from its domination by other forms of consciousness.

There are some interesting entries in the *Record of Yoga*, where Sri Aurobindo noted the immixture of different physical and psychical influences in the progress and control of illness and the crucial role played in overcoming it by the body's own consciousness.[14] Usually, in Indian Yoga practices, the *āsanas* and *prāṇāyāmas* of *haṭha-yoga* are used to control the vital (prāṇic) energies so as to extend the abilities of the body. Through this prāṇic means, one may extend the longevity of the body and bring freedom from illness for a very long period of time. Alternately, the force of concentrated mental will (*tapas*) may be cultivated and used against the action of the forces of disease. But powerful though such practices may be, Sri Aurobindo insists on the awakening of the body's own

14. See, for example, the entry on 1 July 1919. This entry differentiates the various forces at work in an instance of illness. It is also a good example of the action of faith (*śraddhā*), both for and against the disease. RoY, pp. 1106-07.

Śarīra Catuṣṭaya (Perfection of Body) (5.1)

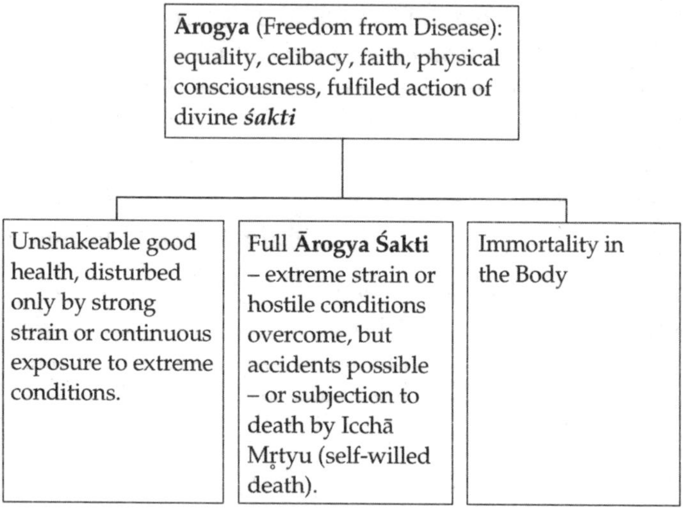
Ārogya (Freedom from Disease): equality, celibacy, faith, physical consciousness, fulfiled action of divine śakti
Unshakeable good health, disturbed only by strong strain or continuous exposure to extreme conditions.
Full Ārogya Śakti – extreme strain or hostile conditions overcome, but accidents possible – or subjection to death by Icchā Mṛtyu (self-willed death).
Immortality in the Body

consciousness. The perfection of the body is to be sought in the ideality of the body's own consciousness, not in the mind or vital trying to help the body.

Finally, there is the fulfilled action of the divine Śakti, the consciousness-force at work in all beings. The divine Śakti is the active force of the Divine that can transform our nature because it is already intelligent and conscious. It knows, what is required at any time or situation, because conscious of our destiny and its steps. Though, initially, we lack an understanding of what it is or what are its actions, our faith in it makes it concretely active in our lives. Though the Śakti is always active and the only true worker in all things, its activity is veiled and indirect; our receptivity enables its direct action. This leads to a progression in which faith is justified by increasing experience and intimacy with the Śakti. We develop a concrete relationship with it as with a person, and come to recognise this relationship as one of closeness and identity with the Divine Mother. The Divine Mother is known to live and act and have her being in us. A settled faith rests in her being and always elicits the necessary response from her in all parts of our nature. This transference allows the transformation of the nature instruments, including that of the body, to occur in us, through the action of the divine Śakti.

Stages to Ārogya

Sri Aurobindo has formulated the development of freedom from disease, *ārogya* in terms of three stages. The first stage is unshakeable good health, disturbed only by strong strain or continuous exposure to extreme conditions.[15] In other words, this is an extension of the body's own healing power. The condition here is, to arrive at a power of faith in the body's own healing and rejuvenation that is so strong that nothing can shake it, except very unexpected adversity or continuous exposure to extreme conditions — in the *Record of Yoga*, Sri Aurobindo mentions examples such as extremes of temperature or of physical strain.[16] Being subject to extreme heat or extreme cold over long periods can wear down the body's natural resistance, and shake its faith in a settled good health. To establish and allow it to grow in power is the first stage in the progress of *ārogya*.

The second stage is what Sri Aurobindo refers to as the full *ārogya śakti*.[17] Here, even conditions of extreme strain or hostile impacts on the body can be overcome but the body is still subject to accidents, plus there is the subjection to death through what he calls *icchā-mṛtyu* (self-willed death).[18] This is an interesting

15. RoY, p. 1477.
16. Ibid. See also RoY, pp. 244, 269, 317, 331, 773, etc.
17. RoY, p. 1477.
18. Sri Aurobindo described his own achievement in these terms to a disciple Nirodbaran in 1935: ". . . I have the power to overcome illness, but accident and poison and the I.M. [Icchā Mṛtyu — self-willed death] still remain as possible means of death." Nirodbaran, *Twelve Years with Sri Aurobindo*, Sri Aurobindo Ashram Trust, 1972, p. 289.

concept with its roots in Indian Yoga psychology and it relates to the fact that a *yogī* may have such a power of mastery over the physical body that no disease can prevail against it. Such a state also implies complete control over environing circumstances. But in spite of this, the law of the earth must be obeyed in that the body must still be abandoned at some time since Nature demands it. For such a being, the abandonment of the body is achieved by will. This is *icchā-mṛtyu*. The *yogī* then chooses the manner, time and place of his/her own death and passes away accordingly. A famous example of this in traditional literature is the death of Bhīṣma in the *Mahābhārata*.[19]

The third stage is the most far-reaching and powerful state of physical perfection — immortality in the body.[20] This of course leads to the very controversial question: why should we seek immortality? It is important to note how Sri Aurobindo formulates the rationale of this stage, so that we may understand his conception of the place of physical immortality.

Physical Immortality

To consider this, let us contemplate once more the three statements on the body by Sri Aurobindo with which we started our study of the *śarīra catuṣṭaya*. According to the first of these statements, the body is the temple of god. Temples of god are dispensable or disposable, one can always make another temple, there is no necessity to conceive of a static temple for all time. The second statement rested on the perception of the body as an instrument for the achievement of the goal of spiritual realisation. In this case too, the body is clearly not conceived as something necessarily permanent — a means can serve its end and then disappear. According to

19. *Mahābhārata*, Book VI (Bhīṣma Parvan), Section CXX.
20. RoY, p. 1477.

the third statement, a divine life in a divine body is the ideal of spiritual realisation. A "divine body" means the body of god — in other words, not only is the body a house of god, but it is itself, a living self-expression of the Divine. If the body is to express the Divine, it must also express the fundamental qualities of the Divine. As Sri Aurobindo points out, the most fundamental quality of the divine is eternity, the divine is eternal. Hence, the body must also express this eternity. Eternity, in terms of the body's life and expression, is equivalent to immortality, the ability to last forever and express its infinite possibilities.

However, to think about the body as a static structure which lasts forever, is very problematic. Here, we find a profound statement by Sri Aurobindo from *The Synthesis of Yoga,* which throws light on his approach to this problem. In the first chapter of this book, titled "Life and Yoga", Sri Aurobindo writes: "To be perpetually reborn is the condition of a material immortality."[21] A material immortality does not imply a static form frozen for all time. It is a structure that constantly renews itself. Now, indeed, this is happening in the case of all living beings throughout life. But, at a certain point, the renewal process stops. Biology tells us that we are subject to the double life processes of constructive regeneration (*anabolism*) and destructive breakdown (*katabolism*). But, with age, the katabolic processes occur faster than the anabolic ones, leading to ageing, disease and death. This is also partly due to the limits to the regenerative powers of the cell. There is a limit to cell division. The failure of the body, to serve as an adequate instrument for the soul's purposes of spiritual realisation and self-expression causes the soul to change its body. This is accomplished through the process of rebirth, by which bodies change, but the soul remains the same. But the

21. SoY, p. 5.

idea of a perpetual rebirth may also be seen as a conscious process. In the natural case, we are subject to it, we are not given a choice in the matter — we are born, we live for a certain number of years, then something happens to the body which results in the breakdown of its functioning and we die. This is followed by an "afterlife" invisible to our external senses, but one in which the soul traverses a certain terrain and reappears in another body. This is the idea of the reincarnated body.

Our surface memory is not conscious of whatever happens between two physical incarnations, but our psychic memory is conscious of it. After the body's separation, the subtler parts or envelopes of our nature — the mental body, the vital body — also fall off in time.[22] Like the physical body, they disintegrate, leaving the part that is eternal, manifesting the eternity of the Divine. This is the soul. It is this which persists from life to life.[23] If this eternal part was to express itself fully in the other instruments, such as the mind and the life-body, we would not lose consciousness at the time of death, nor would our nature sheaths drop off between lives. In other words, *yogins* who have reached this level of psychic integration can either pass out of the body at will, or remain conscious through the process of death, experiencing an afterlife in astral planes without a body, and experiencing also the entry into another body, all as a continuity of consciousness.[24] The *yogin* can thus experience a succession of lives as a continuous awakened state of consciousness through the track of a disappearance and reappearance of bodies. This is a further stage in the perfection

---

22. *Bhagavad-Gītā*, II: 18, 20, 22, 27; *Śvetāśvatara Upaniṣad*, V:11-12, quoted in "The Problem of Rebirth", LD, p. 771.

23. LD, pp. 789-94.

24. See "Memory of Past Lives", The Mother's Questions and Answers, 6 May 1953 as quoted in *The Mother's Vision*, compiled Georges van Vrekhem, Sri Aurobindo Ashram Trust, 2002, pp. 244-45.

of the immortality of the body through a continuity of perpetual rebirths.

Beyond this, we may conceive of a stage in which there wouldn't be the necessity of subjection to death. In other words, as per our earlier discussion, the ability to regenerate the body would be ceaseless, mitigating the necessity for death. The occult intuition of this possibility is present in the primordial layers of human consciousness. This is what is behind the idea of the resurrected body of Christ, for example. Both, Chinese and medieval European alchemy, have concerned themselves with finding psycho-material processes resulting in physical transubstantiation, or immortality through control over the material element of the body. In India, this ideal has been present in several traditions, prominent among which is that of the Tamil *siddhas*.[25] There are notions of this kind in ancient Indian medicine as well, such as in *siddha* medicine. There, we hear of a process called *kāyākalpa,* which means the rejuvenation of the body.[26] But what Sri Aurobindo refers to, is a choice of consciousness, possible to the *yogin* at a certain stage of the perfection of the body. This is what he means when he writes, "to be perpetually reborn is the condition of a material immortality" — to choose to constantly re-new oneself, re-birth oneself, not merely through the automatic processes of cell division, but through the conscious choice of cell division mediated by the natural divine property of eternity being brought into the physical cells as a dynamic consciousness determining its activities.

Experiments of consciousness in this direction at the levels of the cells of the body, were carried out by the Mother, particularly, in the last 20 years of her life. Commenting on an aphorism of Sri Aurobindo pertaining to *ānanda,* the fourth

25. See, for example, R. Venkataraman, *A History of the Tamil Siddha Cult,* Madurai: Ennes Publication, 1990.

26. Ibid.

Śarīra Catuṣṭaya (Perfection of Body) (5.2)

Ārogya (freedom from disease): equality, celibacy, faith, physical consciousness (aspiration and surrender), fulfilled action of divine *Śakti*.

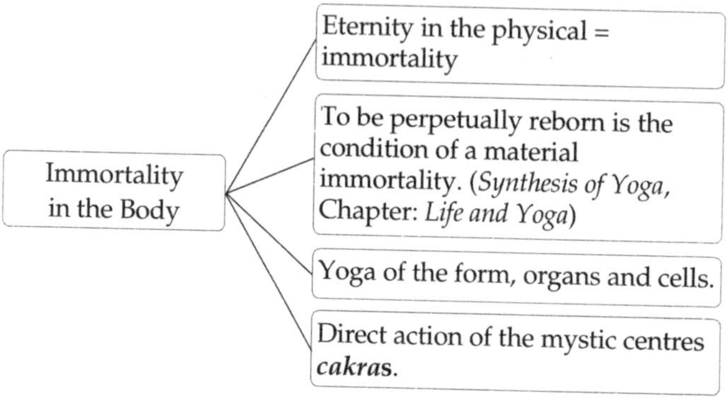
Immortality in the Body
Eternity in the physical = immortality
To be perpetually reborn is the condition of a material immortality. (*Synthesis of Yoga*, Chapter: *Life and Yoga*)
Yoga of the form, organs and cells.
Direct action of the mystic centres *cakras*.

siddhi, in the quartet of the body, she explicates further the notion of "deathlessness" in terms of "perpetual rebirth". The aphorism of Sri Aurobindo, which is referred to here, deals with a form of physical bliss (*raudrānanda*) which we will consider later in this chapter.[27] This passage also bears productive comparison with the quote from Luce Irigaray introduced earlier in the context of sexual continence and physical bliss:

> The deathless state is what can be envisaged for the human physical body in the future: it is constant rebirth. Instead of again tumbling backwards and falling apart due to a lack of plasticity and an incapacity to adapt to the universal movement, the body is undone "futurewards," as it were. . . . [E]ach individual has a different, particular way of organising the cells of his body, and it is this particular way that persists through all the outer changes. All the rest is undone and redone, but undone in a forward thrust towards

27. "Cruelty transfigured, becomes Love that is intolerable ecstasy." EDH, p. 433.

the new instead of collapsing backwards into death, and redone in a constant aspiration to follow the progressive movement of the divine truth.

But for that, the body — the body-consciousness — must first learn to widen itself. It is indispensable, for otherwise all the cells become a kind of boiling porridge under the pressure of the supramental light.

What usually happens is that when the body reaches its maximum intensity of aspiration, or of ecstasy of love, it is unable to contain it. It becomes flat, motionless. It falls back. Things settle down — you are enriched with a new vibration, but then everything resumes its course. So you must widen yourself in order to learn to bear unflinchingly the intensities of the supramental force, to go forward always, always with the ascending movement of the divine truth, without falling backwards into the decrepitude of the body.

That is what Sri Aurobindo means when he speaks of an intolerable ecstasy; it is not an intolerable ecstasy: it is an unflinching ecstasy.[28]

Supermind and the Mind of the Cells

We see from the above that the Mother refers to the action of the supramental consciousness on the cells. According to Sri Aurobindo and the Mother, the psychic transformation of the mental-vital-physical nature cannot achieve the complete process of divinisation, particularly of the physical substance, since the psychic operates within the law of *avidyā* whose foundation is the material Inconscience. The iron law of matter imposes death on all living things, irrespective of any power of immanent consciousness brought to bear on it. However, if this Consciousness transcends the Law of Ignorance which upholds our cosmos, it may conceivably transform the property of Inconscience in matter. Of course, to speak of a

---

28. Entry of 25 November 1959, MA, 1, pp. 332-33.

transcendence in the context of *Brahman*, the one reality there is, it may be better to adapt Gilles Deleuze's infolded metaphysic of absolute immanence, in which he speaks of a "transcendental layer of the immanence", a possibility within the infinity of immanence itself which has not yet manifested. The Supermind is such a principle, which can introduce a new cosmic law, one under which the inconscient property of matter is no longer binding.

This is why, the quartet of knowledge or more accurately, the *vijñāna catuṣṭaya*, is most intimately connected to the quartet of the body and makes its *siddhis* possible. The *siddhis* of the *vijñāna catuṣṭaya* overlap with those of the *śarīra catuṣṭaya* through a criss-cross connection. *Ārogya* of the quartet of the body, is impossible to fully achieve, without the achievement of the quartet of supermind; and the quartet of supermind completes its own objectives with the *siddhis* of the body that are a part of the eight *siddhis*, *aṣṭa-siddhi*. Among these *siddhis* of the body in the *vijñāna catuṣṭaya*, we find one which pertains more particularly to *ārogya* and physical immortality. This is *aṇimā*.[29] Along with other capacities arising from the control of matter in its most primordial atomic state — such as teleportation, materialisation/dematerialisation and invisibility — this *siddhi* also pertains to "invulnerability" and the capacity to "free the body from decay and death".[30]

Returning to the transformation of the body, the psychic and spiritual action can proceed to transform the mental, vital and subtle physical consciousnesses, but finds a resistant residue when it comes to the body. The quartet of the body addresses this in principle, but it is the yoga of the body with which the Mother was concerned in the last 20 years of her life, which dealt concretely with the preparation of this

---

29. RoY, p. 1475.

30. Ibid.

residual content. For this purpose, she addressed the consciousness of the body in terms of three independent but connected levels of consciousness, the consciousness of the physical form, the consciousness of the organs and the consciousness of the cells.[31] The body consciousness at each of these levels must participate in this yoga through its own aspiration and surrender to a divine physicality; other forms of human consciousness cannot substitute for this. A book, *The Mind of the Cells*, was compiled from the Mother's conversations on her experiences and understanding of this area. More about the experiments that she was carrying out in the transformation of the cellular consciousness, can be found in *The Mother's Agenda*. In these texts, she addresses the body consciousness in its various formations, the overall physical form and its functioning in terms of balance, intuitive skill, coordination, lightness, endurance, peace and beauty.[32] In fact, The Mother speaks of such capacities of the body from an early stage, as for example in her talk on "The Four Austerities and the Four Liberations". There she refers to the cultivation of a body which is "beautiful in form, harmonious in posture, supple and agile in its movements, powerful in its activities and robust in its health and organic functioning".[33] One can clearly see how these capacities of the physical form relate to, and can prepare the *siddhi*s of the body, *saundarya* (beauty) in the quartet of the body and *mahimā, laghimā* and *aṇimā* in the quartet of knowledge, *vijñāna catuṣṭaya*. This is also why both the Mother and Sri Aurobindo gave so much importance to physical culture at the *āśrama*.

The first thing to realise here, is that the physical form is

31. CWM: 15, p. 281.

32. "lightness, invulnerability, moving about at will, luminosity at will — all that goes without saying, it's part of supramental qualities", 3 January 1970, MA 11, p. 23..

33. CWM: 12, p. 50.

not fixed, but that behind it is a kind of consciousness that the Mother calls the consciousness of the form. There is a subtle physical aspect to this consciousness of the form; but, even deeper there is a psychic aspect to the consciousness of the form, and high above, what one may call a supramental aspect to it as well. Then, there is the consciousness of the organs: each organ in the body has its own consciousness. And, there is the consciousness of the cells: the cells have their own individual consciousness. As we know so well in the case of cancer, it is at the level of the individual consciousness of the cells that a renegade activity develops. So long as the cells are under nature's conditioning, they work according to the dictates of a mechanical law; but if they break out of that law, they express an anarchic individuality which disrupts the complex functioning of the body. The question is, whether the emergence of individual will at the level of the cells, can lend itself to a voluntary attunement with a higher principle of harmony, as for example, that of the subtle physical body under the control of the psychic and/or overmental/ supramental form.

To become aware of these as independent forms of consciousness, to be identified with these forms of consciousness as aspects of the psychic or higher divine person and to be able to operate harmoniously in this way, the awakening of the powers of aspiration and surrender is the condition of the yoga of the form, organs and cells of the body. In other words, if we were able to experience the form of the body as an aspiration to the form of a higher divine archetype or person from which it may be constantly replenished and regenerated; similarly, if all our organs could experience themselves as forms of aspiration and surrender, to what could be thought of as their functional energy archetypes, and if the cells of our body could similarly surrender and aspire independently and be thus constantly renewed, the yoga of the body would be in continuous dynamic operation. This is the basis for the progression necessary to the appearance of *ārogya* and thus, indestructibility and immortality in the body.

To awaken the consciousness at these otherwise "unconscious" levels of physical functioning and tune then to the divine or overman person, the Mother spoke of silencing the mind, and the emotional and volitional life, or at least finding a way to filter out their interference in the body consciousness. Usually, it is the mental and/or vital consciousness which "speaks for" the body. But, when these can be got out of the way, one experiences the body consciousness in its independence. And here, too, as we see from the Mother's writings, there are independent levels of working. The most primordial level of the body consciousness, thus experienced by the Mother, seems to be a kind of sub-cellular layer of combining vibrations. These vibrations were seen by her to be universal, each cell being a specific "agglomeration, a concentration of [these] vibrations".[34] Moving from the "normal" functioning of the body to the independent functioning of the different levels of body consciousness, implied for the Mother, experimental exercises and operations of consciousness which were unconventional in the extreme and often experienced as what we would call illnesses.[35] Once again, and in the most literal sense, we are brought to Gilles Deleuze's thinking of the "Body without Organs" and his echoing of Spinoza's question regarding the unknown capacities of the body. The Mother, in her experiences with the consciousness of the cells, described repeatedly, the independent working of aspiration and surrender at the level of the cells and her wonder at what the body is capable of:

---

34. Entry of 25 Februray 1961. MA, 2, p. 99.
35. Ibid.

> The body, left to itself without this kind of constant action of the mind upon it, acts like this: as soon as something [in it] gets disturbed, it has immediately an aspiration, a call, an effort to find help. And this is very powerful — if nothing comes in between, it is very powerful. It is as though the cells themselves erupted spontaneously in an aspiration, a call. In the body there are invaluable and unknown treasures. In all cells there is an intensity of life, of the aspiration, of the will to progress, of which usually, one is not even aware.[36]

While dealing with the quartet of knowledge, *vijñāna catuṣṭaya*, we saw how these kinds of experiences may be considered as operations of *iśitā* at the level of the cells. At a more advanced stage, this aspiration in the cells translated itself in the Mother to a spontaneous repetition of the *mantra, oṁ namo bhagavate* going on independently and constantly and calling down the supramental Śakti into the body to organise its activities.[37]

The Mystic Body and Physical Transformation

The process of physical transformation is also seen to involve the direct action of the mystic centres (*cakra*s) within the body. The *cakra*s are the subtle centres for the operations of consciousness within us. According to the psychology of *haṭha-yoga* and Tantra, the entire body structure is backgrounded by a set of nodes of energetic action, action of various forms of consciousness.[38] Each one of these centres is normally, only partially operating in us — this operation maintains the automatisms of the body and the rest of our nature — our minds, wills, feelings, emotions, sensations, skills. All these aspects of nature can become fully conscious and unfold their

---

36. Conversation of 19 May 1954. The Mother, *Questions and Answers 1954*, CWM: 6, p. 140.
37. Entry of 16 September 1958, MA 1, pp. 194-95.
38. RoY, p. 1340.

secret capacities (*siddhis*), if the centres open completely. Thus, the opening up of these centres and their direct action on the body becomes an indispensable aspect of the yoga of the body. With the opening of these centres, we find that it is these energies that lie behind the functioning of the body organs and can eventually transform and replace the automatisms of the organs. The opening of the *cakra*s is also seen as a goal of Tantra.[39] However, in Sri Aurobindo's yoga, such an opening proceeds through a power of descending Śakti, rather than the traditional tāntric method of raising the coiled serpent energy (*kuṇḍalinī*) through *āsana*s and *prāṇāyāma* exercises. Moreover, the traditional tāntric method makes its goal the union (*yoga*) and dissolution (*laya*) of this *kuṇḍalinī śakti* in a superconscient *samādhi* above the brain-mind, in the highest centre, the *sahasradala* (thousand-petalled) lotus. In the Integral Yoga, the complete opening of the *cakra*s and the action of the involved *śakti* in the system is sought instead for a transformed divine working of the nature. For this, the operations of the *cakra*s need to be directed and controlled by a central power, a leader, which also changes through the course of the yoga.[40]

In traditional Tantra, various combinations of *āsana* and forms of *prāṇāyāma* are prescribed to raise the *kuṇḍalinī* at the base of the spine, up the central channel (*suṣumnā*) which carries the mystic centres or *cakra*s within it, as on a stem.[41] But, as with other aspects of yoga, Sri Aurobindo recommends minimising the reliance on automatic procedures and replacing these with more conscious processes, directed by perception, relation, affect, creative choice and will.[42] As a result, though one encounters often the specific terms related to the quartet

39. See John Woodroffe, *The Serpent Power*, London: Dover Publications 1974, pp. 103-256, 317-480. Also SoY, pp. 536-38.

40. SoY, pp. 541-42.

41. Woodroffe, op. cit.; SoY, pp. 536-38.

42. SoY, pp. 542, 612.

of the body in the *Record of Yoga*, there is little direct mention of physical exercises. The Indian tradition of physical yoga (*haṭha-yoga*) with its dependence on *āsana*s, is marked by its relative absence in this text or in Sri Aurobindo's or the Mother's teachings, though much emphasis is laid on developing the body consciousness through physical and psychological attention.

In Sri Aurobindo's own case, as mentioned in the Introduction, he followed a period of *prāṇāyāma* prior to his nirvāṇic experience, but dropped this practice long before the writing of his diary entries. In the *Record of Yoga*, the only *haṭha-yoga* practice he continued, was one of keeping an arm raised for extended periods of time, as part of his attention to the development of the force of lightness and levitation (*utthāpana*). But though, as with the other quartets, the emphasis is on psychological attention, the quartet of the body requires the conscious nexus of physical and psychological activity. For a good part of his stay in Pondicherry, Sri Aurobindo exercised this physical component through many hours of back-and-forth walking in his room everyday, while the Mother regularly played tennis. For the students and disciples at their *āśrama*, they emphasised regular physical activity in conjunction with forms of psychological attention, but left them free to find activities of their choice. Followers at the Sri Aurobindo Ashram, or Auroville, may be seen following a large array of practices ranging from *āsana*s, *ta'i chi*, calisthenics and weightlifting to long distance running, swimming, walking and many forms of sport such as soccer, tennis, badminton and even boxing. What matters in all these cases, is the internal attention and processes brought to bear on the physical activity. The Integral Yoga is meant to be practised in the midst of modern life activities. Though it is not meant to be subject to the conditioned forms of social life prevailing at present, it is meant to develop its own forms of "deterritorialized" society, in which "all life is yoga". Sri Aurobindo's interest in yoga was not one in preserving ahistorical

Śarīra Catuṣṭaya (Perfection of Body) (5.3)
The mystic centres (_cakras_)

	**Above the head**	– ***Sahasradala*** (Knowledge)
	**Between the eyes**	– ***Ājñā cakra*** (perception and will)
	**In the throat**	– ***Viśuddha*** (verbal expression, ***vāk***)
	**In the heart**	– ***Anāhata*** (emotions)
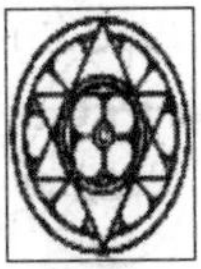	**Behind the anāhata**	**– the soul or psychic centre** (immanent divine)
	**In the navel**	– ***Maṇipūra*** (instincts)
	**Behind the sexual organs**	– ***Svādhiṣṭhāna*** (desires)
	**At the base of the spine**	– ***Mūlādhāra*** (involved consciousness)

"traditions" but in adapting non-modern understandings and practices towards a transformation of modernity.

Here, as generally in the Integral Yoga, the silent mind and its receptivity to a descending current of Higher Consciousness is made the basis of the physical attention for awakening the sleeping centres. The psychic will, acting as an aspiration invoking this higher conscious Śakti, with its origin above the human mind, receives its response in the form of a descent which acts on the different mystic centres, becoming a transformative agent on the nature through them and causing them to open. This descending current establishes a higher consciousness in the nature and in response to it, the sleeping energy (*kuṇḍalinī*) immanent in the being, gradually wakes and sends its ascending force upward to meet and join with the descending *śakti*.[43] This process is one of increasing consciousness and bypasses the dangers of an explosive and chaotic rising *kuṇḍalinī*, which often has side-effects bordering on insanity and needs the presence of an experienced teacher to stabilise the process. Instead, Sri Aurobindo's process relies on the guide or leader within, marked by consciousness. At first this leader, which must emerge and be the controller of the *cakra*s and their activities, is the soul entity, the psychic being; later, with the universalisation of the being, the consciousness rises to and settles in the *sahasradala* and it becomes the spiritual person above; and finally this leader and Master of the secret centres of the nature becomes directly the Supramental *Puruṣa*, the God Being, who takes the place of the immanent divine soul. This direct action of the mystic centres under the control of the Divine Person can transform the body structure itself and push it beyond its limits to a perfect and divine body.[44]

---

43. Sri Aurobindo, *Letters on Yoga I*, SABCL 22, pp. 73-74.
44. SABCL 22, p. 74.

In terms of Sri Aurobindo's terminology, the modes and operations of consciousness connected with each centre can be enumerated. All these centres are located in a subjective or subtle (*sūkṣma*) space, but one which is related to the physical in such a way that the actions and movements of the centres may be experienced as if in certain parts of the physical body, lying in a vertical axis along the spine. The highest of these centres is located above the head and named the *sahasradala*. *Sahasra* means thousand and *dala* means petals, thus, the name of this centre is thousand-petalled lotus. This centre opens to the operations of cosmic mental and supramental consciousness beyond the mentality that has been organised in normal human functioning. Between the eyes is the *ājñā cakra,* which controls mental perception and will. In the throat is the *viśuddha cakra,* which controls verbal expression, the expression of *vāk* — *vāk* is the Sanskrit term for verbal expression. In the heart is the *anāhata cakra,* which controls the emotions. Behind the *anāhata* is a centre where the soul resides with the Divine immanent within us. That is the sense of the "temple" in the first quote from Sri Aurobindo on the body which we considered. The meaning of the body, as the temple of god, springs from the fact that deep within the body, behind the heart, as in a temple, is the soul or psychic centre, with the immanent Divine seated in it. In the navel, is the *maṇipūra cakra,* which controls the vital will and instincts. Behind the sexual organs is the *svādhiṣṭhāna cakra* which controls the desires, greed, jealousy and sensations; and at the base of the spine is the *mūlādhāra*, which again opens (like the *sahasradala* above) to ranges of involved consciousness locked up in subconscience and inconscience. This, in a nutshell, is the map of the *cakra*s.[45] In Sri Aurobindo's yoga, it is the being in the *cakra* behind the heart, the psychic being, which has to emerge and become the leader and controller of all the seven other *cakra*s as the first

45. RoY, p. 1462.

stage towards the transformation of the being. Here, is a quotation from The *Supramental Transformation*, where he details the importance and action of the *cakras*:

> Something there is in us, or something has to be developed, perhaps a central and still occult part of our being containing forces whose powers in our actual and present make-up are only a fraction of what could be, but if they became complete and dominant would be truly able to bring about with the help of the light and force of the soul and the supramental truth-consciousness the necessary physical transformation and its consequences. This might be found in the system of *cakras* revealed by tāntric knowledge and accepted in the systems of yoga, conscious centres and sources of all the dynamic powers of our being, organising their action through the plexuses, and arranged in an ascending series from the lowest physical to the highest mind centre and spiritual centre called the thousand-petalled lotus where, ascending Nature, the Serpent Power of the tāntrics meets the *Brahman* and is liberated into the Divine Being. These centres are closed or half-closed within us and have to be opened before their full potentiality can be manifested in our physical nature. But once they are opened and completely active no limit can easily be set to the development of their potencies and the total transformation to be possible. . . .[46]
>
> There would have to be a change in the operative processes of the material organs themselves, and it may well be in their very constitution and their importance. They could not be allowed to impose their limitations imperatively on the new physical life. To begin with, they might become more clearly outer ends of the channels of communication and action, more serviceable for the psychological purposes of the inhabitant, less blindly material in their responses,

46. Sri Aurobindo, "The Supramental Manifestation on Earth" in EPY, p. 551.

more conscious of the act and aim of the inner movements and powers which use them and which they are wrongly supposed by the material man in us to generate and to use. The brain would be a channel of communication of the form of the thoughts and a battery of their insistence on the body and the outside world where they could then become effective directly, communicating themselves, without physical means from mind to mind, producing with a similar directness effects on the thoughts, actions and lives of others, or even upon material things.[47] The heart would equally be a direct communicant and medium of interchange for the feelings and emotions thrown out for it upon the world by the forces of the psychic centre. Heart could reply directly to heart, the life force comes to the help of other lives and answers their call in spite of strangeness and distance, many beings, without any external communication, thrill with the message and meet in the secret light from one divine centre. The will might control the organs that deal with food, safeguard automatically the health, eliminate greed and desire, substitute subtler processes that draw in strength and substance from the universal life force, so that the body could maintain for a long time its own strength and substance without loss or waste, remaining thus, with no need of sustenance by material aliments and yet continue a strenuous action with no fatigue or pause or sleep or repose. The soul's will or the mind's, could act from higher sources upon the sex centre and the sex organs so as to check firmly or even banish the grosser sexual impulse or stimulus, and instead of serving an animal excitation or crude drive or desire, turn their use to the storing, production and direction towards brain and heart and life force of the essential energy (*ojas*) of which this region is the factory, so as to support the works of mind and soul and spirit and the higher life powers

---

47. As seen when dealing with the quartet of knowledge, this pertains to the *siddhis* of telepathy, *prakāmya* and *vyāpti*. In *Record of Yoga* we find innumerable instances of experiments in this area.

and limit the expenditure of the energy on lower things.[48] The soul, the psychic being, could more easily fill all with the light and turn the very matter of the body to higher uses for its own greater purpose.

This would be a first potent change but not by any means all that is possible or desirable. For, it may well be that the evolutionary urge would proceed to a change of the organs themselves in their material working and use and diminish greatly the need of their instrumentation and even of their existence. The centres in the *sūkṣma śarīra,* of which one would become conscious and aware of all going on in it, would pour their energies into material nerve and plexus and tissue and radiate them through the whole material body; all the physical life and its necessary activities in this new existence could be maintained and operated by these higher agencies, in a freer and ampler way, and by a less burdensome and restricting method. This might go so far that these organs might cease to be indispensable and even felt as too obstructive, the central force might use them less and less and finally throw aside their used altogether. If that happened they might waste by atrophy, be reduced to an insignificant minimum or even disappear. The central force might substitute for them subtle organs of a very different character or, if anything material was needed, instruments that would be forms of dynamism or plastic transmitters rather than what we know as organs.[49]

This might well be part of a supreme total transformation of the body though this too might not be final. To envisage such changes is to look far ahead and minds attached to the present form of things may be unable to give credence to

48. This relates to the discussion on sexual continence earlier in this chapter.

49. The transformation of the organs, which the Mother speaks of in *The Agenda* conversations are referred to here. Deleuze's notion of the "Body without Organs" is pertinent here.

> their possibility. No such limits and no such impossibility of any necessary change can be imposed on the evolutionary urge. . . .[50]

Freedom from Laws of Matter

All of the above were related to the first of the four perfections of the *śarīra catuṣṭaya*, i.e. *ārogya*, but in some ways this is the most profound of the four. The next power enumerated in this quartet is *utthāpana*.[51] This is its literal meaning, but it forms part of the freedom of the body, because the perfection of the body implies its becoming fully conscious and thus, no longer subject to any conditioning that it does not choose. Gravitation is one such primary conditioning factor for the body, part of its material determinism. A perfect body should be able to overcome this determinism because it is not its own choice. So *utthāpana*, in a broader sense, means freedom from subjection to the laws of Matter. This *siddhi*, too, is related to one of the eight *siddhi*s (*aṣṭa-siddhi*) of the *vijñāna catuṣṭaya*. This is *laghimā*, the ability to reduce the weight of things, which Sri Aurobindo refers to as a basis for *utthāpana*.[52] As we saw while discussing the quartet of knowledge (Chapter 4), this is one of the traditional *siddhi*s of yoga and Tantra, as seen in verse 40 of the fourth chapter (Vibhūti Pada) of Patañjali's *Yoga-Sūtras*.

For *utthāpana*, some of the same foundational disciplines considered for *ārogya* are to be cultivated, such as continence, faith and the fulfilled action of the Śakti. Perhaps the most important among these is continence, since this involves the reversal of the direction of natural energy, leading to the development of a force of lightness in the body. But, another very important mastery to develop here is control over the *prāṇa*s. The *prāṇa*s are life energies operating within us which

---

50. EPY, pp. 553-55.
51. RoY, pp. 23, 1477.
52. Ibid., pp. 19, 22, 1473, 1475.

we need to become conscious of. Sri Aurobindo identifies a physical and a subjective *prāṇa* which is at work in the human system. Of these, for the purposes of the quartet of the body, mastery over the physical *prāṇa*s is among the necessities.[53] In traditional yogic disciplines, this is achieved through what is called *prāṇāyāma*. In Sri Aurobindo's own life, he practised some *prāṇāyāma* for about two years and then stopped it. But he does not particularly recommend it (though he doesn't have anything against it either). He rather enjoins becoming conscious of the action of the *prāṇa*s directly by power of consciousness. By withdrawing our consciousness from the body and subjecting it to observation, we become aware of the movement of the different energies inside us, and can control their operations. This is the method towards the awareness and control of the *prāṇa*s.[54]

The Physical Prāṇas

What are the *prāṇa*s? In Indian yogic literature and as Sri Aurobindo describes it, there are five *prāṇa*s which move in specific and characteristic ways within the body.[55] The first of these is called *prāṇa* itself and it moves from the top of the body to the navel. The second is called *apāna*, and moves upwards from the base of the spine, or *mūlādhāra*, to the navel. The third one is *samāna*. *Prāṇa* and *apāna* meet together in the navel and create a new kind of vital current called *samāna*. *Samāna* creates the *bhūta*s, or elemental building-blocks from the food. In other words, there is an energetic component to all that we eat, whether dieticians recognise this or not. Nutrition is not merely a question of balancing proteins, carbohydrates and starch. There is a different level of *bhūta*s that are generated in the subtle body from whatever we eat,

53. SoY, pp. 348-49.
54. Ibid., p. 349.
55. RoY, p. 1462.

Śarīra Catuṣṭaya (Perfection of Body) (5.4)

Utthāpana (Freedom from subjection to physical forces): celibacy, control over *prāṇas*, faith, physical consciousness, fulfilled action of divine *śakti*.

The five *prāṇas* (vital currents) and their Movement in the Body

Prāṇa	• Moves from the top of body to the navel
Apāna	• Move from the base of the spine (*mūlādhāra*) to the navel.
Samāna	• Created by the meeting together of *prāṇa* and *apāna* in the navel centre. Samāna creates *bhūta* (elemental building blocks) from the food
Vyāna	• Moves in the entire body, distributes the *bhūta* created by *samāna* in the body
Udāna	• Moves from the navel to the head carrying *tejas*. – in *yogī*, moves from *mūlādhāra* to *sahasrāra* transforming *retas* to *ojas* (*ūrdhvaretas*).

and this is accomplished through the agency of a prāṇic current called *samāna*; these elements are then distributed throughout the system. This distribution of the *bhūtas* is achieved by another prāṇic current, called *vyāna*. The fifth *prāṇa* is called *udāna*. *Udāna* is related to the word *uḍāna* which means "to fly", it moves from the navel to the head carrying a concentrated energy, *tejas* to the head. *Tejas* is the radiant element inside us, a concentrated force of radiance. In the *yogī* who has mastered the *prāṇas*, this energy of *udāna* moves not just from the navel but from further down, from the *mūlādhāra* to the *sahasrāra*, all the way from the bottom to the top, transforming the crude sexual energy *retas* to its refined and light qualitative form, *ojas*, which is why this movement is called *ūrdhva retas*, in other words, the "upwardisation" of

Śarīra Catuṣṭaya (Perfection of Body) (5.5)

Utthāpana (Freedom from subjection to physical forces): celibacy, control over ***prāṇas***, faith, physical consciousness, fulfilled action of divine ***Śakti***.

Fullness of *prāṇa śakti* – force, lightness and strength in the body – ability to draw energy from Universal Nature.

Freedom from physical weariness and exhaustion of brain or nervous or emotional responses.

Freedom from subjection to the law of gravitation or other physical laws.

Śarīra Catuṣṭaya (Perfection of Body) (5.6)

Saundarya (Beauty and harmony of the physical being): *celibacy, faith, physical consciousness, control of physical substance from soul or spiritual centres, fulfiled action of divine* ***śakti***

Brightness in the body, sweetness of voice, spiritual attractiveness (divine charisma).

Continual youth (aspiration for progress, physical regeneration)

Plasticity of physical form to image of soul (psychic) or spiritual beauty.

the sexual current, the transformation of its quality to a radiance which will uphold the body, give its strength, endurance and ultimately transform it into a divine substance with the powers that we talked about earlier. Thus, control of *udāna* is the primary means to the attainment of *utthāpana*, an anti-gravitational force.[56]

Stages of Utthāpana

Utthāpana also has three stages. The first of these is the fullness of the *prāṇa-śakti*, which means force, lightness and strength in the body.[57] This comes through the ability to draw energy from universal nature. In the quote from Sri Aurobindo carried earlier while considering the action of the *cakra*s, he introduces this idea. The Chinese discipline of physical movement known as *t'ai chi*, for example, is a good preparation leading to this power of drawing *prāṇa* from universal nature, but this can also be drawn directly through the action of the prāṇic currents within us directed by mental awareness and will. This ability to replenish the physical energy through the universal *prāṇa* and ultimately from the higher *prāṇa* above the mind is a necessary power of the *prāṇa-śakti* that needs to be developed for the freedom of the body from its subjection to material aliments. This is what gives fullness of *prāṇa-śakti* to the body.

The second stage is a higher degree of the same; it includes freedom from physical weariness and exhaustion of brain or nervous or emotional response. One has such a tremendous plenitude of *prāṇa*, that there is a constant and immediate replenishment. This regeneration of energy is analogous to the regeneration of the cells which we discussed earlier. Energy is constantly regenerated, because there is a habitual current of exchange established in the nature.[58] In our normal functioning too, there is an invisible and unconscious exchange of energy between individual and environment, which goes on at all times. Children seem to have inexhaustible energy, because they have few mental or vital reservations in the

56. RoY, p. 1462.
57. Ibid., p. 1477.
58. Ibid.

outflow or intake of energy with their environment. Adults, on the other hand, maintain a precarious dynamic balance of energy with their environment, because adult energy is portioned and directed by the will, which has short and long-term investments in certain life goals and exists in a compromised social economy.[59] The nature and quality of human desires and goals, along with mental preferences and social expectations, determines the scope of our prāṇic exchanges.

As we have seen, *prāṇa,* like physical energy, is characterised by quantity, intensity and quality. The child does not discriminate about the quality of energy exchanges, giving and receiving unreservedly. The adult develops an unconscious economy of energy exchange, which supports the quality and intensity of his or her desires and life-goals. This balance can be more or less easily upset, if there is a change in the amount or quality of *prāṇa,* maintaining the economy. This is why, certain contacts or activities may be felt as energising or tiring, or may bring illness to the body. In the quest for a more conscious functioning of the nature, the balance of *prāṇa* undergoes important changes, so that certain energies which were agreeable or even supportive, may no longer agree with it, leaving one exhausted or sick. There thus develops a need to change one's sources of prāṇic support, drawing on subtler and more conscious forms and eschewing more confused, hostile and unconscious forms. An automatic inner balance is facilitated by the Divine Śakti working within the nature; and following its inner directives and intuitions becomes a way by which to progress in the capacity of the *prāṇa-śakti.*[60] Thus, in the *sādhaka* (aspirant) the power of the *prāṇa-śakti* is constantly

---

59. "Energy Inexhaustible". The Mother, *On Education,* CWM: 12, p. 261.
60. Ibid.

calling on some higher divine stream of energy that enters the body in ceaseless currents.[61] It is symbols of this process that we find in Indian mythology, in myths or legends like that of the river Gaṅgā, descending from above as a celestial river. This is really a symbol for the supreme Divine Śakti entering into the human body by the call from below, the constant call of the prāṇic *śakti*.

Finally, the third stage of *utthāpana* is freedom from subjection to the law of gravitation or other physical laws.[62] Sri Aurobindo touches on these but leaves them mostly without elaboration. They also overlap with the physical *siddhi*s of the quartet of supermind, *aṇimā, laghimā* and *utthāpana*, already mentioned, and include such powers as dematerialisation of the physical form, or becoming radiant, radiating light. Sri Aurobindo has many entries in the *Record of Yoga* on freedom from subjection to the law of gravitation. He approached these stages relating to the power of levitation primarily through an *āsana* where he lifted an arm and left it in an upraised position for extended periods of time, using the power of *uḍāna* to maintain its position.[63]

Beauty

The next perfection in the quartet of the body is *saundarya*, which means beauty and harmony of the physical form.[64] This again is an area at odds with much of the traditional formulation of Indian Yoga, according to which the body is a mutating structure subject to ageing and death, and thus, not worthy of attention beyond basic maintenance, so as to support an exclusive attention on the realisation of the transcendental

61. "Energy Inexhaustible". The Mother, *On Education*, CWM: 12, p. 261.
62. RoY, p. 1477.
63. Some examples can be found in *Record of Yoga*, pp. 34, 36, 57, 61, 67, 70, etc.
64. RoY, p. 1477.

spirit, which alone is eternal. Moreover, concern with the beauty of the body is held to be a sign of vanity, an enablement of the ego. But, from Sri Aurobindo's perspective, the physical form is a perpetually regenerating structure which is meant to express divinity. A primary physical attribute of divinity is Beauty. In the Indian conception, this finds expression in the forms of the Purāṇic gods, who are depicted with the bodies of 16-year-olds, described as the epitome of Beauty. The supreme person (*Puruṣottama*) is also the supreme attractor of all beings in the cosmos. Thus, this Divine Beauty becomes an essential aspect of the perfection of the body. Each human being, in his or her essence, is a specific combination of divine qualities. This combination finds its form of expression in the psychic being or soul personality. The physical aspect of this soul personality manifests the specific form of beauty, which is the physical expression of that aspect of divinity. The Mother, in her talks on education titled the Four Austerities and the Four Liberations, makes the aspiration for expressing harmony and beauty a necessary part of physical education for children, preparing for this more esoteric and integral aspect touched on in the quartet of the body:

> A young child should aspire for beauty, not for the sake of pleasing others or winning their admiration, but for the love of beauty itself; for beauty is the ideal which all physical life must realise. Every human being has the possibility of establishing harmony among the different parts of his body and in the various movements of the body in action.[65]

It is this unique qualitative beauty, then, which needs to manifest through the physical structure, dynamically, through all its changes.

Among the primary characteristics, forming the first stage of that qualitative expression, are radiance in the body,

65. The Mother, *On Education*, CWM: 12, p. 16.

sweetness of voice, and spiritual attractiveness.[66] Each of these qualities uplifts the consciousness towards a higher mystic archetype and needs to be distinguished from what is normally called charisma, a vital attractiveness, which stimulates or excites the surface consciousness. The spiritual attractiveness of divine beauty on the other hand, is accompanied by a calm elevation and makes its message felt directly to the soul or psychic being. The second stage in *saundarya,* is perpetual youth. This is related to the aspiration for progress and regeneration in the body, which we have had occasion to consider earlier. Finally, in the progress of this attribute, the consciousness of the physical being reaches a high intensity where the material form becomes plastic to the moulding influence of the psychic being, or higher divine person, imaging one's divine archetype constantly through the body.[67]

Bliss

The fourth and last of the perfections of the *śarīra catuṣṭaya* is *ānanda. Ānanda* recurs in some form in all of the *catuṣṭaya*s and can be thought of as a culminating sign of divine realisation. In the body, *ānanda* becomes established in a variety of forms. *Kāmānanda* is the general rubric of bliss in the body under which all these forms are enumerated by Sri Aurobindo.[68] He also refers to them as *vividhānanda,* (varied forms of bliss) due to, there being a number of them.[69] Sri Aurobindo identifies five forms of *kāmānanda* that are to be established on a constant basis in the body.[70] The first of these is *vaidyutānanda,* which is the coursing of a blissful electricity through the nerves. There is the sense of a blissful electric current, constantly generated

66. RoY, p. 1477.
67. Ibid.
68. Ibid., pp. 1477, 1481, 47.
69. Ibid., pp. 23, 1490.
70. Ibid., p. 1456.

in the body, and coursing through the nerves. One experiences sometimes, a pleasurable tingling in the nerves as part of an experience of physical well-being. Perhaps, *vaidyutānanda* is an enhanced intensity of this experience of sensation.

Śarīra Catuṣṭaya (Perfection of Body) (5.7)

Kāmānanda (Bliss in the physical being): *equality, celibacy, faith, purified physical consciousness, fulfilled action of divine śakti*

Vaidyutānanda	– coursing of blissful electricity through nerves
Raudrānanda	– conversion of painful responses to form of bliss
Tīvrānanda	– experience of ecstatic waves in the physical – form of thrill
Viṣayānanda	– bliss of contact with the One through senses in sense-objects
Maithunānanda	– bliss of union and identity with the One in beings and objects

The second is *raudrānanda*.[71] We came across a reference to this form of bliss earlier in this chapter, while considering the Mother's commentary to one of Sri Aurobindo's aphorisms in the section pertaining to immortality. There are many examples of this recorded by Sri Aurobindo in his diaries and elsewhere.[72] This form of bliss is what one might call a fierce intensity and arises from the subjective conversion of painful responses to forms of bliss. The key to this form of bliss is the

71. RoY, p. 1456.

72. See, for example, RoY, pp. 38 (ant bite), 47 (heat and cold), 60, 497-98 (neuralgia), 609 (blow on elbow), 1025 (burning touch).

establishment of an unshakeable equality in the cells and nerves. When we considered the perfection of equality, we saw that it began with a passive equality, the culmination of which was an imperturbable gladness of acceptance. This led to a more active equality, which progressed through degrees of *ānanda* to ecstasy (*hāsya*). This equality, when applied to the responses of the body also leads through degrees to a fierce intensity of delight, *raudrānanda*.

Since, following the Vedāntic conception, delight is behind all manifestation, what we experience as pain, could be thought of as an intensity of delight, too powerful to bear, which is why the body responds with pain.[73] Technically, therefore, extension of the body's power of consciousness can lead to a transformation of this experience. Here, the extremes of subjection of the physical body that we discussed in *ārogya,* are not only endured, but also converted into forms of delight. In his diaries, Sri Aurobindo makes a number of references to this form of physical bliss. He uses extreme conditions of nature, such as walking barefoot on the hot stones of the courtyard, in the intense heat of Pondicherry in summer, to test this experience.[74] Perhaps, this experience is akin to fire-walking, walking on hot coals. The experience he records, is one of ecstasy instead of pain. Sri Aurobindo has spoken about several other notable experiences of *raudrānanda*. One of these pertains to a scorpion sting, which could have been lethal. Not only did he not suffer any toxic effects, he records his success in converting the experience to one of bliss. He also writes about this in an interesting poem, in which he assumes what seems to be a Vedic persona. The poem is one of a set under the title Meditations of Mandavya:

73. See "Delight of Existence: The Solution" in *The Life Divine*, p. 116; also "He stung Himself with bliss and called it pain" in the poem "Parābrahman", CP, p. 218.

74. Example RoY, p. 48.

While on a terrace hushed
I walked at night,
He came and stung my foot.
My soul surprised
Rejoiced in lover's contact;
But the mind thought of a scorpion
And was snared by forms.
Still, still my soul remembered its delight.
Denying mind, and midst the body's pain,
I laughed contented.[75]

The third form of physical bliss is called *tīvrānanda*.[76] This is the experience of physical thrill, ecstatic waves passing through the body. Thrill seekers, through dangerous sports or adventures, or those experiencing drug-induced ecstasies or extreme amazement, feel a rush of adrenaline and physical symptoms such as hair standing on end, what is sometimes called horripilation in mystic literature. The development of *tīvrānanda* may include a continuous series of ecstatic waves passing through the body. A high intensity of this experience is said to end in a "swoon" of absorption in many ecstatic mystic sects, such as Vaiṣṇavism or Sufism.[77] But, in Sri Aurobindo's practice, the body is made to develop a capacity to remain conscious and unmoved while allowing these experiences to pass through. This is termed *ānanda dhāraṇa sāmarthya* (the capacity to hold *ānanda*).[78] This is facilitated by the emergence of the physical *Puruṣa*.

The next form of bliss is *viṣayānanda*.[79] *Viṣaya* refers to material substance. *Viṣayānanda* is the bliss of contact with

---

75. Sri Aurobindo, CP, pp. 509-10.
76. RoY, p. 1456.
77. Sūfīs designate this condition as *wajd*. See the *Concise Oxford Dictionary of World Religions* 1997, originally published by Oxford: Oxford University Press, 1997.
78. See discussion of *ānandadhāraṇāśakti* in RoY, p. 48.
79. RoY, p. 1456.

material objects. This contact may occur through any or all the senses — sight (*dṛṣṭi*), hearing (*śruti*), smell (*gandha*), taste (*svāda*) and touch (*sparśa*). We had occasion to consider the pure enjoyment (*śuddha bhoga*) of the subtle taste of sense contacts (*rasa grahaṇa*) when considering the purification (*śuddhi*) and enjoyment (*bhukti*) of the mental instrument (*citta, manas* and *buddhi*). In this physical form of *ānanda*, all sense contacts with material objects translate to a direct physical delight, experiencing the intrinsic delight of the One Being, the *Brahman* (*ānanda Brahman*) in Matter. All material objects speak to us in a language of delight in every contact, because one experiences the One self-delighted Being in all of these things. In a poem Sri Aurobindo puts it thus:

> In every contact's deep invading thrill,
> That lasts as if the source was infinite,
> I feel thy touch; Thy bliss imperishable
> Is crowded into that moment of delight.
> The body burns with thy rapture's sacred fire,
> Pure, passionate, holy, virgin of desire.[80]

The final form of physical bliss is *maithunānanda*.[81] The term *maithunānanda*, in common usage, refers to sexual bliss, erotic ecstasy. As Sri Aurobindo uses it here, this refers to a higher intensity of the *viṣayānanda*, in which the sense of the One Being as *Brahman*, is replaced by the concrete physical experience of the Divine Person as the supreme lover, engaging in physical contact through all the objects of the world. We catch a hint of this in the last two lines of the sonnet "Divine Sense" quoted above.[82] Thus, all material objects are here experienced as the physical embrace of the lover in things. This experience includes an erotic charge which spreads

80. "Divine Sense" in Sri Aurobindo, CP, p. 624. See also the poems "The Divine Hearing" and "Divine Sight", CP, pp. 622-23.

81. RoY, p. 1456.

82. CP, pp. 622-23.

through the entire body. It is the bliss of physical union and identity in all beings and objects. In other words, everything is experienced as the Supreme Divine Being, entering into identity and union with one concretely as a physical experience, and this erotic ecstasy of identity is known as *maithunānanda*. In comparison with sexual ecstasy, Sri Aurobindo points out that the *maithunānanda* "is far higher, finer and more intense than the sexual, but of which the sexual is a coarse and excited degradation".[83] It is important to note that complete transcendence of sexual desire is the precondition for the experience of these spiritual *ānanda*s in the physical.[84] In his diary entries, Sri Aurobindo often clubs these physical *ānanda*s with the *ānanda*s, which form part of *bhukti* (enjoyment) in the quartet of perfection, *siddhi catuṣṭaya*. There, he refers to the physical *ānanda*s as *kāmānanda* and the rest as "the subjective *ānanda*s".[85] Each of these *ānanda*s may be occasioned by some cause (*sahaituka*) or, be causeless and spontaneous, that is, experienced without any external or internal stimulus (*ahaituka*), due to the realisation of the intrinsic self-Delight of *Brahman*.

When considering the quartet of equality, we saw how these capacities of experiencing physical bliss in all contacts of the world, relate to the ideas of transformed physical capacity beyond pleasure and pain, in a scale of intensity in the work of the contemporary philosopher Gilles Deleuze. The realisations of the quartet of the body, lend themselves to close comparison with the formation of Deleuze and Guattari's "Body without Organs". The transformation of the body, envisaged by Sri Aurobindo, aims at a similar functional

83. Nirodbaran, *Correspondence with Sri Aurobindo*, Pondicherry: Sri Aurobindo Ashram, p. 795.
84. SoY, p. 595.
85. RoY, p. 1481.

independence of the body parts, as we saw in the discussion of the *cakra*s, a refusal at conditioning, and a conscious and creative participation in all experience, without burnout or breakage. But it goes beyond this in positing the transformed "corps glorieux" or divine body, in which the "organs" are formatious upheld by the direct action of consciousness.

6

The Quartet of Being

In the yoga of integral transformation, the four first limbs — the practices of equality, power, knowledge, and of the body — constitute, what Sri Aurobindo calls the *ādhāra siddhi.* Broadly speaking, *ādhāra siddhi* refers to the perfecting of the psychological make-up. The next three limbs — the *karma catuṣṭaya, brahma catuṣṭaya* and *siddhi catuṣṭaya* — that is, the quartets of action, of being and of yoga, constitute what he calls the general *siddhi*s.[1] They are overarching methods and goals within which the *ādhāra siddhi*s form the more specific processes and goals. In this chapter, we will consider the *brahma catuṣṭaya* (the quartet of being) which is a general *siddhi,* one of the foundational bases of the Integral Yoga. In the order of the *siddhi*s generally followed in his diary notes, the quartet of being is the last but one of the quartets, following the quartet of action and preceding the quartet of perfection. But, Sri Aurobindo's elaboration in the Yoga of Self-Perfection section of *The Synthesis of Yoga* begins with the *siddhi catuṣṭaya,* and since this quartet introduces the most overarching concepts of the practice, we too began our consideration with this. Again, while considering the central core of the quartet of yoga, we saw how this can be thought of as a use of "the method of Vedānta to arrive at the aim of the Tantra".[2] In the language of the *siddhi catuṣṭaya, śuddhi* and *mukti* (purification

1. RoY, p. 23.
2. SoY, p. 612.

and liberation) are the conditions for *bhukti* and *siddhi* (enjoyment and perfection).[3] The "method of Vedānta" implies a reliance on *Puruṣa* or *Brahman*. The "aim of the Tantra" implies perfection (*siddhi*) in Śakti, or a transformed perfection in action and enjoyment. Attainment of integral Being becomes the means to a perfect and integral becoming. Hence, in our consideration here, we will position the *brahma catuṣṭaya* before the *karma catuṣṭaya*; so the *brahma catuṣṭaya* will be the penultimate quartet to be considered by us.

Non-Dual Seeing and the Vision of Reality

Brahma catuṣṭaya, which I have translated loosely as the quartet of being, is also designated by Sri Aurobindo as *brahma darśanam* (vision[4] of *Brahman*). This quartet consists of *sarvam* which means sameness, omnipresence, *anantam*, which means infinity or radical difference, the infinite potency/variety of becoming, omnipotence, *jñānam*, which is omniscience, and *ānandam*, which is delight.[5] Before considering the implications of these terms, it is important to understand what is aimed at in the quartet of Being. As pointed out, the aim of this quartet is *brahma darśanam*. To understand this, we can look more closely at the two terms *brahma* and *darśana*: *brahma* is *Brahman*, which can be translated as Reality or Being. This refers to the fact that we start with the assumption of One Being, or One Reality, that is present everywhere and as all things, that though we enter into a world where we perceive each other as separate, there is, in reality nothing other than the One which expresses through everything, a univocity. Now, we could think about a Being and a Becoming. A Becoming refers to the expression or manifestation of Being. In other words, if all that is manifest is taken away, Being would still

3. RoY, pp. 23, 24, 1478.
4. Ibid., p. 432.
5. Ibid., pp. 23, 1478.

remain. However, within our experience we find that there are processes at work in the world; processes which are not only fixed in the sense that they remain the same or repeat unchangeably in cycles, but also processes which are progressive. In other words, they include a sense of growth. This progressive process, which we participate in, as our phenomenal experience, is what may be called the Becoming. This, we may think of Reality unequivocally as the One Being there is, and that is all that need or can be said about it; but on the other hand, we can also consider that Being as a dynamic self-exploration. This is the very meaning of time, the perception of the eternal as the perennial, through the selective filter of a Real Idea.[6] If we think of *Brahman* in this fashion, the perfection of Being and the perfection of action refer to these two elements of *Brahman* — *Brahman* as a Being and *Brahman* as a Becoming.

Thus, we may think of two sides of the same Reality — there is One Being and it perceives itself as One Becoming, which is the process that defines time for us. We are part of that dual reality, we exist within it, in our own individual and independent ways, but our independence is only an expressive front for the totality of Being-in-Becoming; while at the same time, each of us is that Being and that Becoming. As a result, we may conceive of realising our identity with that Being and with that Becoming. This would form the scope for the term *brahma*.

To continue our consideration of *brahma darśanam*, if *Brahman* is the One Reality there is, the term *darśana* has a number of connotations in the Sanskrit language. In everyday

---

6. Real Idea can be distinguished from conceptual idea in that the former is reality itself embodied as world and its forms. In Sri Aurobindo's words, "The world is therefore not a figment of conception in the universal Mind, but a conscious birth of that which is beyond Mind into forms of itself." LD, p. 125.

language, *darśana* means "to see". But there are also specialised meanings to the word *darśana*. *Darśana* also means spiritual philosophy. All the schools of philosophy in India, are known as *darśanas*. And thirdly, *darśana* is an encounter with an icon or a *guru*. In India, when one says one is going for *darśana* either to a temple or to see a *guru*, a realised Being, what one means is that one is going to see the icon or the *guru*. But there is more to the nature of this seeing which needs consideration. The nature of *darśana* in encountering a *guru* includes the sense that one is seeing and also being seen. It is a mutuality of seeing that is implied. The full connotation of *darśana* goes even beyond this, the moment of true *darśana* occurs in a merging into identity of such mutual seeing. In such a non-dual moment, the seer and the seen, disappear into a purity of sight. In other words, all that remains is the act of seeing which does not belong to any person. Such a moment of transcendence belongs to Being. This is the seeing of Being. This understanding of *darśana* helps to clarify its sense as spiritual philosophy: to see is to be. In philosophical terms we may say, phenomenology is ontology. Identity with Being is the basis of seeing and the resultant description of seeing is the description of Being. In fact, something like this could also be asserted about our everyday existence: we cannot see anything that, in essence, we are not — our seeing is conditioned by our being.[7] But here we go one step further and assert that when we are identified with the One Reality, we see with the eyes of that Reality. This is non-dual seeing.

To arrive at this point, however, we must first acknowledge the fact that we start from a dualistic phenomenal

---

7. This was the direction in which Martin Heidegger attempted to extend the subjectivist phenomenology of Husserl. In Heidegger's ontological extension, states of personal consciousness (phenomenology) were not seen as primordial but rested on and included the totality of Being (ontology) and its determinants.

experience. Our experience is one of an "I" and a "thou", there is always this separation. There is a plurality of beings that are encountering one another. In the encounter with the icon or with the *guru*, the encounter of *darśana* too, we start with a dualism: two states of consciousness encountering one another. But eventually, there is an overcoming of that duality, and this is the moment of *darśana*. Similarly, *darśana* as spiritual philosophy, refers to the expression of a non-dual condition, and a reasoned description of universal reality based on such an experience.

There are a number of *darśana*s in India, and many of these are based on what is called Vedānta. Vedānta is the philosophy of the Upaniṣads, whose foundational basis is the assertion of a single and infinite conscious Reality. That Reality may be seen in different ways in terms of its relations to itself and to its parts, and the philosophical description of these relations, based on the non-dual experience of that Reality is what the Vedāntic *darśana*s describe. So, *brahma darśanam* implies arriving at the constant non-dual seeing of the *Brahman*. Sri Aurobindo has a sentence in *The Synthesis of Yoga* in which he encapsulates the entirety of the integral yoga in terms of *brahma darśanam*. It says, "This realisation of oneness and this practice of oneness in difference is the whole of the yoga."[8]

Mind and The Problem of Duality

This sentence could also be thought of as a succinct statement of the *brahma catuṣṭaya* and a definition of the entire yoga of integral transformation from its perspective. It also touches on the other general perfection — that of *karma catuṣṭaya*. Realisation of oneness is *brahma darśanam*. And the practice of oneness in difference could be thought of as the perfection of action, which is the *karma catuṣṭaya*. Both these are linked to each other. In both cases we find that the yoga is

8. SoY, p. 420.

being described in terms of a movement out of duality, of separation, to a state of non-duality — both in Being and in Becoming.

What are the dimensions of an integral non-duality? This question relates to another more basic one — if all of the *darśanas* are based in the experience of a non-dual reality, why are there differences in their expression? To approach these profound questions, we must go even further in our questioning. Where does the problem arise? Why is it that we experience a world of duality? Where does the separation come from? How deep is the separation? And what are the essential features of that separation? Why is it that we don't experience oneness all the time? Sri Aurobindo tells us that the problem of duality and its experience stems from the Mind.[9] By Mind, it is not the human mind that is meant. Human beings are not the creators of this problem, they are the inheritors of this problem by dint of the possession of mind. By mind is meant the principle of mentation, a universal principle. Human beings find themselves with the faculty of mind, but they also sense the presence of mind in the universe. The very fact that the human mind can describe the natural universe in terms of laws, gives evidence to the presence of mind in the universe. Duality is a property of mental experience. In other words, our experience of the universe is under the determination of mind, and thus, in its basis marked by duality — an experience of being, what in philosophy is called an ontology, which is one of division. The ontology of human experience follows from the ontology of universal experience, which is conditioned by mind. Mind — cosmic mind — is what has created this condition of dualism, because this is the instrument used by *Brahman* to produce multiple individualities. It is a device by which Being can experience

9. See "Supermind, Mind and the Overmind Māyā", Chapter XXVIII, LD, pp. 285-304.

itself as many separate and independent beings. As human beings, we find ourselves in a condition where we experience this in its fullest form: we are individuals who have a very acute sense of being selves, and as selves each of us confronts the world as if it were its own private universe. Everything, and everybody else, is subsidiary or secondary to our personal individual existence. This is the device by which the One has fragmented itself so that it may exist in its latency in each of its infinite portions or possibilities of being.

Let us consider how this becomes possible. We may think of an infinite non-duality, an indivisible Being, but if that indivisible Being is to enter into relations with itself, it develops awareness of itself as possessing "parts", and if it were to make these parts into points of self-prospection and self-experience, we would have a condition in which each part experiences itself as the entire Being. *Brahman* as the self-experience of indivisible being can be co-extensive with its self-experience through its parts. But it could also, by an exclusivity of concentration, produce an experience of being where the parts experience themselves as separate from the totality of Being. We may say that by this device the entirety of *Brahman* becomes latent in each of its self-conceived part(icle)s. This is the condition of being and sentience in our universe and this is our condition.

The instrument of exclusive self-concentration by which *Brahman* produces this condition is the mind. We may ask the question — the logical question that follows from this — why would *Brahman* want to manifest such an experience? What is the need for these particles to experience a separation, which is a painful experience, one may even say, the origin of pain — because the result of the separation is pain?[10] Each of us experiences him/her-self to be a conscious living whole,

10. LD, pp. 622-23.

rubbing against or running into other living wholes that share the same room of space and time in which we find ourselves.

We understand this very clearly because in our own human experience, however small or limited, we can see how easily, once one has tasted of the freedom of a room or a home for oneself, or of one's own car, one's own possessions or relations, it feels insufferable to allow somebody else to share it. This problem of sharing is, at base, an ontological problem, a problem of Being; at its root is the exclusive concentration of indivisible being in its self-conceived parts — what can be thought of as an involution of being in its parts and the consequent fragmentation of Being with the suffering or malaise that has resulted from that.

Why is this necessary? Of course, one can avoid this question by saying that it is irrelevant to *Brahman*. Some *darśanas* have taken this stand. But this would violate the Vedāntic ontology of non-duality, which implies that there is a single self-conscious Reality. If *Brahman* by definition is the only Being there is, and it is conscious, then any act within it can only be a conscious act. Another way to sidestep this question would be to invoke the ultimate incomprehensibility of *Brahman*. Even if *Brahman* is conscious, we can never fathom its purposes. Though it is possible to make such an argument, it violates our deepest intuition of an ideational content to the universe, which mind opens to us.

An Evolutionary Being-in-Becoming

Sri Aurobindo answers this question by seeing this involution of Being in its parts as the basis of an evolutionary process. Again, we can return to the Being and the Becoming. Such an evolutionary process is a form of Becoming, in which each of these possibilities of the One Infinite Being develops in consciousness to the realisation that it is identical with each and all of the Others. Thus, it is not some great sacrifice of "sharing" space and time with others, which is the truth of individual existence, but a realisation of the play of unity in difference which is the significance of this evolutionary Being-in-Becoming.[11]

Let us recollect against this, the aphorism of Sri Aurobindo introduced earlier: "The realisation of oneness and the practice of oneness in difference is the whole of the yoga." It is the movement from the each through the All to the One, which is the process that is generated out of the apparent fragmentation of Being. To explore further the "why" of this Becoming, Sri Aurobindo extends two further ideas which find validation in the Vedāntic tradition: One of these is that this process itself is a form of Delight, the delight of growth and adventure — to experience the widening of horizons, to discover an ever-expanding Infinite richness. This is an essential aspect of Delight, the original and intrinsic Delight of Being at play, in action, in Becoming.[12] The second idea is that this process is a movement towards a certain realisation of *Brahman*, the One Being — a realisation of Oneness in its opposite, multiplicity. That is the condition of the play of the Divine as Delight. If the Divine remained the One without a second, it would not be possible for that Infinite Divine to experience the delight of its infinite possibilities mobilised in play. This is only possible if these infinite possibilities recognise themselves to be individualised infinities. In such an eventuality, each possibility of being in these self-conceptions of Being is a singularity, unique individualised form of the One Reality there is, and each experiences its non-duality with the rest of the universe and with every other Being, which is the essence of *brahma darśanam*. This realisation creates the conditions for another kind of life on earth. Sri Aurobindo calls this the Divine Life. The Sanskrit name for this Divine Life, or play of

11. LD, pp. 121-22.
12. Ibid., pp. 118-19.

Brahman's Delight, is *līlā*. This is why we find that the *karma catuṣṭaya* is alternately called by Sri Aurobindo *līlā catuṣṭaya*. This also leads to an understanding of the evolutionary Becoming as a personal growth into the divine Person for each one of us; and for that Person, the Divine Person, to be at play in and as its many selves — in other words, *brahma darśanam* itself has to be seen not merely as a non-dual realisation of the impersonal principle of *Brahman*, but also of *Brahman* as the One Person – *Puruṣa, Īśvara, Puruṣottama*, the Supreme Person. In the *Record of Yoga*, Sri Aurobindo sometimes refers to this Divine Person as *Līlāmaya Puruṣa* or *Līlāmaya Kṛṣṇa*.[13]

The One and the Infinite

To return to the four aspects of the perfection of Being, Sri Aurobindo defines these as *sarvam, anantam, jñānam* and *ānandam*.[14] The first two of these present us with a radical duality within Being. That radical duality lies in the fact that *Brahman* is One and *Brahman* is also infinite. It is the infinite One. If we contemplate this phrase — the infinite One — in its radical fullness, we recognise why it is so difficult to grasp. Logic fails before it. We can conceive of one. One is just the beginning of a series that proceeds unendingly if we want to encompass infinity. But infinity is not a number. Infinity is something indefinable, immeasurable. How can that which numerically initiates measure, the number one, be equated with that which is outside of all measure — the infinite? This is a fundamental paradox to our logical experience. We immediately see the fact that as mind-creatures (mental beings) we cannot grasp this duality. How then are we to deal with it? We find that this proposition of the Infinite One splits into two separate realisations for us, and this duality in the experience of *Brahman* as One and as Infinite, confronts us

13. RoY, pp. 106, 398, 432, 433, 446, 461, etc.
14. Ibid., pp. 23, 1478.

with a central problem in world religions. The history of religions has often been one of violent animosity in the name of god. Each claims to be the truth, and each one is right. The problem is that they assert different aspects of truth. At the level of mind we see contradictions and we cannot resolve them, but these aspects can coexist in a Reality that is beyond mind. This is also the problem of the different *darśana*s in Indian spiritual thought. The *darśana*s each conceive, experience and realise the non-duality of Being in terms of oneness, infinity, and a variety of positions in between. But this is a problem of mind. In a chapter titled "The Difficulties of the Mental Being" in *The Synthesis of Yoga*, Sri Aurobindo describes this problem of the mind which confronts us when we try to encompass the oneness and the infinity of *Brahman* in one *darśana*:

> [T]he mind is an inveterate divider of the indivisible, and its whole nature is to dwell on one thing at a time to the exclusion of others, or to stress it to the subordination of others. Thus, in approaching *Saccidānanda* it will dwell on its aspect of the pure existence, *sat*, and consciousness and bliss are compelled then to lose themselves or remain quiescent in the experience of pure infinite Being which leads to the realisation of the quietistic monist.[15]

Saccidānanda is a synonym for *Brahman*, naming it by its three primary attributes — *sat*, *cit* and *ānanda*. *Sat* means Existence and relates to *sarvam*, all-ness or oneness or the One Reality there is, in terms of its indivisibility. *Cit* refers to consciousness and relates to *anantam* because it is the consciousness of the One Being, that can shape or assume its innumerable and infinite forms. The mobilisation of consciousness gives rise to the infinite variety of forces that are at work in the world. *Ānandam*, delight, the third principle, refers to the intrinsic self-delight of *Brahman*, and *jñānam* refers to Supermind, the

15. SoY, p. 398.

knowledge which is intrinsic to and arises from the self-consciousness of Being.

One sees in the enumeration of this quartet, that Sri Aurobindo is drawing attention to the problem of the mind in its approach to the qualities of *Brahman*. It can experience, realise and describe *Brahman* in terms of any one of these primary qualities and put the other two aside. This is why Sri Aurobindo says that in the first case when the mind casts its attention on pure existence, *sat*, consciousness and bliss are compelled to lose themselves or remain quiescent in the experience of pure Being. This leads to the realisation of the quietistic monist. Monism is the philosophy (*darśana*) which describes *Brahman* as the One Being there is, but ignores or renders as illusory its infinite manifesting capacity or its creative Delight.

Sri Aurobindo continues:

> Or it will dwell on the aspect of consciousness, *cit*, and existence and bliss become then dependent on the experience of an infinite transcendent power and conscious force which leads to the Realisation of the tāntric worshipper of energy.[16]

This refers to another *darśana*, that of Tantra, which sees Force of Consciousness (*cit-śakti*) as the primordial Godhead.

> Or it will dwell on the aspect of delight, *ānanda*, and existence and consciousness then seem to disappear into a bliss without basis of self possessing awareness or constituent Being which leads to the realisation of the Buddhistic seeker of *nirvāṇa*.[17]

In other words, here, there is an extinction of Being and of Consciousness. What remains is a trance of indefinable and ineffable bliss in which one loses oneself.

---

16. SoY, p. 398.
17. Ibid.

> Or it will dwell on some aspect of *Saccidānanda* which comes to the mind from the supramental Knowledge, Will, or Love and then the infinite impersonal aspect of *Saccidānanda* is almost or quite lost in the experience of the Deity,[18] — the personal God — which leads to the realisations of the various religions and to the possession of some supernal world or divine status of the human soul in relation to God. And for those whose object is to depart anywhither from cosmic existence this is enough since they are able, by the mind's immergence into or seizure upon any one of these principles or aspects to effect through status in the divine planes of their mentality or the possession by them of their waking state this desired transit.[19]

The drift of this is that the mind's exclusive conception of the Divine or contact with an exclusive aspect of the Divine leads it to an experience in which this aspect accounts for the whole of its Reality, other aspects being subordinated to it or seen as latent, illusory or non-existent. Sri Aurobindo begins the following paragraph with the desideratum and its ultimate difficulty:

> But the *sādhaka* of the Integral Yoga has to harmonise all, so that they may become a plenary and equal unity of the full realisation of *Saccidānanda*. Here the last difficulty of mind meets him: its inability to hold at once the unity and the multiplicity.[20]

What Sri Aurobindo has described here is the experience of *Brahman* conditioned by the consciousness of Mind. He has described *Brahman* in terms of its primary intrinsic properties as nominated in Vedānta as *Saccidānanda* — i.e. a single infinite Being having the attributes of Existence, Consciousness and Bliss. He also includes the creative Knowledge-Will aspect of *Brahman* as *vijñāna* (Supermind). One can see how the fourfold

---

18. SoY, p. 398.
19. Ibid.
20. Ibid., p. 399.

Brahma Catuṣṭaya (Perfection of Being) (6.1)

Impersonal/Personal

Sarvam (Sameness, Oneness): Realisation of permanent omnipresence of Being – static or passive ***Brahman*** (***Vidyā/Avidyā*** = ***Sat***/Matter).	***Anantam*** (Infinity): Realisation of infinite force and quality at play in all forms – active or dynamic ***Brahman*** (***Vidyā/Avidyā*** = ***Cit***/Life).	***Jñānam*** (Knowledge): Realisation of knowledge by identity of properties and laws of all things and relations between them – Knowledge ***Brahman*** (***Vidyā/Avidyā*** = ***Vijñāna***/Mind).	***Ānandam*** (Delight): Realisation of omnipresent, omnipotent and omniscient Delight of Being – Delight ***Brahman*** (***Vidyā/Avidyā*** = ***Ānanda***/Psychic Being) – Personal: ***Līlāmaya Puruṣottama***.

perfection of the *brahma catuṣṭaya* relates to these primary attributes of *Brahman*. *Brahman* as purity of existence, *sat*, is experienced as pure Presence, present everywhere; it is the eternal present in past, present and future and the standing presence in every location. Thus, its experience is best characterised as omnipresence. This is also the realisation of *Brahman* as *sarvam, sarvam brahma*, the transcedental presence behind the cosmic whole and all its parts. *Brahman* as consciousness (*cit*) is a dynamic power which by concentration (*tapas*) can bring into becoming the infinite potentialities of being. It is thus experienced as a conscious creative energy manifesting infinite forms and qualities in the cosmos. Thus, its experience is best characterised as omnipotence. This is also the realisation of *Brahman* as *anantam, anantam brahma*, the transcendental power behind the whole cosmos and all its becomings. *Brahman* as self-knowledge figuring itself in idea can order itself in becoming in terms of symbol, meaning, correspondence, law and causation. Thus, its experience is best characterised as omniscience. This is also the realisation of *Brahman* as *jñānam, jñānam brahma*, the transcendental Real Idea behind the whole cosmos and its becomings. Finally, *Brahman* as pure self-existent bliss (*ānanda*), is experienced as the causeless delight intrinsic to all existence and expressive in all its becomings. Thus, its experience is best characterised as omniqualitative bliss. This is also the realisation of *Brahman* as *ānandam, ānandam brahma*, the transcendental bliss behind the cosmos mobilised as creative delight in all its becomings.

The Passive Brahman

In the example provided above, Sri Aurobindo considers the problem of approaching *Brahman* in the *avidyā* through exclusive concentration on any one of these attributes. This is a radical problem of the mind in *brahma darśanam*. Taking, particularly, the first two realisations, how are we to realise the infinity of Being and the oneness of Being, without reducing one to the other? It is only when this problem is overcome that one may hope to arrive at true *jñānam*, the supramental knowledge status, in which one can know God as God knows himself — One and infinite at the same time. But to even arrive at the co-existence of *sarvam* and *anantam*, one has to start where we are — from a dualistic experience governed by mind. This is how Sri Aurobindo himself began and realised at first the *sarvam*, the Sameness or Oneness in the experience of *nirvāṇa*. In *nirvāṇa* he experienced the unreality of the world. All differentiated phenomenal experience dropped away and all that remained was the sense of an intangible permanent behind the manifest world. Sri Aurobindo later expressed this realisation in a sonnet titled *Nirvāṇa*:

> All is abolished but the Mute Alone.
> The mind from thought released, the heart from grief
> Grow inexistent now beyond belief;
> There is no I, no Nature, known-unknown.
> The city, a shadow picture without tone,
> Floats, quivers unreal; forms without relief

Flow, a cinema's vacant shapes; like a reef
Foundering in shoreless gulfs the world is done.

Only the illimitable Permanent
Is here. A Peace stupendous, featureless, still,
Replaces all — what once was I, in It
A silent unnamed emptiness content
Either to fade in the Unknowable
Or thrill with the luminous seas of the Infinite.[21]

This is the condition of *sarvam*, in which all phenomena disappear and there is only an undifferentiated illimitable Permanence sensed in the background. The sense of self is also vacated and becomes a hiatus: either to disappear in some extinction of Being or for something inconceivable to express itself. This was a condition in which Sri Aurobindo lived for a long time, while conducting a very active struggle for political freedom, a revolutionary movement to rid India of colonial rule.[22] That action was carried out — here again we touch on the quartet of action — not by personal agency, but by being a silent channel for a power that acted through him.[23] He remained a witness to the action of force (*śakti*) through him. But, this condition led in him to the next realisation, which was that of the *anantamaya*, the infinite fertility or manifesting aspect of the Divine.[24] Later Sri Aurobindo would refer to these two aspects of *Brahman* as the passive and the active or static and dynamic *Brahman* respectively.[25] In mental consciousness, we can realise either of these to the exclusion of the other, or else the two can co-exist without integration. A part of our consciousness may dwell in the *sarvam*, while another part experiences the *anantam*. Sri Aurobindo further explains this condition in *The Synthesis of Yoga:*

21. "*Nirvāṇa*" in CP, p. 561.
22. OH, p. 260.
23. Ibid., p. 259.
24. AN, p. 94.
25. Ibid.

> The integral yoga of knowledge demands a divine return upon world existence, and its first step must be to realise the Self as the All, *sarvam brahma*. First, concentrating on the Self-existent, we have to realise all of which the mind and senses are aware as a figure of things existing in this pure Self that we now are to our own consciousness. This vision of the pure Self translates itself to the mind-sense and the mind-perception as an infinite Reality in which all exists merely as name and form, not precisely unreal, not a hallucination or a dream, but still only a creation of the consciousness, perceptual and subtly sensible rather than substantial.[26]

Thus, the entities and phenomena of the world are experienced as constructions of consciousness, projections of ideas, lacking substance, "a cinema's vacant shapes" as he phrases it in the poem:

> In this poise of the consciousness all seems to be, if not a dream, yet very much like a representation or puppet-show taking place in the calm, motionless, peaceful, indifferent Self. Our own phenomenal existence is part of this conceptual movement, a mechanical form of mind and body among other forms, ourselves a name of Being among other names, automatically mobile in this Self with its all-encompassing, still self-awareness. The active consciousness of the world is not present in the state to our realisation, because thought has been stilled in us and therefore our own consciousness is perfectly still and inactive, whatever we do, seems to be purely mechanical, not attended with any conscious origination by our active will and knowledge.[27]

Let us recollect that this is the condition in which Sri Aurobindo was conducting the freedom struggle, or rather,

26. SoY, p. 401.
27. Ibid., pp. 401-02.

was bearing witness to something conducting it in him. Elsewhere, he has written of the specific circumstances following on his experience of the *nirvāṇa* : He was scheduled to deliver a political speech, and told the *guru* who had taught him the meditation technique through which he had his nirvāṇic experience, that he had no motive left to initiate any action. His teacher asked him to pray. But, Sri Aurobindo did not have even the will or impulse to pray, and told his *guru* so. The teacher then told him he himself would pray along with some others and urged him to fold his hands "to Nārāyaṇa", and stand in front of the audience, assuring him that a voice would speak through him. Sri Aurobindo records that he did as directed and observed himself giving a talk.[28] He gave a political speech, but was not the agent of the speech, he was the witness of the speech being given through him. In this condition Sri Aurobindo lived for months until phenomenal experience regained its reality as the formations of a single Energy and he knew the *anantam*.

So he writes:

> The basis of this status of consciousness is the mind's exclusive realisation of pure self-existence in which consciousness is at rest, inactive, widely concentrated in pure self-awareness of Being, not active and originative of any kind of becoming. Its aspect of knowledge is at rest in the awareness of undifferentiated identity; its aspect of force and will is at rest in the awareness of unmodifiable immutability. And yet it is aware of names and forms, it is aware of movement; but this movement does not seem to proceed from the Self, but to go on by some inherent power of its own and only to be reflected in the Self. In other words, the mental Being has put away from himself by exclusive concentration the dynamic aspect of consciousness, has

28. A.B. Purani, *Evening Talks with Sri Aurobindo*, 13 April 1923, Sri Aurobindo Ashram Trust 1982, pp. 72-73.

> taken refuge in the static and built a wall of non-communication between the two; between the passive and the active *Brahman* a gulf has been created and they stand on either side of it, the one visible to the other but with no contact, no touch of sympathy, no sense of unity between them.[29]

This is an exprience occurring within the consciousness of Mind and subject to its law of exclusive concentration. It is not something determined by human volition, but part of the natural constitution of the human. He continues:

> If we rest here, there are only two possible attitudes toward the world. Either we must remain as mere inactive witnesses of the world-play or act in it mechanically without any participation of the conscious self and by mere play of the organs of sense and motor-action.[30]

Sri Aurobindo points out that the second attitude, that of action without personal agency, which seems so outrageously impossible to the modern mind, hyped with its self-importance and its humanist hubris of necessity to the universe, is in fact, perfectly possible. The sense of personal agency is largely the mental construction of a surface identity, an identification with a puppet persona which is part of natural conditioning by which we live the illusion of being doers in this world. This is the ego self, but the functions of nature through the mental-vital-physical instrumentality can continue with or without it.[31]

The Active Brahman

But the experience of the still self and the unreality of world and personality is not the only realisation of *Brahman*, of which

---

29. SoY, p. 402.
30. Ibid., pp. 403.
31. Ibid.. pp. 403-04.

the human being is capable. Or that given, it is possible to shift from that realisation to one of the realisation of infinite force and quality at play in all forms, *Brahman* as *anantam*. But for this we need to exercise a specific form of attention. To better understand this, let us recollect once more Sri Aurobindo's aphoristic definition: "The realisation of Oneness and the practice of oneness in difference is the whole of the yoga." The key to the *anantam* is the attention required to sustain the practice of oneness in difference. Sri Aurobindo elaborates:

> [T]his poise of a perfect activity founded upon a perfect inner passivity is that which the *yogin* has to possess. [I]n place of an aloof indifference to the works of the active *Brahman* we have to arrive at an equal and impartial delight in them; in place of a refusal to participate lest our freedom and peace be lost we have to arrive at a conscious possession of the active *Brahman* whose joy of existence does not abrogate His peace, nor His lordship of all workings impair His calm freedom in the midst of His works.[32]

But the problem of mind pursues our experience. If the exclusive concentration of the mental being on the plane of pure existence is sought to be overcome by an inclusion of its power of activity, there is the likelihood of an exclusive mental affirmation of the *anantam* and a loss of the *sarvam*. In Sri Aurobindo's words: "Here the difficulty is that mind is likely to precipitate itself into the consciousness of Force instead of possessing it."[33] — This, in fact, is the ontology of "normal" human experience. Our mental identification is subject to the action of the forces of Becoming, *anantam* and this surface identification is what we take to be ourselves as doers.

---

32. SoY, pp. 405-06.
33. Ibid., p. 406.

> The extreme mental state of precipitation into Nature is that of the ordinary man who takes his bodily and vital activity and mind-movements dependent on them for his whole real existence and regards all passivity of the soul as a departure from existence and an approach towards nullity. He lives in the superficies of the active *Brahman*. . . .[34]

We all live within the realisation of *anantam*, the active *Brahman*, except that we don't possess it but are driven by its conditioning forces, carried on its surface waves, assuming its conditioning identification to be ourselves:

> He lives in the superficies of the active *Brahman* and while to the silent soul exclusively concentrated in the passive self all activities are mere name and form, to him they are the only Reality and it is the Self that is merely a name. In one the passive *Brahman* stands aloof from the active and does not share in its consciousness; in the other, the active *Brahman* stands aloof from the passive and does not share in its consciousness nor wholly possesses its own. Each is to the other in these exclusivenesses an inertia of status or an inertia of mechanically active non-possession of self, if not altogether an unreality.[35]

Extending the Oneness

So, for the person who has realised the permanence of the static Self, the *sarvam*, Sri Aurobindo says:

> [T]here is the likelihood of a partial, superficial and temporary relapse into the old mental movement when he attempts again to ally himself to the activity of the world. To prevent this relapse or to cure it when it arrives, he has to hold fast to the truth of *Saccidānanda* and extend his realisation of the infinite One into the movement of the infinite multiplicity. He has to concentrate on and realise

34. SoY, p. 406.
35. Ibid.

> the One *Brahman* in all things as conscious force of Being as well as pure awareness of conscious Being. The self as the All, not only in the unique essence of Being, but in the manifold form of things, not only as containing all in a transcendent consciousness, but as becoming all by a constituting consciousness, this is the next step towards his true possession of existence. In proportion as this realisation is accomplished, the status of consciousness as well as the mental view proper to it will change. Instead of an immutable Self containing name and form, containing without sharing in them the mutations of Nature, there will be the consciousness of the Self immutable in essence, unalterable in its fundamental poise, but constituting and becoming in its experience, all these existences which the mind distinguishes as name and form. All formations of mind and body will be not merely figures reflected in the *Puruṣa*, but the real forms of which *Brahman*, Self, conscious Being is the substance and, as it were, the material of their formation.[36]

This, then, is the condition of the overcoming of the division between *sarvam* and *anantam*, and it is not easy. As Sri Aurobindo says, one may have the realisation of the one or the other or of both, as separate realisations not integrated, but it takes an entry into a different poise of Being to realise them as the one Reality with its two sides, or aspects. Such a realisation takes the *yogin* beyond the subjection to the exclusivities of the mind, and into the status of *Brahman* which Sri Aurobindo calls Supermind. This status is also the source of that knowledge, knowing which all may be known, by identity and by extension of identity — which leads us to the third *siddhi* of the *brahma catuṣṭaya*, that is *jñānam*, *Brahman* knowledge.

Knowledge

This is the necessary transition that must intervene: out of

36. SoY, p. 407.

our experience of *Brahman* in the *avidyā* to our experience of *Brahman* in the *vidyā*. *Avidyā* is the state of consciousness determined by the power of mind and its law of exclusionary divisions; *Vidyā* is a state of consciousness which transcends the mind in the law of unity, integrality and identity characterising Supermind. This movement leads to the realisation of knowledge by identity of the properties and laws of all things and the relations between them. This is *jñānam brahma, Brahman* as knowledge. Here, one knows the One by identity and the Many by extension of identity. One knows by being the infinite One and entering into relations with its own possibilities how that Being is disposed towards, or relates to, its infinite multiplicity of names, forms and forces. One knows by identity, the proportion in the deployment of energy or how it is measured out, or what the links are between the Self and its relata. One perceives by identity cosmos as Being in action, as Being's self-becoming. This knowledge cannot be had without the realisation of *jñānam brahma* or Supermind, as Sri Aurobindo calls it. This is the transition from *avidyā* to *vidyā*, or from Mind to Supermind.

Correspondences

Undoubtedly, this transition is very distant from our normal human condition of subjection to mind. But, through the practices noted in his *Record of Yoga*, Sri Aurobindo provides us with some initiating pointers in everyday life towards these realisations. For this, we need to understand that each of the higher principles in the *vidyā* are represented in some corresponding principle in the *avidyā*. A concentration on these principles, which are accessible to us in our everyday experience, can lend us a key to the realisation of the higher attributes of *Brahman*. For example, *sarvam*, which is based in *sat* of *Saccidānanda*, finds its corresponding representation in matter in our world, which has the nature of ignorance (*avidyā prakṛti*). By dint of its very unconsciousness and insentience, it exclusively represents a purity of existence. All we can assert of matter is that it is. Consciousness and Delight could be said to be latent in it. So, by reducing all experiences to their materiality and focusing on these material forms as a sameness of material existence, an insistent dwelling of the mind on a kind of spiritual materialism, one may arrive at *sarvam* within the *avidyā*. This is a form of constant meditation on the *Brahman*. Similarly, *anantam,* the basis of the power of consciousness mobilised as force, is represented correspondingly in life — life which is so manifold in its diversity and expresses an infinite plenitude of dynamic forces and qualities. Through an exclusive concentration on the qualities and energetics of living beings as a single Conscious Force at work and play in the world, we may arrive at an experience of *anantam* within the *avidyā*.

Similarly, we find that there is not only a dumb, brute material reality to the world, nor is there only action of conscious force in the world, but there is also an ideational content to the world. We find that there is significance, meaning and law in the cosmos; objects and events are related to each other in structures and processes that have a symmetry of logical and analogical patterns and lend themselves to epistemological and causational systematisations and problematics of development and evolution. This ideational aspect of *Brahman* is what finds its corresponding reality in the ignorance as mind. Thus, by an exclusive and insistent concentration on the rationality of the world, its powers of law, order, proportion, symmetry, relation we may approach a realisation of *jñānam* in the *avidyā*. Each of these — *sarvam, anantam, jñānam* — through exclusive focus or concentration on the principles of matter, life, or mind, grants us a certain degree of the experience of *Brahman* in the *avidyā*.

Interestingly, this is the kind of process described in the

Taittirīya Upaniṣad in the chapter on Bhr̥gu's Tapasyā.[37] The principles referred to here, under exclusive concentration of mind, can be realised independently; but one may also add experience to experience — that is, one may take care to retain the realisation of *sarvam,* while concentrating on *anantam* as the diversity which springs from a material sameness. Similarly, one may retain the grounding in this consolidated realisation while concentrating on the ideational content of the world as *jñānam*. This kind of disciplined process moves towards an integral realisation, though still within the *avidyā*.

However, if we are to open to a higher possibility of the idea-force of mind, if we realise that, that which expresses itself as law, process, order, harmony, relation, proportion, measure in this universe, ultimately draws its origin from a supreme infinite creative power of which these measures are the expression, then we can open ourselves to *vijñānam* or Supermind. Mind can open to its origin, through a surrender to its creative infinity. This is the meditation that can bring us closer to the higher possibility of *jñānam* in the *vidyā*. This is *vijñāna*, the supramental knowledge aspect of *Brahman*. Further, when *jñānam* is realised in this transition from *avidyā* to *vidyā,* and established as a knowledge by identity, then the origin of this *vijñāna,* this creative ordering knowledge principle, is seen not as a giver of laws, but a player of the creative harmonies of the infinite that is *ānandam* (the delight). We come to realise that it is *Brahman* as delight that has become all these things. *Ānanda,* causeless creative delight is then realised as the original power of the Becoming — the realisation of the omnipresent, omnipotent and omniscient delight of Being. As mentioned earlier, this is the process of Bhr̥gu's Tapasyā as narrated in the *Taittirīya Upaniṣad* and it culminates in the realisation of the *ānanda Brahman*. Once more, we find a progression from *mukti* to *bhukti* which is the hallmark of all

37. "Bhr̥gu Vallī", *Taittirīya Upaniṣad* III.

the seven quartets and summarised in the quartet of perfection or yoga, *siddhi catuṣṭaya*.

Bliss, Impersonal and Personal

For Sri Aurobindo, this *ānanda* consciousness also has two stages or grades in its realisation. The first stage in the dawning of the *ānandamaya Brahman* is its appearance as an impersonal principle. This is realised as the creative principle which has projected itself in all the other aspects of *Brahman* that have preceded it in the progression of *Brahman* realisation. But, beyond this impersonal delight, there is experienced an increasing sense of the *ānandam Brahman* as person (*puruṣa*) someone we can relate to, not merely a trascendence very distant from us, but seated in our own hearts, the most essential, though indescribable name and form of ourself and all things. In thinking of the expression of univocity as difference and differentiation, Gilles Deleuze, following Gilbert Simondon, notes the primacy of individuation: "It is the individual which is above the species, and precedes the species in principle."[38] The principal of the individual motives, the continuous and perpetual individuation of the cosmos and its constituents. But, this individual has to be understood as the paradoxical nexus of compossible elements, a matrix of infinite discrete differentiations, yet irreducible and indivisible. Such a paradoxical matrix of infinite personality is what we come across in the self-disclosure of Kṛṣṇa in the *Bhagavad-Gītā*.[39] One may think of this as the foundation of the pre-individual basis of all discrete individuation, carried in its entirety in each individual, and the trans-individual horizon of the superman. In Simondon's words:

> Participation, for the individual, is the fact of being an

38. Gilles Deleuze, *Difference and Repetition*, trans. Paul Patton, New York: Columbia University Press, 1994, p. 250.
39. *Bhagavad-Gītā* XI: 19-26.

> element in a much vaster individuation, through the intermediary of the stock of pre-individual reality that the individual contains, that is, thanks to the potentials it harbours.[40]

This person seated in the heart of all beings as the personified integral delight principle is, what Sri Aurobindo calls *Līlāmaya Puruṣottama* or *Līlāmaya Kr̥ṣṇa*.[41] The entire universe, including ourselves and all else in it, is then seen as the self-multiplication of this Bliss Person undertaken for the delight of *līlā*. All experiences of quality in this universe, good, bad, happy, sorrowful, pleasant, unpleasant, ecstatic, painful are seen as the play of delight emanating from the person who is pure bliss and whose bliss cannot be changed or diminished by any experience. Sri Aurobindo calls this aspect of *brahma darśana* Kr̥ṣṇa *darśanam,* since this Supreme Person (*Puruṣottma*) goes by the name of Kr̥ṣṇa for him.[42] Thus, *Kr̥ṣṇa darśanam* becomes the culmination of the *brahma catuṣṭaya,* and leads into the next general quartet, the *karma catuṣṭaya* also known to Sri Aurobindo as the *līlā catuṣṭaya,* the play of the *Puruṣottama,* with its own infinite energy (*Parā-Prakr̥ti*), with all beings as agents in this cosmic Becoming. This, indeed, is the essence of action, *karma,* in (and as) the universe. Considering the above from the viewpoint of a transpersonal psychology, one can see that what lies beyond the separate individual subject (the

40. Gilbert Simondon, *L'individuation psychique et collective*, Paris: Aubier-Montaigne, 1989, p. 11; translated and quoted in Bernard Stiegler, *Acting Out*, Stanford: Stanford University Press, 2009, p. 5.

41. See, for example, entry of 3 July 1914: "At present all is *ānanda Brahman* in a general bright mentality but the Kr̥ṣṇa *dr̥ṣṭi* is implied in it, not yet entirely possessed of it." RoY, p. 529. Also, RoY, pp. 538, 565, 569, 664, etc. As may be seen from these entries, Sri Aurobindo often distinguishes even finer degrees in the transition from the impersonal to the personal realisation of *ānanda Brahman*.

42. This is also dealt with under the Quartet of Works, *karma catuṣṭaya* as one of its *siddhis*. RoY, pp. 437, 447, 833, 839, 841, etc.

ego) is not necessarily non-personal or impersonal but includes a transcendental personalism.

Sri Aurobindo himself practised this progression of *Brahman* realisation described above and noted its results in his *Record of Yoga*. Let us end with a perusal of one such diary entry, which perhaps, best encapsulates the entire process:

> March 24, Tuesday, 1914 — *Saguṇa Brahman dṛṣṭi* has now practically taken the place of the *nirguṇa* which is now perceived only as a foundation for the action of the *saguṇa*.[43]

Saguṇa and *nirguṇa* relate to personal and impersonal aspects of *Brahman* respectively. In terms of our consideration, *saguṇa* refers to *Brahman* with qualities and thus, points to *Brahman* as Person, *Puruṣottama; nirguṇa* refers to *Brahman* without qualities or the impersonal *Brahman*. Thus, this statement relates to *Kṛṣṇa darśanam*, the last phase of *Brahma darśana*. "It is seen that the *sarvam Brahma* is prominent when the *tapas* of mental *caitanya* is fixed on matter." – *Tapas* of mental *caitanya* may be translated as "concentration of mental consciousness". Let us recollect our discussion on the fixing of the attention on matter as a meditation leading to *brahma darśana* of *sarvam* in *avidyā*. *Tapas* of mental *caitanya,* then refers an insistent dwelling by the mind on the idea of the omnipresent substance of *Brahman*. It is interesting to note how Sri Aurobindo uses this empirical and phenomenological method to stabilise this foundational aspect of *brahma darśanam*. "It is seen that sarvam Brahma is prominent when the *tapas* of mental *caitanya* is fixed on Matter, all else being felt as undifferentiated consciousness, and Matter alone as real to the mind, unreal to the *dṛṣṭi*." "Real to the mind, unreal to the *dṛṣṭi*", in other words, there is no substantial reality to matter in the vision, but reality to the mind as an omnipresent principle. — "Sarvam anantam is felt . . ." that is, the two

43. RoY, pp. 397-98.

together, *sarvam* and *anantam* are experienced together; *sarvam* has been allowed to settle and *anantam* has been added to it, so that the infinite potency of manifesting force is experienced as an action of omnipresent Substance.

> . . . *Sarvam anantam* is felt when the tapas is fixed on matter and life. All else being felt to be a sea of consciousness out of which life and matter proceed. *Sarvam anantam jñānam* when the tapas is fixed on life, matter and mind, with *vijñānam* felt behind vaguely as the source of mind.

Here, the concentration is focused on the consolidated principles of matter, life and mind — that is, *sarvam* and *anantam* are allowed to settle into constancy in the consciousness and *jñānam* is added to them as the ideational element in the cosmos. This ideational element in the *avidyā* carries within it the intuition of some higher and integral source, *Brahman* as Real Idea or Knowledge-Will, *vijñānam*. "But, when the *jñānam* increases and is sun-illumined, then the *ānandam* also appears and the *Saguṇa Brahman* becomes the *līlāmaya parā-puruṣa*." Thus, with the transition out of the *avidyā* into the *vidyā*, where the source of mind is allowed to become manifest by "sun-illumining" the realisation of knowledge, that is, when *jñānam* as Supermind emerges in the consciousness, the *ānanda Brahman* is experienced behind it and the whole is seen in terms of individuation proceedings from an infinite Person. He ends with a note on the *anantam*:

> "The *anantam* has also two *bhāvas*, one in which the infinite force acts as if it were a mechanical entity, knowledge standing behind from it, the other in which life-force and knowledge act together and the infinite force is an intelligent or a conscious force.

In experiencing the transition from *avidyā* to *vidyā*, the action of the Consciousness-Force, *cit-śakti* at work in all becomings, *anantam*, also reveals itself as having two modalities, which are now seen in the light of the qualitative Delight consciousness, *Saguṇa ānanda Brahman* as two qualities, *bhāvas*. One of these is what is known as *Prakṛti*, the action of a seeminlgy blind Nature force in the cosmos, working through the mechanical laws of physics and chemistry in material nature, and other automatisms of biology, ecology, logic or behavioural psychology. However, behind these automatisms, the human mind also intuits larger ideas — symmetries, progressions, symbolic or analogical correspondences. Thus, this *avidyā Prakṛti* is *anantam*, which presents the appearance and manifests the *bhāva* or subjective consciousness/mood of a "mechanical entity, knowledge standing behind from it". The other is the *bhāva* or consciousness of *Parā-Prakṛti*, the unveiled self-conscient Energy or Śakti of Puruṣottama or *Parā-Puruṣa*, the personal centre of *ānandam Brahma*. In this action of *anantam*, Knowledge is spontaneously and instantaneously self-revealed in Will, Real Idea in Becoming. Sri Aurobindo calls this "the other in which life-force and knowledge act together and the infinite force is an intelligent or a conscious force". Just as at the heights of *Brahman* realisation, "*Saguṇa Brahman* or *Brahman*-with-qualities becomes the *līlāmaya parā-puruṣa*", a movement from the impersonal to the person, so too the *cit-śakti* as *Parā-Prakṛti* becomes Devī (the Divine Mother) from this vantage of *vidyā*, all becomings are revealed as the play of the *līlāmaya* Kṛṣṇa with its own self-conscious *Ādyā Śakti* (Kālī). These are the elements of the *Brahma catuṣṭaya*, the perfection of Being, leading to the *darśana* of *Brahman* in all things and in oneself, the One Reality there is, the One and the infinite, the self-knowing Being, who has delight in itself and in all things.[44] Its delight is mobilised in the Being and the

---

44. Kṛṣṇa and Kālī are also two of the founding elements in the *karma catuṣṭaya*. In the Quartet of Being, these pertain to the realisation of Being; in the Quartet of Action, they pertain to the dynamic realisation of the Becoming of Being.

Becoming as the Delight of the *līlāmaya Puruṣottama*, in his play with his supreme *Śakti, Parā-Prakṛti*.

Transcendental Empiricism

This powerful meditation may be analogically compared with the tripartite division of immanence foundational to Gilles Deleuze, adapted from the philosophy of Spinoza and to some extent, Henri Bergson. Deleuze translates Spinoza's tripartite division of reality into substance, attribute and mode to his own conceptual economy as the field of immanence, the virtual and the actual.[45] Making extensive use of these categories to derive his philosophical methodology, which he calls transcendental empiricism, Deleuze elaborates in *Difference and Repetition* that these three fields of reality can be seen as two forms of "repetition" with a zone of "difference" in between.[46] A fruitful correspondence (not identity) of this can be attempted with Sri Aurobindo's phenomenological reduction pertaining to the three modalities of *sarvam, anantam* and *jñānam*; or of the operation of *Prakṛti* as *anantam* in the *avidyā* characterised as a "mechanical entity, knowledge standing behind from it" with *Puruṣa* standing further behind.

The field of the empirical can be related to *sarvam* in matter or to the mechanical action of *Prakṛti*. It is characterized by a mechanical repetition and elaboration of differences, as of molecules, *guṇa*s, predictable movements (though each of these carries the entire cosmos potentially in itself). The field of the virtual is the zone of difference — here one intuits an infinitely fertile force proliferating in the form of variety or multiplicity. This can be related to the field of life as *anantam*, or of the life-ideas which manifest as actualities in the empirical field. Finally, Deleuze's field of Immanence is characterised

45. Gilles Deleuze, *Difference and Repetition*, op. cit., pp. 283-304.

46. Ibid.

by the repetition of an univocal infinity (Nietzsche's "eternal recurrence of the Same") grounding and manifesting through virtuality and actuality. Deleuze, following Spinoza's characterisation of Substance, attributes "univocity" to this and speaks of it as the "real subject of repetition" and "pronominal", differentiating it from the empirical repetition:

> We are right to speak of repetition when we find ourselves confronted by identical elements with exactly the same concept. However, we must distinguish between these discrete elements, these repeated objects, and a secret subject, the real subject of repetition, which repeats itself through them. Repetition must be understood in the pronominal.[47]

This can be seen to correspond to *vijñāna* or *Puruṣa*, originary plane or (pronominal0) Being of identity who/which is the One infinite that becomes all there is in potential and fact.

---

47. Gilles Deleuze, *Difference and Repetition*, op. cit., pp. 23-24.

7

The Quartet of Action

KARMA *Catuṣṭaya* (the quartet of action) is enumerated in the *Record of Yoga,* as the first of the general perfections. However, from a certain perspective, this quartet can be seen as the capstone of the general perfections and the test of their fulfillment. To see how perfection of action can be thought of as the test of the integral yoga and its esoteric goal, we need to pursue the consequence of the question, why the One Reality would wish to fragment itself into all these struggling beings caught between the two stools of Matter and Spirit. The answer is that this is the way by which That can become self-conscious in each of its infinite part(icle)s. Each possibility of this reality can thus, know itself as the entire reality; and such an individually self-conscious plurality becomes the condition for the play (*līlā*) of the divine life.[1] Thus, this may be seen as a culminant *siddhi* (a cosmic perfection of action). The arrival at the point where each particle of god can know itself to be entirely god, is a cosmic realisation of Being — what can be thought of as the *brahma catuṣṭaya* (quartet of being) — realised as Becoming in the cosmos. Such a realisation is the foundational condition for a transformed dynamic world, where the One is at play in/as every particle; and we are in conscious identity with that play. Beyond a static self-consciousness — we are, each one of us is, more — we constitute that manifestation of the One at play in this world.

1. LD, pp. 1096-98.

That is the cosmic culmination of the quartet of action. At the individual level, too, the quartet of action brings into expression the realisation of Being as a realisation of Becoming. Sri Aurobindo enumerates the four *siddhi*s of Action in terms of four Ks — *Kṛṣṇa, Kālī, Karma* and *Kāma*.[2]

Personal Gods and an Integral Karma-Yoga

The quartet of action relates to the traditional Indian form of *karma-yoga,* just as the quartet of being could be said to relate to *jñāna-yoga*. But, Sri Aurobindo puts forward a modified version of these yogas in his quartets, in keeping with the integrality of their aims. Thus, an integral *karma-yoga* includes the integral possibilities of action. And these possibilities include the possibility of identity in knowledge, in will, and in delight. All these are parts of the total scope of an integral *karma-yoga* (the quartet of *karma*). Sri Aurobindo expands this limb of yoga into its four parts in an unusually enigmatic way, since this quartet includes for the first time, the names of some personal Hindu deities. In general, one seldom comes across the names of personal deities or gods in Sri Aurobindo's public writings. But, in the *Record of Yoga,* being his diaries, he refers directly to certain deities in terms of *siddhi* (perfection) and therefore, we have to take them as belonging to his personal practice. However, the question remains, what do these deities mean in his practice? Do they bear any resemblance to their traditional descriptions and expressions? To unravel their significance, it is better for us to approach them in their more general forms rather than any assumption of sectarian tradition, or of cultic form for these deities, any iconic idea of what they may mean. Perusing the diaries and his other writings, it becomes clear that Sri Aurobindo's approach to these deities is often couched in alternate terms.

The *Record of Yoga* follows the system of the *sapta catuṣṭaya,*

2. RoY, pp. 23, 1478.

and here he uses a personal approach to forms or forces of Being that play a key part in his yoga. Here, we can bring to mind what Sri Aurobindo has had to say about the foundational role of faith (*śraddhā*) in his yoga and of the object of that faith. One of the first things that is necessary for any journey into the unknown, is faith in the leader of the path, as a being who is aware of our possibilities, preferences and difficulties and knows, too, the path to be travelled and even if we cannot see him, is leading us onward. To that leader of the path, Sri Aurobindo gave the name, the Master of the Yoga.[3] That Being, the Master of the Yoga, may be completely invisible or unknown to us. But *śraddhā* in the Master of the Yoga is the first step in embarking on the journey of yoga. Also, though Sri Aurobindo uses the gendered term master, this object of our surrender is to be seen as a biune male-female Being. Not only does the Master of the yoga guide and lead us, offer us advice and solace and prepare the circumstances for our progress, but s/he also enters into the mind and life forces that drive us, and can order the processes of our becoming. In this more intimate, subjective and dynamic aspect, we experience her more as the Creative Consciousness at work in us as well as in all things — the Divine Śakti. Thus, it is both the Master and the Divine Mother, in whom we are called upon to have faith.

Kr̥ṣṇa

It is this biune reality or principle, a goal, an attractor, a magnet, but at the same time an impersonal person, one beyond all forms, but who can take any form, and also bears the mystery of the form of supreme attraction. This is the significance of the term Kr̥ṣṇa. Kr̥ṣṇa is the supremely attractive person — as the teacher and guide, his role in the *Gītā*, he is the attractor of knowledge; as the king and diplomat

3. See RoY, pp. 49, 50, 52, 66, 71, 76, 132, 153, etc.

in the field of cosmic world energies, his role in Mathurā and Dwārkā, as in the battle of the Kurus, he is the attractor of power; and as the Lord of the heart, the enchanter of souls, because the source of the *līlā* of delight, his role among the cowherds and *gopīs* of Vṛndāvan, he is the attractor of bliss. The Sanskrit word for attraction is *ākarṣaṇa*, and considering the mantric or vibratory quality of the Indo-European sound-root *kṛṣ* behind this word, we find that both words *Kṛṣṇa* and "attraction" carry this vibrational quality of "attraction".

Looking at Sri Aurobindo's speeches and writings, we find that he refers to Kṛṣṇa in a number of places. For example, in 1909, talking of his experience at the Alipore Jail, where he was interned for a year, serving a sentence on suspected grounds of anti-colonial terrorism, he refers to Śrī Kṛṣṇa's intervention and participation in hisyoga.[4] This participation culminated in the experience where he attained to *darśana* of Śrī Kṛṣṇa in all beings and things. He saw Kṛṣṇa in the judge, in the prosecutor, in his own counsel, in all the members of the jury — seated in everybody he saw Kṛṣṇa. His description of this experience goes beyond human beings to the experience of Kṛṣṇa in trees, in the prison bars and in his bed, indeed in all things he laid eyes on.[5] We hear of Kṛṣṇa in a number of other later contexts as well. In 1926, Sri Aurobindo attained to the full realisation, down to his physical being, of the plane of consciousness which he called overmind. He refers to this realisation in terms of identity with Kṛṣṇa. In this case, he relates Kṛṣṇa to the personal aspect of the overmind consciousness, the overmental godhead.[6]

But, in *Record of Yoga*, Kṛṣṇa is equated with the person aspect of *Brahman*, non-dual Being.[7] We saw, while considering

4. Sri Aurobindo, "Uttarapara Speech" *Karmayogin*, CWSA 8, pp. 3-12.

5. CWSA 8, pp. 6-7.

6. Sri Aurobindo, OH, pp. 35, 272-73.

7. See, for example, the entry of 26 March 1914, RoY, p. 408.

the *brahma catuṣṭaya,* how the last of its *siddhi*s is *ānanda* (bliss) which carries in itself two stages — first, the delight of the one as an impersonal reality (*nirguṇa*) and beyond that, the realisation of the one supremely attractive Person (*saguṇa*) whom Sri Aurobindo refers to as *līlāmaya Kṛṣṇa*. This establishes the significance of the cosmos as a Becoming of *Brahman,* in terms of *līlā,* the play of divine personal relationship emanating from *Brahman* in the form of the supremely attractive Person, who has unfolded this play for his own self-delight. While considering this aspect of the quartet of being, we noted its intimate relationship with the quartet of action, *karma catuṣṭaya.* If the *brahma catuṣṭaya* established the significance of Being in itself and in the Becoming, the *karma catuṣṭaya* deals with the Power of Becoming in itself and in its manifold relations with Being. Understanding this relationship between these two quartets, illuminates for us the symmetry intended by Sri Aurobindo in both ending the *brahma catuṣṭaya* and beginning the *karma catuṣṭaya* with Kṛṣṇa. We may also note that the last term in both quartets, their culminant realisation deals with delight — the bliss of identity in Being, *ānanda Brahman* in the case of the *brahma catuṣṭaya,* and enjoyment of the bliss of divine relationship, *kāma,* in the case of the *karma catuṣṭaya.*[8]

Kālī

The second *siddhi,* in the quartet of action, is enumerated in terms of a second deity, Kālī. Sri Aurobindo seldom refers to the Goddess Kālī in his other writings. In his early years in Pondicherry, we find Sri Aurobindo using this name to sign some of the letters which he was writing incognito to his collaborators in the freedom struggle when under surveillance by the British in Pondicherry.[9] One may think of this as a

8. RoY, pp. 23, 1478.
9. See, for example, letters to Motilal RoY in Sri Aurobindo, AN, pp. 175-234.

mere disguise, but there may be further significance to it because at this same time, he was referring to Kālī in the *Record of Yoga*. At this time, he was also writing in his *Thoughts and Aphorisms*, of his attainment of identity with both Kṛṣṇa and Kālī.[10]

Who is Kālī to Sri Aurobindo? While considering the perfection of being we saw that Sri Aurobindo used the name Kālī for the conscious force, *Brahman*'s power of consciousness. Just as Kṛṣṇa represented for him the person aspect of Being, Kālī is for him the person aspect of Becoming, the power of consciousness that manifests the cosmos and its constituents. This is what emanates in the quartet of power (*śakti catuṣṭaya*) as the four major Goddesses (the *mahāśaktis*).[11] In other words, Kālī in the *Record of Yoga* subsumes the four *mahāśaktis*. Of course, we have Mahākālī as one of the *mahāśaktis*, but here the integral Śakti from whom the four emanate, is referred to as Kālī. We know of the traditional association of Kālī with the intensity of conscious force. It is the most intense conscious force that Sri Aurobindo was bringing to bear on his own yoga.[12] Perhaps, for this reason, he invoked this particular goddess as the supreme name of the conscious force, of energy, of *prakṛti*.

These are the first two realisations of the *karma catuṣṭaya* enumerated by Sri Aurobindo, Kṛṣṇa as *Īśvara* or Lord, the Master of the Yoga, the Person aspect of *Brahman* itself, and Kālī as Śakti or power of consciousness, the person aspect of all Becoming. The highest goal of the *karma catuṣṭaya* is realisation of identity in difference with Kṛṣṇa, the Supreme Person as the True Self and in the relation of Master and Lord

---

10. See "Thoughts and Aphorisms" nos. 216, 427, 476, 519 and 540 in EDH, pp. 12, 454, 483, 490, 496, 499.
11. RoY, pp. 94, 1455, 1471.
12. Ibid., p. 12.

with all beings, taking delight in all action. Next comes the realisation of Kālī, and this refers to identity with the Person aspect of the dynamic creative power which is at work in all Becoming. These two realisations may be seen to correspond to the first two realisations of the *brahma catuṣṭaya*.

In our consideration of the *brahma catuṣṭaya*, we have seen how the realisation of *sarvam*, its first *siddhi*, has two stages to it — as an impersonal Being, passive *Brahman* and as a Person. This person aspect of *sarvam* is identical with Kṛṣṇa. Similarly, we may extend the analogy and see two stages to the realisation of *anantam* — as the transcendental and universal conscious force of Becoming, active *Brahman* and its person aspect. This person aspect of *anantam* is Kālī. This then emanates four qualities of Becoming, which in their person aspects are enumerated by Sri Aurobindo in the *śakti catuṣṭaya* as Māheśvarī, Mahākālī, Mahālakṣmī and Mahāsarasvatī with their four *Puruṣa*s or Lords. Hence, we can see that in the quartet of action, Sri Aurobindo proceeds with the culminating realisations of the *brahma catuṣṭaya*, realisation of identity with the transcendental person who forms the centre of Being and the transcendental person who forms the centre of Becoming. These two persons are ultimately One and to be realised in their unity and difference, just as in the case of *sarvam* and *anantam*, in the quartet of Being. This is why our faith in the yoga is directed to this biune Being and why Sri Aurobindo sometimes refers to these two deities in a hyphenated form — Kṛṣṇa-Kālī[13] — and sometimes as a single name, Kṛṣṇakālī,[14] as one person, the two-in-one. So Kālī is Śakti or Divine Mother and the goal there is realisation of identity in difference with the Supreme Śakti as nature force and in the relation of Divine Mother of all beings carrying out all actions for the delight of *Īśvara*.

13. RoY, pp. 77, 230, 571, 711, 734, etc.
14. Ibid., pp. 96, 97, 247, 275, 277, 750, 767 etc.

Puruṣa and Prakṛti

The realisations of Kṛṣṇa and Kālī, can be explored further in terms of their relationship with *sarvam* (omnipresence) and *anantam* (omnipotence) in the Perfection of Being, or of *sat* (being) and *cit* (consciousness) of *Saccidānanda*. While dealing with the quartet of Being, we saw how *sarvam* and *anantam* appear in human experience as a radical duality, due to the nature of the mind. Similarly, the appearance of Kṛṣṇa and Kālī in the *avidyā* of mental existence, takes on the appearance of a radical duality which has been traditionally recognised in the Indian *darśana* of Sāṁkhya by the names of *puruṣa* and *prakṛti*. We experience these as a duality because, due to the exclusive attention of the mind, we can either detach our consciousness from all phenomenal activity, which are then experienced as unreal with a static witnessing Presence in the background that alone is experienced as real; or we can plunge ourselves into a cosmic dynamism in which we are subject to the energies that are driving all things in the world. These are thus, experienced as separate poises of being, one a being-without-becoming, inert, the other a being-as-becoming, conditioned. These two experiences may coexist in the same human being, but they do so as watertight realities, without integration. From the viewpoint of *puruṣa*, *prakṛti* is an illusion or a mechanical automatism. From the viewpoint of *prakṛti*, *puruṣa* remains always beyond reach.

The philosophies that have theorised this dichotomy between *puruṣa* and *prakṛti*, start from the recognition of human existence as a condition of imprisonment. In this prison in which we find ourselves, we are under the compulsion of *prakṛti* — the laws of matter and of life, of physics and chemistry and the processes of anabolism and catabolism, our emotions and the emotions of others, the ambitions and wills of people all around us and our own uncontrollable desires, and the compulsion of our thinking — the rational justifications and ideological preferences of the mind. We cannot know reality as it is, because we are shut in our own constructions and compulsions. The philosopher, Immanuel Kant highlighted this nature of human imprisonment under the bell jar of mental constructions, though he considered the human ability to create schemas of an essentially unknowable world for our mutual handling to be the legitimate function of mind.[15] These forms of compulsion are automatisms, and all these automatisms compose our imprisonment in the world. In the Sāṁkhya philosophy, this imprisonment is attributed to *Prakṛti.*[16]

In other words, *Prakṛti* is a Nature Force active in matter, life, emotions, sensations, thoughts, intuitions. But, the quality of human consciousness is such that it makes us aware of our subjection to *Prakṛti* and makes us struggle against this subjection. Human beings have an intuition and aspiration for freedom and for knowledge of identity with pure consciousness. This is the source of discontent in human existence, why there is a haplessness or helplessness to human life. If we were entirely like animals, we would be subject to *Prakṛti* without questioning it or feeling its subjection. But human consciousness is discontent with its subjection, which implies an intuition of freedom beyond conditioning. This intuition arises from the latent awareness of *Puruṣa,* the pure unconditioned root of consciousness in us, independent of all mutating influence of Nature Force, free from its imprisonment.[17] But though such a discovery of *Puruṣa* is possible, we soon realise that this freedom comes with a cost. The exclusive purity of *puruṣa* repels the play of *Prakṛti* and loses the bliss of becoming; the prison disappears, but so does the world.

---

15. See Kant's definition of Transcendental Idealism in his *Critique of Pure Reason,* A365.
16. Īśvara Kṛṣṇa, *Sāṁkyha-Kārikā,* pp. 62-63.
17. Ibid, pp. 64-68.

Kṛṣṇa-Kālī and the Delight of Becoming

But, life as a prison is not the only way of viewing human existence in the world. In fact, the majority of human beings do not experience life as a prison, or do not experience it thus most of the time. The common human experience of life is that of a desirable state. Few human beings would wish to put an end to their lives due to the subjection of nature, whether their own or others'. Human beings are marked by hope and the willingness to pay any price to live another day, because the experience of life is intrinsically delightful, even the neutrality of an uneventful life is marked by the undertone of happiness.[18] To breathe air, to see the world and to receive sunlight in sight and touch, is a delight. The sense of imprisonment is only one aspect of the experience of Nature Force. The other aspect is that it expresses the delight of Becoming; it is the Becoming of a self-delighted Being. If we recognise this, then our question of realisation reconfigures itself to one of how we can enjoy the delight of Becoming and yet not feel imprisoned by its conditioning forces. This is the problem of realising simultaneously the first two perfections of the *karma catuṣṭaya*, the realisation of Kṛṣṇa-Kālī, of arriving at a power of action arising out of the freedom and mastery of Being. The forces of *prakṛti* are then no longer experienced as compulsions but powers we handle creatively. This creative power does not arise from our surface individualities as ego, separate from other beings and at odds with the world, but out of the realisation of the One Being and its Creative Energy. This, in its most personal aspect, is the essence of Kṛṣṇa-Kālī.

How are we to arrive at this dynamic experience of Kṛṣṇa and Kālī as one biune being? Here again, we may recollect the transition discussed in the quartet of being, a transition from *avidyā* to *vidyā* — out of subjection to the cosmic power of

18. "Bhṛgu Vallī", *Taittirīya Upaniṣad*, III.1; LD, pp. 106-07.

mind, where all our experience, even spiritual experience is divided into exclusive realities, to a world in which there is infinite indivisible being that can experience itself as one and two and many at the same time. This is a transition to Supermind. In Supermind, the duality of *Puruṣa* and *Prakṛti* becomes resolved to an experience of unity in difference of the One as Two. This is the realisation of Īśvara-Śakti or Kṛṣṇa-Kālī. The *karma catuṣṭaya* is the way of action to arrive at this realisation of Kṛṣṇa and Kālī as the supramental biune Being and the way of expression to manifest the play of that Being (*līlā*).

Work

The Way of Action proceeds through work in our everyday active lives. The *karma* in *karma catuṣṭaya* translates literally as "work", and Sri Aurobindo enumerates the third of the four realisations of the *karma catuṣṭaya* as *karma* (work).[19] The fundamental question then becomes, what is work? What we usually call work, pertains to our professional life, what we do for our living. If we are fortunate, what we do for a living is something we have chosen, not a compulsion but a creative choice. But even there, is this the significance of work? This concern saturates the *Bhagavad-Gītā*, where it is raised as the issue of "the work to be done" or the "acceptable sacrifice", *kartavyam karma* or *niyatam karma*.[20] The many interpreters of the *Bhagavad-Gītā*, laid down their opinions of what this means. Some say, work is duty: either charity or being faithful to one's parents or one's family or company or nation or religion or ideal. But, the significance of work goes beyond this. We find that the world is full of the sense of struggle and labour, which is the essence of work. Work is the effect of a cosmic energy, which is pushing all things to express ever more of the Whole; this is the urge of Kālī pushing towards the

19. RoY, pp. 23, 1478.
20. *Bhagavad-Gītā* III:8.

Karma Catuṣṭaya (Perfection of Action) (7.1)
Kṛṣṇa (Lord), *Kālī* (Divine Śakti),
Karma (Work), *Kāma* (Enjoyment).

Kṛṣṇa **(*Īśvara*, Lord):**	Realisation of identity in difference with Supreme Person as true self and in relation of Master and Lord with all beings, taking delight in all action.
Kālī **(*Śakti*, Divine Mother):**	Realisation of identity in difference with Supreme ***Śakti*** as Nature Force and in relation of Divine Mother with all beings, carrying out all actions for the delight of ***Īśvara***.
Karma **(Work):**	At first preparation, then egoless instrumentality of Divine ***Śakti***. Steps: (1) Consecration of work; (2) Renunciation of fruit; (3) Eradication of ego — of worker and of instrument; (4) Perfection of nature and identity with the Master of Works in Supermind.
Kāma **(Enjoyment):**	Delight of instrumentality, delight of relation with Divine Mother and Lord of Works, delight of identity with ***Īśvara-Śakti***.

realisation of the Person who attracts the entire cosmos and stands at its fount, the integer who is self-revealed as Kṛṣṇa but equally as Kṛṣṇa-Kālī, the two-in-one, whose *līlā* is all Becoming.[21]

In Supermind, these stand revealed as One, just as work, the struggle and labour of Ignorance also stands revealed there as the play of love.[22] It is for this reason that *karma* is literally *līlā* for the person who has realised the perfection of action

21. LD, p. 371.
22. Ibid.

within the *avidyā*. Work then, is not experienced as a compulsion but the creative self-choice of the Divine and the very synonym for Becoming. Becoming is revealed as the Being of the Divine, choosing to manifest itself in a creative play of all its possibilities, each recognising its own complete identity with the Divine in itself and as all the others. The Divine is infinite, it can explore itself infinitely, it is not bored by its sameness as we are, because it is marked by horizonless difference. To it, every aspect of itself, every mirror of itself is unknowable — not only unknown, but unknowable, because it is truly infinite. Every name by which Śakti can call *Īśvara,* is an infinity of exploration and wonder, a continent ever to be discovered. The Divine can multiply itself into infinite infinities at play, that is the mobilisation, the creative action of Delight. This is *karma,* the basis of the quartet of action. It is seen in its root to be nothing other than *līlā,* the play of Kṛṣṇa and Kālī.[23] Thus, *līlā* is the attractor of work. *Līlā* is the name in the *vidyā* for what we call work, *karma* in the *avidyā*. Everything in the cosmos, whether in the past, present or future, is at once *līlā* and *karma*.

Choice of Work

Still, the question remains, how should we choose our field of work? The *Bhagavad-Gītā* offers two levels of answers to this question, both of which are represented in the Seven Quartets. At the outset, the *Gītā* draws attention to the idea of *svabhāva* and *svadharma,* or soul quality and psychic law of becoming, respectively. *Svadharma* in the *Gītā* is explained in terms of the *cāturvarṇa* (the four castes) of Vedic thought. We have seen while discussing *śakti catuṣṭaya,* how Sri Aurobindo interprets these "castes" in terms of the four manifesting Śaktis, Māheśvarī, Mahākālī, Mahālakṣmī and Mahāsarasvatī. The *varṇa* (caste) in each individual case is related in some

23. RoY, pp. 1138-39.

predominant way to one of these *mahāśaktis*. Thus, the psychic power of becoming closely tied to Māheśvarī, the goddess of wideness and Knowledge is that manifested by the brāhmaṇa; that tied to Mahākālī, the goddess of power, passion and intensity is manifested by the kṣatriya; that tied to Mahālakṣmī, the goddess of mutuality, commerce and harmony is manifested by the vaiśya and that tied to Mahāsarasvatī, the goddess of skill, service and labour, is manifested by the śūdra.[24]

These *varṇas*, or castes, are psychic laws of becoming arising from a soul quality, possessed by each individual. In the view of the *Gītā*, the way of action, Karma-Yoga is most properly served by following one's *svadharma*.[25] This is taken by many to mean an adherence to the social status and role into which one is born. However, taking a historical and spiritual view of the *Gītā*'s injunction, Sri Aurobindo contests this interpretation, indicating instead, the need for each individual to discover his or her innate *svadharma*.[26] But, to arrive at this inner law of becoming, one must first be free of the conditionings of upbringing, culture, environment, as well as desires which drive one's decisions. An inner desirelessness is the condition for bringing one into contact with this psychic law of becoming. In our fiercely competitive world, where such a premium is placed on "proficiency", it is easy to distort the seeking for *svadharma* into an obsession. Ironically, *svadharma* reveals itself best when we are least concerned with it.

This brings us to the deeper level at which both, the *Gītā* and Sri Aurobindo, answer the question of "the work to be done". The *Gītā*'s approach is one of an unconditional surrender to the Divine Person. In a chapter titled "The Divine Work" in

24. RoY, pp. 1471, 1455.
25. *Bhagavad-Gītā*, III:35
26. EoG, pp. 513-14.

The Synthesis of Yoga, Sri Aurobindo elaborates on this, writing about the "work" of the person who has realised the goals of the quartet of being as a prelude to the quartet of action:

> Work cannot be fixed by any mind-made rule or human standard, for his consciousness has moved away from human law and limits and passed into the divine liberty, away from government by the external and transient into the self-rule of the inner and eternal, away from the binding forms of the finite into the free self-determination of the Infinite. "Howsoever he lives and acts", says the *Gītā*, "he lives and acts in Me". The rules, which the intellect of men lays down cannot apply to the liberated soul. By the external criteria and tests which their mental associations and pre-judgements prescribed such a one cannot be judged. He is outside the narrow jurisdiction of these fallible tribunals. It is immaterial whether he wears the garb of the ascetic or lives the full life of the householder, whether he spends his days in what men call holy works or in the many-sided activities of the world, whether he devotes himself to the direct leading of men to the light, like Buddha, Christ or Śaṅkara, or governs kingdoms like Janaka, or stands before men like Śrī Kr̥ṣṇa as a politician or a leader of armies; what he eats or drinks; what are his habits or his pursuits; whether he fails or succeeds; whether his work be one of construction or of destruction; whether he supports or restores an old order or labours to replace it by a new; whether his associates are those who men delight to honour or those whom their sense of superior righteousness outcastes and reprobates; whether his life and deeds are approved by his contemporaries or he is condemned as a misleader of men and a fomenter of religious, moral and social heresies. He is not governed by the judgements of men or the laws laid down by the ignorant; he obeys an inner voice and he is moved by an unseen power. His real life is within and this is its description that he lives, moves and acts in God, in the Divine, in the Infinite.

> But, if his action is governed by no external rule, one rule it will observe that is not external; it will be dictated by no personal desire or aim, but will be part of a conscious and eventually well-ordered, because self-ordered divine working in the world. The *Gītā* declares that the action of the liberated man must be directed not by desire but towards the keeping together of the world, its government, impulsion, maintenance in the path appointed to it.[27] This injunction has been interpreted in the sense that the world being an illusion in which most men must be kept since they are unfit for liberation, he must so act outwardly as to cherish in them an attachment to their customary works laid down for them by the social law.[28]

This refers to a misinterpretation by illusionist schools of the word *loka saṁgraha*, that is, the liberated man must not attempt to foment a widespread desire for liberation in people because the world will become non-functional as a result. He must try to encourage people to do their social duty. But, as one can see here, Sri Aurobindo contests this view. He continues,

> If so, it would be a poor and petty rule and every noble heart would reject it to follow rather the divine vow of Amitābha Buddha, the sublime prayer of the *Bhāgavata*, the passionate aspiration of Vivekananda. But, if we accept rather the view that the world is a divinely guided movement of nature, emerging in man towards God and then this is the work in which the Lord of the *Gītā* declares that he is ever occupied although he himself has nothing ungained that he has yet to win, then a deep and true sense will appear for this great injunction. To participate in that divine work, to live for God in the world will be the rule of the *karmayogin*; to live for God in the world and therefore so to act that the Divine may more and more manifest himself, and the world go

---

27. The *Gītā* uses the term *loka saṁgraha*, means the keeping together of the world. *Bhagavad-Gītā*, 3.25.
28. SoY, pp. 271-72.

> forward by whatever way of its obscure pilgrimage, and move nearer to the divine ideal.[29]

This becomes the key to the work to be done. Sri Aurobindo concludes this train of thought with these words, "It is altogether from within that must come the knowledge of the work that has to be done."[30]

A major part of the quartet of action is about finding this perfect guidance, the perfect way of action. Sri Aurobindo points to the need for purification and desirelessness to arrive at this:

> We cannot, however, easily distinguish this true inner law of our being; it is kept screened from us so long as the heart and intellect remain unpurified from egoism. Till then, we follow superficial and impermanent ideas, impulses, desires, suggestions and impositions of all kinds from our environment, or work out formations of our temporary mental, vital, physical personality — that passing experimental and structural self which has been made for our interaction between being and the pressure of a lower cosmic nature.[31]

It is interesting to note here Sri Aurobindo's definition of the ego. He spells out the various compulsions of *Prakṛti* that drive us, from around and from within, behind which one may contact the conscious force of Kālī or Śakti.

> In proportion as we are purified, the true being within declares itself more clearly, our will is less entangled in suggestions from outside or shut up in our own superficial mental constructions. Egoism renounced, the nature purified, action will come from the soul's dictate, from the depths or the heights of the Spirit, or it will be openly

29. SoY, p. 272.
30. Ibid.
31. Ibid., p. 274.

> governed by the Lord, who was all the time seated secretly within our hearts. The supreme and final word of the *Gītā* for the *yogin,* is that he should leave all conventional formulas of belief and actions, all fixed and external rules of conduct, all constructions of the outward surface nature, *dharmas*, and take refuge in the Divine alone. Free from desire and attachment, one with all beings, living in the infinite truth and purity and acting out of the profoundest deeps of his inner consciousness, governed by his immortal divine and highest self, all his works will be directed by the power within through that essential spirit and nature in us which, knowing, warring, working, loving, serving, is always divine, towards the fulfilment of God in the world and expression of the eternal in time.[32]

Stages Towards True Choice

This becomes the key to understanding the divine work, the acceptable sacrifice. The stages to arrive at it include purification, consecration, eradication of the ego and the emergence of the soul or psychic being as the governing agent of nature. It calls for becoming intuitional beings and replacing our nature by the divine nature. Sri Aurobindo draws largely on the *Bhagavad-Gītā* to elaborate the steps needed to achieve these stages. This involves, first and the foremost, the acknowledgement of our ignorance regarding the work to be done, the way to its achievement and its consequences. The *Gītā* approaches this problem of true works, primarily through a consecration of all works and a sacrifice of the consequences. The acknowledgement of our ignorance can be turned into a renunciation of personal ownership. The consequence of our acts then do not belong to us and is of no importance to us; it belongs to and is important only to the cosmic Being in its Becoming. The real significance of each action and its consequences belongs not to the individual who performed

32. SoY, p. 274.

it, but to the cosmic work of leading the universe towards a Divine realisation. This becomes the *Gītā*'s lever of initiation into divine action, through an offering of all individual predilections, preconditions and preferences to the supreme Śakti and the Supreme Lord, Kṛṣṇa-Kālī. This consecration of work is to be performed with each action, since the scope of work includes every movement of Śakti. Whatever one does, is to be seen as work, not merely the work for which one is paid or even the work which one performs as duty or charity, but work includes every activity, including waking up in the morning, performing one's ablutions, walking, eating, even breathing is a work and calls for consecration. This is one way of understanding Sri Aurobindo's epigram. "All life is *yoga*." One wakes in the morning and gathers oneself, as much as one can, into a concentrated consciousness of self and one offers it to the Divine. One says, I give myself and all I have and all I will do, to You; let all that is done by me be inhabited by You, so that You are the action and the enjoyer of the action and its consequence — that is consecration of the work.

The second major step consists of a renunciation of the fruit of action. This renunciation means divesting oneself from the sense of ownership over the results of action and offering them to the Divine Śakti and the Divine Lord, to use, according to their wisdom in the cosmic Becoming. The result then belongs to the Divine and success and failure lose their personal significance. Its good is no longer a personal good, its good is whatever the Divine feels is good. Therefore, one may make a conscious prayer of this nature:

> I, in my ignorance, have no knowledge of what value the results of my actions have to my progress, the cosmic Becoming and the Divine Will. Whatever the result, I will not be attached to it, I will accept it as your will, because the fruit of my action is yours, not mine.

This key step of renouncing the fruits of action is taken by many to be the goal of the *karma-yoga*, but this is not true. It can certainly be thought of as the most powerful lever of the *karma-yoga*. It is that which breaks the backbone of egoism and the practice which allows us to become detached in the midst of work. If it is done in a conscious and systematic manner, the more one becomes aware of it pervading one's life, the closer one comes to a concrete sense of the disinterested Worker inside us, the presence of the one cosmic Person at work in the world. And, it is only when that disinterested Being becomes prominent in us, can the promptings of the Divine be heard and the work proceed from within.

The third step is the eradication of the ego. The eradication of the ego proceeds from the renunciation of consequences. Here, too, Sri Aurobindo points to two important stages. The first is the eradication of the ego of the worker, that is, the sense that, "I am the person initiating and executing this work". As one loses the sense of being the beneficiary of the fruits of one's works, one also increasingly becomes a witness to one's works. One is no longer the active egoistic doer but an instrument and a witness who observes the Śakti at work within one, through whose agency one's works are accomplished. This often carries a sense at the end of the day as if one did nothing, yet many things were done through one's instrumentation. That is a sign of the thinning of the sense of the worker, and leads to the eradication of the ego of the worker.

But, there is another very important step beyond this — because, as this sense develops (and in some cases, this experience may be innate) — the sense of one's capacity to do work also gets expanded, greater energies may use one's instrumentality, one may find oneself put to greater responsibilities. This enlarged capacity for action, belongs to, what the *Gītā* calls the *vibhūti*. The loss of sense of the small personal ego may equip one to open to a much larger cosmic power of action — that of the *vibhūti*. With this enhanced capacity there may enter another and more dangerous kind of egoism: the ego of the instrument. The *yogin* needs to be aware of this possibility and eradicate it too if and when it arises. This is what Sri Aurobindo writes about this form of ego and how to deal with it:

> Even when we become aware of all as the working of one cosmic force and of the divine behind it, that too need not liberate. If the egoism of the worker disappears, the egoism of the instrument may replace it or prolong it in a disguise. The life of the world has been full of instances of egoism of this kind and it can be more engrossing and enormous than any other. There is the same danger in yoga. Our nature must house the cosmic force, but not in its lower aspect, or in its rājasic or sāttvic movement. It must serve the universal will but in the light of a greater liberating knowledge. There must be no egoism of any kind in the attitude of the instrument even when we are fully conscious of the greatness of the force within us. Every man is knowingly or unknowingly the instrument of a universal power, and, apart from the inner presence, there is no such essential difference between one action and another, one kind of instrumentation and another as would warrant the folly of an egoistic pride. The breath of divine power blows where it lists and fills today one and tomorrow another with the sword of the puissance. If the potter shapes one pot more perfectly than another the merit lies not in the vessel but in the maker. The attitude of our mind must not be "This is my strength", or, "Behold God's power in me", but rather "A divine power works in this mind and body and it is the same that works in all men and in the animal, in the plant and in the metal, in conscious and living things and in things appearing to be inconscient and inanimate. This large view of the One working in all and of the whole world

> as the equal instrument of a divine action and gradual self-expression, if it becomes our entire experience will help to eliminate all rājasic egoism out of us and even the sāttvic ego sense will begin to pass away from our nature.[33]

This constitutes the eradication of the ego. With the ego eradicated, one arrives at the experience of the One Worker in all things. As Sri Aurobindo describes in the last part of the quoted passage above, the elimination of the ego-sense is accomplished by the meditation on the entire cosmos and its constituents as the instrument(s) of the One Worker and the One Work. This includes the mental fixation on the idea that there is one Being and that Being's Becoming, and this is the "work" that is being accomplished by all things in the cosmos. As this sense of the One Worker, working in and through us, increases and grows more concrete to an inner sense, we also begin to become aware of a Being whose presence upholds all works and towards whom all works proceed from the worker in the world. This awareness and identification in consciousness with the Becoming and the Being, is our entry into contact through works with the deities referred to as the first two *catuṣṭaya*s, Kr̥ṣṇa and Kālī. Kālī is the Supreme Energy and the One Worker that is at work in all things; she is the Divine Mother, creatrix of the cosmos and present in it as its subjective dynamism. Kr̥ṣṇa is the Divine Lord, whose Will Kālī serves and who is the destination of all Becoming — an infinite distance like the vanishing point of a perspective and yet intimately present in every step and standing beyond all destining as identity and attractor. Kr̥ṣṇa as destination is the attraction at the head of all destiny, whose attraction will never cease, who will draw from the unfathomable depths of his own radical infinity, ever more into manifestation through the Power of Kālī, the Divine Śakti. The growth of this inner

33. SoY, p. 250.

perception and sense is a sign of the approach towards perfection, *siddhi*, of the *karma catuṣṭaya*.

Surrender to the Divine Śakti

This inner sense may develop as a duality in the *avidyā* of our given human condition — the sense of a static transcendental presence outside us that is observing and sanctioning, and the sense of a dynamic Being within us and all things, the energy, whether mechanical or conscious, subjective or objective, at work in the cosmos. This dualism, in some form, is inevitable, given the cosmic ignorance within which it is experienced; and it needs to be transformed into an experience of unity and identity in the Supermind. In the *brahma catuṣṭaya* we saw that one way of approaching this transformation of experience is through knowledge, identification with the Idea-principle in the world whose origin is Supermind. Mind is that in us, which is aware of the ideational content in the universe, but mind cannot arrive at integrality. Hence, by opening the mind to a higher power, and allowing that to transform the mentality and thereby, arrive at an integral vision of things, ultimately takes us into the consciousness of Supermind. In the quartet of action, this experience of integrality is approached differently and in a more generally approachable way. This is through a surrender of the active being to what Sri Aurobindo calls Kālī here, or the Divine Mother, in his later writings. If we can conceive of this conscious power as one which is luminous above but veiled below, then a surrender to the unveiled source of that power can lead us through our dynamic processes, preparing our nature instruments and transforming us. The "work" will then become progressively conscious, a work in which we are guided through inner intimations and outer circumstances, towards the illumination of the entire being and into a state in which the Śakti or Kālī is experienced in an unveiled form as a power of, and ultimately in inseparable identity with *puruṣa*, or Kṛṣṇa. Here, we'll find ourselves lifted up into identity with this integral two-in-one, Kṛṣṇa-Kālī. This is the realisation in Supermind.

As Sri Aurobindo put it later in his book *The Mother*, this surrender to the Divine Mother is what will prepare the human instrument which otherwise would find it impossible, by its unaided effort, to cross over from its mind-bound experience in *avidyā* to an integral experience in *vidyā*. He says there:

> The supramental change is a thing decreed and inevitable in the evolution of the earth-consciousness; for its upward ascent is not ended and mind is not its last summit. But that the change may arrive, take form and endure, there is needed the call from below with a will to recognise and not deny the light when it comes, and there is needed the sanction of the Supreme from above. The power that mediates between the sanction and the call is the presence and power of the Divine Mother. The Mother's power and not any human endeavour and *tapasyā* can alone rend the lid and tear the covering and shape the vessel and bring down into this world of obscurity and falsehood and death and suffering Truth and Light and Life Divine and the immortal's *ānanda*.[34]

In the quartet of action, the progressive surrender to the Divine Mother and faith in her, become the keys to the transition of human consciousness from *avidyā* to *vidyā* through a dynamic process. We have seen earlier how the development of an intuitive consciousness is part of this transition. Faith in the Śakti operating in the performance of works, leads progressively to this intuitional development in the dynamic parts of the mind, will and instrumental physical being, and its replacement of the habitual operations of these parts. In

34. Sri Aurobindo, *The Mother*, SABCL 25, pp. 40-41.

this progress, the thinking and planning mind, the acquired skills and training of specialised tasks, the operational methods of the will are made silent, surrendered and receptive to the Śakti through a faith in her ability to use these as her instruments. As in the working of inspiration in creative activity, a faith in the human agent opens the action of a higher power and its pure transmission through its instrumentality. With experience, this faith grows and comes to depend with increasing substantiality on the higher force. Depending on the power of this faith, we say that a creative person has command over his or her inspiration. A similar process establishes the dependence of the entire active instrumentality on the Divine Mother, who one invokes in all one's works and experiences, as providing the inspired ideas and intuitive skills in each instance. This effects the replacement of the normal ego-dependence on one's own labouring and struggling processes by a confident active surrender to the Śakti and its ability to use one infallibly to achieve its ends. As this experience regularises itself, one loses the sense of the doer and witnesses the Divine Mother from above acting in and through one. The sense of identity with this Śakti, grows in the instrumental being as they become faithful channels of her action, while the experience of all the works being offered to the Lord, also grows, along with the identity of the witnessing self with this Lord or *Īśvara*.

Thus, the fulfilment of the two primary realisations of the fourfold perfection of the *karma catuṣṭaya,* is the union of *Īśvara* and Śakti, or Kr̥ṣṇa and Kālī, realised as an integral identity in Supermind, where they are, forever, two sides of the same Reality, the Supreme Lord ever loosing forth his own conscious creative energy, who is at work creating the conditions for ever-greater manifestations, as the Becoming of Infinite Being.

Kāma

The *siddhi* of the *karma catuṣṭaya*, its fourth realisation, is *kāma*. This is the delight in the play of Kṛṣṇa and Kālī, *līlā*. *Kāma*, in the *karma catuṣṭaya*, can be said to encompass three forms of delight or *ānanda*: the delight of the instrument, the delight of relation with the Divine Mother (Kālī) and the Lord of Works (Kṛṣṇa), and the delight of identity with Īśvara-Śakti (Kṛṣṇa-Kālī).

The first of these can be realised upon renunciation of attachment to the results of work. The common understanding of work is that it is undertaken for the enjoyment of its results. Work seems to be tied to a motivational goal. But, if we are to consciously reject or renounce the fruit of our works, we find a replacement of this deferred delight by the spontaneous delight of the instrument in the work. As Sri Aurobindo puts it, the delight of the instrument is in experiencing the beautiful and perfect notes of the Śakti, as they manifest through it. This is the first level of delight in works. Secondly, there is the realisation of the delight of relationship with the hand that uses our instrumentality, the One that plays the instrument. This relationship itself is a complex, consisting of our relationship with the Energy or Śakti which uses us, our relationship with the Master of the Works or Divine Lord and our awareness of the relationship of the Śakti and the Lord. We enjoy our relationship with the Divine Mother, to whom we are surrendered, as She moulds us; we enjoy too, our relationship with the Divine Lord, who is the Master and Goal of our Works and our Becoming; and we enjoy the relationship of the Divine Mother with the Divine Lord by being the hyphen in between, the instrument through which that *līlā* of relationship is being manifested. And, finally, as our experience of delight in relationship converges in Supermind, in an identity, in which our own being knows itself to be one with the One Worker, the Divine Śakti, working within us; and knows too identity with the Master of Works as the One from whom all work and its enjoyment proceeds, we attain to the delight of identity with and of Īśvara-Śakti, (Kṛṣṇa-Kālī), the supramental Delight of the One Being in its Becoming.

Identity in Difference

We see then, that this goal of *kāma* takes in its ambit the identity with Kṛṣṇa and Kālī, but also the relationship with Kṛṣṇa and Kālī and between them. Let us recollect the words of Sri Ramakrishna, "I don't want to be sugar, I want to eat sugar". This is the mystic justification of the dualist, the sweetness of relationship. But, in the *karma catuṣṭaya*, the idea is one of both being and eating the sugar. Knowing identity with Kṛṣṇa brings Kṛṣṇa's self-delight; knowing identity with Kālī, brings the delight of relationship with Kṛṣṇa. This is the realisation of identity in difference. During the same period that Sri Aurobindo was writing the *Record of Yoga*, he was also writing his *Thoughts and Aphorisms*. In this text, we come across some lines which relate to the experience of this dual and integral delight:

> I did not know for some time whether I loved Kṛṣṇa best or Kālī; when I loved Kālī, it was loving myself, but when I loved Kṛṣṇa, I loved another, and still it was my Self with whom I was in love. Therefore, I came to love Kṛṣṇa better even than Kālī.[35]

This realisation is beyond logic. This is why one of the great *yogī*s and metaphysicians of India following the mystic Sri Caitanya, called his path of Divine Love, *acintya bhed-abheda*, (unthinkable unity in difference). This realisation of identity in difference is the dynamic aspect achieved through the Becoming of what Sri Aurobindo has introduced in the *brahma*

35. EDH, p. 483.

catuṣṭaya in terms of Being: "the realisation of oneness and the practice of oneness in difference is the whole of the yoga". Identity in difference with the Supreme Person, *Īśvara* or Kṛṣṇa as the true self and in relation of Master and Lord with all beings, taking delight in all action; identity in difference with the supreme *Śakti* or Kālī as nature force in relation of Divine Mother with all beings, carrying out all action; and identity in difference of the Śakti as power of consciousness of *Īśvara*, identical and in relation with the Supreme Lord carrying out His Will for his Delight — this is the culmination of the quartet of action.

8

Attitudes of Self-Discipline

HAVING concluded our consideration of the seven major quartets of the yoga of integral transformation, we can attempt to synthesise their gains. As we proceeded through these quartets, we noticed elements of convergence and overlap. These overlaps arose because, as pointed out at the outset, the fractal or integral nature of the system makes each of these seven quartets constitute the entire yoga. Each one of these approaches brings into itself several aspects of the rest. But, Sri Aurobindo splits these approaches into seven, so as to open seven simultaneous and interacting lines of attention. In a way, it is like taking a slew of threads and discovering that they are one at the end. Thus, we find that each one of these quartets overlaps with others. It then becomes natural to try and connect the overlaps, so as to arrive at some general ideas cutting across or, through the practice of this system. This attempt to synthesise the approaches would give us a more holistic or "integral" grasp, which would equip us to look at some of the entries of Sri Aurobindo's *Record of Yoga* and see how he uses the terminology of the seven quartets to study his own progress. Sri Aurobindo, in these entries, often approaches the quartets in a synthetic or even syncretic fashion, so as to experiment in a systematic way, and like a scientist, record his progressions, retrogressions, expected and unexpected results. This is the kind of expression we find in the *Record of Yoga*. To understand it, let us try to distinguish some of the general areas.

Attitudes of Self-Discipline

One such general line of approach concerns attitudes of self-discipline. This is also an attempt for us to understand how we can proceed to tie these various approaches in a self-practice. The first question to ask then, is, what attitudes are we required to practise? In making our approach, the first thing to remember is Sri Aurobindo's epigram at the start of *The Synthesis of Yoga*: "All Life is Yoga". In other words, at the outset of our approach, this epigram tells us that there is no segregated practice, nothing prescribed in terms of routines, but, that the practice is undertaken on the run. This is particularly relevant today, when the luxury of a secluded existence belongs only to the commodified packaging of leisure, in the tight circulations of a global economy, and all so-called private time is "accounted" and surveilled. The yoga is not meant to be a pastime as in a visit to the yoga studio, a meditation room or an intensive retreat. It's a 24-hour practice of subjectivation — one is to do it while preparing to go to work, while working, while resting, while eating, while enjoying; one is to do it in sleep and in recreation: everything is yoga. This is the idea behind the epigram, "All Life is Yoga". So, when we think of attitudes of self perfection, we are looking for the inculcation of central principles that will be like threads running through life as a practice of becoming. In trying to draw out these threads from a consideration of commonalities in the seven quartets, I would also like to bring them into alignment with certain source texts of the integral yoga. One of these, which we have been referring to often, is Sri Aurobindo's *The Synthesis of Yoga*. But, for the consideration of commonalities of attitude, I will also consider a text, which has been given to us by the Mother, Sri Aurobindo's partner and collaborator. This is a simple but powerful text titled *The Four Austerities and the Four Liberations*; it presents many of the major ideas that we've considered so far, in a very focused and practical way. This text spells out a number of these commonalities of attitude without naming these difficult Sanskrit terms.

Resolution and Sincerity

The first of these attitudes of self-perfection, which I would like to bring to attention, is resolution and sincerity of practice. One has to make a resolution to transform oneself, or "become-other" in Deleuze's term, an investment of one's life to the project of supermanhood, because before this, life may be full of beautiful experiences, or it can be full of hopes and aspirations, but, there is no glue to it other than what conditions the subject through the technologies of power and capital. What is missing is resolution. This resolution is a central turning of the being, the Heideggerian *kehre* or ontological turn, whose preparation is the analysis of the constitution of the subject, but whose practice is the illimitable trajectory of self-fashioning and self-exceeding as an instrument of the will to power as evolution. There's something inside us that says yes, it's now, everything changes from now — the clock starts ticking from now. This resolution is not something we can decide or determine in advance. It has to come by itself, as an act of the soul. But, even an act of the soul needs the support of the conscious and unconscious beings/parts in us, especially, the support of that which is the most active agent of our conscious lives, the mind. So, when the inner being is ready, when the dweller within knocks on the gates to indicate the time for resolution, the mind must give its adherence and unreserved assent. That is the resolution.

With resolution comes the need for sincerity of practice. Sincerity may be thought of as the central attitude in the practice of the yoga of integral transformation. If one is not willing to be sincere, one should not take the step. The Mother has something simple to say about this in the text mentioned above. She writes about discipline, about the fact that once one has decided, one has to follow one's own discipline, not a discipline given by anybody else. No teacher, no school, no monastery should tell one, what one is supposed to do. You will tell yourself what discipline you'll follow, it's your own inner guidance, but you have to follow that guidance with sincerity. In this respect, she says,

> There must be no little exceptions to the rule that are indulged in just for once, but which are repeated very often, for as soon as one yields to temptation, even just for once, one lessens the resistance of the will-power and opens the door to every failure.[1]

This lesson is very important for us to keep in mind. It is so critical because our central aid in our personal enterprise is will-power. The power of will, and this discipline of the will, the ability to keep the will focused, to concentrate the will and not let it flag, is the first absolute essential attitude of integral becoming. The will cannot be allowed to forget that it has taken the resolution and that its life is given, surrendered to an ideal. This is sincerity and why it becomes the decisive practice. Earlier, we had occasion to consider Michel Foucault's adulation of the Stoics in ancient Greece for their self-discipline as part of an ethics and aesthetics of existence, without reference to externally or institutionally determining forces, such as religion, state or social norms. Such a "care of the soul" demands the *askesis* of personal resolution and "truth-telling", a prefect sincerity. The text that forms the centre of our consideration here — Sri Aurobindo's *Record of Yoga* — is itself the trace of such a practice of truth-telling, a transaction between one's present and future selves, contingent upon an act of resolution and sincerity. It engages a hermeneutics of the self and creates its own milieu at the same time.

1. The Mother, "The Four Austerities and the Four Liberations" in *On Education*, CWM:12, p. 51.

This attitude is also emphasised in a term that is common to the general field of yoga. This is *abhyāsa*. The word *abhyāsa* means practice. In *The Synthesis of Yoga,* Sri Aurobindo introduces the idea of the four aids in a chapter by that name. The first of these aids is the Śāstra or teaching. In this case, the system of the seven quartets is itself the Śāstra which Sri Aurobindo received from "the Master of the Yoga" and followed scrupulously. As we noted, this is not a set of prescriptions, but a system of experimentation that needs to be interpreted through creative will and increasing consciousness. In his treatment of Śāstra in *The Synthesis of Yoga*, Sri Aurobindo does not refer to this or any other text as such, but indicates that the text of the Śāstra is within each person, in keeping with his view (discussed here in the chapter on the quartet of knowledge) that all knowledge is contained within each person:

> For the *sādhaka* of the integral yoga, it is necessary to remember that no written Śāstra, however great its authority, or however large its spirit, can be more than a partial expression of the eternal Knowledge. He will use, but never bind himself even by the greatest Scripture. . . . [I]n the end he must take his station, or better still, if he can, always and from the beginning, he must live in his own soul beyond the limitations of the word that he uses.[2]

Regarding the practice, he writes:

> An absolute liberty of experience and of the restatement of knowledge in new terms and new combinations is the condition of its self-formation. . . . By this yoga, we not only seek the Infinite, but we call upon the Infinite to unfold himself in human life. Therefore, the Śāstra of our yoga must provide for an infinite liberty in the receptive human soul. A free adaptability in the manner and the type of the

---

2. SoY, p. 55.

> individual's acceptance of the Universal and Transcendent into himself is the right condition for the full spiritual life in man. . . . Meanwhile, certain general lines have to be formed which may help to guide the thought and practice of the *sādhaka*. But these must take, as much as possible, the form of general truths, general statements of principle, the most powerful broad directions of effort and development rather than a fixed system, which has to be followed as a routine.[3]

The second aid, mentioned in this chapter, is *utsāha*. *Utsāha*, rightly translated, means enthusiasm, but what Sri Aurobindo means by it is a kind of energy, a powerful positive energy and inspired passion, the Greek *enthusiasmos*, in making progress. But, he couples *utsāha* with personal effort, *abhyāsa*. *Abhyāsa* stands for disciplined practice, not practice that is externally imposed, but practice that is self-imposed. *Abhyāsa* is described by Sri Aurobindo in terms of three stages. We must remember that the aim of the yoga of integral transformation is a "becoming-other", which implies a transformed ontology and a transformed agency.

> There must be, first, the effort towards at least an initial and enabling self-transcendence and contact with the Divine; next, the reception of that which transcends, that with which we have gained communion, into ourselves for the transformation of our whole conscious being; last, the utilisation of our transformed humanity as a divine centre in the world.[4]

The third aid is the *guru*. As most people know, *guru* is the teacher. In *The Four Aids*, Sri Aurobindo clarifies that the *guru* — whoever it may be on the outside — is actually the divine presence within the aspirant. The *guru* is the One Divine who is within all beings. It may start off as guidance from an

3. SoY, pp. 56-57.
4. Ibid., p. 58.

external teacher, but this teacher should be internalised, the *guru* moves from being without to being within. Finally, one recognises the teacher everywhere.[5] The fourth aid is time. Sri Aurobindo says that *kāla* (time) is the fourth aid, because it is that which chases us, we find ourselves constantly struggling against the clock. On the other hand, the *yogī* is meant to dwell in eternity. Thus, it is the dialectic between eternity and time that we enact in our lives through *sādhanā,* because we are time-hunted beings, and at the same time a part of us is eternal, and the relationship between these two is guided by the Time Spirit, *kāla* — the giver of the synchronicities of the cosmic participation. This awareness and friendship with time, the eternal whose self-exploration we participate in, makes it the aid, the help — time itself is our guide:

> The ideal attitude of the *sādhaka* towards time is to have an endless patience as if he had all eternity for his fulfillment and yet to develop the energy that shall realise now and with an ever-increasing mastery and pressure of rapidity till it reaches the miraculous instantaneousness of the supreme divine transformation.[6]

Aspiration

The second attitude of self-perfection is related to *utsāha* and appears under the *śakti catuṣṭaya* of the *Record of Yoga.* This is *lipsā. Lipsā* has a variety of meanings, a common one being attachment. This would be a surprising use, since attachment is something we are normally asked to reject in yoga: we are asked to be disinterested, unattached. But, Sri Aurobindo gives a different sense to the word *lipsā,* because — like the term *kāma* which means desire — Sri Aurobindo uses this word in the sense of its transformed potential. When *lipsā* is purified,

---

5. SoY, pp. 61-63.
6. Ibid., p. 68.

it reveals itself not as attachment but as a pure psychic or soul power, which we can more properly translate as adherence or aspiration, an impersonal will. Thus, "aspiration" is the second attitude of self-perfection that runs through the yoga of integral transformation. The aspiration can also be called a will to progress in integral becoming. It is something that the aspirant is seeded with. Once the resolution is made, there burns something within the heart which must be constant, adhering to the goals of the seven quartets. This is the will to progress in integral becoming.

To help us understand what this means, we can look at two quotes. The first one is from Sri Aurobindo's text *The Mother*, where he talks about the power of the Divine Śakti guiding and leading us, and in fact, doing the yoga within us. We feel we are making the effort, but that is only because the ego translates the guidance and agency of the Divine Śakti into its own terms. As we progress, this sense transfers itself into more of an intimate relationship with this guiding power, and finally, we realise that it is that power that does everything. We are merely a witness and enjoyer of its action. The text, *The Mother*, introduces the term aspiration in its very first line. Further, it describes the aspiration:

> An aspiration vigilant, constant, unceasing, the mind's will, the heart's seeking, the assent of the vital being, the will to open and make plastic the physical consciousness and nature. . . .[7]

In this statement, we become aware of a necessary attitude at all levels of the being, an integral approach relating to the seven quartets. We see the mind's will which is the discipline of the mind, the mind which is trying to arrive at the truth of knowledge. The mind must be unflagging in its aspiration for

---

7. Sri Aurobindo, *The Mother with Letters on the Mother*, SABCL 25, pp. 6-7.

arriving at knowledge. The heart's seeking — this indicates the emotional being — which thirsts for the fullness of the Divine Love, must also have its power of aspiration for the Divine, constantly present. The assent of the vital being, — this indicates the power of the will, constantly urging the being towards various ideals, and here the assent of the vital being implies that the ideal be one-pointed and approached with one's full enthusiasm — this returns us once more to the *utsāha* of the *Four Aids* — the assent of the vital elicits the enthusiasm of the entire being for the ideal. Finally, the body or physical consciousness, which is addressed in the *śarīra catuṣṭaya* — the will to open and make plastic the physical consciousness, is also part of this active and integral aspiration.

The second quote to consider, comes from the text written by the Mother, introduced earlier — *The Four Austerities and the Four Liberations.* It pertains to the practice of the aspiration or the will to progress in integral perfection, through action. How are we to practise this in our everyday lives? This question becomes an important one because we are full of choices and preferences, and these are the preferences of ignorance. So the Mother says in this text:

> It is said that one only does well what one is interested in doing. This is true, but it is truer still that one can learn to find interest in everything one does, even in what appear to be the most insignificant chores.[8]

This is a practical aspect of the integral aspiration. Whatever comes to us in the stream of circumstance, can we respond enthusiastically with the will to progress? This can also be seen as an illustration of the dynamic aspiration that's implied in Sri Aurobindo's aphorism, "All Life is Yoga".

---

8. SABCL: 25, p. 54.

Constant Remembrance

The third common attitude to practise in the yoga of integral perfection is constant remembrance of and delight in the One infinite Being and Person. This is something, repeatedly drawn attention to, in the quartets. Sri Aurobindo draws our attention to the fact that our focus must never shift from the attention on the One Infinite — that there is only one Being, one Being in many bodies, many things, a being which is never the same, one Being fragmented in a variety of contrary, appearances throughout the universe — but one Being. To keep the focus of one's affect on that One infinite Being, to love the one Being and Person in all our contacts and relations, and to delight in that Being is a central thread in the yoga of integral transformation. To remember that Being alone confronts us in all things and all beings, that the one Being surrounds us, guides us, and it's the only Being we are responsible to — this is to be our delight. To hold to this delight, a constant remembrance and delight in the One, is *prema,* which means love. Sri Aurobindo uses this term in the seven quartets: the universalised love for the One, everywhere and in everything, needs to be kept in the front of the consciousness.[9] Every specific relation and activity will then be a channel through which the One will come to us.

If *prema* is the active affective component of this attitude, *ānanda* (bliss) is its receptive component. Sri Aurobindo introduces and insists on the practice of this attitude in a number of places, prominently in the *brahma catuṣṭaya* and the *samatā catuṣṭaya*. Whatever the taste of things, whatever our preferences, whatever our natural proclivities of cultural upbringing, we must strive for an equal delight in all things. That, which is bitter, has the delight of bitterness, that which is sweet, has its own delight. It is delight in all its forms that

9. RoY, p. 1470.

we must be able to experience impersonally and to differentiate the various qualities within it. In our consideration of the *śarīra catuṣṭaya*, the quartet of the body, we saw Sri Aurobindo referring to *raudrānanda*, delight in pain. The aim was to transform the experience of pain to bliss, to experience it as an intensity of delight. We habitually respond with pain to this intensity. But, the power of consciousness can intervene to change our natural conventions of response to pain so as to experience the same as delight, even in the experience of the senses. Even physical reactions of pain would then be experienced as *sparśa*, the blissful touch of the One. The remembrance of Bliss in the One, is something that universalises itself in all experiences if one practises it. We have earlier had occasion to consider Sri Aurobindo's statement in *The Synthesis of Yoga*, where he says, "the realisation of oneness and the practice of oneness in difference is the whole of the yoga".[10]

Equality

Some of these primary attitudes of practice come more directly from our studies of the seven quartets. The first of the *ādhāra siddhi*s, equality (*samatā*) assumes paramount importance in the practice of integral transformation. Equality is to be practised constantly as we move along. In all our experiences, at every level, we must attempt to establish equality. In other words, all things are valued the same — the value of oneness, the equality of the Divine. *Samatā* is a very powerful practice. As with oneness, there are many places where Sri Aurobindo draws attention to this. This is also a primary emphasis in the *Bhagavad-Gītā*, where, at one place, yoga is equated to equality: *samatvam yoga uccyate* (equality is spoken of as yoga).[11] It will be instructive to think of the kinds of equality which

---

10. SoY, p. 420.
11. *Bhagavad-Gītā*, II:48.

should be practised. One of these is mental equality, the equality to ideas. This is a very sensitive area. Even without being conscious of it, there are often a number of ideologies determining our mental preferences: we give our support to one principle over another. Mental equality would consist of being conscious of ideologies and being able to accept the value in all ideas. Sri Aurobindo has an interesting personal note on this: He says,

> The capital period of my intellectual development was when I could see clearly that what the intellect said may be correct and not correct, that what the intellect justifies is true and its opposite also is true. I never admitted a truth in the mind without simultaneously keeping it open to the contrary of it. And the first result was that the prestige of the intellect was gone.[12]

This is related to the practice of equality in ideas.

Then, there is equality to the circumstances of life. This kind of equality is well discussed in the quartet of equality or peace (*samatā catuṣṭaya*), where an equality to the dualities of life experience is enjoined — equality in happiness and suffering, attraction and repulsion. This is not easy to achieve. One may accept the sorrows of life with resignation or stoic fortitude, but we eagerly pursue the things which bring happiness. And, on obtaining these, we seldom stop to think about equality. Sri Aurobindo wrote of this superiority to the experiences of life in terms of active and passive powers of equality. As we saw in our consideration of the quartet of equality, he mentions three major passive qualities (*titikṣā, udāsīnatā, nati*), moving into their active counterparts. Of these passive powers of equality, the first is *titikṣā* (endurance). Endurance is how we respond to that which is not so palatable

---

12. A.B. Purani, *Evening Talks with Sri Aurobindo*, Pondicherry: Sri Aurobindo Ashram Trust, 2007, p. 199.

or bearable. Sri Aurobindo says that great endurance is possible to the human spirit because God dwells in him. We can find something in us equal to any adversity. This is a profound lesson of humanity. We see in human history, how the most impossible adversities have been endured, because the person going through the experience has discovered in himself or herself something which is equal to it. Human beings are not aware of their own capacities of endurance until they are challenged with what exceeds their expectations, and then we often realise that we find the power to endure. This is the first and most basic of the powers of equality to be cultivated.

The second level of passive equality is superiority to experience. The Sanskrit term, which Sri Aurobindo uses, is *udāsīnatā*, which literally means "to be seated above". If endurance is an action of equality at the same level as one's experience, *udāsīnatā* refers to a vertical transcendence. In other words, there is a dimension of experience which remains untouched by one's physical or vital responses. This isn't endurance, but transcendence. The emergence of the mental *puruṣa*, the witness self, can provide the beginnings of this experience; but the entry into the spiritual consciousness can bring its fulfilment. A good example can be had from the life of the great Yogī Ramaṇa Maharṣi. Though suffering from painful cancer in his last months, he gave *darśana* to hundreds of visitors, with the same beatific smile and radiant eyes and with no visible expression of pain. This was because he was identified with the divine Self, and felt himself unmoved by the experience of the body. This is *udāsīnatā*: the ability to fully transcend nature's experience. Even though, there is suffering in the body or the feelings, something in the consciousness is so much above it, that it is experienced as if far away. It is free from the experience of both happiness and pain.

The third stage of passive equality is glad acceptance *(nati)*. This is not merely a neutrality, but a positive condition. To endure and to be seated above are neutral forms of equality, but glad acceptance is the fulfillment of receptive equality. It is where the Divine is concretely present in one's experience so that, one is able to experience all events and encounters as the contacts of the Divine. This relates to the earlier discussion on *ānanda*, in receiving all contacts of the world as the bliss of the touch of god. Apart from these aspects of equality, that is equality to ideas and circumstances of life, there are one's tastes — by taste one may think not only of sensory tastes, e.g. the tastes of one's tongue, but aesthetic taste, the tastes of one's mind. Mental preferences of taste are, in some ways, more difficult to bring equality to. We have touched on this also in our consideration of Delight in the One. Then, there is the area of equality in one's relations. Here too, there must develop a dimension of experience in which all relations are forms of the One. Friendship, enmity, etc. are flavours of relationship, but behind them, there is the One. If one can experience this, it is a great progress. The *Gītā* says, friend and foe, brāhmaṇa and dog, outcaste or king, are all the same to the *yogin*.[13] All is one, but there is a differentiation of oneness . . . the *yogī* not only sees everything as One, but also sees the unlimited differentiations of the one consciousness.

Then, there is equality in the responses of the nerves and body. The responses of the nerves is a matter of importance, because the transformation of pain to delight, touched on earlier, starts with this equality. The nerves give a conditioned response to the contacts of stimuli. But, if the impetus towards equality can be communicated to the nerves, there is an enlargement of capacity, their conditioning changes, and they translate the impacts into values of neutrality. This is a turning

13. *Bhagavad-Gītā*, V:18.

point. The point of bringing equality into the body, lies in being able to experience sensory stimuli in terms of neutrality. Neutrality is the gate to divine enjoyment. An active reception of the value of divine delight can only come after the ability to neutralise nature's conditioned responses. Neutrality deepens into ecstasy.

These are the ways by which equality can be practised: in the activities and tastes of the mind, in the responses we give to fate and the circumstances of life, in our relations, and in the responses of the body in the nerves and the cells.

Purification

Next in the attitudes of integral transformation is purification (*śuddhi*). As we saw when we dealt with the quartets of perfection and of equality, much of purification depends on equality. But, there is another component to purification: this is rejection. Rejection is an act of will, and Sri Aurobindo writes about rejection as one of the primary practices in his book, *The Mother*. Here, he writes about three principal powers of practice in the very first chapter — these are aspiration, rejection and surrender. But, in the seven quartets, he does not use the term rejection. What translates to rejection in the *Record of Yoga*, or in *The Synthesis of Yoga*, is an aspect of purification or *śuddhi*. *Śuddhi* includes the rejection of desires — which Sri Aurobindo calls *vāsanās*.[14] These are the various intrinsic seeds, desires that are seeded in the subconscient. They come partly from our natural conditioning as human beings, partly from the recycled materials of universal nature of which we are constituted, partly from our genetic inheritance and partly from past lives. Even prior to this life's experiences, the seeds, *saṁskāras* of past lives and of universal nature already provide us with propensities towards desires of various kinds.

14. RoY, p. 1478.

These must be observed, understood and repeatedly rejected, till, finding no support in the will, they drop off. Equality, which we have just discussed, is also a power of purification, but rejection is an act of will, hence more dynamic. To know how to reject is also part of this discipline (*abhyāsa*). To the rejection of compulsions (*vāsanās*) in the life energies (*prāṇas*) must be added rejection of attachment, which Sri Aurobindo calls *āsakti* and rejection of longing which is called *kāmanā*.[15] There is also the rejection of preference — this preference can be in the mind, in the life force, the vital, or in the body, the physical — and the rejection of the dualities of attraction and repulsion, which in Sanskrit are called *rāga* and *dveṣa*. We often tend to speak or act without thinking, driven by desire or emotion. Sri Aurobindo says about this: "Prohibit and inhibit by will all action or speech that starts blindly from the passions or emotions surging in the heart."[16] Then, there are the habitual responses of the sense mind, based on the natural conventions of the senses and the heuristics of expectation based on memory. These too need to be consciously rejected, or rather suspended, and referred to the higher intelligence, which in turn needs to be purified progressively into an instrument of perceptive intuition.

Replacements

Next come a set of replacements. Perhaps, the most important of these comes from the *Gītā* and relates to one's action. Sri Aurobindo draws repeated attention to it. This is the replacement of the motives of one's action through desirelessness in works. Normally, we assume that works are performed for some motive, a reward which we expect from it, or to avoid some punishment. This game of reward and punishment, is how the animal life operates — what Sri Aurobindo calls the vital. But, if we make a conscious rejection

15. RoY, p. 1478.
16. Ibid., p. 1479.

of that entire field of play, reject the desire for reward and reject the fear of punishment, then we find another source of action. That motive power is desirelessness in works. It is not that we lose the power of motive, there is a change in the power of motive. It turns into an offering, a sacrifice, servitude to a higher power. Sri Aurobindo uses the term *dāsya* for this — the joy of surrendered desireless works. This performance of selfless works is not a self-deprivation or denial, it is the condition of divine enjoyment. This is why Sri Aurobindo points to this as the way to *lipsā*, which is defined as readiness to take and enjoy whatever the Master of the Yoga gives. This will result in pure enjoyment, also known as *śuddha bhoga*. Again, this may also come from equality — equality in seeing the delight in all things. But, the replacement of the motives of action, through desirelessness in works is a dynamic way, the way of the will.

Faith

The next aspect among attitudes of self-discipline is faith. Faith is a great power — it appears in the *Record of Yoga* in the *śakti catuṣṭaya* as *śraddhā*, and it also appears in the book *The Mother*, as part of another triad, which is an inner condition for the action of the Grace of the Divine Mother. The Divine Grace is the Śakti, or higher energy, that is at work within us; it becomes active as soon as we make the resolution. When something in the centre of our being makes a resolution to follow this process of becoming, though we may be unaware of it, something responds and begins working in and through us. This is the Śakti. In its working, it also makes certain demands of our nature. Sri Aurobindo writes about this in his book *The Mother*. Here, he writes that for the grace to act there is an inner condition which is necessary: "an inner state made up of faith, sincerity and surrender".[17] We have touched

17. *The Mother and Letters on the Mother*, SABCL: 25, p. 9.

on sincerity, and will soon consider surrender. But faith is a keystone among the attitudes of integral transformation.

Faith is given the Sanskrit term *śraddhā*. Sri Aurobindo devotes a chapter to it in *The Synthesis of Yoga*. Faith is divided by him into three kinds. First, there is faith in oneself. Any action, even one of following one's ambition in the world, is based on faith. This is why, the *Gītā* defines human identity in terms of faith. It says, you are what your faith is, *yo yacchraddhaḥ sa eva saḥ*.[18] This is because we are not stationary beings, we are beings of destiny, progressing towards a goal, not established by our minds, but carried within us as an intuition; and we have a faith that we can achieve it. Thus, faith is the power to achieve. The resolution needed to start any yoga, is already an activation of this faith. When one turns towards this becoming, there is something deep inside us, an innermost being, which carries a certitude in the will to achievement.

Going to the root of this, Sri Aurobindo points out that this faith is not something personally generated by us. Human beings are creatures of ignorance; faith carries an intuition beyond ignorance. In this, it also needs to be distinguished from foolhardy with fulfilment. Faith belongs in its depths to the evolutionary intelligence. It is the Divine Mother's ability to achieve this goal through us. Though it may start as a faith in our personal will to achieve, it is gradually revealed to us as a power not stemming from our limited self or ego, taking on impossible odds, but with its origin in the Divine; a faith that the Divine can achieve through us because it is the veiled Divine, who has become each of us. Each of us is an emanation of the Divine, and ultimately, nothing other than the Divine. This leads naturally to the second aspect of faith. This is faith in the Divine guidance. This is a critical aspect of the yoga,

18. *Gītā*, XVII:3

because we find ourself walking blind; we have entered a forest without any clarity on the step ahead, and what it will demand of us. Without faith in a guidance, however appoximate, we cannot take the first step in this path. That guide who motives our path, is the Lord (*Īśvara*) or the Supreme Being. With faith in the divine guidance, we open ourselves to an invincible Being — invincible though invisible — leading us, and we move in the knowledge that He can lead us. As a natural extension of this, is faith in the power of this Being — this is the Divine Śakti, the Divine Mother. Faith in the Divine Mother goes beyond guidance; it is faith in an active power at work within us and in our circumstances. It is a trusting faith that every miracle is possible, because it is Her powers in us that we offer back to Her, and it is She who acts through us.

This is the triple *śraddhā,* which needs to be practised. This involves reminding oneself that the yoga is possible because that which leads us and that which is in us — both as a presence and as a power — can do it, whatever the odds, since it is its pre-individual and impersonal drive in the cosmos. This, in its most fundamental sense, is the meaning of the epigram already referred to: "All Life is Yoga". The next attitude to develop, is the opening to sources of intuition and identity. By this, I mean those kinds of practices that lead us to knowledge. Faith also leads in this direction. In analysing faith, Sri Aurobindo points to two components of faith: the force of faith and the illumination of faith. The force of faith is what one might call blind faith. It is that which we have even when we don't know the step in front of us. Sri Aurobindo says, "At first one must have force of faith, but it will reveal itself to be an illumined faith as one proceeds."[19] Faith becomes enlightened through experience and the

---

19. RoY, p. 13.

development of consciousness as we progress. This is the illumination of the faith.

This is also related to our entry into knowledge, what we have discussed earlier as the *vijñāna catuṣṭaya*. Knowledge there, is not information. It is not the possession of an external archive or encyclopaedia by which we can understand things that are outside us. True knowledge is knowledge by identity of consciousness: we know because we are. We can know because there is only One and it knows its oneness. We can be one with that One. In other words, through identity with the One, we can know whatever we need to know: that is the ultimate fount of knowledge. But, to get there from where we are, our condition of separative knowledge, which rests on the crutch of external data, and depends on the division between subject and object, we need to pass through a process. This process involves opening to sources of intuition and identity.

Its first requirement is that we quiet the mind. The presumptions of the mind stand in the way of this — it thinks it already knows, it plans ahead, it is full of its own opinions and plans. It refuses to cede authority because it knows no other source of knowledge. Thus, it must be replaced by a different source of knowing. The inner discipline towards this, is to gradually silence the mind through refusal of thoughts, because it is these thoughts that we take to be our own, which give us the sense of personal choice, our personal knowledge. Adapting Descartes' famous dictum, our minds believe that we know because we think. But, if we stop the thought at its root, then we find that there is a silence in which we see much more directly than our thoughts could show us and we can act from this sight. Perception comes to us, various inner faculties of knowledge open up in us, the senses reveal inner dimensions: we see with inner sight, hear with inner hearing, and can also perceive directly through the mind, receiving intuitions which reveal a full picture of what is needed, what has to happen. This opening to the intuition through the quieting of the mind, and ultimately, the silencing of the mind, is the transition to a point where one arrives at identity, and experiences the self-knowledge of the One that is a result of its self-consciousness.

Quiet Mind and the Discipline of Speech

It is normal to think that the establishment of a quiet mind is achieved through the practice of meditation. Indeed, it is greatly aided by the practice of meditation, but it can be achieved dynamically, in the thick of activity. The way to this achievement is an active surrender of all one's preconceptions and thoughts to the higher Śakti. We can practice a continual surrender of our thoughts so that the thought disappears, and every such disappearance brings in its place, either silence or another light — a perception or intuition. The Mother approaches this discipline in a very practical way, not through traditional meditation, but through the control of speech. Instead of worrying about silencing one's thoughts, she advises becoming conscious of speech. She refers to this as the austerity of speech and writing.[20] Often, there is no need to say anything. In such cases, instead of the compulsion to speak, it is best to enjoy the silence. We often feel compelled to say things due to environmental conditioning. The Mother enjoins becoming conscious of this and refusing the conventional. Sometimes, we find that we can say things in a minimal way and they are even better understood, because these are lacking in the confusion of excess. We can practise this economy of speech. The Mother points out how this becomes more potent if there is a community of people practising this. Those, who are given to habitual chatter with one another, can discover that they share much more deeply through silence, and through

20. *The Mother*, SABCL: 25, p. 57.

a minimal expenditure of words. In this conversational practice, when something is said, it is understood at a deeper level; and when nothing is said, there is an eloquent silence. Austerity of speech is a powerful aid in opening to sources of intuition. The Mother also says, when asked a question, it is better to stop for a moment before replying. It is best not to presume that one knows the answer; or to repeat an answer heard from someone else or, read somewhere or, even thought of or said earlier. She recommends making oneself silent and asking for guidance. What one says through this practice is always surprising, because it is spontaneous and guided by a higher force. This is an oracular faculty, an aspect of intuition that we can regularise through practice.

Sri Aurobindo, following the Veda, uses the image of lightning for the intuition.[21] He says that it lights up the darkness of the ground in a flash. But lightning is a sporadic power. It comes once in a while and it casts its light in flashes. So, the yoga of intuition, lies in our being able to draw on these lightnings with such regularity that it becomes an uninterrupted chain of lightnings, a constant flow of lightnings. Whenever needed, they can come. As this action becomes regular, it changes its nature from lightning to a glow of luminosity from the source of light. And, what is illuminated is no longer a succession of linked ideas but large tracts of ground, global thinkings. Each of these stages, in the development of intuition, takes us to higher ranges of functioning of the cosmic mind planes. Ultimately, one enters into the home of light. One sees the truth. Whatever has to be known is known directly through perception, not even through intuition. This is *dṛṣṭi*, as it is called, seeing. *Dṛṣṭi* is the penultimate stage before identity, before entering the very body of the One and knowing things by the self-consciousness

---

21. SoY, "Vijñāna or Gnosis", p. 479.

of the One. This is the yoga of intuition and identity. Thus, the key practices in this process include, the establishment of a quiet mind and openness to the guidance of the divine Śakti, acting from the cosmic mind planes. This also requires a great faith, initially a blind faith, because the mind does not believe that it's possible without experience.

Austerity in speech and writing is a great aid and the opening of the inner senses is made possible through this practice and through the establishment of the quiet mind; to the degree that the mind becomes quiet, the senses start flowering within. The faculties of clairvoyance, or clairaudience, or knowing things directly by mental contact, what is called the sixth sense, become active due to the opening of the inner senses. Finally, there is the concentration on the essence of oneness in the objects of knowledge. Here, we turn to the ultimate form of knowing for which the practice is a constant remembrance in consciousness that there is only the One in all things, that all is the play of the One. In our conscious and our unconscious parts, it is that one focus that will open the doors of knowledge to us. This is the way to the arrival at *jñāna*.

Surrender

The final and the most important general attitude of integral transformation is surrender, for which Sri Aurobindo uses the Sanskrit term *ātmasamarpaṇa* in the *śakti catuṣṭaya*. Surender is the acknowledgement of a transpersonal agency, the "going under" which Nietzsche sees as the precondition for the overman.[22] As we saw, in each one of the seven quartets, there is some form of surrender involved, and Sri Aurobindo has a number of terms for these. In the active and dynamic part of

22. Friedrich Nietzsche, "*Thus Spoke Zarathustra*", Walter Kaufmann tr., *The Portable Nietzsche*, New York: Penguin Books, 1976, pp. 127-28.

the being, utilised in our works, it is a submission to the divine Will, for which he uses the term *nati* in the *samatā catuṣṭaya*. *Nati* literally means to humble oneself. This submission of the self is made to the being, whom Sri Aurobindo calls the Master of the Yoga. This is the divine guide, *Īśvara*, and the divine Mother (Śakti). The constant perception, that we are being led, and that we surrender ourselves to Him who is guiding us, and to Her who is acting through the circumstances, is that submission to the divine will or *nati*.

In one's practice of action, this also implies the surrender and selfless service to the Divine, in Him/Her-self, and to the Divine in all beings. It is important to distinguish these two even as forms of the Divine, because, we must not lose the One for the Many or the Many in the One. There is a kind of ethical platitude which says that service to humanity is the same as service to God, because in serving humanity we serve God in man. But, Sri Aurobindo makes it clear that in serving humanity without serving God in himself, you are missing the One in your attempt to find the One in the Many. Yet, it is much easier to discover a limiting One (cultism) or a transcendental One (refusal of the ascetic) than to extend the practical infinity of the One in all beings and events. It must be the primary focus on the One, that then can translate itself to the service to the One in the Many. This is where we find that submission and selfless service to the Divine in himself and in all beings, which is called *samarpaṇa*.

Then, there is surrender to the action of the Yoga Śakti, the power that acts in the yoga. This is similar to our submission to the divine Will, except that this is not made only to the power which controls the circumstances which we experience as our fate, but that which responds to circumstances from within us. What is inside us is also the Divine Śakti, the Śakti of Yoga, and to that Agent within our sense of agency, that invisible and myserious other in the self, we surrender ourselves. Not only our will, but our sense of personal identity must be surrendered to that Other within us. That, which acts in us is not our ego. It is not what we take ourselves to be. It is the Divine, the Unpredictable, the Conscious Being hidden behind our fragmentation. It is to That, we surrender the fount of our own being and action. This will bring a different experience, not only of our world, but of ourselves. The question — who am I? — will receive an entirely new answer, once we can surrender our sense of doership and the fount of our action, to the Divine Mother. With this practice, one finds an increasing intimacy of relationship with the Master of the Yoga and the Divine Śakti, a kind of reciprocity within us all the time, the experience of being in relation with the Divine, that sense that the Divine and we are at play. It is this relationship that becomes the predominant sense of one's identity, no longer the ego, but a transpersonal sense of oneself as a structure of relationship, a servant of god, a slave of the Divine. Again, in the quartet of power, Sri Aurobindo uses the term *dāsyam* (slavery for this).

Sri Aurobindo describes this experience of relationship with the Divine Mother springing from surrender, in a passage from the book, *The Mother*. Here he writes:

> [A] time will come when you will feel more and more that you are the instrument and not the worker. For first by the force of your devotion your contact with the Divine Mother will become so intimate that at all times you will have only to concentrate and to put everything into her hands to have her present guidance, her direct command or impulse, the sure indication of the thing to be done and the way to do it and the result. And afterwards you will realise that the divine Śakti not only inspires and guides, but initiates and carries out your works; all your movements are originated by her, all your powers are hers, mind, life and body are conscious and joyful instruments of her action, means for

her play, moulds for her manifestation in the physical universe. There can be no more happy condition than this union and dependence; for this step carries you back beyond the border-line from the life of stress and suffering in the ignorance into the truth of your spiritual being, into its deep peace and its intense *ānanda*.

While this transformation is being done it is more than ever necessary to keep yourself free from all taint of the perversions of the ego. Let no demand or insistence creep in to stain the purity or the self-giving and the sacrifice. There must be no attachment to the work or the result, no laying down of conditions, no claim to possess the Power that should possess you, no pride of the instrument, no vanity or arrogance. Nothing in the mind or in the vital or physical parts should be suffered to distort to its own use or seize for its own personal and separate satisfaction the greatness of the forces that are acting through you. Let your faith, your sincerity, your purity of aspiration be absolute and pervasive of all the planes and layers of the being; then every disturbing element and distorting influence will progressively fall away from your nature.

The last stage of this perfection will come when you are completely identified with the Divine Mother and feel yourself to be no longer another and separate being, instrument, servant or worker but truly a child and eternal portion of her consciousness and force. Always she will be in you and you in her; it will be your constant, simple and natural experience that your thought and seeing and action, your very breathing or moving come from her and are hers. You will know and see and feel that you are a person and power formed by her out of herself, put out from her for the play and yet always safe in here, being of her being, consciousness of her consciousness, force of her force, *ānanda* of her *ānanda*. When this condition is entire and her supramental energies can freely move you, then you will be perfect in divine works; knowledge, will, action will become sure, simple, luminous, spontaneous, flawless, an outflow from the Supreme, a divine movement of the eternal.[23]

The Triple Dāsyam

To conclude, let us look at a passage from the *Record of Yoga* which deals with Sri Aurobindo's own experience of this surrender. This diary entry comes from 1 July 1912. This jotting is a long one, and it begins with his announcement to himself that he has completed seven years of *sādhanā*. We will look at a section of this entry where he writes about his surrender in terms of *dāsyam* (slavery or servitude to the Divine). However, before this undertaking, we need to consider some of the specialised Sanskrit terms with which he describes his experience to himself. We have already come across the term *dāsyam*; it means servitude. In this passage he distinguishes three stages to this form of complete surrender and calls them the primary, secondary and tertiary *dāsyam*s or alternately single, double and triple *dāsyam*s. He also uses the terms *aśraddhā*. We have encountered the term *śraddhā*, which means faith. *Aśraddhā* is the opposite of this, lack of faith, in other words, doubt. He uses this term with reference to what he calls *nāstikya buddhi*. Literally, this means an agnostic intelligence. A part of his intelligence doubts a message (*ādeśa*) which he received while he was serving his long jail sentence, while being tried for "crimes against the crown". Then he uses the term *akalyāṇa*. In the quartet of power, we came across the usage *kalyāṇa-śraddhā* to refer to a faith in positive consequences. *Akalyāṇa* is the opposite of *kalyāṇa*, what we may think of as misfortune. *Vāk* refers to the hearing of divine messages. Then he comes to what constitutes the heart of the entry and has to do with the three statuses of the *Puruṣa*, the central divine person representing itself in the nature. In this entry, the first reference to this *Puruṣa* is to be found when Sri

23. Sri Aurobindo, *The Mother*, SABCL: 25, pp. 16-18.

Aurobindo writes about *anumati* (sanction). He uses the phrase "the unhappy independence of the soul" in this regard. He is referring to the ego, but seeing the ego as an exteriorisation of the *Puruṣa* in the personality. Later, he draws attention to these statuses of the *Puruṣa* more explicitly and relates them to the three stages of the *dāsyam*. In the first stage, the *Puruṣa* is said to be *kartā* and *anumantā* (doer and giver of sanction). He says this is the servant of God, but not his slave. Evidently, by *Puruṣa* here, he is referring to the appearance of *Puruṣa* in *Prakṛti*, or the ego of the doer and the chooser. *Kartṛtva abhimāna*, the renunciation of which marks the second stage, means egoism of the doer. Thus, in the second stage, one renounces the sense of being the doer of actions and becomes the witness of *Prakṛti* as the doer of one's own and all acts. But, it is only when the *abhimāna* or egoism of the *anumantā* or sanctioner of acts is renounced, that the fullness of the *dāsyam* becomes realised. There is then, a consciousness of the Divine Lord, *Īśvara* or *Parameśvara* in his freedom allowing the *parāśakti* or Divine Mother to determine action freely using one's nature as her instrument. This is a condition of irresistible slavery to the Divine Force, without even the possibility of self-determination, due to the tertiary surrender of the *Puruṣa*:

> Even now the *dāsyam* though complete in action, is not free of an intellectual questioning. But this last leaven of *aśraddhā*, of *nāstikya-buddhi*, is confined to the truth or untruth of the *ādeśa* given in the jail, the apprehension of certain forms of *akalyāṇa*; it is not capable any longer of positiveness and even at its highest is unable to generalise itself. For the rest the triple *dāsyam* of body is active beyond doubt, the last shadowy effigies of the double *dāsyam* is fading away in the mind and feelings there is not the same clearness; for the shadow of the double *dāsyam* still persists by the strength of the *aśraddhā*, but the express thought, the *vāk* of the divine communication, the experiences and feelings (all except the depression due to doubt) are ordinarily independent of the

anumati. Only the perceptions present still a field to the unhappy independence of the soul, its triste liberty to doubt and revolt against God, and from this field the others are sometimes temporarily affected.

The three forms of *dāsyam* ar0e now distinct and well marked. The simple *dāsyam* is that obedience to the divine impulsion which is self-chosen and depends on the individual's intelligence of God's will and his consent, his readiness to obey. The *Puruṣa* is still *kartā* and *anumantā*, a servant of god, not his slave. The great step bridging the transition from the simple to the double *dāsyam* is the renouncement of the *kartr̥tva abhimāna*, by which we perceive that *Prakr̥ti* is the only doer of all our actions voluntary or involuntary from the most deliberately concerted endeavour even to the simplest trifle and, in consciousness, are aware of the impulse of *Prakr̥ti* in every movement physical or mental. At first the consciousness tends to make a false division claiming the movement itself to be our own although the determining impulse is felt as a driving or a pressure proceeding from infinite nature above or around us. The wearing away of this division marks a farther attenuation of servanthood and deepening towards the divine servitude. But so long as the *anumantā* keeps his *abhimāna* and reserves his right of individual lordship (*Īśvara*) over *Prakr̥ti*, we have not passed the stage of simple *dāsyam*. For between the various impulses of *Prakr̥ti*, we have the sense of choosing, of an active and constant freedom, and although we choose what we understand to be God's will, it is still our choice that determines the action in the *ādhāra* and not his direct and imperative will. In the double *dāsyam* on the contrary there is no active and constant freedom, but only a general and ultimate freedom which is used little or only exceptionally. We are aware of ourselves as *Īśvara* and *anumantā*, the individual ruling and sanctioning authority, but, although we still have the power of refusing our sanction to any particular impulse of *Prakr̥ti* if we choose, we do not choose; we make no choice, we do not determine what is god's will and act thereby or order *Prakṛti* to act thereby, but leave everything to god to determine; the whole responsibility is his and a given impulse of *Prakṛti* fulfils itself or not as He chooses without our interference. If the will is used, it is used by *Prakṛti*. We are aware of it as being not our will, but the wll in the *ādhāra* used by *Prakṛti*. In the triple *dāsyam*, even this potential freedom disappears. Whatever impulse of infinite nature comes, we could not interfere with it if we wished, any more than the drifting leaf can deny itself to the storm or the engine to the force that works it. We are aware of our body as a whole and in its various parts being moved not by will in the body but by a will or force outside the body; our thoughts, feelings, will-power similarly. Each of these stands perfectly apart from the others and is worked separately by nature. The will wills and has done; it does not try to determine action but leaves the action to happen or not as nature pleases; the thought thinks and is done, it does not try to determine either the movement of the will or the movement of the action; the feelings equally live for themselves, *ātmatṛpti*, not striving to compel action and emotion or thought and feeling to agree. What harmony is necessary is determined by the Parā-Śakti that drives us, which we feel always as a force driving us. But this force is itself only an instrument of a conscious will driving it, the will or *anumati* of the *Puruṣottama*, who is Parameśvara and universal *anumantā*.[24]

---

24. RoY, pp. 74-76.

9

The Conditions of Being and Knowledge

HAVING completed our consideration of the seven quartets through which Sri Aurobindo structures his yoga psychology and practice of integral transformation, we took up the general attitudes for practice in the last chapter. Earlier, we had touched on the ontology of self-perfection while considering the *brahma catuṣṭaya*. Here, I will elaborate on the quartet of being and explore how this relates to the other lines of the yoga, particularly, the quartet of knowledge (*vijñāna*). We considered the Vedāntic basis of knowledge acquisition followed by Sri Aurobindo as a knowledge by identity. In other words, one knows because one is. Thus, knowledge by identity rests on being. To be something is to truly know what it is. We can see how knowledge is intimately linked with the being. Within the quartet of being we have *jñānam*, which refers to omniscience, as its third element. We start with a consideration of this element. Later, we will see how the other elements of the quartet of being relate to force or action, and delight, which form the other two major goals of the yoga of integral transformation.

Intuition and Identity

When we considered the quartet of knowledge, we saw that knowledge by identity is not something common to our experience. Commonly, we acquire knowledge through our senses. This implies a dualism between the knower and the object of knowledge. We try to understand things from the outside. But if we start with a faith that it is possible for us to know things from their inside, then one can think of a transition, a progress from our normal mode of knowing to a mode of knowledge by identity. This transition is mediated by intuition. Gradually, our external sense knowledge is to be replaced by an increasingly unerring intuition. Ultimately, the intuition realises its basis in identity.

We can receive intuitions about a thing only if we are intimately connected, at some level, with that thing. Since oneness is the basis of the universe, through a focused openness to this oneness, we can enter into intimate contact with whatever we seek knowledge of. For this transition, Sri Aurobindo utilised a variety of means for developing intuition. For example, one of these means was what he called "sortilege". This is the use of an external aid to arrive at intuitive knowledge. Sortilege is not something uncommon; many have some awareness of it and may have practised it sporadically, maybe absentmindedly. Sortilege involves opening a book at random and allowing one's eyes to fall on some text. This text is then noted as if it held a message. The process can be more consciously directed sometimes, as when there is a specific problem to which one seeks an answer. One may concentrate on the problem, invoke a higher power and open a book which one trusts for guidance, taking the text on which the eyes fall as a message answering one's question.

This was one among many processes that Sri Aurobindo was experimenting with in his exercising of intuitive knowledge. We'll see some of these methods among the entries in his diary notes. But, to start our consideration of intuitive knowledge acquisition based on identity, I would like to draw attention to a comment he makes in relation to one such entry on sortilege. This is a note dated 22 March 1914, on a sortilege conducted on the *Kaṭha Upaniṣad*. He records the specific edition and translator — a scholar named Apte — and the page number. He then notes the Sanskrit text which is the result of the sortilege, and comments on it. This comment is instructive in approaching the enterprise of developing the faculties of knowledge acquisition in the yoga of integral transformation. Sri Aurobindo writes:

> Since the entire oneness can be realised here and it is only by that complete realisation of God in everything in this world that absolute liberty is possible — for the idea of Him as something separate manifesting here is an error — therefore the final word is that an effort must be made to realise God the Spirit here, absolutely, so that nothing else may be seen, felt, smelt, heard, tasted.[1]

In other words, all our senses should give us evidence only of the One. What this implies is a complete embodiment of the realisation of oneness, an embodiment that brings us knowledge of oneness within and without, not only in essence but also in sense.

Puruṣa

Thus, the ontology of integral transformation rests on fullness of identity with *Brahman* (Absolute Immanance), the One Being there is. But it's interesting to note that the way in which Sri Aurobindo understands this realisation is somewhat different from the common Advaitic (transcendental) understanding of *Brahman* realisation. According to Advaita, one may experience a divine Person, *Īśvara*, Lord, or God. But this is considered a stage, what may be called an anthropic stage. It is supposed that beyond this Divine Person there is a formless transcendental Reality that is One, infinite, and conscious — this is *Brahman*. In Sri Aurobindo's own case, he was not theistic

1. RoY, p. 396.

by proclivity. He did not start with belief in a personal god, and arrived at his initial realisation as the result of a meditation practice. He identified this realisation as *nirvāṇa*. He described this in a poem called *nirvāṇa* which we considered earlier. Here he wrote of how whatever he perceived through his senses was unreal. The substantiality of the world disappeared and all he experienced around him were as shadows. But, behind these shadows there was something permanent, that couldn't be defined, but was the essence of an unchangeable something. This experience fits well the traditional descriptions of the Buddhist *nirvāṇa* or the Advaitic *Brahman*. Certainly, in this case, the senses did not give any evidence of god, rather the opposite.

This sense of unreality persisted in Sri Aurobindo's experience for quite sometime, but through this he continued conducting political activity to rid India of British colonial occupation. However, by the time he was to make the entry we just considered in the *Record of Yoga*, he had passed through other radical experiences which resulted in a modification of the condition of unreality with which he started. Particularly, during his one year of solitary confinement while undergoing trial, he experienced the fullness of a Divine Being and Person behind the veil of unreality and within all things. This was now seen to be the density of Presence at the centre of the cosmos with its reality dispersed in gradations of consciousness, stretching to the visible material universe. There was a centre to this infinite manifestation, and that centre of being, the focus of all this infinity was a Person, *Brahman* as the dimension of density and quality. In other words, this divine presence was the centre of a circumferenceless circle. As per the *Aitareya Upaniṣad*, it is this divine person, *Puruṣa*, for whose self-experience the cosmos is exteriorised and it is this person in whose image the human being is made, so that his instruments of external knowledge, the senses, may give evidence of his own reality.[2] The person who projects his infinite possibilities as nature and sees himself everywhere, finds a being in nature who can mirror him in its senses, and see as he sees.[3] This is yoga, union, where the circle finds its hermeneutic return, the serpent bites its own tail. Thus, it is this kind of embodied seeing of the person within the creation and through the senses which becomes the goal of knowledge for Sri Aurobindo. This also gives a new approach to the theistic aspect of the Divine. The Divine Being is a Divine Lord, there

Ontology of Self-Perfection (9.1)

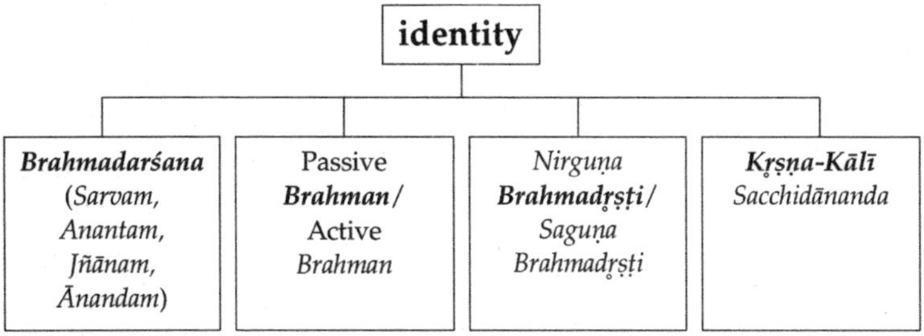

is a person, mysterious, hidden behind the infinite reality of *Brahman*. The very soul of *Brahman* is *Puruṣottama*, or *Īśvara*, the Lord.

Integral Realisation of Brahman

Sri Aurobindo had these realisations prior to his arrival in Pondicherry, and by the time he started the *Record of Yoga* — which is four or five years later — he was working at settling all the powers and implications of these realisations systematically in his own experience. An experience in consciousness takes time and application to bring into all the parts of the being and in integral relation with what exists.

2. *Aitareya Upaniṣad*, I.I.1-4.
3. Ibid., I.II.1-5.

This is what Sri Aurobindo was working at — to consolidate his experiences integrally through practice. The basis of realisation behind this integrality of knowledge is *Brahmadarśana* (the realisation of *Brahman*) which, as we saw, he divided into *sarvam, anantam, jñānam* and *ānandam*. Loosely speaking, *sarvam* means everything, it is the One Being in all things. *Anantam* means infinity: not only is it the One Being, a univocity, but He is infinite, a continuous variation and a radical differentiation. *Jñānam* means knowledge, and *ānandam* means delight. *Jñānam*, is a natural attribute of this reality because it is self-conscious. That, which is conscious of itself can apply its consciousness to itself and arrive at self-knowledge. In other words, knowledge is not automatic, but knowledge is intrinsic. Similarly, *ānandam*, is also intrinsic. Sri Aurobindo illustrates this by pointing out that our own experience as finite beings in the world demonstrates to us that whenever a limit is overcome, a boundary crossed in our experience and knowledge of self, we experience delight. This is the essence of delight. If we can then conceive of Being without limits or boundaries, one in whose self-conception any horizon is only an occasion for a greater horizon, delight would be intrinsic to such self-experience, since delight is the subjective form of freedom.

Sri Aurobindo's diary notes provide us with both the formulation of the theory and goals (*darśana*) and the record of the practice and its results (*yoga*) related to the experience of being with its four intrinsic attributes, *sarvam, anantam, jñānam* and *ānandam*. We find an example of this in his entry from 1914, dated 24 March, Tuesday.[4] We have considered this entry earlier, while dealing with the *brahma catuṣṭaya*, but here we will revisit it in some more detail. Here he writes, "*saguṇa brahma dr̥ṣṭi* has now practically taken the place of the *nirguṇa*, which is now perceived only as a foundation for the

4. RoY, p. 397.

action of the *saguṇa*". *Guṇa* means quality, *nirguṇa* means having no qualities, beyond qualities. What we came across in Sri Aurobindo's description of his initial brāhmic or nirvāṇic experience could be thought of as *nirguṇa*. In other words, it is *Brahman* free from qualities. *Saguṇa* means that which has qualities. In other words, in this entry, he is recording a transition from an impersonal to a personal realisation; his sense of the diffusion of Oneness in the world is giving place to a sense of the concentration of Oneness in a Person. That is, one Person in all things rather than one Consciousness in all things. Thus, the attributeless diffusion of the One, its dimension of extension is now seen as a foundation only for the action of the qualitative presence of the concentration of the One as person, its dimension of density. This is why, Sri Aurobindo writes, that the *nirguṇa* has receded to the background as the foundation of the action of the *saguṇa*.

He continues: "It is seen that *sarvam brahma* is prominent when the *tapas* of mental *caitanya* is fixed on matter, all else being felt as undifferentiated consciousness and matter alone as real to the mind, unreal to the *dṛṣṭi*." *Sarvam* means everything, all things, the entirety. *Dṛṣṭi* means sight, and *tapas* is concentration of consciousness. In other words, when his mental consciousness is concentrated on matter, *Brahman* as the One-in-All is prominent to the mind as the reality of matter, but materiality as he knew it has become unreal to the sight. One may call it a kind of "divine materialism". In *The Life Divine,* Sri Aurobindo has a chapter on matter which has some bearing on this.[5] What he is practising here, is a systematic meditation on pure matter.

This may attract a comparison with the method of science, since science starts with similar foundations. According to science, all forms of consciousness are seen as epiphenomena

5. LD, Book I, Chapter XXIV, pp. 245-53.

of matter, accidents which happen to arise, with no basis outside of matter. But, Sri Aurobindo's exercise here, is a deliberate use of this materialist assumption as a form of spiritual concentration. By assuming all experience to be based in matter, we can arrive at an experience of the consciousness of matter. Everything, aside from materiality is rejected in this meditation as mere bubbles arising from the physics and chemistry of things. The result of this meditation is the equation of our consciousness with the sameness of matter which we intuit all around us. This is *sarvam* — the same in all. This consistent reduction of everything to matter in the mind is, what Sri Aurobindo refers to as *tapas* of the mental *caitanya*. By exercising this persistent reduction, he arrives at the realisation of a reality which is one in all things (*sarvam*). The mind experiences the concrete sense of this reality of matter, even as the eyes see the differentiated world of matter as unreal. This, in a sense, is a systematic recapitulation of his very first major realisation — that of *nirvāṇa*. At the same time, one may say, he is confirming what modern physics (particularly quantum physics) tells us — that the substantiality of matter is illusory, but that there is a substratum of indivisible oneness behind all material things. We could call this "*Brahman* as Matter".

This bears comparison with a section of an Upaniṣad called the *Taittirīya Upaniṣad*. Here, there is a sequence titled Bhr̥gu Vallī, which is often quoted but not well understood. The section is about a sage, Varuṇa and his son, Bhr̥gu.[6] Bhr̥gu asks his father, "What is *Brahman*?" His father asks him in turn to meditate and report his findings to him. Bhr̥gu meditates and returning to his father, declares "Matter is *Brahman*." The common interpretation for this is that Bhr̥gu makes the obvious error of materialism because he is absorbed

6. *Taittirīya Upaniṣad*, III.

like most people, in the materiality of the world. But this interpretation is already based on a dualism between matter and spirit. Bhṛgu's father does not agree or disagree, but asks him to return to his meditation and report to him his findings. Bhṛgu continues his meditation and returns after awhile to say, "It is *Prāṇa* (life-force) that is the *Brahman*". His father sends him back again to his meditation. This process is repeated a number of times with Bhṛgu successively reporting that mentality, causality and eventually, delight are the *Brahman*. With his arrival at this point, Varuṇa affirms that delight (*ānanda*) is indeed, the *Brahman* and asks Bhṛgu now to return to his prior experiences, assimilating them to this new foundation. We may say Sri Aurobindo's practice follows closely the lines of this story from this Upaniṣad. The first part of the entry that we read from his diary, initiates a process of progressive *Brahman* realisation through different states of consciousness, which shed light on the meaning of the Upaniṣadic story. According to this, what Bhṛgu realised in his first meditation is what Sri Aurobindo is tracking systematically — that Matter is indeed the *Brahman* and nothing else. Through meditation on matter as *Brahman*, he arrives at the realisation of *sarvam*.

Plurality of Life

The diary entry continues: "*Sarvam anantam* is felt when the *tapas* is fixed on matter and life, all else being felt to be a sea of consciousness out of which life and matter proceed."[7] We see here, that Sri Aurobindo has added the world of Life to his original exclusive mediation on matter, and as a result, has arrived at a double realisation of *Brahman* — *sarvam anantam*. *Anantam* means infinity. By including the principle of Life to his original meditation on matter as *Brahman*, he arrives at the realisation of both, the sameness and the infinity

7. RoY, op. cit.

of *Brahman*. With the emergence of life, we see the persistence of differentiation, as a continuously variable state of experience[8] and an infinite diversity of forms which struggle to retain their separate identities. With this intuition, we can return to matter and see it too as differentiated, irreducible in its diversity of types and instances. Earlier historical periods in civilisation recognised this primacy of life in matter as animism. In this perception, everything is animated, everything has life in it, life pushes through matter controlling and determining its forms and their behaviours — tree, rock, and mountain are all seen to express some livings qualities. The pitch of expression is further amplifed in plants and animals, and all creatures are products of living matter. This is the infinite diversification of the substance called matter. So, infinity — not merely infinity as a kind of amorphous reduction to matter and its distribution, but a persistent breaking of matter into life-forms with names and shapes — this differentiation into new, ever-changing yet persistent realities that are infinite, this infinite world of living things opens up as reality, when we concentrate on the primacy of the life-principle in the material world.

In other words, just as we could call the first form of meditation a kind of divine materialism, we can call this a divine animism. However, the sameness of matter, though lending itself to the plurality of life to the extent of seeming to be dominated by it, has nevertheless, its independent reality, a difference in kind. The intuition of this is carried in the saying: "We are of dust and to dust we return".[9] Matter may lend itself temporarily to the mutations of life, but it eventually reverts to its inert sameness. By retaining in our meditation, the independence of these principles, we can

8. "You cannot step twice into the same river." Heraclitus, fragment 41, quoted by Plato in *Cratylus*.

9. "Dust you are and to dust you will." *Genesis* 3:19.

experience *Brahman* as both *sarvam* and *anantam*, one and infinite at the same time, the protean creativity of the *Brahman* along with the foundational static reality of the *Brahman*. However, as considered when dealing with *Brahma darśana* in the quartet of being — in mental experience, these principles are experienced as independent realities, as if *Brahman* presents itself in two entirely different ways. Matter and life, sameness and difference, may have relations with each other, may condition each other, but remain ultimately separate and independent. This is why the human history of religion is marked by assertions of exclusive descriptions of ultimate reality. It is easy to assert either of *sarvam* or *anantam* to be true, and the other to be false. But, Sri Aurobindo is proceeding along a systematic progression whose nature could be called additive. The realisation of *sarvam* is retained while adding to it the realisation of *anantam*. These realisations may not be harmonised or integrated, but they are made to co-exist in experience.

He continues: "*Sarvam, anantam, jñānam* when the *tapas* is fixed on life, matter and mind, with *vijñānam* felt behind vaguely as a source of mind."[10] *Jñānam* is knowledge. What he is adding to his earlier realisation here, is once more related to the method of science in terms of its faith. Indeed, we are justified in speaking of science as a kind of religion, with a faith to it. The faith of science is that the world is rational, that there are laws to the universe that the mind can understand because these laws, right down to matter, are logically coherent. This is the dimension that Sri Aurobindo is bringing here into his meditation : there is a unitary basis in matter, an infinite creative and diversifying force in life, to these is added the sustained perception of the power of causation and law which consistently maps every phenomenon

10. RoY, pp. 397-98.

and entity of this creation down to its material basis. Then, we realise that *Brahman* is *sarvam, anantam* and *jñānam*, all three at once. Sri Aurobindo also introduced here the intuition of *vijñānam* behind *jñānam*, supermind behind mind, because mind can intuit the presence of something perfect, integral and infinite, which exceeds it but is its origin.

By nature, mind cannot but approach reality in fragments. This is one of the problems of mind. We can at best aspire to piece together a systems theory of reality, but we cannot arrive at a holism of reality with the mind. Our piecemeal totality will never be complete. This is the tragedy told in the old ditty of humpty-dumpty. The fall of humpty-dumpty, is the story of the appearance of mind in a holistic universe. The mind breaks the indivisible into fragments. And, just as all the king's horses and all the king's men can't put humpty-dumpty together again, we too, cannot reconstruct an indivisible whole of seamless relations. However, we can intuit this supramental whole. We know that there is a wholeness; behind the weird phenomena of quantum physics we intuit it, in our seeking for a unified field theory we intuit it, but with mind, we cannot grasp it. What is needed to grasp this is the *vijñānam* behind the *jñānam*. This is the higher faculty of knowledge, supermind, that is infinite, and yet can mobilise things in laws, through a power of causality which Bhr̥gu described to his father as the fourth state of *Brahman* – matter, life, mind, causality, *sarvam, anantam, jñānam* with *vijñānam* behind it.

Bliss as Origin: Impersonal and Personal

Sri Aurobindo's diary entry goes on: "But when the *jñānam* increases and is sun-illumined, then the *ānandam* also appears."[11] This takes us into the fourth term, where the *ānandam* appears behind the *vijñānam* (sun-illumined). Here,

11. RoY, p. 398.

there is a sense of the causality of things opening into a greater supramental pitch of the infinity and unity of this causal law. This is the intution behind the visions of great scientists and philosophers, who believe that the universe is coherent, governed by massive laws; that there is an ungraspable infinite intelligence at work in the world, something we cannot comprehend but can intuit. This is the "sun-illumined" condition of *jñānam*. As this dawns, we move from beauty to sublimity, from order to wonder. The philosopher Immanuel Kant makes the distinction between beauty and sublimity. The sense of beauty is our intuition of miraculous order in created things. But, the sense of sublimity takes us one step further: it includes the overwhelming presence of infinity, the awesomeness of the creation beyond order and chaos, the feeling of wanting to prostrate oneself. Behind this, the miraculous freedom of creative delight, the delight of infinity, *ānandam* makes its appearance.

Sri Aurobindo concludes his entry: "Then the *ānandam* also appeared and the *Saguṇa Brahman* becomes the *līlāmaya parā Puruṣa*."[12] *Saguṇa Brahman* is *Brahman* with qualities. The *līlāmaya parā-puruṣa* is the Supreme Person in his aspect of creative play. Behind the qualitative *Brahman*, the Person to whom these qualities belong, stands self-revealed. From the impersonal, we move to the personal. The *Saguṇa Brahman* is self-revealed as the Supreme Person who, for the joy of his play with his own infinity, multiplies himself innumerably in the forms of the universe.

Sri Aurobindo wraps up with a final comment on the active power of *Brahman*, the *anantam*, now self-revealed in two qualitative forms or *bhāvas*:

> The *anantam* has also two *bhāvas*, one in which the infinite force acts as if it were a mechanical entity, knowledge

12. RoY, p. 398.

> standing back from it; the other in which life force and knowledge act together and the infinite force is an intelligent or at least a conscious force.[13]

These are the two aspects of what he calls elsewhere the active *Brahman* or *Prakṛti*, the Creative Will of *Brahman*, also known as the Divine Mother. There is a lower action, the one that we encounter in our common experience, where we are faced with the unconscious automatisms of nature. This is what is known as the *aparā-Prakṛti*, where "the infinite force acts as if it were a mechanical entity, knowledge standing back from it". The other *bhāva* is what is called *parā-Prakṛti*, in which "life force and knowledge act together and the infinite force is an intelligent, or at least, a conscious force". It is this conscious action of the *Parā-prakṛti*, which is natural to supermind. Since knowledge and force are inseparable in it, Sri Aurobindo refers to it as knowledge-will. This is the *śakti* or Creative Force of *līlāmaya Parā-puruṣa*, and it is this power which is invoked for the transformation of the lower or *aparā-Prakṛti*. This is also what Sri Aurobindo calls *Kālī* in the *karma catuṣṭaya* and *Parāśakti* elsewhere. This concludes the systematic meditation for arriving at the integral vision (*darśanam*) of *Brahman* that Sri Aurobindo follows and the kind of knowledge, force and delight it brings him.

Just as the *anantam* reveals itself, in its higher potency to be *Kālī*, the *ānandam* reveals its *saguṇa* source to be *līlāmaya parā-puruṣa*, who he calls *Kṛṣṇa* in the *karma catuṣṭaya*. Sri Aurobindo seldom uses the names of these personal deities elsewhere in his writings. This is because Sri Aurobindo is careful to avoid the possible misunderstanding of cultism towards particular gods, though in his own practice, he relates in a personal way to these deities as dual aspects of the One being, Īśvara and Śakti, Lord and his own Will or Energy.

13. RoY, p. 398.

This is, thus, a transition out of *brahma darśana* as an impersonal single reality to an experience of a dual divine Being. On the one hand, an impersonal-personal Being — Kṛṣṇa — on the other hand, an energy of that Being doing everything in this world — Kālī. This double perception, perceiving these two at once, all the time, by the selves and in all things, is the culmination of the ontology of self-perfection. In the entries of the *Record of Yoga*, he refers to this realisation as *Kṛṣṇa-Kālī Saccidānanda*. This is the nature of the ultimate realisation of identity, and he identifies himself with these, each of these two, and with both together. Not only are they everywhere in all things but in him also. He is witness to his identity with Kālī and her action proceeding from Kṛṣṇa through him.

The Divine Master

Earlier, we had considered a passage about *dāsyam*. In this passage, we stopped where Sri Aurobindo noted the characteristic condition of slavery of the "triple *dāsyam*" — that the *Puruṣa* is incapable of initiating any action and only witnesses the parts of the nature being used as needed by the Divine Mother or Parā-Śakti.[14] In the continuation of this passage, he elaborates further on this realisation of Kṛṣṇa-Kālī. The entry belongs to 1 July, 1912. Where we stopped in our earlier consideration, his entry recorded: "What harmony is necessary is determined by the Parā-Śakti that drives us, which we feel always as a force driving us."[15] We can see that this Parā-Śakti is identical with Kālī and will be equated with Kālī, the Supreme Energy. What orchestrates the harmony of coordinated action in the *jīva* is no longer any personal impulsion, but this Parā-Śakti, which the experiencer feels always as a force driving him.

He continues: "But this force is itself only an instrument

14. RoY, pp. 74-75.
15. Ibid., p. 76.

of a conscious Will driving it, the Will or *anumati* [sanction] of the *Puruṣottama* who is *Parameśvara* and universal *anumantā*."[16] *Puruṣottama* is the Supreme Person, *Parameśvara*, the Supreme Lord, and *anumantā*, the bestower of sanction. Thus, it is the sanctioned Will of the Supreme Person and Lord, which is carried out by the Parā-Śakti. This is how the entry ends: "This consummation is also attended by a ripening realisation of the Divine Master." This is the *Puruṣottama* or *Parameśvara*, Śrī Kr̥ṣṇa. Thus, the ripening realisation of the triple *dāsyam*, is not only the knowledge of the Parā-Śakti as the sole mover and doer of actions in him, but of *Puruṣottama*, the master whose will is being effected in all cases by the Parā-Śakti. He continues: "Formerly, I realised the impersonal god, Brahma or *Saccidānandam*" — grammatically, a neuter form referring to the impersonal aspect of *Saccidānanda* — "separately from the personal, *Īśvara* or *Saccidānanda*. Brahma has been thoroughly realised in its absolute infinity and as the material and informing presence of the world and each thing it contained — *yat kiñca jagatyam jagat*".[17] — This Sanskrit phrase is a quotation from the *Īśa Upaniṣad* meaning "whatever moves in this moving universe".[18] — "But the sense of the One has not been applicable utterly and constantly. There have been lacunae in the unitarian consciousness, partly because the personality has not been realised with equal thoroughness, or at one with the impersonality." Thus, he notes that *Brahman* as an impersonal Being present everywhere is constantly seen in all things, but its personal aspect, the *Puruṣottama*, is not as thoroughly realised.

By his phrasing, we may intuit that the impersonal *Brahman* which he has realised thoroughly is the aspect of pervasion, the single substance everywhere and in all things (*sarvam*). It

16. RoY, p. 76.
17. Ibid.
18. *Īśa Upaniṣad*, I.

is interesting here that he contrasts this with the aspect of the One which implies density instead of pervasion. This is why he sees the source of this lacuna somewhat in the incompleteness of realisation of the One Person behind and at the heart of all things. Continuing his reflection: "Hence, while dwelling on the *parātman*" — another aspect of the impersonal *Brahman*, the Supreme Self — "the mind, whenever the *jīvātman* manifested itself in the *sarvam Brahman* has been unable to assimilate it to the predominant realisation and an element of *dvaita bhāva* — of Viśiṣṭādvaita has entered into its perception."[19] Dvaita stands for duality. Here, he uses the name of one of the philosophic schools of Vedānta: Viśiṣṭādvaita. Viśiṣṭādvaita is a school which holds to the realisation of the One Being in all things as known through its phenomena, not as the One known by itself. One may call this Being-in-Becoming. That is, the reality of the individual self as a manifestation of the One Person is inadequately experienced; instead, the individual is experienced as a wave or formation of the One Substance, an aspect of the Being-in-Becoming rather than the Being in itself manifested individually.

He elaborates this further:

> Even when the assimilation is partly effected the *jīva* is felt as an individual and local manifestation of the impersonal *caitanya* and not as an individual manifestation of *caitanya* as universal personality.[20]

In other words, the monadisation of impersonal substance rather than the self-replication of Divine Person, the water in the beaker condensing into drops rather than Being as a Drop extending an instance of itself. Sri Aurobindo's assumption here, based on his realisation of theistic non-dualism, is that *Brahman* is a Supreme Person and we as individual beings (*jīva*)

19. RoY, pp. 76-77.
20. Ibid. p. 77.

are created in the image of this Person or *Puruṣa*. Our fulfillment lies in reproducing in our own personal essence the personhood of the Supreme Person, towards which an impersonal realisation may be a stage but not a culmination. This is what he means as the individual manifestation of *caitanya* as universal personality. "On the other hand the universal Śrī Kṛṣṇa or Kṛṣṇa-Kālī in all things animate or inanimate has been realised entirely but not with sufficient constancy."[21] This pertains to the realisation of the Universal Person in its single and dual aspects in the world rather than in the self. Here, in this entry, Sri Aurobindo says that he has realised this but not with sufficient constancy. — "and latterly with little frequency. The remedy is to unify the two realisations, and towards this consummation I feel the Śakti to be now making."[22]

This amazing honesty of perception and analysis meets us throughout in the *Record of Yoga;* the kind of diary writing as truth-telling in the Foucauldian sense, where one sees him recording for himself exactly what he is experiencing and where he stands in terms of the goals he has set for himself.

Evidence of the Senses

Let us further consider the realisation of knowledge with which we began — a knowledge in which even the senses participate in giving exclusive evidence of the One Being. The third attribute of *Brahma darśana* is *jñāna*. From the realisation of *Brahman* comes knowledge, and, as we have seen, this is a knowledge by identity, because if one is identified with the One Being, by extension s/he can know that One Being anywhere and in anything. This sounds somewhat incredible, but even in our times there have been those with experiences which attest to this. Here, I'm referring not only to mystics

21. RoY, p. 77.
22. Ibid.

but professionals in the secular world. An experience I'd like to draw attention to is described by the 1983 Nobel Prize awardee in medicine, Barbara McClintock. McClintock's work on gene expression in maize is path-breaking and its implications remain revolutionary. Her entire career as a scientist was marked by an intuitive communication with her subjects and many of her most brilliant findings, such as that of the "jumping genes", which brought her the Nobel award, were received through an inner knowledge which is close to an experience of identity. Here is what she has to say of this experience with chromosomes within the maize cell:

> I found that the more I worked with them the bigger and bigger [they] got, and when I was really working with them I wasn't outside, I was down there. I was part of the system. I was right down there with them, and everything got big. I even was able to see the internal parts of the chromosomes — actually everything was there. It surprised me because I actually felt as if I were right down there and these were my friends.[23]

This kind of extension of identity can arise because of the underlying unity of all things in *Brahman*. Sri Aurobindo, when he was once asked whether he could know everything, replied that this was possible in principle, but in each instance it would need to be exercised. Thus, even for one with *Brahman* realisation, specific knowledge is a *siddhi*, a special effort is needed to extend the unity consciousness and know things by identity. Barbara McClintock had an innate faculty for this kind of knowledge at the cellular level of the maize, a faculty intensified by her empathy for her subject. This has been brought out well in the most popular biography of the scientist by Evelyn Fox Keller, which is titled, *A Feeling for the Organism*.

23. Evelyn Fox Keller, *A Feeling for the Organism: The Life and Work of Barbara McClintock*, New York: A.W.H. Freeman/Owl Books, 1984, p. 117.

Ontology of Self-Perfection (9.2)

Knowledge

Knowledge by Identity — realisation (*pratibodha*): perception of things through *bhāva* — *bhāva* of being or sat realising truths of being *bhāva* of knowledge of cit realising truths of thought, *bhāva* of force or tapas realising truths of action, *bhāva* of love or *ānanda* realising truths of emotion, sensation and bliss.	**Intuition** — Four faculties of discrimination, intuition (*śruti*) and truth-seeing (*dṛṣṭi*). Operation of these 4 to world of ideas — *Jñānam* or Divine Thought; to temporal facts and events of the material world — *Trikāladṛṣṭi*	Develop consistency of **discrimination** (judgement of right and wrong) and intution (direct conclusion) for the other two to establish themselves.	**Purification** (***śuddhi***) of the senses and the mental instrument — equality in preferences, tastes, social conditioning and emotional reactions, absence of hatred, desire, fear, disgust, passions.

Sri Aurobindo refers to this aspect of knowledge by identity as realisation of *pratibodha*, the perception of things through *bhāva*, through their intrinsic sense of being.[24] He writes of *bhāva* of being (*sat*) realising truths of being, and *bhāva* of knowledge (*cit*) realising truths of thought. Being establishes identity, but active consciousness brings identity into awareness through application of reflexivity. To be able to "know" that one is something, already implies a reflexive action of consciousness, knowledge by consciousness, the acquisition of formal properties that have been objectified to oneself. This is the utility of the *bhāva* of *cit*, consciousness in

24. RoY, p. 16.

realising truths of thought. Then, there is *bhāva* of force, of *tapas*, realising truths of action. In other words, one may become identified in mobility with things. All things in the universe are in reality in motion and one can know the truths of action through identification in will with the force of action. Finally, there is *bhāva* of love or *ānanda*, realising truths of emotion, sensation and bliss. Elsewhere, he calls this *saṁjñāna*. This is the way by which one can know things from within, by their affective condition — the specific vibration of delight within them, through the *bhāva* of love, or *ānanda*. These are the four ways by which knowledge by identity may be developed and acquired. Using Sri Aurobindo's adopted terminology from the *Aitareya Upaniṣad*, we may say *bhāva* of *sat* is *vijñāna*, *bhāva* of *cit*, *prajñāna*, *bhāva* of *tapas*, *ājñāna* and *bhāva* of emotion, *saṁjñāna*.

The Intuitive Faculties

This could be seen as the culmination of the knowledge by identity. But to arrive there, we need to start where we are, and first acquire intuition. I introduced this while dealing with the quartet of knowledge, but here I draw attention to this once more: development of intuition involves the faculties of discrimination, intuition, truth-hearing and truth-seeing.[25] Sri Aurobindo writes about discrimination as the judgement of right and wrong; he points out that we are constantly judging things, and this judgement has primarily a practical and, only secondarily, a moral dimension to it — what is the right thing to do, what should I do and what should I not, how should I act, how should I not act. Human beings are perpetually involved in these kinds of judgements, using their minds to arrive at conclusions. But, in order to develop intuitive discrimination, we need to quieten the mind and open ourselves with the faith that a higher judgement will reveal what is to be done.

25. RoY, pp. 17-18.

But, as Sri Aurobindo shows us by example in the *Record of Yoga*, this process needs to be established by testing each step. Before such a process can become dependable, there is need for some healthy scepticism and some common sense. One must always be open to possibility, yet one must develop purity of consciousness before one can fully depend on a judgement which claims to be higher than the rational. Through this process, our goal must be to develop more and more of this intuitive faculty of discrimination. In fact, this reliance on an intuitive discrimination is not altogether alien to ordinary human activity. What we call creativity, whether in exceptional gifted "artists" or in quotidian acts of ordinary people, carries in itself the mark of such intuitive judgements, which we recognise as the sense of inevitability. Creative expression brings us into contact with a miraculous power of ordering, where everything seems to be in its right place making up the aesthetics of the whole. If we could cultivate this kind of tact as a general condition of existence, we would find the settlement of discrimination in us. But usually, gifted artists are endowed with this kind of intuition only in some specialised domain and are seldom able to extend it to decisions of social or political life. Here is where the yogic cultivation of this faculty becomes important.

The second of these faculties is what he calls intuition or direct conclusion, given a mass of data, to arrive directly at an understanding which also reveals the interpretation of the data. We normally use logical, deductive and inductive processes to arrive at these results. But, with the operation of intuition, the result can be grasped directly, as a fact. Sri Aurobindo points out that we all have both discrimination and intuition of this kind to some degree. The dominance of mental reason is largely responsible for a loss of confidence in these abilities. The fear of the irrational closes the doors on these possibilities. But, Sri Aurobondo points to this development as a necessary step in conscious evolution. This kind of practice has, in fact, a long history in all the traditions of the world. We find Plato giving examples of the operation of a practical intuition of this kind from the life of his teacher, Socrates, who used to depend on it. He speaks of this as Socrates' Daemon; the voice within him that gave him directions.[26]

Socrates, for example, came across a bifurcation in the street and found two ways to reach the same destination, one shorter and one longer, one more logical and one illogical, but the Daemon asked him to take the longer route. Since he has developed this intuition to a point of dependability, he follows its guidance, but his travelling companion takes the shorter route and is trampled by a pack of wild boar. Sri Aurobindo enjoins the development of discrimination and intuition until they become dependable in us; he sees this as a necessary step in arriving at knowledge by identity. As these two faculties are established and become active, two more emerge on their own, he says. These are truth-hearing and truth-seeing, hearing and seeing truth instead of inferring it or even intuiting it without grasping it. With truth-hearing and truth seeing, the inner senses become instruments to bring evidence of truths. This is a further step towards knowledge by identity, an intimacy with reality using the senses, presaging Sri Aurobindo's words with which we started our consideration:

> Since the entire oneness can be realised here and it is only by that complete realisation of god in everything in this world that absolute liberty is possible — for the idea of him as something separate manifesting here is an error — therefore, the final word is that an effort must be made to

26. Plato, *Apology of Socrates*, 31c-d, 40a. John Burnet, *Plato: Euthrypho, Apology of Socrates and Crito*, Clarendon Press, 1977, p. 16.

realise God the Spirit here, absolutely, so that nothing else may be seen, felt, smelt, heard, tasted.[27]

Purification of the Mental Instrument

These four forms of intuition give us two levels of knowledge. When we apply them to the world of ideas we get *jñānam* (divine thought). When we apply them to the world of temporal facts and events of the material world, we arrive at the knowledge of the three times (*trikāladr̥ṣṭi*). This includes the knowledge of the universal past and the power of prophesy. We can intuit, understand and see the past of things before us, the present of things beyond what meets the eye, and the future of things which are yet to come. To develop these kinds of intuition in the form of truth-seeing and truth-hearing, Sri Aurobindo writes of the *śuddhi* of the senses and of the mental instrument. The mental instrument includes the various aspects of our reasoning as well as of our sensing. This purification is effected through the cultivation of equality in preferences, social conditioning, and emotional reactions and the absence of hatred, desire, fear, disgust and passions. Undoubtedly, this sounds like a tall order, but what is meant here in this specialised sense, is not merely the ridding of these things from the mental consciousness, but rejecting them also from the localised consciousness of the senses. In other words, these can be seen as perversions of the senses. Earlier, I quoted Blake, and that quotation of his about the doors of perception, is most appropriate in this case: "When you can cleanse the doors of perception you will see the world as it truly is, infinite." Once the purification of the senses is achieved, the doors of perception become cleansed and perfect equality settles in the sensing.

It may be useful to reflect some more on this. Normally,

---

27. RoY, p. 396.

our senses are conditioned, and work in a selective fashion: we see at and hear certain things, we filter out certain things. This selection is determined by a variety of factors — genetics, upbringing, past lives, peer pressure, advertising of all kinds, politics, to name some. All these factors and more, play their part to form the preferences of our senses. If we can unravel these consciously, if we can become aware of what we are attracted towards, or what we abhor as repulsive, fearful or distasteful, we realise that these are values given by our sensing to certain external elements. This study and realisation, is the starting point for becoming free from these conditioned values through the conscious development of equality in the senses. This equality brings liberation to the sensory apparatus of the mental instrument, so that, the intuition can work directly through the senses bringing us truth-hearing and truth-seeing.

The fulfilled, constant and dependable working of discrimination, intuition, truth-seeing and truth-hearing constitutes the establishment of an intuitive mentality for Sri Aurobindo. Beyond this, lies knowledge by identity; beyond all forms of consciousness, subjective or instrumental. That, of course, is what the *brahma catuṣṭaya* is all about. But, if knowledge by identity is to exercise itself in the phenomenal world, it is the intuitive mentality which it can use as its instrument, not only through the inner activity of the senses, but even through its outer evidence. It is here, that we can say with fullness what Sri Aurobindo holds out for himself as the goal of knowledge: "to realise God the Spirit here, absolutely, so that nothing else may be seen, felt, smelt, heard, tasted".

10

Power and Enjoyment

In this last chapter, we will consider the power and enjoyment of integral transformation. As we saw at the outset, the goals of integral transformation are twofold — liberation and enjoyment. In the previous chapter, we considered Being and Knowledge, which relate to the goal of liberation. In the quartet of perfection, *siddhi catuṣṭaya,* Sri Aurobindo uses the term *mukti* for liberation and *bhukti* for enjoyment. Liberation and enjoyment are the two poles between which all human effort is concentrated. All schools of spiritual or mystical practice operate somewhere between these two poles, either affirming one over the other or in a synthesis of various kinds and degrees. Somewhat facetiously, this may be related to the commonsensical wisdom that all human beings can be divided into pessimists and optimists. Those, who prioritise the first, *mukti,* assume a pessimistic attitude towards life, seen as an imprisonment. This has birthed all the philosophies that see the goal of existence as escape from life, cessation of the chain of rebirth and escape from the wheel of *saṁsāra.* There is a truth to this perception, because indeed, our life experience confronts us in the guise of an imprisonment, a conditioning and there is something in us that is desirous of absolute freedom from all subjection. This desire arises, as we saw when considering the quartet of being, *brahma catuṣṭaya,* because the spirit is absolutely free.

But the need to escape is a partial understanding of the

human urge, because the spirit remains free even in its bondage. It is purely by choice of creative self-delight, that the spirit has become this universe and its creatures. It is a form of delight, not a necessity that has made it assume this appearance of imprisonment. This is why, within the understanding and need for liberation, there is also the experience of delight. Addressing this reality of experience, Sri Aurobindo adapts Jean-Jacques Rousseau's famous statement "Man was born free, and he is everywhere in chains" in terms of a paradox of existential experience: "The whole world yearns after freedom, yet each creature is in love with his chains." Yet, one may say there is a justification for this, because life is both an imprisonment and a field of enjoyment. Instead of demanding an escape from life, it is possible to think of freedom as the condition for an untroubled experience of the delight of life. This is how, Sri Aurobindo views the relation between *mukti* and *bhukti* and how these two become twin goals in the yoga of integral transformation. In this chapter, we will turn our attention to the "other pole" of power and enjoyment. This may be called the earthly pole or the pole of magic. Going back to the premise that all spiritual practice is bounded by these two poles, we may rename these as the pole of spirituality and the pole of magic. The pole of spirituality takes us outside the world of forms and their phenomenal existence in time; the pole of magic takes us into forms and their temporal manifestations, so as to control and enjoy them. Some schools see this pole of magic as undesirable or illegitimate, while other schools see it as the true goal of human existence. The question is: Is there a divine reality to it? Is it possible to include these goals in a divine life, an integral oneness, as Sri Aurobindo conceives of it here? Sri Aurobindo's answer is an emphatic yes. This is why, power and enjoyment can be seen as leitmotifs repeating in a variety of ways throughout his seven quartets of integral becoming.

The Goals of Magic

Apart from power and enjoyment, there is a third goal often associated with the primeval aspiration of magic. This is the search for immortality. Most archaic systems of magic concern themselves centrally with these three goals. For one, there is power. Animistic practices are developed to address this aspiration and gain power over the beings and entities of the material and non-material worlds. Another goal is delight or ecstasy. How can we maximise our experience of bliss as embodied beings? This becomes a major concern. The third is immortality. The seeking for immortality, which our modern material sense finds impossible and incredible, is nevertheless a part of the human aspiration. This seeking is intrinsic to the human as a spiritual being, because spirit is eternal. Of course, this is what liberation is supposed to address, freedom from transient phenomena through identity, with the eternity of spirit. But, there is also a part of us that seeks the eternity of the form, because if we are integrally divine, the form also seeks to partake of the eternal.

We may say an essence of form, that which distinguishes us as person, belongs to the soul, and partakes of the eternal nature of the Divine. That is, through reincarnations we take different bodies, but there is a continuation of the form of the soul personality, what Sri Aurobindo calls the psychic being. Thus, seen from this standpoint, immortality is already a reality, since soul is not conditioned by the temporary disappearance of a body. But, the idea of immortality in archaic civilisations arises from the wish to be master of this process. In other words, why should we be subject to this disappearance and re-appearance? Why should the control of this process not be within our power? This becomes the rationale behind the seeking for immortality. While dealing with the quartet of the body, we considered Sri Aurobindo's saying, that the condition of a material immortality is to be reborn perpetually in time.[1] Nothing remains constant, the very meaning of time is change. This is why, we have to integrate change and permanence through rebirth. But, this constant rebirth in time does not need to be an imposition upon us without our consent, which is what death is, as is birth, for that matter. It could be a choice of the consciousness, a choice of the being within this life. To renew ourselves, regenerate ourselves in a succession without end, is the notion of immortality. This becomes the third concern of the active or dynamic pole. Thus, when thinking about energy and its formations, we find power, enjoyment and immortality to be the three major goals of Śakti.

Karma and the Law of Oneness

In our study of the quartets, we found two dealing directly with power (*śakti*) — the quartet of power, *śakti catuṣṭaya* and the quartet of action, *karma catuṣṭaya*. *Karma* is a complex philosophical term in India, but here it is used in a more specific sense to stand for work or action. Any action has consequences. These causal chains are not necessarily moral. The idea of *karma* as the law of causation, proposes that we receive objective circumstances and subjective experiences, which are commensurate with whatever we do, inevitably, as a universal law, like the law of conservation of mass and energy. For there to be truth to this, it must spring from the law of oneness. The truth of *karma* is not so much an equation of good and evil; rather its morality, if one wishes to use that term, lies in its adherence to the law of oneness. To understand this, we can recollect the sacrifice of *Puruṣa* and its consequence — the One Person has fragmented itself, and this secret oneness continues to be the truth governing the reality of fragmentation and differentiation in the depths, hidden from surface appearances and acts. Thus, we realise that in the truth of things, it is this univocity expressing in everything that is

1. SoY, p. 5.

done in this world, with each of its many human agents, like an actor, enacting some aspect of its works.

The law of *karma* implies that this is not only an unconscious truth of the action of entities, but that these entities are meant to become conscious of this truth in their acts. If, indeed, we are to be conscious of embodying the one Being, thus, reconstituting the One Person in being and action, our acts themselves provide us with subjective experiences meant to awaken this realisation in us. We are made to go through a process of realising that whatever we do to any other, we do unto ourselves. *Karma,* as a law of causation derives from this. Our actions and reactions provide the subjective experiences for the soul to evolve in power so as to impose this consciousness of oneness on the nature. *Karma* as a process, proceeds from a secret pact or contract, between the soul and nature whereby the being moves towards the realisation of its oneness through a process of repeated actions and reactions, until "the lesson is learned". This is why, we often speak of *karma* in terms of being stuck in a groove. We may find similar circumstances coming to us for lifetimes. Through these experiences, the soul, which retains the memory of experiences, arrives at a point where it can illuminate the nature, or seen in reverse, the nature becomes receptive to the message of the soul and there is a moment of liberation, a moment of knowledge that the circumstances one receives in life are one's own choice. It is one's choice because arriving, in active nature, at a realisation of the oneness of all beings is the choice of the soul and its meaning in the evolution. The liberation that comes from the soul's imposition of the consciousness of unity on some aspect of the nature causes the falling away of that kārmic construct, and yields a power to deal with the same circumstances in a new, free and creative manner. What seemed like an imprisonment and an impossibility, now feels easy to deal with; one recovers wisdom, mastery and creativity under the same circumstances.

We can extend this understanding of *karma*, because *karma* stands not only for action but also for work. The idea of work comes from the knowledge of a goal and the exertion of energy to achieve it. If we are to take our life on earth as a form of work, this implies a teleological view of *karma*. This goal or telos, is not chosen by ourselves in the unconsciousness of our nature, but chosen by our soul and the cosmic power of manifestation. The goal is that of arriving at the identity of the One. So the notion of work is that all action is meant to bring us and the world one step closer to the realisation of that identity. This would be the reconstitution of the sacrificed body of *Puruṣa* in being and action.

To have a clearer understanding of the power driving this process, we return to the idea of the One Being and the One Becoming. The law of oneness, active secretly within the fragmentation of Being, is driving that process towards its self-realisation in cosmic and individual nature. Thus, it is the One Being that is behind this process of Becoming, and there is One Energy that is driving it and working it out. The meaning of the cosmos becomes that of a play of hide-and-seek and of union, identity, of the One who has chosen to fragment and immerse Himself in his own opposite. We are agents in that game, facilitating it through our journeys from ignorance to knowledge. The exertion of energy in this process, constitutes the notion of work. Work is the action of the One Energy trying to reveal the One Being to itself, in us and through us.

To understand work in this way, implies a revision of our normal understanding. Our normal and unconscious understanding of work is that we are thrown into this world, given certain conditions to live, we must work to survive and to be responsible for the fulfilment of our social duties. Beyond this, we work for pleasure, mostly the fulfilment of vital desires but also, the fulfilment of creative delight. To make all this possible, we need to work, so that work becomes a conditioning incumbent on our lives as stumbling human beings bounded by a birth and a death. But in fact, our work is part of a universal work. And the delight of that work is not the goal of seeking various material fulfilments, but the delight of the growth of consciousness in every step that it takes towards the realisation of the individual and cosmic identity of the One. This is the truth of the delight of work.

Delight of Action

In our consideration of the quartet of action, we saw how Sri Aurobino relates *karma* (work) to the personal aspects of the One Being and the One Energy — Kṛṣṇa and Kālī, in his formulation. The one worker is Kṛṣṇa and the one energy at work is Kālī. When one arrives at identity with these godheads, one knows the universal will acting through one's nature and the Divine Presence upholding that will. This becomes the structure of human existence and the basis of delight. In this, Sri Aurobindo orients us towards the teaching of the *Gītā*, which says that the goal of all work belongs to the One. As individuals bound by partial knowlege, we have no access to the knowledge of a goal beyond our personal concerns. But, each personal goal belongs to the universal Becoming, the one Becoming of the one Being. The understanding of the significance of the goals or fruits of our actions in that Becoming eludes us. Thus, the delight of the goal does not belong to us as we are constituted in our nature, since we cannot respond with the values of truth to the results of our action. The true value of each result is known by the One Being and thus, its proper enjoyment belongs to Him. But the delight in the work belongs to us, and the delight in the instrumentation belongs to us, the delight in lending or surrendering ourselves — that belongs to us. This becomes the basis of the idea of work and the identification with the

Being, and the Energy of work as the power and the delight in dynamic action.

The Four Cosmic Powers

Another aspect to the performance of work in the yoga of integral transformation merits our consideration. This pertains to the qualitative forms of the Consciousness-Energy in its universal action. In the *śakti catuṣṭaya,* Sri Aurobindo describes four major qualitative aspects of universal Energy. He calls these the four *mahāśaktis*, represented in each human being, as four soul powers. In his later writings, such as *The Mother,* Sri Aurobindo elaborates on these four aspects of the Mother. The Divine Mother is the primary or transcendental consciousness-force, who is the one energy, will and intelligence through whose action all manifestation is made possible. The Divine Mother emanates four cosmic personalities of herself to manifest different primary qualities of her action.

In our study of the seven quartets, we have encountered these four goddess forms while considering the *siddhi* of *vīrya* in the quartet of power, *śakti catuṣṭaya*. But, here Sri Aurobindo also introduced four *puruṣa*s or forms of being for each of these energies, gendered male in correspondence with the feminine *śakti*s. These gods seldom find mention in his later works, there is no mention of them, for example, in the book *The Mother*. These four gods (*Puruṣa*s *or Īśvara*s), belong to an early form of Indian Vaiṣṇavism, known as Pāñcarātra. In this form of Vaiṣṇavism, there is the concept of emanation. In other words, from the one integral godhead, Vāsudeva, there are four primary emanations which, in their joint action, are behind all cosmic manifestation. The Pāñcarātra texts also attribute forms of conscious force or *śakti*s to each of these emanations. Though not many texts of the Pāñcarātra sect are in existence at present, the *śakti*s enumerated in what remain, are roughly equivalent to the four aspects of the Mother, which form a cornerstone to the quartet of power, and to Sri Aurobindo's yogic teaching.[2]

The Pāñcarātra sect is also interesting for the aspects of Vāsudeva or *Puruṣottama* which it describes. These are *parā*, *vyūha*, *vibhāva*, *antaryāmin* and *arcā*. The *parā* form represents the absolute; the *vyūha* form the absolute as cosmic, represented by an emanationism; the *vibhāva* form the incarnation or direct and free manifestation of the absolute as individual in the cosmos (*avatāra*); the *antaryāmin* form, the psychic being or manifestation of the absolute in the cosmic, subject to the laws of Māyā; and the *arcā* form, the manifestation of the absolute in nature through ritual. Of these, it is the *vyūha* or cosmic manifestation, which relates to the four *Īśvaras* (lords) and *mahāśakti*s (executive powers). These are also relevant in the psychic or *antaryāmin* form as the soul forces or "virtues" (*vīrya*). Here, it is worth noting that the emanationism of Pāñcarātra is not a system of hierarchic representation at different removes from the Absolute, as in the relation between Platonic Ideas and the world, but the Absolute itself, present entirely in its emanated forms.

These four *Īśvara*s or gods forming the beings of the cosmic operations in the Pāñcarātra, and as given by Sri Aurobindo, are Mahāvīra, Balarāma, Pradyumna and Aniruddha. The *māhaśakti*s corresponding to these are Māheśvarī, Mahākālī, Mahālakṣmī and Mahāsarasvatī, respectively. Māheśvarī is the aspect of *jñānam* and *mahimā*, — *jñānam* means knowledge and *mahimā* stands for greatness or vastness. She is wide and all-encompassing and all knowledge belongs to her. She is the mother of Knowledge. Mahākālī is the mother of Power, strength (*balam*), heroism (*vīryam)* and fierceness (*raudram*).

2. See *Lakshmi Tantra: A Pañcarātra Text*, ed. and tr. Sanjukta Gupta, New Delhi: Motilal Banarsidass, 2007.

Thus, power of intense concentrated energy is the aspect of Mahākālī. The attributes of Mahālakṣmī — as given in the *Record of Yoga* — are *prema* and *dānam*. *Prema* means love, and *dānam* is giving. The unrestrained giving of the self in love, compassion, oneness — these are the powers of Mahālakṣmī. The attributes of Mahāsarasvatī are *kāma* and *karma*. *Kama* is enjoyment of service, and *karma* is work. Mahāsarasvatī is connected with the laborious construction of things. These four aspects of the Divine Mother are related to Oneness in four different ways, though each contains the entirety of the Divine Śakti.

Māheśvarī is the intrinsic self-power of the One. She is the spatialisation of Oneness, vast, wide, infinite in extension. If Māheśvarī's power can be thought of as the spatialisation of Oneness, Mahākālī's is more properly the temporalisation of Oneness, with the fragmentation and differentiation implicit to the Sacrifice of *Puruṣa,* which initiates Time and the power of passionate intensity and concentrated force, which forces the condition of division towards Oneness. Mahālakṣmī's approach to oneness is one of mutuality, of exchange or affective interchange which affirms the Oneness secret within the condition of division. And Mahāsarasvatī's approach to oneness is skilful construction. The oneness which has been fragmented, is pieced together by the ingenuity and skill of Mahāsarasvatī. These four goddesses correspond to the four soul types that we find in Hinduism as the caste system. These castes are presently deformed hierarchic social differentiations, based on heredity, but Sri Aurobindo points out that the castes are properly psychological soul-types. Related to Māheśvarī is the type of the brāhmaṇa, or the seeker after knowledge. Related to Mahākālī is the kṣatriya, the forceful warrior for the truth. Related to Mahālakṣmī is the type of the vaiśya, who is today mainly the trader. But, if we are to see this more broadly, this man of commerce is the person whose modality of being is that of exchange. And Mahāsarasvatī is related to the vaiśya or the labourer, the one who works from ground up, who puts together the edifice. This is the engineer, the labourer, the skilled workman, the person who uses tools is the attribute of Mahāsarasvatī.

Personal Law of Becoming

Thus, in reinterpreting the *varṇa*s or castes in this fashion, Sri Aurobindo aligns them to each individual's soul-choice, oriented towards expressing some quality of consciousness in its evolving development. This quality of becoming forms what is known as *svadharma. Svadharma* — we come across this term in the *Gītā* where Śrī Kṛṣṇa says to Arjuna, "Your *svadharma* is that of a warrior, hence, your virtue is to fight for the truth."[3] The traditional interpretation of this is that Arjuna was born into the warrior caste, but in Sri Aurobindo's interpretation, this is not the case. Rather, Kṛṣṇa says to Arjuna that his soul-type is to fight for the truth, and he cannot escape it because that's what he chose as his modality of expression and development. We can see this kind of differentiation among people all around us in the world. There are doers, there are thinkers, there are lovers, there are craftsmen. All these kinds of beings are there around us, and when somebody fully realises their potential, we find that they express a number of these attributes, but they are organised around some predominant quality. This is the *svadharma*.

The law of being extends its law of becoming. The soul being and becoming, are designated as the couplet *svabhāva* and *svadharma* in the *Gītā*. The qualitative being of each individual is seen, following Pāñcarātra, as *antaryāmin* form of Vāsudeva, and thus, directly related to one of the four *vyūha* gods or conscious beings controlling the soul powers forming the *svadharma* through its Mahāśakti. Thus, we find,

3. *Bhagavad-Gītā*, II:3138.

in the case of Māheśvarī, we have Śiva, or from Pāñcarātra, Mahāvīra. With Mahākālī we find Rudra, a fierce attribute of Śiva, or from the Pāñcarātra system, Balarāma. With Mahālakṣmī we have Viṣṇu, or Pradyumna from Pāñcarātra. And with Mahāsarasvatī, we find Kāma, the god of love, an Indian counterpart of the Greek Cupid, or Aniruddha following Pāñcarātra. Realisation of these beings and powers in ourselves, becomes the basis of work in each of us. One aspect of this work is to grow into the knowledge of what are the primary qualities that are to manifest in us, what is our *svadharma*.

This may not be an easy question to answer, because we start with a different conception of work. We grow up trying to enter certain professions which we hold to be desirable due to external conditioning. The desire of parents and elders, peer pressure or social biases, push us in the direction of certain goals. Desire for money or for approbation, the need for name and fame may motivate us. All these are distortions of the true work potential in each of us. So, we may conceive of a yoga of undoing which precedes the awareness of *svadharma*. If we can become equal to the pressures of external conditioning, our *svadharma* will reveal itself in the spontaneous choices which arise in us. It is hardly through thinking about it that there develops an awareness of *svadharma*, Rather, it arises dynamically, in the awareness of inner choices. For some this comes easily. Souls like Arjuna, are given circumstances, befitting the work they are supposed to do. They find themselves fulfilled in what they are given to do. But, for most, the inner awareness and manifestation of *svadharma* accompanies the development of an equality in works. For one, who detaches himself or herself from conditionings, the spontaneous choices of life develop a momentum of becoming; there develops an accumulation of results from the acts, which one finds oneself undertaking, in the greater freedom which one experiences. This puts one in the flow of a work-field. One discovers the flowering of *svadharma,* in the freedom which comes from equality to the pressures of conditioning. One looks behind, in retrospect, and realises that one is fulfilled in one's work.

Ādeśa and Karma for Sri Aurobindo

Svadharma deals with the manner and the general field of one's work. But, arriving at a specific form of work may also come through a revelation of the work to be done, what the *Gītā* refers to as *kartavyam karma*. These kinds of revelations put one in direct relationship with certain larger forms of becoming. In the case of Sri Aurobindo we find that, at a certain point, when he had perfected a complete detachment and surrender, he relied for initiation of action entirely on the messages that came to him. In the last chapter, and while considering the quartet of knowledge, we considered truth-seeing and truth-hearing as vehicles for such messages. This is the basis of the messages on which he relied, acting from these foundations. These directions through truth-audition is, what he called the *ādeśa. Ādeśa* refers to the hearing of a voice. This may be heard within as we hear fully formed thoughts clothed in language or, it may be words heard by the external ear. It is important here to learn to distinguish between different kinds of "voices" one may hear. Sri Aurobindo points out that it takes preparation and purification to recognise the voice of truth, but also that this voice, once recognised, cannot be mistaken, because it comes with its own self-evidence. Self-evidence is the ultimate proof of truth. All things that can be doubted are not self-evident; that which cannot be doubted is self-evident. However, self-evidence is not something recognisable without purification.

This is the essence of the *ādeśa*. Sri Aurobindo received *ādeśa*s that moved him from field to field of work, including his withdrawal from political action and movement to found his āśram in Pondicherry. This *ādeśa* came, as a single short command: "Go to Pondicherry."[4] Sri Aurobindo had developed the consciousness which allowed him to follow these *ādeśa*s simply, without vacillation, though this transformed functioning came through a careful purificatory process, including doubt (*aśraddhā*).[5] While he was awaiting trial at the Alipore jail of Calcutta, he received such an *ādeśa* regarding his work for the future. This was not a directive for immediate action, but rather a general guidance orienting him towards certain forms of work. This is what concretised for him, four lines of action given to him, as the specific kinds of energies that would flow through him and were to be his *karma*. He enumerated these four lines as *sāhitya* (literature) *kr̥ti* (politics), *samāja* (society) and *dharma* or *daiva* referring to spirituality.[6]

All of Sri Aurobindo's writings could be spoken of as *sāhitya* (literature). The literary power of his remarkable writings was acknowledged in the nomination of Sri Aurobindo for the Nobel Prize in literature, in 1943 and a petition for the same in the year of his passing, 1950. A number of Nobel laureates in literature, such as Pearl Buck, Gabriela Mistral and Aldous Huxley, were among those who put forward this petition, proposing him for this highest literary award, not for any novel that he wrote, but for his *magnum opus* of philosophy, *The Life Divine*.[7] Sri Aurobindo himself may have considered *Savitri*, his epic poem, to be his prime contribution to world literature.

4. AN, pp. 89-90.
5. Ibid. *Record of Yoga* has many entries relating to the doubt (*aśraddhā*) that was part of the process of the establishment of *ādeśa siddhi*, perfection in truth-hearing.
6. See, for example, the entry under *Śraddhā* in RoY, p. 311. Also, RoY, pp. 314, 1290.
7. Peter Heehs, *The Lives of Sri Aurobindo*, New York: Columbia University Press, 2008, p. 404.

Another line of work, shown to him by the *ādeśa,* was politics. This, of course, is what had brought him to the prison in the first place — his active participation in the national struggle to free India from British colonial rule. But, in the *Record of Yoga,* we find, that though he left this field of Indian politics to move to his *āśrama* in Pondicherry, he continued his political action, now not merely in India, but in an experimental world action. One finds in the *Record of Yoga* very interesting entries on political world events of the early twentieth century. This is, in fact, a critical point in world history, because through the period of the *Record of Yoga*'s writing, the First World War was preparing to erupt and then entered its active stage. We find entries recording political events related to the war in Turkey, Ireland, England, Germany. In these entries, he is (a) making predictions, and (b) recording the effects of applying yogic force in these instances of world politics.[8] These experiments may be considered parapsychological, and relate to the quartet of knowledge in the development of its capacities of knowledge and power through a form of telepathy (*aṣṭa-siddhi*).

The third aspect of *karma* which the *ādeśa* revealed to him, was *samāja.* This pertains to his ideas on social reconstruction and transformation. This work was ideational and practical — ideational through his writings on society in works such as, *The Ideal of Human Unity* and *The Human Cycle;* and practical, in the development of the Ashram, which he saw as a spiritual laboratory, where all life, and representatives of all humanity would be included as an experiment in spiritual evolution.[9]

Finally, the fourth aspect of his *karma,* shown to him by the *ādeśa* was spirituality (which he often refers to in the *Record*

8. RoY, pp. 38, 112, 120, 128, 216-17, 334, 502, 528, etc.
9. Sri Aurobindo's collaborator, the Mother's founding of the international city of Auroville in 1968, may be seen as a further development of this *karma.*

of Yoga as "religion"). He defined this as the inner work towards the establishment of a new rung of consciousness on earth, which he called the supramental, and a new species to embody it. In the diary entries, he also records instances of personal influence on the spiritual advance of others under this category (*dharma* acting through communicative *vyāpti*).[10]

Karma and the Four Śaktis

These were the four lines along which Sri Aurobindo conducted his work, utilising the cosmic energies that worked in him. We'll look at a passage, from November 1912, in the *Record of Yoga*, where he writes about these energies, identifying the two primary goddesses at work in his own case to be Mahāsarasvatī and Mahākālī. He identifies the Īśvara-Śakti pair Aniruddha-Mahāsarasvatī as the basis, because his work proceeded in a meticulous and thorough fashion. We can see this as obvious in the records maintained by him in his diary, where the experiments and experiences are subject to scrutiny and proceed by rigorous testing, so as to establish the work brick by brick. But, he says that if it were left only to Mahāsarasvatī, "this method would render success in this life impossible".[11] Hence he looks to Balarāma-Mahākālī:

> The method chosen for preparation has been Mahāsarasvatī's, but the method chosen for fulfilment is Mahākālī's in the Mahāsarasvatī mould. Mahākālī's method is vehemence, force and swiftness, attaining knowledge by swift intuitions, moving to success in action by forceful strides. It is vehement in *lipsā*, violent in method, headlong in accomplishment. It seeks to attain the whole and then only returns upon the details. This vehemence, violence and precipitate rapidity has to be established in

10. RoY, pp. 482, 560, 574, 649, etc.
11. Ibid., p. 170.

the *prāṇa, citta* and *buddhi,* so as to govern feeling, thought and action (there have been plenty of isolated instances and brief periods of it in the past of the *sādhanā*) and justified by success; but the basis of hidden calm and self-possession in the Māheśvarī-bhāva of Mahāsarasvatī has to be maintained and all has to be in the [Mahāsarasvatī] mould which demands thoroughness, perfect [contrivance], faultless elaboration of detail in the consummate whole.[12]

Power and Enjoyment of Self-Perfection (10.1)

- **Power** (*Śakti*):
  - ***Karma*** based on realisation of Kṛṣṇa-Kālī and the 4 soul powers of the ***Daivī Prakṛti*** (*svabhāva/svadharma*):
    - Mahāvīra/Śiva-Maheśvarī (*jñānam, mahimā*)
    - Balarāma/Rudra-Mahākālī (*vīryam, raudryam*)
    - Pradyumna/Viṣṇu-Mahālakṣmī (*prema, dānam*)
    - Aniruddha/Kāma-Mahāsarasvatī (*kāma, karma*)
  - Aṣṭa-siddhi (Eight Occult Powers):
    - *Vyāpti* (receptive/communicative)
    - *Prakāmya* (intuitive or direct perception)
    - *Vaśitā* (control by concentration of will)
    - *Aiśvarya* (direct operation of will)
    - *Iśitā* (control of objects/.events by mere thinking)

Thus, Mahāsarasvatī and Mahākālī, are the two primary goddess *śakti*s at work in Sri Aurobindo's *karma* at this point; and Māheśvarī and Mahālakṣmī are realised as subsidiary powers. This is one aspect of the operation of Power, in the entries of the *Record of Yoga*.

---

12. RoY, p. 170.

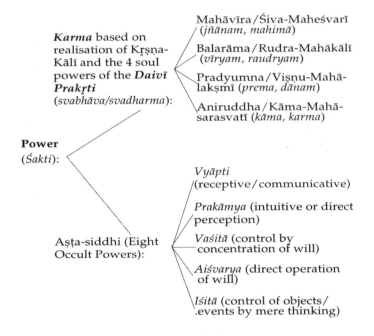

Capacities of Remote Knowledge and Power

We considered earlier Sri Aurobindo's remote experiments in knowledge and power on the stage of world politics. This aspect of Power in the *Record of Yoga,* occurs in the entries pertaining to what Sri Aurobindo calls the eight occult powers, (*aṣṭa-siddhi*). We encountered these when considering the quartet of knowledge, *vijñāna catuṣṭaya*. In the *Record of Yoga,* there are many entries pertaining to his development and testing of these powers. These entries are very interesting from the viewpoint of parapsychology, because he develops this theme in great detail. We may recollect some of these powers from our earlier study. First, there are two powers of knowledge through forms of telepathy, called *vyāpti* and *prakāmya*. *Vyāpti* can be either receptive or communicative and, *prakāmya* can also be of two kinds, intuitive or direct perception. To refresh our memory about these powers, we can look at the section on *aṣṭa-siddhi* in the scribal notes of disciples whom Sri Aurobindo addressed about the details of the yoga:[13] "There are two *siddhi*s of knowledge, three of power, and three of being. All *siddhi*s exist already in nature. They exist in you." — In other words, these powers are natural, they are already at work in us. — "Only owing to habitual limitations you make a use of them, which is mechanical and limited. By breaking these limitations, one is able to get the conscious and voluntary use of them."[14] Following this, he speaks of the powers of physical control, such as levitation, abnormal strength, appearance and disappearance, etc. and then about the powers of knowledge and power. While dealing with the powers of knowledge, he elaborates on *vyāpti* and *prakāmya:*

> Consciousness in itself is free to communicate between one

---

13. RoY, p. 1473.
14. Ibid.

> mind and another without physical means consciously and voluntarily. The two *siddhis* by which this is done, are called *vyāpti* and *prakāmya*. . . . *Vyāpti* is when the thoughts, feelings, etc. of others, or any kind of knowledge of things outside yourself are felt coming to the mind from those things or persons. This is the power of receptive *vyāpti*. There is also power of communicative *vyāpti* — when you can send or put out your own thought, feeling, etc. into someone else.[15]

As one can see, this constitutes the locus of telepathy — receiving and sending thoughts directly by mind action.

> *Prakāmya* is when you look mentally or physically at somebody or something and perceive what is in that person or thing — thoughts, feelings and facts about them. There is also another kind of *prakāmya* which is not of the mind but of the senses. It is the power of perceiving smells, sounds, contacts, taste, light, colours, and other objects of sense, which are either not at all perceptible to ordinary people, or beyond the range of your ordinary senses.[16]

This is the range of extrasensory perception, something Sri Aurobindo was developing experimentally as evidenced in his diary entries in the *Record of Yoga*. His disciples have recorded several further instances of the use of such powers in his later life. Earlier, we had considered an example of sortilege, but Sri Aurobindo also has entries recording the seeing of things written before him in colours or coloured lights, and of receiving messages in this manner. Just as messages came to him in the form of *ādeśa*s as truth-audition (Śruti), these may be understood as truth-vision (*dṛṣṭi*). These forms of writing go by the name *lipi* in the *Record of Yoga*.[17]

The three *siddhi*s of power or will, among the *aṣṭa-siddhi*s

---

15. RoY, pp. 1473-74.
16. Ibid., p. 1474.
17. Ibid., pp. 50, 52, 54, 55, 61, 64, etc.

are *vaśitā, aiśvarya* and *iśitā*. Sri Aurobindo has many entries in the *Record of Yoga*, pertaining to the use of these powers; and continued to use them throughout his life. In the *Record of Yoga*, we find him using *vyāpti* and *prakāmya* to receive knowledge from his surroundings as well as from great distances, things happening in remote lands. But, he was also using *vaśitā, aiśvarya* and *iśitā* to influence and control events and things around him[18] and at great distances, as with spiritual action (*dharma*)[19] and world politics (*kṛti*).[20] If we are to admit the truth of these possibilities, one of the major questions that arises is about the legitimacy of this kind of action. One could appreciate its danger — undoubtedly, it is dangerous. But, the modern world is full of many kinds of dangers: to possess weapons is a danger and the power of destruction in the hands of contemporary humans is unprecedented. So, as with technological powers, the question of responsibility is of utmost importance. This is why, the development of these powers is conditional, in Sri Aurobindo, on the purification of consciousness and the realisation of Oneness.

In the section pertaining to the quartet of knowledge, Sri Aurobindo begins with a long essay on the legitimacy or illegitimacy of the use of such occult powers.[21] He introduces the idea of responsible use, but more importantly, he sees these powers as natural to a higher evolution of consciousness in humanity. He does not discourage the development or use of these powers, because he feels that they are natural to a greater consciousness. But, for growth of consciousness to be fruitful, he feels that human beings must put themselves in contact with the power of Oneness, and put these powers at

18. RoY, pp. 42-43, 82, 176, etc.
19. Ibid., pp. 165, 179, etc.
20. Ibid., pp. 118, 165, 177, 179, 209, etc.
21. Ibid., pp. 14-16.

the service of that higher realisation, one may say using his terminology, use them for the *karma* of Kṛṣṇa-Kālī. To return to the *siddhi*s of power, *vaśitā* is control by concentration of will. In other words, by concentratating one's will on somebody or something, an event occurs, one influences the occurrence of an event by the power of concentration. *Aiśvarya* is a further stage of power where one doesn't need to concentrate any more, the will operates directly. One can will an occurrence without concentration, through a direct act of will. And *iśitā* is the third stage of this faculty, where one can control objects and events by mere thinking. One can see how powerful this thinking must become for that to happen and how responsible one must be in one's thinking. One cannot afford to have any stray thought, which is not entirely conscious. As soon as one thinks it, it comes to pass, or is set to happen irreversibly in the future. Thus, these are the gradations of the *siddhi*s of power.[22]

Empiricism of the Records

In exemplification, let us look at a very interesting passage dealing with several of these powers. It also takes up the action of the *śakti*s that are at work in him and the meaning of that work. The entry in question is, from 30 December 1912, and the diary jotting is titled *trikāladṛṣṭi,* which refers to the knowledge of past, present and future.[23] In this case, it is more the practice of the faculties of predictive knowledge, of knowing beforehand, using *vyāpti* and *prakāmya,* but also the higher degree of direct knowledge of the three times, *trikāladṛṣṭi:*

1. A squirrel on the roof which descends the angle of the tiles leaps on to the wall of the next house, runs along it and

---

22. RoY, pp. 20-22.
23. Ibid., p. 169.

ascends its roof. The first motion seen in the squirrel's mind, *prakāmya,* before it is executed. The second, ditto. The third by *trikāladṛṣṭi,* without any data; objective or subjective.

2. The leaf-like insect, put yesterday on the smaller tree, stated yesterday by S, to be no longer on the tree, suggested that it was back among the green leaves. While searching for it with the eyes today — *trikāladṛṣṭi*: that it was not in the green plant and was still on the tree. No data. The certainty was absent. Half an hour later it was shown by N, still on the tree.

3. A crow approaching the verandah. Another upon it. The idea of coming on the verandah seen in the crow's mind, but a suggestion of *trikāladṛṣṭi* that it would fly away to the wall on the left before reaching it. Uncertainty and false *viveka,* mistaking the intention for the event, suggestion at the last moment, when the crow had paused just below the verandah to eat something, that something would happen to send it away, rejected obstinately by the false *viveka.* The next moment, the first crow flew away to the wall on the left and the object of observation followed it. These three instances show the state of the *trikāladṛṣṭi.* Everything observed is the rendering in thought of a truth of tendency, intention or event, but everything is not yet put easily in its correct place. And uncertainty about te actual event is the normal state of the mental being who cannot distinguish between the correct decision and a false choice. This stage has to be exceeded before a clear and reliable *trikāladṛṣṭi* can be established.[24]

S and N referred to here, are two of the revolutionaries who were staying with Sri Aurobindo at the time, and formed part of his intimate circle. *Viveka* is discrimination. We discussed earlier the development of discrimination as a form of intuition. Sri Aurobindo here, is trying to use his intuitive

---

24. RoY, p. 169.

discrimination, but it is false, and he is recording this fact and its effects. We see this record as his conclusion on the state of his realisation in the quartet of knowledge.

From this entry we receive a good insight into Sri Aurobindo's method in yoga. It is not a superhuman person that we encounter, who has arrived full blown with myriad occult powers, but someone assiduously engaged in their development as part of human or perhaps transhuman, development. We can see the scientific rigour with which he proceeds, a subjective science that he is establishing for himself, in keeping with his own definition, "yoga is nothing but a practical psychology". Here is the entry pertaining to the next stage:

> 31 December.
>
> Yesterday it seemed as if the rudimentary equipment of the immediate life and its bare necessities were acquired with a lacuna, with inconvenient effects of the past confusion with a precarious source, but still, if it is maintained it stands as the first real triumph of the power in overcoming this obstinate difficulty.[25]

We may recollect that Sri Aurobindo writes about the centrality of faith, *śraddhā*, and optimism is the natural consequence of this faith. In the *Record of Yoga*, we see him practising this optimism born of faith. He notes to himself that a certain power or realisation is deficient, something went wrong, or something expected didn't happen. The very next entry has him noting that what he perceived as a defect or deficiency, was the first step towards its achievement, it's success is assured, he has been given the certainty of its achievement. An unbounded optimism, based on faith in himself and the Divine Mother is at work.

---

25. RoY, pp., 169-70.

Yesterday's *lipi* indicated that outward *tyāga* (outward) must be entirely abandoned and *bhoga* fully accepted; "submission to desirability" or some equivalent phrase was used. Another *lipi* ran: "violent purposes have to be justified" and is interpreted in the sense that although hitherto all the more vehement uses of the *aiśvarya* have been abortive and only moderate demands have been satisfied, the vehement Mahākālī use of the *aiśvarya* and *iśitā,* have not therefore, to be abandoned but must be insisted on till they succeed. Aniruddha and his Śakti, Mahāsarasvatī have been satisfied; the *yogasiddhi* has been justified and the *ādeśasiddhi* is beginning to be justified by slow, small and steadily progressive processes. This is Aniruddha's method, the method of the patient intellectual seeker, and the patient and laborious contriver, who occupies knowledge and action inch by inch and step by step, covering minutely and progressively all the grounds, justifying himself by details, and through the details arriving at the sum, but if continued, this method would render success in this life impossible. The method chosen for preparation has been Mahāsarasvatī's, but the method chosen for fulfilment is Mahākālī's, in the Mahāsarasvatī's mould. Mahākālī's method is vehemence, force and swiftness, attaining knowledge by swift intuitions, moving to success in action by forceful strides. It is vehement in *lipsā,* violent in method, headlong in accomplishment. It seeks to attain the whole and then only returns upon the detail. This vehemence, violence and precipitate rapidity has to be established in the *prāṇa, citta* and *buddhi* so as to govern feeling, thought and action and justified by success. But, the basis of hidden calm and self-possession in the Māheśvarī-*bhāva* of Mahāsarasvatī has to be maintained (there have been plenty of isolated instances and brief periods of it in the past of the *sādhanā*) and justified by success; but the basis of hidden calm and self-possession in the Māheśvarī-bhāva of Mahāsarasvatī, has to be maintained and all has to be in the [Mahāsarasvatī] mould which demands thoroughness, perfect [contrivance], faultless elaboration of detail in the

> consummate whole. The literary work, the subjective action on others, the outward physical speech and action have all to be done with this swift elaboration and violent minuteness. At first the Māheśvarī-*bhāva* will retain some prominence but will afterwards become implicit only in its Mahāsarasvatī continent. The first necessity is, however, that the Mahākālī method should be justified in the result so that the intellectual sceptic and critic in Mahāsarasvatī may be assured of the correctness of the instructions given.[26]

Lipi is the astral writing that Sri Aurobindo was seeing as a form of *ādeśa*. *Tyāga* means renunciation; Sri Aurobindo asserts at the outset that he cannot renounce anything. He states that he is meant to accept life in its fullness. He then proceeds to record and interpret some *lipis*. Then comes a part on *aiśvarya* — the most direct of the *siddhis* of power, achievement of results through mere thought — and the *śaktis* involved in its action. Mahākālī is the Goddess of Power, Mahāsarasvatī of Construction. As we saw early in this chapter, Mahāsarasvatī and Aniruddha proceed through gradual, tentative steps, testing every movement. The *ādeśasiddhi*, Sri Aurobindo refers to here, is the perfection of consciousness required to receive constant and dependable directions through *Śruti*. As we noted, this is a process which Sri Aurobindo refers to in various places in the *Record of Yoga*, noting the prevalence of doubt (*aśraddhā*) which he encountered in a number of cases.[27] We also saw at the beginning of the chapter how Sri Aurobindo invoked Mahākālī as the necessary Śakti to bring success through swift bounds, building on Mahāsarasvatī's slow preparations. He lays emphasis on this here, saying that there can be no violence without calm as its basis. This is how Sri Aurobindo approached and oriented himself in his *karma* and the modalities of his action, testing its steps.

---

26. RoY, pp. 170-71.
27. Ibid., pp. 66, 74, 83, 88, 93, etc.

Bliss

To conclude, let us look at an entry dealing with the aspect of delight. We find that delight is a property of experience which runs through all the seven quartets like a constant stream. In each case, Sri Aurobindo addresses some aspect of delight as a goal. One can summarise this trend and be justified in saying that delight is one of the consummating goals of the yoga of integral transformation. In the aspect of quartet of being, *brahma darśana,* or the *brahma catuṣṭaya,* it forms the fourth limb. As we have seen, it is *ānandam brahma* of the quartet *sarvam, anantam, jñānam, ānandam. Ānandam brahma* is the bliss of *Brahman*. As we saw in the ontology of self-perfection, this can be either *nirguṇa* or *saguṇa,* unqualified or qualitative, impersonal or personal. Of these, Sri Aurobindo prioritises the Person as the centre, focal point and concentration of delight of the infinite: the Being of Delight — *Ānandamaya Puruṣa,* as he calls it. A term he uses for this is *līlāmaya darśana,* the perception of that One Being of Delight at play in the world in innumerable forms. This involves seeing this Being of Delight, *Ānandamaya Puruṣa* in all beings and things. Sri Aurobindo had his first experience of this while in the Alipur Jail in Calcutta, while he was still a leader in India's struggle for Independence. Here, he saw Śrī Kr̥ṣṇa in everybody and everything — in inanimate objects like the bed, the door, the walls, non-human animate objects like trees, and in human beings like the prosecutor, the judge, the jury, the other accused persons — in everybody he saw Kr̥ṣṇa.[28]

In the *Record of Yoga,* he has entries pertaining to the regularisation of that experience of the *līlāmaya darśana.* We find him working on making this settled and permanent. Sri Aurobindo describes this Being of *ānanda* as:

> Our playmate in the great world game who has disguised

28. Sri Aurobindo, *Karmayogin,* CWSA:8, p. 7.

> himself throughout as friend and enemy, helper and opponent, and in all relations and in all workings that affect us, has led our steps towards our perfection and our release.[29]

Elsewhere, he describes this Being similarly and relates the transformed aspirant by likeness (*sādṛṣya*) to Him:

> [N]either is he merely an impersonal indeterminate, nor a mere stuff of conscious existence for all determinations and personalisings to draw upon for their material, but a supreme Being, the one original conscious Existent, the perfect Personality capable of all relations even to the most human, concrete and intimate; for he is friend, comrade, lover, playmate, guide, teacher, master, ministrant of knowledge or ministrant of joy, yet in all relations unbound, free and absolute. This too the divinised man becomes in the measure of his attainment, impersonal in his personality, unbound by quality or action even when maintaining the most personal and intimate relations with men, unbound by any *dharma* even when following in appearance this or that *dharma*.[30]

Kṛṣṇa-Darśana

One could think of this experience of Kṛṣṇa-*darśana*, as such an ecstatic experience that one loses all sense of distinction between beings in it. It was an experience of this kind which made the famous nineteenth-century Bengali mystic, Sri Ramakrishna, offer the flower meant for the deity in ritual worship, to the cat, the prostitute and to himself. One could lose all sense of structure with it. But, Sri Aurobindo's rigorous and scientific mind continues to remain active in developing a taxonomy of stages even to this experience. Thus, we find him writing about three intensities of Kṛṣṇa-*darśana* in human beings, applicable with modifications to all things and beings

29. Sri Aurobindo, "The Master of the Work", in SoY, pp. 256-57.
30. EoG, p. 141.

in the *Record of Yoga*. An example of this is described in the entry of 30 May 1915:

> The Kr̥ṣṇa-*darśana* is re-established in its first intensity; the difficulty of the unbeautiful face concealing the Sarvasundara is conquered in fact, though it attempts to return and does recur as a reminiscent experience. The second intensity is now more frequent and more secure as founded on a firmer foundation of the first intensity.
>
> Preliminary — Kr̥ṣṇa sensed behind the disguise
> 1st intensity — Kr̥ṣṇa seen behind the human mask.
> 2nd intensity — Kr̥ṣṇa seen in the human being
> 3rd intensity — The human being seen in Kr̥ṣṇa
> Consummation. The human being = Kr̥ṣṇa.
>
> *The same rule holds with all things and beings.*[31]

The first is the preliminary stage — "Kr̥ṣṇa sensed behind the disguise". This involves the constant practice of the thought "Everybody is a disguise for the One Being of Delight, Kr̥ṣṇa". This leads to a kind of mental sense, that though people are acting in a variety of ways, good, bad or neutral, it is the One Being that is disguised behind them. The establishment of this sense becomes the first and key step. From this comes the seeing of Kr̥ṣṇa behind the human mask. This involves the opening of the inner occult sight. The second stage or intensity is Kr̥ṣṇa seen in the human being. And, the third intensity is the human being seen in Kr̥ṣṇa. That is, there is only the Being of Delight and all beings are manifestations of that One Being as its self-multiplied forms. Now, this third intensity also has three degrees for Sri Aurobindo: the vision of *sarvamaya, anantaguṇamaya*, and *ānandamaya* Kr̥ṣṇa — these are the three degrees leading to the consummation, the human being is

31. RoY, p. 856.

Power and Enjoyment of Self-Perfection (10.2)

• Delight *(Ānanda)* :

Brahma darśana: Ānandam Brahman – Nirguṇa/Saguṇa – Līlāmaya Darśana

The three intensities of ***Kṛṣṇa darśana:*** (1) "***Kṛṣṇa*** *seen* behind the human mask" (2) "***Kṛṣṇa*** seen in the human being", and (3) "The human being seen in ***Kṛṣṇa***" leading to the consummation: "The human being = ***Kṛṣṇa***."

Samatā: Sama Ānanda (*Rasa, Bhoga – Śuddha Pravṛtti*), ***Ātmaprasāda*** or ***Hāsya***

Karma: Kāma/Bhukti – ***Kṛṣṇa***-Kālī realisation in works.

Śuddha Bhukti –
with three states — ***rasagrahaṇa, bhoga*** and ***ānanda*** — each with three intensities — ***rati, ratna*** and ***ratha*** — on each of seven levels corresponding to the seven planes of existence — *Kāmānanda (śarīra), Premānanda (citta), Ahaitukānanda (manas), Cidghanānanda (vijñāna), Śuddhānanda (ānanda), Cidānanda (cit-tapas), Sadānanda (sat).*

equal to Kṛṣṇa.[32] This becomes the culmination of *Kṛṣṇa-darśana*, or the ontology of Being seen as the Puruṣa of Delight. Sri Aurobindo describes these three degrees of the third intensity of Kṛṣṇa-*darśana* shortly after the above diary entry. Just prior to this, on 15 June 1915, he notes:

> In *Kṛṣṇa-darśana* the vision of everything as a form of Kṛṣṇa Kālī seems fixed. *Darśana* of Kṛṣṇa Kālī ranges between the various intensities down to non-intensity.[33]

Then, 16 on June he writes:

> An enormous progress in *Kṛṣṇa-darśana*, which has fixed itself rapidly, first in the mere *darśana*, then in the first intensity, then in the third where it varies between the first and third in the third. The first in the third is *sarvamaya*, the second is *anantaguṇamaya* and the third is *ānandamaya* Kṛṣṇa.[34]

One may note the resemblance of these three intensities with three of the *siddhis* of the *brahma catuṣṭaya* — i.e., *sarvam, anantam* and *ānandam brahma*. The first intensity could then pertain to seeing Kṛṣṇa as the One Being in all beings; the second to a seeing of the infinite possibilities of manifestation of Kṛṣṇa; and the third would be a seeing of the One pure infinite and creative Being of Delight in every form of manifestation and beyond it.

Samatā

How can we conceive of such experiences? Apart from the practice of the meditation of seeing all beings as the One Being in disguise, Sri Aurobindo has introduced us to several other methods as well. One, which also returns to us from all sides

---

32. RoY, p. 872.
33. Ibid.
34. Ibid.

in his quartets, and can never be overemphasised, is *samatā* or equality. Neutrality becomes the gate of entry into the garden of divine bliss. One can bring to mind the *Gītā*'s teaching of inner renunciation, *tyāga* and of the *Īśa Upaniṣad*'s paradoxical initiating line: *tena tyaktena bhuñjītha*, by renunciation do thou enjoy. We are pushed and pulled by the currents of attraction and repulsion. Developing a superior equality to these currents brings us to the threshold of the condition for experiencing all things as bliss. In this context, this would also imply the enlargement of one's capacity for enjoyment through the maintenance of a perfect equality in all experiences of enjoyment. Unconditional delight, contenment (*ātmaprasāda*) or ecstasy (*hāsya*), arises from an equal delight taken in all that, in our natural condition, attracts us and all that repels us. Sri Aurobindo describes this constant and active equal delight as "the image of the smile of Śrī Kṛṣṇa, playing *balavat*, like a child, as the eternal *bālaka* or child, and *kumāra*, youth, in the garden of the world".[35] This is the fountain of immutable happiness that we should have within us at all times and under every circumstance, and the quartet of equality, is the key to that realisation.

Another aspect of *bhukti* which we have discussed is the Kṛṣṇa-Kālī realisation in works: one is the instrument of the works of delight carried out in the manifestation by the Being and Śakti of delight. Here, in being a pure instrument, one experiences the delight taken by the Being in the instrument, and the delight of the Śakti flowing through the instrument in its actions. The quartet of action, *karma catuṣṭaya* holds the key to this realisation of dynamic and creative delight.

Finally, there is *śuddha bhukti*, the enjoyment of our liberated being, which arises from union with the Supreme. This is the third member of the quartet of perfection, *siddhi*

35. RoY, p. 6.

catuṣṭaya, resulting from *śuddhi* and *mukti,* and consisting of the realisation of the delight of existence, independent of all experience and extending itself to all experiences.[36] The Divine is free from need, because possessed of delight intrinsic to his infinity, completely fulfilled, *pūrṇa,* in him/her/itself. That is the causeless delight of existence that we must aim to realise, as the foundation of our being. This realisation has three stages, *rasagrahaṇa* (mental taste or mood), *bhoga* (vital enjoyment or relish) and *ānanda* (spiritual bliss), each with three intensities — *rati, ratna* and *ratha,* on each of seven levels corresponding to the seven planes of consciousness. Thus, at each of the levels of consciousness we can experience this intensive delight of being, extending itself in its experiences of the world in these three kinds — *rasagrahaṇa, bhoga* and *ānanda* — firstly in the body as the five forms of *kāmānanda* (*tīvrānanda, raudrānanda, vaidyutānanda, viṣayānanda* and *maithunānanda*) or physical bliss, discussed in the *śarīra catuṣṭaya;* in the *citta* or the emotions as *premānanda* or the bliss of love; in the *manas* or the sense-mind as *ahaitukānanda,* which means desireless and causeless or spontaneous bliss. The forms of delight continue, as we have seen, on planes presently distant from us — *cidghanānanda* in the ideal consciousness of *vijñāna* or Supermind, *śuddhānanda* in the plane of delight, *cidānanda* in the plane of *cit* or pure consciousness, and *sadānanda* in the plane of *sat* or pure existence. This entire spectrum of the symphony of bliss is the subjective fulfilment of the yoga of integral becoming and transformation, and this fulfilment is Sri Aurobindo's invitation to humanity, to follow in his footsteps in the endeavour to exceed itself through the stages of an experimental system aiming for the divine man or superman.

The third goal of the pole of power or magic was enumerated as immortality. This goal was covered under *ārogya*

36. RoY, p. 23.

of the quartet of the body. It is among the furthest fringe objects of the seven quartets of supermanhood and consists of two realisations — the realisation of the eternal being in the human system (*kāraṇa*) and the extension of its immortality to the instruments (*karaṇa*) of mind, life and body. The preparation of the instruments, particularly the body, through the amplification of its faith in its own unceasing health and energy and the supplementation of this through the descent of a higher divine Śakti, are the steps to this distant goal. But, the preliminary step is to free the body from its subjection to the interference of the mind and the life-being, with their own expectations of the body and its capacities. The immanence of divinity in the body was hinted at by the enlightenment philosopher, Baruch Spinoza (and echoed by Gilles Deleuze) when he raised the open-ended existential question of becoming "Of what is a body capable?" and, in the practice of Sri Aurobindo and the Mother, we find the practical development of this question through experiments of consciousness down to the cells of the body. Against the grain of a technological overdetermination, this potential of growth in unlimited consciousness and radical experiment, held out in their lives, is their invitation for the future of humanity.

Index